Egypt
a country study

Federal Research Division
Library of Congress
Edited by
Helen Chapin Metz
Research Completed
December 1990

On the cover: A representation of Tutankhamen (1347–
1337 B.C.), pharaoh of the New Kingdom, on his throne

Fifth Edition, First Printing, 1991.

Library of Congress Cataloging-in-Publication Data

Egypt: a country study / Federal Research Division, Library of
Congress ; edited by Helen Chapin Metz. — 5th ed.
    p.   cm. — (Area handbook series, ISSN 1057-5294) (DA
pam ; 550-43)
    Previous ed. has statement of responsibility: Foreign Area
Studies, the American University : edited by Richard F. Nyrop.
    ''Research completed December 1990.''
    Includes bibiliography (pp. 369-391) and index.
    ISBN 0-8444-0729-1
    1. Egypt. I. Metz, Helen Chapin, 1928-   . II. Library of
Congress. Federal Research Division. III. Series. IV. Series:
    DA pam ; 550-43.
DT46.E32   1991   91-29876
962—dc20   CIP

Headquarters, Department of the Army
DA Pam 550-43

For sale by the Superintendent of Documents, U.S. Government Printing Office
Washington, D.C. 20402

Foreword

This volume is one in a continuing series of books prepared by the Federal Research Division of the Library of Congress under the Country Studies—Area Handbook Program sponsored by the Department of the Army. The last page of this book lists the other published studies.

Most books in the series deal with a particular foreign country, describing and analyzing its political, economic, social, and national security systems and institutions, and examining the interrelationships of those systems and the ways they are shaped by cultural factors. Each study is written by a multidisciplinary team of social scientists. The authors seek to provide a basic understanding of the observed society, striving for a dynamic rather than a static portrayal. Particular attention is devoted to the people who make up the society, their origins, dominant beliefs and values, their common interests and the issues on which they are divided, the nature and extent of their involvement with national institutions, and their attitudes toward each other and toward their social system and political order.

The books represent the analysis of the authors and should not be construed as an expression of an official United States government position, policy, or decision. The authors have sought to adhere to accepted standards of scholarly objectivity. Corrections, additions, and suggestions for changes from readers will be welcomed for use in future editions.

Louis R. Mortimer
Chief
Federal Research Division
Library of Congress
Washington, D.C. 20540

Acknowledgments

The authors wish to acknowledge the contributions of the writers of the 1983 edition of *Egypt: A Country Study,* edited by Richard F. Nyrop. Their work provided general background for the present volume.

The authors are grateful to individuals in various government agencies and private institutions who gave of their time, research materials, and expertise in the production of this book. These individuals included Ralph K. Benesch, who oversees the Country Studies—Area Handbook program for the Department of the Army. The authors also wish to thank members of the Federal Research Division staff who contributed directly to the preparation of the manuscript. These people included Thomas Collelo, the substantive reviewer of all the graphic and textual material; Sandra W. Meditz, who reviewed all drafts and served as liaison with the sponsoring agency; and Martha E. Hopkins and Marilyn Majeska, who managed editing and book production.

Also involved in preparing the text were editorial assistants Barbara Edgerton and Izella Watson; Richard Kollodge and Ruth Nieland, who edited chapters; Beverly Wolpert, who performed the prepublication editorial review; and Joan C. Cook, who compiled the index. Linda Peterson of the Library of Congress Composing Unit prepared the camera-ready copy under the supervision of Peggy Pixley.

Graphics were prepared by David P. Cabitto, and Timothy L. Merrill reviewed map drafts. David P. Cabitto and Greenhorne and O'Mara prepared the final maps. Special thanks are owed to Marty Ittner, who prepared the illustrations on the title page of each chapter, and David P. Cabitto, who did the cover art.

The authors would like to thank Ly H. Burnham, who assisted with demographic data. Finally, the authors acknowledge the generosity of the many individuals and public and private agencies, especially the Press and Information Bureau of the Arab Republic of Egypt, who allowed their photographs to be used in this study.

Contents

List of Figures

Preface

This edition of *Egypt: A Country Study* replaces the previous edition published in 1983. Like its predecessor, the present book attempts to treat in a compact and objective manner the dominant historical, social, economic, political, and national security aspects of contemporary Egypt. Sources of information included scholarly books, journals, and monographs; official reports and documents of governments and international organizations; and foreign and domestic newspapers and periodicals. Relatively up-to-date economic data were available from several sources, but the sources were not always in agreement.

Chapter bibliographies appear at the end of the book; brief comments on some of the more valuable sources for further reading appear at the conclusion of each chapter. Measurements are given in the metric system; a conversion table is provided to assist those who are unfamiliar with the metric system (see table 1, Appendix). Landholdings, however, are presented in *feddans,* a unit of measure that remains in general use although Egypt officially uses the metric system. One *feddan* equals 1.038 acres. The Glossary provides brief definitions of terms, such as *feddan,* that may be unfamiliar to the general reader.

The information available on ancient and modern Egypt is detailed and voluminous. Limitations of space and time, however, precluded the presentation of anything more than a short survey.

The transliteration of Arabic words and phrases posed a particular problem. For many of the words—such as Muhammad, Muslim, Quran, and shaykh—the authors followed a modified version of the system adopted by the United States Board on Geographic Names and the Permanent Committee on Geographic Names for British Official Use, known as the BGN/PCGN system; the modification entails the omission of all diacritical markings and hyphens. In numerous instances, however, the names of persons or places are so well known by another spelling that to have used the BGN/PCGN system may have created confusion. For example, the reader will find Cairo rather than Al Qahirah, Giza rather than Al Jizah, Suez rather than As Suways, and Gamal Abdul Nasser rather than Jamal Abd an Nasr. For some place-names, two transliterations have been provided (see fig. 1).

Country Profile

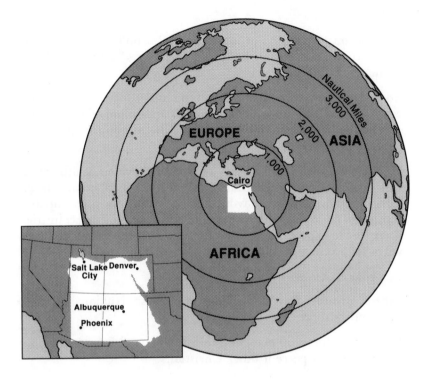

Country

Formal Name: Arab Republic of Egypt.

Short Form: Egypt.

Term for Citizens: Egyptians.

Capital: Cairo.

Geography

Size: Approximately 1 million square kilometers.

Topography: Four major regions: Nile Valley and Delta, where about 99 percent of population lives; Western Desert; Eastern Desert; and Sinai Peninsula.

Climate: Except for modest amounts of rainfall along Mediterranean coast, precipitation ranges from minimal to nonexistent. Mild winters (November to April) and hot summers (May to October).

Society

Population: Estimated at more than 52.5 million in mid-1990, mostly concentrated along banks of Nile River. Annual growth rate estimated at 2.6 percent.

Education and Literacy: Education compulsory for basic nine-year cycle but attendance not enforced; approximately 16 percent of school-age children did not attend. Literacy approximately 45 percent in 1990.

Health and Welfare: Ministry of Health provided health care at variety of public medical facilities. Urban-rural distribution of health care generally biased in favor of larger cities. Average nutrition compared favorably with most middle- and low-income countries. Average life expectancy at birth fifty-nine years for men and sixty years for women in 1989.

Language: Arabic.

Ethnic Groups: Egyptians, beduins, Greeks, Nubians, Armenians, and Berbers.

Religion: Almost 90 percent Sunni Muslims, 8.5 percent Coptic Christians, 1.5 percent other Christians.

Economy

Gross Domestic Product (GDP): US$45.08 billion, or US$867 per capita in 1988. Economy experienced sluggish growth after mid-1980s.

Agriculture: Single largest source of employment; contributed 15 percent of GDP in 1987. Major crops by area planted (in descending order): clover for livestock feed, corn, wheat, vegetables, rice, cotton, and fruit. Heavily dependent on food imports. Some reforms in pricing implemented in 1980s.

Industry: Contributed 34 percent of GDP in 1987. Share of manufacturing in GDP 12 percent; sector stagnated in 1980s. Manufacturing produced mainly consumer goods but also some basic industries such as iron and steel, aluminum, and cement. Manufacturing dominated by public sector; consensus that sector needed reform. Oil share of GDP fell considerably with crash of oil prices in late 1985. Oil production averaged 42.7 tons per year between 1984 and 1988. Gas acquiring added importance in 1980s.

Exports: US$4.8 billion in 1988, of which oil was US$3.1 billion. Textiles US$458 million and other manufacturing US$810 million. Cotton (major export before late 1970s) US$310 million. Exports stagnated in 1980s.

Imports: US$10.6 billion, of which intermediate goods US$3.7 billion, capital goods US$3 billion, consumer goods US$2 billion, and food and agriculture US$1.7 billion. Trade deficit increased rapidly in first half of 1980s and stabilized in second half.

Debt: Civilian US$35 billion in 1988 (forecast); military US$10.8 billion. Negotiations with International Monetary Fund continuing in early 1990 on debt rescheduling and economic restructuring.

Currency: Egyptian pound (£E) consists of 100 piasters. In early 1990, worth between US$1.00 and US$1.50 depending on applicable exchange rate.

Fiscal Year: Since July 1, 1980, July 1 through June 30.

Transportation and Communications

Railroads: More than 4,800 kilometers of track, 950 kilometers of which double-tracked. Bulk of system standard gauge (1.435 meters), but 347 kilometers narrow gauge (0.75 meter). Twenty-five-kilometer suburban transit link between Cairo and industrial suburb of Hulwan electrified. Southern part of Cairo Metro opened 1987; northeast line opened 1989. Ferry at Aswan connects Egyptian Railways to Sudanese system.

Roads: More than 49,000 kilometers, of which about 15,000 kilometers paved, 2,500 kilometers gravel, 31,500 kilometers earthen.

Inland Waterways: About 3,500 kilometers, consisting mainly of Nile River and several canals in Delta.

Suez Canal: About 160 kilometers for international shipping between Red and Mediterranean seas. Reopened in 1975. Capable of handling ships of 150,000 deadweight tons laden and 16 meters draft. In 1987 17,541 ships transited canal with 257,000 tons of cargo, earning Egypt US$1.22 billion.

Ports: Alexandria main port. Port Said and Suez other two large ports. Phosphates shipped from Bur Safajah on the Red Sea. Port near Alexandria remained under construction in 1990.

Pipelines: About 1,400 kilometers for domestic crude oil and refined products plus about 600 kilometers for natural gas.

Airports: Sixty-six airfields but only Cairo and Alexandria handled international traffic.

Telecommunications: Well developed radio and television facilities; shortage of telephones. Numerous international communications links.

Government and Politics

Government: Constitution of 1971 delegates majority of power to president, who dominates two-chamber legislature—lower People's Assembly and upper Consultative Council, created in 1980 from the old Central Committee of the Arab Socialist Union—and judiciary, although each constitutionally independent. President possesses virtually unrestricted power to appoint and dismiss officials, including vice president or vice presidents, prime minister and members of Council of Ministers, military officers, and governors of the twenty-six administrative subdivisions known as governorates.

Politics: President Husni Mubarak (1981–), former military officer, as were his predecessors: Gamal Abdul Nasser (1954–70) and Anwar as Sadat (1970–81). Nasser was leader and Sadat member of Free Officers' group that overthrew monarchy in 1952 Revolution. President dominated National Democratic Party formed in 1977. Opposition composed of number of secular and religious parties in legislature, of which Muslim Brotherhood was the chief, and some nonparliamentary Islamic extremist groups.

International Organizations: Member of United Nations and its specialized agencies; Organization of African Unity; and Nonaligned Movement. Founding member of League of Arab States (Arab League), headquartered in Cairo until after Egypt signed peace treaty with Israel in March 1979. Arab League expelled Egypt and moved headquarters out of country. In 1990 Arab League headquarters returned to Cairo.

National Security

Armed Forces (1989): Total personnel on active duty 445,000, including draftees mostly serving for three years. Reserves totaled about 300,000. Component services: army of 320,000 (estimated 180,000 conscripts), navy of 20,000 including 2,000 Coast Guard (10,000 conscripts), and air force of 30,000 (10,000 conscripts). Air Defense Force separate service of 80,000 (50,000 conscripts).

Major Tactical Military Units (1988): Army: four armored divisions, six mechanized infantry divisions, two infantry divisions, four independent infantry brigades, three mechanized brigades, one armored brigade, two air mobile brigades, one paratroop brigade, Republican Guard armored brigade, two heavy mortar brigades, fourteen artillery brigades, two surface-to-surface missile (SSM) regiments, and seven commando groups.

Navy: Twelve submarines, one destroyer (training), five frigates, twenty-five fast-attack craft (missile), eighteen fast-attack craft (torpedo), minesweepers, and landing ships.

Air Force: About 440 combat aircraft and 72 armed helicopters; force organized into one bomber squadron, ten fighter-ground attack squadrons, thirteen fighter squadrons, two reconnaissance squadrons, and fifteen helicopter squadrons, plus electronic monitoring, early warning, transport, and training aircraft. Air Defense Force organized into more than 230 battalions of antiaircraft guns and SAMs.

Military Equipment (1989): Tanks and armored personnel vehicles a mix of older Soviet and newer United States models. Other major equipment included Soviet artillery and mortars; Soviet, French, United States, and British antitank rockets and missiles; and mostly Soviet tactical air defense weapons. Egypt planned to coproduce with United States 540 Abrams M1A1 tanks beginning in 1991. Air force fighters included F–16s and F–4s from United States and Mirage 2000s from France, backed by large number of older Soviet designs. Most fighting ships of Soviet or Chinese origin, although fleet included two modern frigates built in Spain and six British missile boats. Air Defense Force had more than 600 Soviet SA–2 and SA–3 SAMs plus 108 improved Hawk SAMs from United States.

Defense Budget: Authoritative data not available although minister of defense claimed spending £E2.4 billion or 10 percent of total government outlays in 1989. Other sources believed defense expenditures twice as high as claimed, even excluding US$1.3 billion in military aid from United States, aid from Saudi Arabia, and income from other sources such as foreign sales of domestic defense industry.

Internal Security Forces: Principal security agencies—national police force of more than about 122,000 members and Central Security Forces, a paramilitary body of about 300,000, mostly conscripts, which augmented regular police in guarding buildings and strategic sites and controlling demonstrations. Several other government agencies had own law enforcement bodies. General Directorate for State

Security Investigations main intelligence organization monitoring suspected subversive and opposition groups and suppressing Islamic extremists.

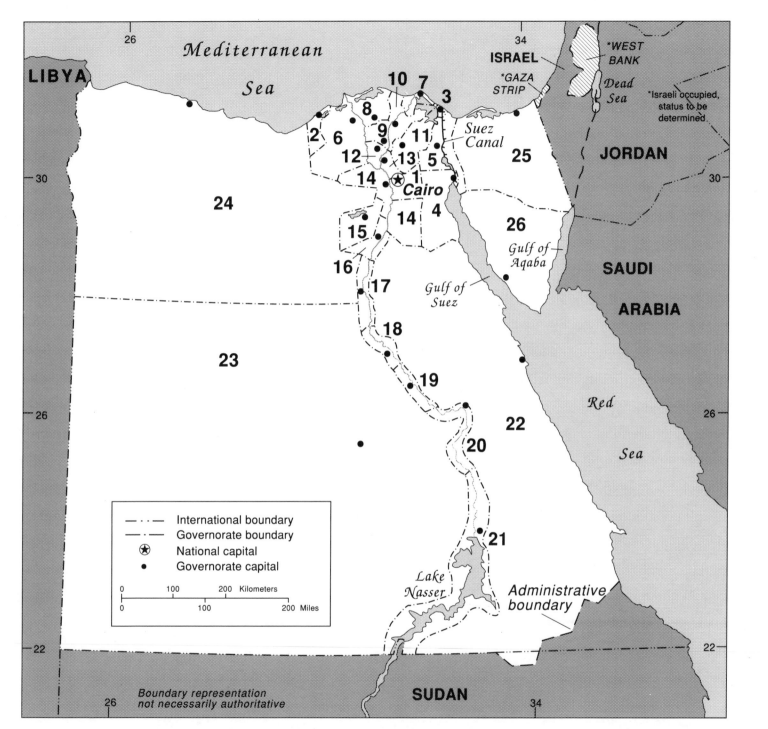

Administrative Divisions of Egypt

GOVERNORATES	GOVERNORATE CAPITALS
City Governorates	
1. Cairo (Al Qahirah)	Cairo
2. Alexandria (Al Iskandariyah)	Alexandria
3. Port Said (Bur Said)	Port Said
4. Suez (As Suways)	Suez
Lower Egypt	
5. Ismailia (Al Ismailiyah)	Ismailia
6. Al Buhayrah	Damanhur
7. Damietta (Dumyat)	Damietta
8. Kafr ash Shaykh	Kafr ash Shaykh
9. Al Gharbiyah	Tanta
10. Ad Daqahliyah	Al Mansurah
11. Ash Sharqiyah	Az Zaqaziq
12. Al Minufiyah	Shibin al Kawm
13. Al Qalyubiyah	Banha
Upper Egypt	
14. Giza (Al Jizah)	Giza
15. Al Fayyum	Al Fayyum
16. Bani Suwayf	Bani Suwayf
17. Al Minya	Al Minya
18. Asyut	Asyut
19. Suhaj	Suhaj
20. Qina	Qina
21. Aswan	Aswan
Frontier Governorates	
22. Red Sea (Al Bahr al Ahmar)	Al Ghardaqah
23. New Valley (Al Wadi al Jadid)	Al Kharijah
24. Matruh	Marsa Matruh
25. North Sinai	Al Arish
26. South Sinai	At Tur

Source: Based on information from *Gazetteer of Egypt*, Washington, August 1987, v.

Figure 1. Administrative Divisions of Egypt, 1990

Introduction

OCCUPYING A FOCAL GEOGRAPHIC bridge linking Africa and Asia, contemporary Egypt is the inheritor of a civilization dating back more than 6,000 years. The unification of Upper Egypt and Lower Egypt in the third millennium B.C. required the development of administrative and religious structures, and the monuments that remain demonstrate the mathematical, astronomical, and architectural skills attained in constructing rock tombs, temples, and pyramids—the latter dedicated to the divine kings, the pharaohs.

Egypt's strategic location has made it the object of numerous conquests: by the Ptolemies, Romans, Greeks, Arabs, Fatimids, Mamluks, Ottomans, and Napoleon Bonaparte. The most recent conquerors, the British, granted Egypt partial independence in 1922 and withdrew completely in 1954. Of these foreign rules, the Arab Muslim conquest, by its arabization and Islamization, had the greatest impact on Egyptian life and culture, resulting in the rapid conversion of the overwhelming majority of the population to Islam and the spread of Sunni Muslim religious and educational institutions. Shia Islam, represented by the Fatimid conquest in 969, led to the founding the same year of Al Azhar, later transformed into a Sunni theological school, and in the 1990s still regarded as the outstanding interpreter of Islamic religious law (sharia).

The rule of Muhammad Ali (1805–48), an Albanian officer in the army of the Ottoman sultan, who succeeded in detaching Egypt from Ottoman control, represented another major influence on Egypt's history. Muhammad Ali encouraged the development of Egypt by introducing long-staple cotton as a major crop; by expanding Egypt's infrastructure through a network of canals, irrigation systems, and roads; and by promoting secular education. His efforts to create a manufacturing sector failed, however, in part because Britain's tariff policies were designed to favor the import of raw materials to be processed in Britain.

For contemporary Egypt, the Free Officers' 1952 Revolution, spearheaded by Gamal Abdul Nasser, has clearly been the formative event. Nasser's charismatic leadership institutionalized the role of the military and created an authoritarian state that pursued goals of "Arab socialism." These goals centered on the implementation of agrarian reform, nationalization of key industries, a one-party state (the Arab Socialist Union—ASU) domestically, and closer ties with the Soviet Union and Eastern Europe internationally.

Major events of Nasser's regime included the construction of the Aswan High Dam with Soviet aid; the take-over of the Suez Canal in 1956, which led to the 1956 War and the British-French-Israeli Tripartite Invasion of the Sinai Peninsula (also known as Sinai); and the short-lived Egyptian-Syrian union as the United Arab Republic (1958–61). Egyptian participation in the June 1967 War with Israel resulted in Egypt's loss of the Gaza Strip and Sinai and the so-called War of Attrition along the Suez Canal in 1969–70.

Nasser's death brought to office his vice president, Anwar as Sadat, also a military man but more conservative in political outlook than his predecessor. Sadat's rule has been characterized as patriarchal, a return to a traditional method of government that relied on clientelism. Sadat demilitarized the state in favor of the bourgeoisie and opened Egypt to capitalism and to the West through the *infitah* (opening or open door; see Glossary) in 1974. Sadat also moved toward some democratization and constitutionalism, represented by the Constitution of 1971, which, however, concentrated power in the hands of the president. Sadat's early successes in the October 1973 War with Israel made him a popular hero and psychologically boosted the morale of Egyptians. In an attempt to end the state of war with Israel, Sadat journeyed to Jerusalem in November 1977; as a next step, through the mediation of United States president Jimmy Carter, he signed the Camp David Accords in September 1978 and the Egyptian-Israeli peace treaty in March 1979. These actions, however, and Sadat's increasing repression of domestic opposition, resulted in Egypt's being cut off from the rest of the Arab world and ultimately led to Sadat's assassination by a Muslim extremist group, Al Jihad (Holy War), in October 1981.

Husni Mubarak, Sadat's vice president, took over the government and was initially regarded by many as an interim president. He demonstrated a commitment to gradualism aimed at modifying and preserving the best elements of his predecessors' accomplishments while building domestic consensus, tolerating opposition, promoting an equal partnership between the public and private sectors, allowing greater democracy and constitutionalism, and relying on technocrats for advice. In addition, through skillful diplomacy he gained Egypt's return to the Arab fold in 1987 and assumed a leadership role in the Arab world. Simultaneously he maintained good relations with the West and improved relations with the Soviet Union.

Mubarak's gradualism seemed to many observers a useful leadership characteristic for contemporary Egypt. For example, he strove to prevent the small but growing number of Muslim extremists, sometimes referred to as fundamentalists, from exercising disproportionate influence over the moderate body of Muslims, who in

November 1990 constituted approximately 90 percent of the country's population of about 56 million persons. (In announcing the population figure, the Census Bureau stated that the population has increased by 1 million persons in nine months and seven days.) Although concerned about the intimidation of Christian minorities, mainly Copts, at the hands of Muslim extremists, as of mid-1991, the government has been unable to prevent young Coptic Christians from acting on their own to counter acts of violence against their religious centers and property.

Since the 1952 Revolution, the government has appointed the functionaries of mosques and Islamic religious schools. The growth of Islamic political movements, especially the Muslim Brotherhood, and of Islamic associations in universities resulted in increased pressure on the government in the 1980s for application of the sharia in legal decisions. Mubarak acceded to the gradual application of the process.

The 1952 Revolution also expanded secular education, and from 1964 to 1974 the government was obliged by law to hire all those with higher education degrees. The practice led to an overstaffed and ineffective bureaucracy. The *infitah* ended this hiring requirement, but by the mid-1980s unemployment among university graduates was estimated to be as high as 30 percent.

The 1952 Revolution initiated free health care at public health facilities. Although these services continued in the early 1990s, facilities often lacked adequate medical personnel. In addition, a social security program was begun in the 1960s.

The 1952 Revolution had given priority to economic development and had made the state the prime economic agent of Arab socialism. The National Charter of 1962 clearly spelled out the state's role. The role of the private sector, however, was considerably enlarged by the *infitah* after the October 1973 War, and private-sector employees on average received three times the salaries of government workers. Mubarak encouraged private investment but funds flowed largely into the service sector and agriculture rather than into industry, despite government development plans (1982–86, 1987–91) designed to promote the latter. The shortage of skilled personnel, especially in the technical and industrial spheres, also had a major impact on the economy.

Agricultural production had not benefited significantly from the development process. By 1990, although production had shifted away from concentration on long-staple cotton to such crops as rice, fruits, and vegetables, self-sufficiency had fallen below the 1960 level. Only approximately 3 percent of Egypt's land was suitable for agriculture. Despite postrevolutionary land reforms, increased mechanization, and land reclamation programs following the construction of the Aswan High Dam—a program underway in 1991 involved 300,000 *feddans* (see Glossary) to be worked jointly with Sudan—Egypt's agricultural output did not keep pace with population growth. Although pricing reforms and the elimination of government quotas for most crops helped increase output, production remained insufficient. Part of the problem was lack of proper drainage and consequent reduction of optimum yields. In general, a major challenge facing Egypt was better exploitation of its water resources, including exploration for new underground water, particularly in the Western Desert, and improved irrigation technology. Government development plans also sought to promote generation of electricity and other energy sources such as oil, gas, and coal as well as to improve further the transportation network of roads, railroads, and canals and to update telecommunications.

Egypt's major sources of foreign exchange used for development projects and for needed imports were oil revenues, Suez Canal tolls, tourism income, and workers' remittances from the approximately 2.5 million Egyptians working abroad. Added to these were capital grants from other Arab states after the October 1973 War and, as well, economic and military grants from the United States and loans from the Paris Club (the informal name for a consortium of eighteen Western creditor nations) after the conclusion of the 1979 peace treaty with Israel.

Egypt faced a serious economic situation in the late 1980s and early 1990s: stagnation and ultimately negative economic growth in addition to heavy indebtedness. After two years of negotiations with the International Monetary Fund (IMF—see Glossary), the Egyptian government finally concluded a preliminary agreement in October 1990 that enabled it to reschedule its US$18 billion debt to Paris Club members. The agreement required Egypt to increase prices of certain basic commodities such as gas, fuel oil, gasoline, electricity, flour, and rice by eliminating or reducing subsidies. Mandated, as well, were the devaluation and unification of the Central Bank exchange rate and the exchange rate of commercial banks, raising of the interest rate, and reforming of the foreign investment law. Egypt also sought to promote privatization of the industrial public sector—one of the recommendations of the World Bank (see Glossary)—and announced in October 1990 that it would establish nine new industrial "free zones" to encourage investment and create more jobs. Some officials recognized that, additionally, the government needed to restructure management style in the public sector and banking to encourage greater efficiency and productivity. Another economic problem facing Egypt was rising inflation, which between 1987 and 1989 had increased between 20 and 25 percent annually. In early 1991, inflation was estimated to have dropped to 11 percent, but it nevertheless had a severe impact especially on lower income groups.

Egypt also endeavored to improve its trade and financial situation by concluding barter agreements that eliminated the need to expend foreign currency. For example, in August 1990 it reached a five-year agreement with the Soviet Union that was worth £E5 billion, with other supplemental agreements to follow.

Egypt's economic situation became particularly critical in 1990 because of the Persian Gulf crisis. In October, before the crisis developed into a war, the World Bank had calculated that Egypt would lose US$2.4 billion in remittances from workers in Iraq and Kuwait, US$500 million from the loss of exports to Iraq and Kuwait, US$500 million from tourism, and US$200 million from Suez Canal tolls. In addition, Egyptian minister of international cooperation Maurice Makramallah estimated that Egypt would require a further US$900 million to meet the needs of Egyptians repatriated from Iraq and Kuwait. In early April 1991, after the war, Egyptian officials announced that 700,000 Egyptians who had worked in Iraq and Kuwait had returned home jobless. Estimates of unemployment in early 1991 varied, with some figures as high as 20 percent, despite the approximate 684,000 visas issued to Egyptians for work in Saudi Arabia after the Persian Gulf crisis began.

The estimated costs did not take into account actual war costs of sending about 35,000 Egyptian armed forces personnel to Saudi Arabia and provisioning them. Saudi Arabia, which in December promised US$1.5 billion, and Kuwait, together with several European Economic Community (EEC) member nations, had agreed to contribute to these costs and to the losses incurred by Egypt's economy, but funds were slow in arriving. President George Bush of the United States proposed in September that the United States forgive Egypt its approximately US$7 billion military debt because of Egypt's help in the Persian Gulf crisis; Congress subsequently endorsed this proposal. This action relieved Egypt of annual repayments amounting to more than US$700 million. Other countries such as Canada, several EEC member states, the Persian Gulf countries and Saudi Arabia also forgave Egypt's debt obligations. By early November 1990 the total debt cancellation stood at about US$14 billion.

In subsequent action, Egypt sent a delegation in mid-April 1991 to the IMF requesting an eighteen-month standby agreement and a loan. When United States secretary of state James A. Baker III visited Cairo in March, he had promised that the United States, grateful for Egypt's support in the war with Iraq, would put in a good word for Egypt with the IMF. In mid-May the IMF approved the standby agreement and granted Egypt a US$372 million loan, but imposed certain additional conditions on the Egyptian economy. The IMF agreement paved the way for Egypt to obtain favorable terms from the Paris Club for its debt to member countries. On May 25, it was announced that Egyptian government debts would be reduced 50 percent and advantageous terms granted on the remainder. In mid-June the World Bank agreed to an additional US$520 million loan to Egypt.

Meanwhile, with regard to economic development Egypt signed an agreement at the end of May 1991 with the African Development Bank for a US$350 million loan to finance part of the Kuraymar power station. This sum was supplemented by contributions of US$100 million from the Arab Fund for Social and Economic Development, US$100 million from the World Bank, and US$10 million from the Islamic Bank for Development. On July 10 the Egypt Consultative Group, consisting of thirty countries and institutions, pledged US$8 billion in aid to Egypt over the next two years, more than twice the minimum Egypt had suggested. The World Bank, which organized the group, stated that the donors had determined on "massive support" for Egypt's reform program, which it described as "daring" and "exhaustive." It estimated that Egypt had lost approximately US$20 billion as a result of the war in the Persian Gulf.

The endorsement of Egypt's policies represented by the action of this World Bank-affiliated group was an encouraging sign. In summary, however, Egypt's prospective economic situation depended upon several factors: the successful implementation of the IMF agreement, its capacity to promote itself as an investment and financial center, its role in the region as well as its position as a partner of the West, and perhaps most critically, its ability to follow through on necessary economic reforms.

The role of government was prominent not only in Egypt's economic life but also in other spheres, such as political parties, parliamentary organization and elections, the judiciary, and the military. The Constitution of 1971 validated a mixed presidential-parliamentary-cabinet system with power concentrated in the hands of the president, who had extensive opportunities to bestow patronage, including the appointment of the prime minister, and who could legislate by decree in emergencies. Whereas the People's Assembly, the elected lower house, theoretically could exercise a check on the president, in reality this did not occur, and the assembly had no role in foreign affairs or defense matters. The upper house, the Consultative Council, was an advisory body created in 1980 when the Central Committee of the Arab Socialist Union, then the only legitimate political party, became the nucleus of the council.

Under Mubarak the People's Assembly acquired greater authority over minor matters of state and more freedom of debate; assembly committees also exercised an oversight role with regard to cabinet ministers. The dominant political party remained the National Democratic Party (NDP), which had succeeded the ASU, but it was largely an appendage of the government. The new Electoral Law in 1984 limited opposition seats in the assembly to parties that obtained at least 8 percent of the vote, thereby eliminating representation on the part of some of the small fringe parties. In May 1990, however, Egypt acquired several new parties: the Green Party, the Democratic Unionist Party, and the Young Egypt (Misr al Fatah) Party became eligible to run for election. The Supreme Administrative Court rejected, however, the application for party status of the Nasserite Party on the ground that its program was totalitarian. A similar request for party recognition by the Muslim Brotherhood in January 1990 had been rejected because the body had been formed on a religious basis.

In May 1990, the Supreme Constitutional Court ruled that the People's Assembly elected in May 1987 was invalid. It so ruled because a 1986 amendment to the 1972 Electoral Law was judged unconstitutional by reason of its discrimination against independent candidates through use of the closed list system of proportional representation, requiring selection of a single slate. As a result, assembly legislation passed up to June 2 would stand, but new elections had to be held under the second-ballot system, in which, if no individual received an absolute majority, a run-off was held between the top two candidates. Mubarak adjourned the existing assembly and called a referendum for October 11 on whether the assembly should be dissolved. The referendum resulted in new assembly elections called for November 29, with nine legal parties authorized to participate.

In fact, the Muslim Brotherhood and three of the major opposition parties—the right-of-center New Wafd Party, the left-of-center Socialist Labor Party, and the centrist Liberal Party—declined to take part in the elections. They refused because of amendments to the 1972 Electoral Law forbidding unified lists (the Muslim Brotherhood had combined with the Socialist Labor Party for election purposes) and preventing NDP members from changing allegiance. Other reasons for the abstention of these parties was the government's refusal to lift the state of emergency or to allow judicial bodies to supervise the election. As a result, in a very low voter turnout estimated at between 8 and 25 percent of those eligible, the NDP claimed to control 79.6 percent of the new assembly, with independents holding 19 percent and the left 1.4 percent. The NDP percentage included, however, ninety-five independents affiliated with the NDP, indicating that party control was not as strong as it might seem. An internationally known Egyptian political analyst has said that the 1990 elections showed that local issues and loyalties counted for more in party politics than political platforms and that unless the NDP is separated from the government, Mubarak's desire for reorganization of NDP structure in the interests of increased democratization cannot occur. The November election was further clouded by the October 12 assassination by Muslim extremists of assembly speaker Rafat al Mahjub, constitutionally next in line to the president.

The Persian Gulf crisis and the ensuing war resulted in quandaries for various Egyptian parties other than the NDP. For example, divisions occurred among Islamist groups with some supporting Saudi Arabia and Kuwait and others backing Iraq. The Muslim Brotherhood decided to end its alliance with the Socialist Labor Party and seek to gain party status of its own. The leftist parties also experienced confusion, with some members of Tagammu supporting each side in the Persian Gulf war.

Evidence of the greater role of constitutionalism was the growing independence of the judiciary under Mubarak. Judges increasingly defended the rights of citizens against the state. The Ministry of Interior, however, often ignored court decrees.

On the foreign affairs front as well, Mubarak followed a policy of gradualism. He continued the friendly relations with the West established under Sadat but sought a more independent course for Egypt. For instance, he improved relations with the Soviet Union and rejected United States president Ronald Reagan's proposal to take joint military action against Libya.

A number of events reflected Mubarak's growing confidence in asserting his personal role and that of Egypt on the Middle East scene. In September 1989, he proposed ten points to enable direct Palestinian-Israeli talks on Israeli prime minister Yitzhaq Shamir's election plan. The points included international observers for the election, withdrawal of the Israel Defense Forces from the balloting area, an end to Israeli settlement activities in the West Bank (see Glossary), and the participation of East Jerusalem residents in the election. The Israeli Labor Party endorsed the proposals, but the Likud government sharply opposed them.

Egypt's more prominent role in the international sphere was also reflected in Mubarak's April 1990 visits to various Asian and European capitals: Beijing, Pyŏngyang, Moscow, and London. He focused primarily on economic matters, seeking debt relief and expanded export markets for Egypt. His purpose also included a request for political action condemning Israel's settlement of Soviet Jewish immigrants in the occupied territories and banning weapons proliferation in the Middle East.

The major event affecting Egypt's relations with the Arab world and the broader international sphere was clearly its decision to side with Saudi Arabia and the United States in opposing Iraq's invasion of Kuwait on August 2, 1990. Earlier Mubarak had sought unsuccessfully to mediate between Iraq and Kuwait. Egyptians were unsympathetic with Iraq despite the presence there of nearly 1 million Egyptian workers because of numerous instances of mistreatment of Egyptians by Iraq and disenchantment with Saddam Husayn's Baath socialism and his authoritarian actions. Mubarak's condemnation of Iraq's occupation of Kuwait, therefore, was initially popular in Egypt; as the crisis developed into war, however, popular support appeared to wane somewhat although observers believed Egyptians supported Mubarak's position approximately three to one.

Even before Iraq invaded Kuwait, its threats to that country began producing a realignment in the Arab world. In mid-July Syrian president Hafiz al Assad paid a historic visit to Cairo after thirteen years of separation between the two nations; both countries shared a concern about Iraq's growing bellicosity. The visit led to the creation of a joint ministerial committee to further cooperation in the economic, industrial, petroleum, energy, agricultural, education, and information fields. (At the beginning of April 1991, after the war, Mubarak and Assad met again in Cairo and announced their opposition to breaking up Iraq.) In mid-October Libyan president Muammar al Qadhafi visited Cairo, as an aftermath of which a number of cooperation agreements were also signed.

A further indication of the new alignment was the majority vote in early September 1990 of League of Arab States (Arab League) members to return Arab League headquarters to Cairo. Egypt had been expelled from the Arab League in 1979 after signing the peace treaty with Israel. Readmitted to the Arab League proper in 1989, Egypt had subsequently joined several League-affiliated bodies such as the Arab Atomic Energy Organization and the Organization of Arab Petroleum Exporting Countries. The vote indicated the split in the organization because only twelve of the twenty-one members, those supporting the condemnation of Iraq's invasion of Kuwait, sent their foreign ministers to the Cairo meeting; representatives of Iraq, Jordan, Libya, Sudan, Yemen, and the Palestine Liberation Organization, among others, were conspicuously absent.

The rift was underscored by Egypt's announcement of its decision in mid-September not to participate further in the Arab Cooperation Council, a primarily economic body formed in 1989 by Egypt, Jordan, Iraq, and the Yemen Arab Republic (North Yemen, prior to the May 1990 union of North and South Yemen). In December Mubarak proposed the creation of a new Arab alliance consisting of Egypt, Saudi Arabia, and Syria, presumably as a replacement for the Arab Cooperation Council, and warned pro-Iraqi Sudan that Egypt would act if Iraqi weapons were transferred there.

Whereas it supported the United States, Egypt's stance in the Persian Gulf crisis was a moderate one. It advocated the ouster of Iraq from Kuwait, but in early November 1990, Mubarak sent word to President Bush that sanctions should be given two to three more months to work before any military attack on Iraq. In a speech to the joint session of the People's Assembly and the Consultative Council on January 24, 1991, Mubarak stated that he had made twenty-six unavailing appeals to Saddam Husayn and had eventually sent a force of 35,000 Egyptians to Saudi Arabia in conformity with the provisions of the Arab Mutual Defense Pact signed in 1950. Also in January, Mubarak sent Minister of Foreign Affairs Ismat Abdul Majid to Washington with a message indicating, among other points, that if Iraq withdrew from Kuwait, Egypt considered Saddam Husayn's remaining in power acceptable.

As the war was ending, Mubarak again addressed a joint legislative session on March 3, 1991. He stated that Egypt was prepared to help rebuild Iraq as well as Kuwait with Egyptian labor and set forth a nine-point program, which he described as a "pan-Arab appeal." The points included that there should be no vengeance, that border disputes must be settled, that the Middle East must be freed of weapons of mass destruction, that the Arab-Israeli dispute must be settled, and that the basis for participation of all Arab citizens in democracy should be expanded. As time passed, however, Egypt became disillusioned by the responses of Kuwait, particularly, and, to a lesser extent, Saudi Arabia to Egypt's offers of manpower assistance. Egypt had agreed to serve with Syria in a Persian Gulf peacekeeping force proposed by the six-nation Gulf Cooperation Council, in accordance with the Damascus Declaration of March 6. Kuwait had made public promises to grant contracts to Egyptian firms and to hire Egyptian workers for its reconstruction efforts. It granted minimal awards to Egypt, however, and implied that Egyptians were fit only for menial labor. In addition, Kuwait indicated its preference for United States rather than Egyptian troops on its territory.

Informed observers believed that Mubarak's announcement on April 8 that Egyptian forces would be withdrawn from the Persian Gulf was the cumulative result of these factors. The United States was shocked by Mubarak's decision and expressed its displeasure to Kuwait, indicating that only a minimal number of United States forces would remain in the area. As a result of United States pressure, Kuwait modified its position, and Egypt agreed in principle with United States secretary of defense Richard B. Cheney to send peacekeeping and border patrol troops to Kuwait. In mid-June the number of such troops remained to be worked out, but Mubarak's visit to Kuwait on July 18 indicated that relations between the two countries had improved. Other evidence of improved Egyptian relations with all Arab states was the unanimous election of Ismat Abdul Majid as secretary general of the Arab League in May.

In the broader international sphere, Secretary of State Baker paid several post-Persian Gulf war visits to Cairo in the first half of 1991, and Egypt was among the first Arab states to indicate its acceptance of the Baker plan for a twofold approach to Middle East talks. The plan proposed that the United States and the Soviet Union jointly sponsor an opening session to be followed by direct negotiations between Israel and its Arab neighbors. On July 19, in a further step toward easing Middle East tensions, Mubarak proposed that Israel suspend the expansion of settlements in the occupied territories, in return for which the Arab states would end their economic boycott of Israel. Saudi Arabia and Jordan soon afterward indicated agreement with this proposal.

Mubarak's domestic policy has been summarized as one of limited liberalization, limited Islamization, and limited repression. These three factors all impinged on national security, a sphere in which Mubarak emphasized the maintenance of domestic stability, probably a more important concern after the 1979 peace treaty with Israel than external threats. Egypt had a professional officer corps but a shortage of well trained enlisted personnel, especially noncommissioned officers, because of the attraction of higher paying civilian employment. Conscripts, based on the 1955 National Military Service Law, served for three years in one of the four services: army, navy, air force, or Air Defense Force, or they might be assigned to the police, prison guard service, or the military economic service. Until the Persian Gulf crisis of late 1990–91, the last war in which the armed services had seen action was the October 1973 War.

Egypt's defense spending was proportionately less than that of most Middle Eastern countries, but it represented 11 percent of gross national product (GNP—see Glossary) in 1987, or 32 percent of total government spending. In addition, Egypt benefited to a substantial degree from foreign military assistance. From 1955 to 1975, this aid came primarily from the Soviet Union, with the result that Egypt had much Soviet military equipment in its inventory. From the signing of the peace treaty with Israel in 1979 onward, the United States became Egypt's main military supplier, and the orientation of the armed forces became Western. Egypt's defense industry was the largest in the Arab world, producing arms, ammunition, artillery, and other military goods and assembling aircraft and armored vehicles for domestic use or export to Third World countries.

With reference to internal security, the military were called out to join the police and the paramilitary police, the Central Security Forces (CSF), to suppress dissent when occasions warranted. This occurred during the 1977 food riots and the 1986 riots by the CSF. The police and intelligence services kept a watchful eye on right-wing Islamic groups, of which the Muslim Brotherhood was the chief, but Al Jihad was one of the most extreme—the organization's leader in Bani Suwayf in Upper Egypt was killed in a riot in late June 1991. Left-wing factions were kept under surveillance as well, although the Communist Party of Egypt had been officially banned since the early 1950s. Former Minister of Interior General Zaki Badr was responsible for the arrest of as many as 20,000 persons charged with being dissidents during his four-year tenure; this figure included arrests in April 1989 of 1,500 persons accused of acts of Muslim extremism against Christian churches and businesses. Moreover, human rights organizations brought accusations of torture on a regular basis against Egypt's internal security forces. Mubarak relieved Badr of his post in early January 1990; his successor, General Muhammad Abd al Halim Musa, stated that he considered the opposition to be "part of the mechanism" of government. This statement encouraged popular hope for a more liberal internal security policy. Restrictions remained, however, and in September 1990, a group of Muslim activists and leftists was barred by the government from traveling to Iraq and Saudi Arabia on a peace mission.

Part of Egypt's internal security concern related to its neighbor to the south, Sudan, which staged a massive pro-Iraqi demonstration in Khartoum on January 19, just after the Persian Gulf war began. Egyptian security forces had been keeping a watchful eye on a number of Sudanese activists, and 500 of them were rounded up and deported on January 23 as representing a threat to Egyptian security. Although public demonstrations have been outlawed in Egypt, about 2,000 Cairo University students staged an antiwar demonstration on February 24, which Cairo police broke up with tear gas. No serious injuries were reported.

The government's continuing concern over national security was but one aspect of the problems posed by the Persian Gulf war. The war had far-reaching political, economic, and diplomatic implications for Egypt's future. In mid-July 1991, it remained to be seen whether Egypt would continue to evolve democratic political institutions, to reform governmental administrative structures, and to promote economic reforms designed to further agricultural and industrial development. Also in question was whether Egypt could resume the position of Arab leadership it had gained under Nasser, now that Syria's Hafiz al Assad was reasserting his regional leadership role, and whether the realignment resulting from the war would work in Egypt's favor.

July 23, 1991   Helen Chapin Metz

Chapter 1. Historical Setting

Sphinx and pyramids at Giza (Al Jizah)

THE ROOTS OF EGYPTIAN civilization go back more than 6,000 years to the beginning of settled life along the banks of the Nile River. The country has an unusual geographical and cultural unity that has given the Egyptian people a strong sense of identity and a pride in their heritage as descendants of humankind's earliest civilized community.

Within the long sweep of Egyptian history, certain events or epochs have been crucial to the development of Egyptian society and culture. One of these was the unification of Upper Egypt and Lower Egypt sometime in the third millennium B.C. The ancient Egyptians regarded this event as the most important in their history, comparable to the "First Time," or the creation of the universe. With the unification of the "Two Lands" by the legendary, if not mythical, King Menes, the glorious Pharaonic Age began. Power was centralized in the hands of a god-king, and, thus, Egypt became the first organized society.

The ancient Egyptians were the first people of antiquity to believe in life after death. They were the first to build in stone and to fashion the arch in stone and brick. Even before the unification of the Two Lands, the Egyptians had developed a plow and a system of writing. They were accomplished sailors and shipbuilders. They learned to chart the heavens in order to predict the Nile flood. Their physicians prescribed healing remedies and performed surgical operations. They sculpted in stone and decorated the walls of their tombs with naturalistic murals in vibrant colors. The legacy of ancient Egypt is written in stone across the face of the country from the pyramids of Upper Egypt to the rock tombs in the Valley of the Kings to the Old Kingdom temples of Luxor and Karnak to the Ptolemaic temples of Edfu and Dendera and to the Roman temple to Isis on Philae Island.

The Arab conquest of 641 by the military commander Amr ibn al As was perhaps the next most important event in Egyptian history because it resulted in the Islamization and Arabization of the country, which endure to this day. Even those who clung to the Coptic religion, a substantial minority of the population in 1990, were Arabized; that is, they adopted the Arabic language and were assimilated into Arab culture.

Although Egypt was formally under Arab rule, beginning in the ninth century hereditary autonomous dynasties arose that allowed local rulers to maintain a great deal of control over the country's

3

destiny. During this period, Cairo was established as the capital of the country and became a center of religion, learning, art, and architecture. In 1260 the Egyptian ruler, Qutuz, and his forces stopped the Mongol advance across the Arab world at the battle of Ayn Jalut in Palestine. Because of this victory, Islamic civilization could continue to flourish when Baghdad, the capital of the Abbasid caliphate, fell to the Mongols. Qutuz's successor, Baybars I, inaugurated the reign of the Mamluks, a dynasty of slave-soldiers of Turkish and Circassian origin that lasted for almost three centuries.

In 1517 Egypt was conquered by Sultan Selim I and absorbed into the Ottoman Empire. Since the Turks were Muslims, however, and the sultans regarded themselves as the preservers of Sunni (see Glossary) Islam, this period saw institutional continuity, particularly in religion, education, and the religious law courts. In addition, after only a century of Ottoman rule, the Mamluk system reasserted itself, and Ottoman governors became at times virtual prisoners in the citadel, the ancient seat of Egypt's rulers.

The modern history of Egypt is marked by Egyptian attempts to achieve political independence, first from the Ottoman Empire and then from the British. In the first half of the nineteenth century, Muhammad Ali, an Albanian and the Ottoman viceroy in Egypt, attempted to create an Egyptian empire that extended to Syria and to remove Egypt from Ottoman control. Ultimately, he was unsuccessful, and true independence from foreign powers would not be achieved until midway through the next century.

Foreign, including British, investment in Egypt and Britain's need to maintain control over the Suez Canal resulted in the British occupation of Egypt in 1882. Although Egypt was granted nominal independence in 1922, Britain remained the real power in the country. Genuine political independence was finally achieved between the 1952 Revolution and the 1956 War. In 1952 the Free Officers, led by Lieutenant Colonel Gamal Abdul Nasser, took control of the government and removed King Faruk from power. In 1956 Nasser, as Egyptian president, announced the nationalization of the Suez Canal, an action that resulted in the tripartite invasion by Britain, France, and Israel. Ultimately, however, Egypt prevailed, and the last British troops were withdrawn from the country by the end of the year.

No history of Egypt would be complete without mentioning the Arab-Israeli conflict, which has cost Egypt so much in lives, territory, and property. Armed conflict between Egypt and Israel ended in 1979 when the two countries signed the Camp David Accords. The accords, however, constituted a separate peace between Egypt

4

and Israel and did not lead to a comprehensive settlement that would have satisfied Palestinian demands for a homeland or brought about peace between Israel and its Arab neighbors. Thus, Egypt remained embroiled in the conflict on the diplomatic level and continued to press for an international conference to achieve a comprehensive agreement.

Ancient Egypt

The Predynastic Period and the First and Second Dynasties, 6000–2686 B.C.

During this period, when people first began to settle along the banks of the Nile (Nahr an Nil) and to evolve from hunters and gatherers to settled, subsistence agriculturalists, Egypt developed the written language, religion, and institutions that made it the world's first organized society. Through pharaonic (see Glossary) Egypt, Africa claims to be the cradle of one of the earliest and most spectacular civilizations of antiquity (see fig. 2).

One of the unique features of ancient Egyptian civilization was the bond between the Nile and the Egyptian people and their institutions. The Nile caused the great productivity of the soil, for it annually brought a copious deposit of rich silt from the monsoon-swept tableland of Ethiopia. Each July, the level of the Nile began to rise, and by the end of August, the flood reached its full height. At the end of October, the flood began to recede, leaving behind a fairly uniform deposit of silt as well as lagoons and streams that became natural reservoirs for fish. By April, the Nile was at its lowest level. Vegetation started to diminish, seasonal pools dried out, and game began to move south. Then in July, the Nile would rise again, and the cycle was repeated.

Because of the fall and rise of the river, one can understand why the Egyptians were the first people to believe in life after death. The rise and fall of the flood waters meant that the "death" of the land would be followed each year by the "rebirth" of the crops. Thus, rebirth was seen as a natural sequence to death. Like the sun, which "died" when it sank on the western horizon and was "reborn" in the eastern sky on the following morning, humans would also rise and live again.

Sometime during the final Paleolithic period and the Neolithic era, a revolution occurred in food production. Meat ceased to be the chief article of diet and was replaced by plants such as wheat and barley grown extensively as crops and not gathered at random in the wild. The relatively egalitarian tribal structure of the Nile Valley broke down because of the need to manage and control

5

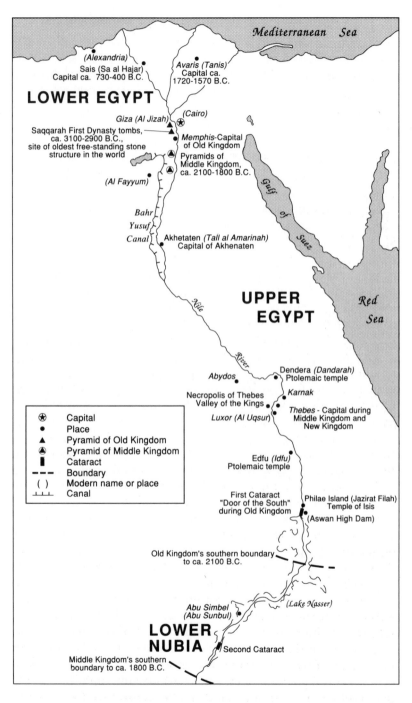

Figure 2. Ancient Egypt

the new agricultural economy and the surplus it generated. Long-distance trade within Egypt, a high degree of craft specialization, and sustained contacts with southwest Asia encouraged the development of towns and a hierarchical structure with power residing in a headman who was believed to be able to control the Nile flood. The headman's power rested on his reputation as a "rainmaker king." The towns became trading centers, political centers, and cult centers. Egyptologists disagree as to when these small, autonomous communities were unified into the separate kingdoms of Lower Egypt and Upper Egypt and as to when the two kingdoms were united under one king.

Nevertheless, the most important political event in ancient Egyptian history was the unification of the two lands: the Black Land of the Delta, so-called because of the darkness of its rich soil, and the Red Land of Upper Egypt, the sun-baked land of the desert. The rulers of Lower Egypt wore the red crown and had the bee as their symbol. The leaders of Upper Egypt wore the white crown and took the sedge as their emblem. After the unification of the two kingdoms, the pharaoh wore the double crown symbolizing the unity of the two lands.

The chief god of the Delta was Horus, and that of Upper Egypt was Seth. The unification of the two kingdoms resulted in combining the two myths concerning the gods. Horus was the son of Osiris and Isis and avenged the evil Seth's slaying of his father by killing Seth, thus showing the triumph of good over evil. Horus took over his father's throne and was regarded as the ancestor of the pharaohs. After unification, each pharaoh took a Horus name that indicated that he was the reincarnation of Horus.

According to tradition, King Menes of Upper Egypt united the two kingdoms and established his capital at Memphis, then known as the "White Walls." Some scholars believe Menes was the Horus King Narmer, whereas others prefer to regard him as a purely legendary figure.

With the emergence of a strong, centralized government under a god-king, the country's nascent economic and political institutions became subject to royal authority. The central government, either directly or through major officials, became the employer of soldiers, retainers, bureaucrats, and artisans whose goods and services benefited the upper classes and the state gods. In the course of the Early Dynastic Period, artisans and civil servants working for the central government fashioned the highly sophisticated traditions of art and learning that thereafter constituted the basic pattern of pharaonic civilization.

The Old Kingdom, Middle Kingdom, and Second Intermediate Period, 2686–1552 B.C.

Historians have given the name "kingdom" to those periods in Egyptian history when the central government was strong, the country was unified, and there was an orderly succession of pharaohs. At times, however, central authority broke down, competing centers of power emerged, and the country was plunged into civil war or was occupied by foreigners. These periods are known as "intermediate periods." The Old Kingdom and the Middle Kingdom together represent an important single phase in Egyptian political and cultural development. The Third Dynasty reached a level of competence that marked a plateau of achievement for ancient Egypt. After five centuries and following the end of the Sixth Dynasty (ca. 2181 B.C.), the system faltered, and a century and a half of civil war, the First Intermediate Period, ensued. The reestablishment of a powerful central government during the Twelfth Dynasty, however, reinstituted the patterns of the Old Kingdom. Thus, the Old Kingdom and the Middle Kingdom may be considered together.

Divine kingship was the most striking feature of Egypt in these periods. The political and economic system of Egypt developed around the concept of a god incarnate who was believed through his magical powers to control the Nile flood for the benefit of the nation. In the form of great religious complexes centered on the pyramid tombs, the cult of the pharaoh, the god-king, was given monumental expression of a grandeur unsurpassed in the ancient Near East.

Central to the Egyptian view of kingship was the concept of *maat,* loosely translated as justice and truth but meaning more than legal fairness and factual accuracy. It referred to the ideal state of the universe and was personified as the goddess Maat. The king was responsible for its appearance, an obligation that acted as a constraint on the arbitrary exercise of power.

The pharaoh ruled by divine decree. In the early years, his sons and other close relatives acted as his principal advisers and aides. By the Fourth Dynasty, there was a grand vizier or chief minister, who was at first a prince of royal blood and headed every government department. The country was divided into *nomes* or districts administered by *nomarchs* or governors. At first, the *nomarchs* were royal officials who moved from post to post and had no pretense to independence or local ties. The post of *nomarch* eventually became hereditary, however, and *nomarchs* passed their offices to their sons. Hereditary offices and the possession of property turned these

officials into a landed gentry. Concurrently, kings began rewarding their courtiers with gifts of tax-exempt land. From the middle
of the Fifth Dynasty can be traced the beginnings of a feudal state
with an increase in the power of these provincial lords, particularly in Upper Egypt.

The Old Kingdom ended when the central administration collapsed in the late Sixth Dynasty. This collapse seems to have resulted
at least in part from climatic conditions that caused a period of
low Nile waters and great famine. The kings would have been discredited by the famine, because pharaonic power rested in part
on the belief that the king controlled the Nile flood. In the absence
of central authority, the hereditary landowners took control and
assumed responsibility for maintaining order in their own areas.
The manors of their estates turned into miniature courts, and Egypt
splintered into a number of feudal states. This period of decen-
tralized rule and confusion lasted from the Seventh through the
Eleventh dynasties.

The kings of the Twelfth Dynasty restored central government
control and a single strong kingship in the period known as the
Middle Kingdom. The Middle Kingdom ended with the conquest
of Egypt by the Hyksos, the so-called Shepherd Kings. The Hyksos were Semitic nomads who broke into the Delta from the northeast and ruled Egypt from Avaris in the eastern Delta.

Pyramid Building in the Old and Middle Kingdoms

With the Third Dynasty, Egypt entered into the five centuries
of high culture known as the Pyramid Age. The age is associated
with Chancellor Imhotep, the adviser, administrator, and architect
of Pharaoh Djoser. He built the pharaoh's funerary complex, including his tomb, the Step Pyramid, at Saqqarah. Imhotep is famed
as the inventor of building in dressed stone. His architectural genius
lay in his use of durable, fine-quality limestone to imitate the brick,
wood, and reed structures that have since disappeared.

The first true pyramid was built by Snoferu, the first king of
the Fourth Dynasty. His son and successor, Kheops, built the Great
Pyramid at Giza (Al Jizah); this, with its two companions on the
same site, was considered one of the wonders of the ancient world.
It contained well over 2 million blocks of limestone, some weigh-
ing fifteen tons apiece. The casing stones of the Great Pyramid
were stripped off to build medieval Cairo (Al Qahirah).

The building and equipping of funerary monuments represented the single largest industry through the Old Kingdom and, after
a break, the Middle Kingdom as well. The channeling of so much
of the country's resources into building and equipping funerary

monuments may seem unproductive by modern standards, but pyramid building seems to have been essential for the growth of pharaonic civilization.

As Egyptologists have pointed out, in ancient societies innovations in technology arose not so much from deliberate research as from the consequences of developing lavish court projects. Equally important, the continued consumption of so great a quantity of wealth and of the products of artisanship sustained the machinery that produced them by creating fresh demand as reign succeeded reign.

The pyramids of the pharaohs, the tombs of the elite, and the burial practices of the poorer classes are related to ancient Egyptian religious beliefs, particularly belief in the afterlife. The Egyptian belief that life would continue after death in a form similar to that experienced on earth was an important element in the development of art and architecture that was not present in other cultures. Thus, in Egypt, a dwelling place was provided for the dead in the form of a pyramid or a rock tomb. Life was magically recreated in pictures on the walls of the tombs, and a substitute in stone was provided for the perishable body of the deceased.

The New Kingdom and Third Intermediate Period, 1552–664 B.C.

Around the year 1600 B.C., a semi-autonomous Theban dynasty under the suzerainty of the Hyksos became determined to drive the Shepherd Kings out of the country and extend its own power. The country was liberated from the Hyksos and unified by Ahmose (ruled 1570–1546 B.C.), the son of the last ruler of the Seventeenth Dynasty. He was honored by subsequent generations as the founder of a new line, the Eighteenth Dynasty, and as the initiator of a glorious chapter in Egyptian history.

During the New Kingdom, Egypt reached the peak of its power, wealth, and territory. The government was reorganized into a military state with an administration centralized in the hands of the pharaoh and his chief minister. Through the intensive military campaigns of Pharaoh Thutmose III (1490–1436 B.C.), Palestine, Syria, and the northern Euphrates area in Mesopotamia were brought within the New Kingdom. This territorial expansion involved Egypt in a complicated system of diplomacy, alliances, and treaties. After Thutmose III established the empire, succeeding pharaohs frequently engaged in warfare to defend the state against the pressures of Libyans from the west, Nubians and Ethiopians (Kushites) from the south, Hittites from the east, and Philistines (sea people) from the Aegean-Mediterranean region of the north.

Toward the end of the Twentieth Dynasty, Egyptian power declined at home and abroad. Egypt was once more separated into its natural divisions of Upper Egypt and Lower Egypt. The pharaoh now ruled from his residence-city in the north, and Memphis remained the hallowed capital where the pharaoh was crowned and his jubilees celebrated. Upper Egypt was governed from Thebes.

During the Twenty-first Dynasty, the pharaohs ruled from Tanis (San al Hajar al Qibliyah), while a virtually autonomous theocracy controlled Thebes. Egyptian control in Nubia and Ethiopia vanished. The pharaohs of the Twenty-second and Twenty-third dynasties were mostly Libyans. Those of the brief Twenty-fourth Dynasty were Egyptians of the Nile Delta, and those of the Twenty-fifth were Nubians and Ethiopians. This dynasty's ventures into Palestine brought about an Assyrian intervention, resulting in the rejection of the Ethiopians and the reestablishment by the Assyrians of Egyptian rulers at Sais (Sa al Hajar), about eighty kilometers southeast of Alexandria (Al Iskandariyah) on the Rosetta branch of the Nile.

Art and Architecture in the New Kingdom

As historian Cyril Aldred has said, the civilization of the New Kingdom seems the most golden of all the epochs of Egyptian history, perhaps because so much of its wealth remains. The rich store of treasures from the tomb of Tutankhamen (ruled 1347–1337 B.C.) gives us a glimpse of the dazzling court art of the period and the skills of the artisans of the day.

One of the innovations of the period was the construction of rock tombs for the pharaohs and the elite. Around 1500 B.C., Pharaoh Amenophis I abandoned the pyramid in favor of a rock-hewn tomb in the crags of western Thebes (present-day Luxor). His example was followed by his successors, who for the next four centuries cut their tombs in the Valley of the Kings and built their mortuary temples on the plain below. Other wadis or river valleys were subsequently used for the tombs of queens and princes.

Another New Kingdom innovation was temple building, which began with Queen Hatshepsut, who as the heiress queen seized power in default of male claimants to the throne. She was particularly devoted to the worship of the god Amun, whose cult was centered at Thebes. She built a splendid temple dedicated to him and to her own funerary cult at Dayr al Bahri in western Thebes.

One of the greatest temples still standing is that of Pharaoh Amenophis III at Thebes. With Amenophis III, statuary on an enormous scale makes its appearance. The most notable is the pair of

11

colossi, the so-called Colossi of Memnon, which still dominate the Theban plain before the vanished portal of his funerary temple.

Ramesses II was the most vigorous builder to wear the double crown of Egypt. Nearly half the temples remaining in Egypt date from his reign. Some of his constructions include his mortuary temple at Thebes, popularly known as the Ramesseum; the huge hypostyle hall at Karnak, the rock-hewn temple at Abu Simbel (Abu Sunbul); and his new capital city of Pi Ramesses.

The Cult of the Sun God and Akhenaten's Monotheism

During the New Kingdom, the cult of the sun god Ra became increasingly important until it evolved into the uncompromising monotheism of Pharaoh Akhenaten (Amenhotep IV, 1364–1347 B.C.). According to the cult, Ra created himself from a primeval mound in the shape of a pyramid and then created all other gods. Thus, Ra was not only the sun god, he was also the universe, having created himself from himself. Ra was invoked as Aten or the Great Disc that illuminated the world of the living and the dead.

The effect of these doctrines can be seen in the sun worship of Pharaoh Akhenaten, who became an uncompromising monotheist. Aldred has speculated that monotheism was Akhenaten's own idea, the result of regarding Aten as a self-created heavenly king whose son, the pharaoh, was also unique. Akhenaten made Aten the supreme state god, symbolized as a rayed disk with each sunbeam ending in a ministering hand. Other gods were abolished, their images smashed, their names excised, their temples abandoned, and their revenues impounded. The plural word for god was suppressed.

Sometime in the fifth or sixth year of his reign, Akhenaten moved his capital to a new city called Akhetaten (present-day Tall al Amarinah, also seen as Tell al Amarna). At that time, the pharaoh, previously known as Amenhotep IV, adopted the name Akhenaten. His wife, Queen Nefertiti, shared his beliefs.

Akhenaten's religious ideas did not survive his death. His ideas were abandoned in part because of the economic collapse that ensued at the end of his reign. To restore the morale of the nation, Akhenaten's successor, Tutankhamen, appeased the offended gods whose resentment would have blighted all human enterprise. Temples were cleaned and repaired, new images made, priests appointed, and endowments restored. Akhenaten's new city was abandoned to the desert sands.

The Late Period, 664–323 B.C.

The Late Period includes the last periods during which ancient

Egypt functioned as an independent political entity. During these years, Egyptian culture was under pressure from major civilizations of the eastern Mediterranean and the Near East. The socioeconomic system, however, had a vigor, efficiency, and flexibility that ensured the success of the nation during these years of triumph and disaster.

Throughout the Late Period, Egypt made a largely successful effort to maintain an effectively centralized state, which, except for the two periods of Persian occupation (Twenty-seventh and Thirty-first dynasties), was based on earlier indigenous models. Late Period Egypt, however, displayed certain destabilizing features, such as the emergence of regionally based power centers. These contributed to the revolts against the Persian occupation but also to the recurrent internal crises of the Twenty-eighth, Twenty-ninth, and Thirtieth dynasties.

The Twenty-sixth Dynasty was founded by Psammethichus I, who made Egypt a powerful and united kingdom. This dynasty, which ruled from 664 to 525 B.C., represented the last great age of pharaonic civilization. The dynasty ended when a Persian invasion force under Cambyses, the son of Cyrus the Great, dethroned the last pharaoh.

Cambyses established himself as pharaoh and appears to have made some attempts to identify his regime with the Egyptian religious hierarchy. Egypt became a Persian province serving chiefly as a source of revenue for the far-flung Persian (Achaemenid) Empire. From Cambyses to Darius II in the years 525 to 404 B.C., the Persian emperors are counted as the Twenty-seventh Dynasty.

Periodic Egyptian revolts, usually aided by Greek military forces, were unsuccessful until 404 B.C., when Egypt regained an uneasy independence under the short-lived, native Twenty-eighth, Twenty-ninth, and Thirtieth dynasties. Independence was lost again in 343 B.C., and Persian rule was oppressively reinstated and continued until 335 B.C., in what is sometimes called the Thirty-first Dynasty or second Persian occupation of Egypt.

Ptolemaic, Roman, and Byzantine Egypt, 332 B.C.–A.D. 642

The Alexandrian Conquest

The Persian occupation of Egypt ended when Alexander the Great defeated the Persians at the Battle of Issus (near present-day İskenderun in Turkey) in November 333 B.C. The Egyptians, who despised the monotheistic Persians and chafed under

Egypt: A Country Study

Persian rule, welcomed Alexander as a deliverer. In the autumn of 332 B.C., Alexander entered Memphis, where, like a true Hellene, he paid homage to the native gods and was apparently accepted without question as king of Egypt. Also like a true Hellene, he celebrated the occasion with competitive games and a drama and music festival at which some of the leading artists of Greece were present. From Memphis, Alexander marched down the western arm of the Nile and founded the city of Alexandria. Then he went to the oasis of Siwa (present-day Siwah) to consult the oracle at the Temple of Amun, the Egyptian god whom the Greeks identified with their own Zeus.

The Ptolemaic Period

After Alexander's death of malarial fever in 323 B.C., the Macedonian commander in Egypt, Ptolemy, who was the son of Lagos, one of Alexander's seven bodyguards, managed to secure for himself the *satrapy* (provincial governorship) of Egypt. In 306 B.C., Antigonus, citing the principle that the empire Alexander created should remain unified, took the royal title. In reaction, his rivals for power, Ptolemy of Egypt, Cassander of Macedonia, and Seleucus of Syria, countered by declaring themselves kings of their respective dominions. Thus came into existence the three great monarchies that were to dominate the Hellenistic world until, one by one, they were absorbed into the Roman Empire.

The dynasty Ptolemy founded in Egypt was known as the line of Ptolemaic pharaohs and endured until the suicide of Cleopatra in 30 B.C., at which time direct Roman control was instituted. The early Ptolemies were hardheaded administrators and business people, anxious to make the state that they created stable, wealthy, and influential. The Ptolemies had their eyes directed outward to the eastern Mediterranean world in which they sought to play a part. Egypt was their basis of power, their granary, and the source of their wealth.

Under the early Ptolemies, the culture was exclusively Greek. Greek was the language of the court, the army, and the administration. The Ptolemies founded the university, the museum, and the library at Alexandria and built the lighthouse at Pharos. A canal to the Red Sea was opened, and Greek sailors explored new trade routes.

Whereas many Egyptians adopted Greek speech, dress, and much of Greek culture, the Greeks also borrowed much from the Egyptians, particularly in religion. In this way, a mixed culture was formed along with a hybrid art that combined Egyptian themes with elements of Hellenistic culture. Examples of this are the grandiose temples built by the Ptolemies at Edfu (present-day Idfu) and Dendera (present-day Dandarah).

The last of the Ptolemies was Cleopatra, the wife of Julius Caesar and later Mark Antony. During her reign, Egypt again became a factor in Mediterranean politics. Cleopatra was a woman of genius and a worthy opponent of Rome. Her main preoccupations were to preserve the independence of Egypt, to extend its territory if possible, and to secure the throne for her children. After the ruinous defeat at Actium in 31 B.C., Cleopatra was unable to continue the fight against Rome. Rather than witness the incorporation of Egypt into the Roman Empire, she chose to die by the bite of the asp. The asp was considered the minister of the sun god whose bite conferred not only immortality but also divinity.

Egypt under Rome and Byzantium, 30 B.C.–A.D. 640

With the establishment of Roman rule by Emperor Augustus in 30 B.C., more than six centuries of Roman and Byzantine control began. Egypt again became the province of an empire, as it had been under the Persians and briefly under Alexander. As the principal source of the grain supply for Rome, it came under the direct control of the emperor in his capacity as supreme military chief, and a strong force was garrisoned there. Gradually, Latin replaced Greek as the language of higher administration. In 212 Rome gave the Egyptians citizenship in the empire.

The emperor ruled as successor to the Ptolemies with the title of "Pharaoh, Lord of the Two Lands," and the conventional divine attributes assigned to Egyptian kings were attributed to him. Rome was careful, however, to bring the native priesthood under its control, although guaranteeing traditional priestly rights and privileges.

Augustus and his successors continued the tradition of building temples to the local gods on which the rulers and the gods were depicted in the Egyptian manner. The Romans completed the construction of an architectural jewel, the Temple of Isis on Philae Island (Jazirat Filah), which was begun under the Ptolemies. A new artistic development during this period was the painting of portraits on wood, an art that originated in the Fayyum region. These portraits were placed on the coffins of mummies.

The general pattern of Roman Egypt included a strong, centralized administration supported by a military force large enough to guarantee internal order and to provide security against marauding nomads. There was an elaborate bureaucracy with an extended system of registers and controls, and a social hierarchy based on caste and privilege with preferred treatment for the Hellenized population of the towns over the rural and native Egyptian population. The best land continued to form the royal domain.

The empire that Rome established was wider, more enduring, and better administered than any the Mediterranean world had known. For centuries, it provided an ease of communication and a unity of culture throughout the empire that would not be seen again until modern times. In Western Europe, Rome founded a tradition of public order and municipal government that outlasted the empire itself. In the East, however, where Rome came into contact with older and more advanced civilizations, Roman rule was less successful.

The story of Roman Egypt is a sad record of shortsighted exploitation leading to economic and social decline. Like the Ptolemies, Rome treated Egypt as a mere estate to be exploited for the benefit of the rulers. But however incompetently some of the later Ptolemies managed their estate, much of the wealth they derived from it remained in the country itself. Rome, however, was an absentee landlord, and a large part of the grain delivered as rent by the royal tenants or as tax by the landowners as well as the numerous money-taxes were sent to Rome and represented a complete loss to Egypt.

The history of Egypt in this period cannot be separated from the history of the Roman Empire. Thus, Egypt was affected by the spread of Christianity in the empire in the first century A.D. and by the decline of the empire during the third century A.D. Christianity arrived early in Egypt, and the new religion quickly spread from Alexandria into the hinterland, reaching Upper Egypt by the second century. According to some Christian traditions, St. Mark brought Christianity to Egypt in A.D. 37, and the church in Alexandria was founded in A.D. 40. The Egyptian Christians are called Copts, a word derived from the Greek word for the country, *Aegyptos*. In the Coptic language, the Copts also called themselves "people of Egypt." Thus the word *Copt* originally implied nationality rather than religion.

In the third century A.D., the decay of the empire gradually affected the Roman administration of Egypt. Roman bureaucracy became overcentralized and poorly managed. The number of qualified applicants for administrative positions was sharply reduced by Roman civil war, pestilence, and conflict among claimants to imperial power.

A renaissance of imperial authority and effectiveness took place under Emperor Diocletian. During his reign (284–305), the partition of the Roman Empire into eastern and western segments began. Diocletian inaugurated drastic political and fiscal reforms and sought to simplify imperial administration. Under Diocletian, the administrative unity of Egypt was destroyed by transforming Egypt from one province into three. Seeing Christianity as a threat to Roman state religion and thus to the unity of the empire, Diocletian launched a violent persecution of Christians.

The Egyptian church was particularly affected by the Roman persecutions, beginning with Septimius Severus's edict of 202 dissolving the influential Christian School of Alexandria and forbidding future conversions to Christianity. In 303 Emperor Diocletian issued a decree ordering all churches demolished, all sacred books burned, and all Christians who were not officials made slaves. The decree was carried out for three years, a period known as the "Era of Martyrs." The lives of many Egyptian Christians were spared only because more workers were needed in the porphyry quarries and emerald mines that were worked by Egyptian Christians as "convict labor."

Emperor Constantine I (324–337) ruled both the eastern and western parts of the empire. In 330 he established his capital at Byzantium, which he renamed Constantinople (present-day Istanbul). Egypt was governed from Constantinople as part of the Byzantine Empire. In 312 Constantine established Christianity as the official religion of the empire, and his Edict of Milan of 313 established freedom of worship.

By the middle of the fourth century, Egypt was largely a Christian country. In 324 the ecumenical Council of Nicea established the patriarchate of Alexandria as second only to that of Rome; its jurisdiction extended over Egypt and Libya. The patriarchate had a profound influence on the early development of the Christian church because it helped to clarify belief and to formulate dogmas. In 333 the number of Egyptian bishops was estimated at nearly 100.

After the fall of Rome, the Byzantine Empire became the center of both political and religious power. The political and religious conflict between the Copts of Egypt and the rulers of Byzantium began when the patriarchate of Constantinople began to rival that of Alexandria. The Council of Chalcedon in 451 initiated the great schism that separated the Egyptian Church from Catholic Christendom. The schism had momentous consequences for the future of Christianity in the East and for Byzantine power. Ostensibly, the council was called to decide on the nature of Christ. If Christ were both God and man, had he two natures? The Arians had already been declared heretics for denying or minimizing the divinity of Christ; the opposite was to ignore or minimize his humanity. Coptic Christians were Monophysites who believed that after the incarnation Christ had but one nature with dual aspects. The council, however, declared that Christ had two natures and that he was equally human and equally divine. The Coptic Church refused to accept the council's decree and rejected the bishop sent to Egypt. Henceforth, the Coptic Church was in schism from the Catholic Church as represented by the Byzantine Empire and the Byzantine Church.

For nearly two centuries, Monophysitism in Egypt became the symbol of national and religious resistance to Byzantium's political and religious authority. The Egyptian Church was severely persecuted by Byzantium. Churches were closed, and Coptic Christians were killed, tortured, and exiled in an effort to force the Egyptian Church to accept Byzantine orthodoxy. The Coptic Church continued to appoint its own patriarchs, refusing to accept those chosen by Constantinople and attempting to depose them. The break with Catholicism in the fifth century converted the Coptic Church to a national church with deeply rooted traditions that have remained unchanged to this day.

By the seventh century, the religious persecutions and the growing pressure of taxation had engendered great hatred of the Byzantines. As a result, the Egyptians offered little resistance to the conquering armies of Islam.

Medieval Egypt
The Arab Conquest, 639-41

Perhaps the most important event to occur in Egypt since the unification of the Two Lands by King Menes was the Arab conquest of Egypt. The conquest of the country by the armies of Islam under the command of the Muslim hero, Amr ibn al As, transformed Egypt from a predominantly Christian country to a Muslim country in which the Arabic language and culture were adopted even by those who clung to their Christian or Jewish faiths.

The conquest of Egypt was part of the Arab/Islamic expansion that began when the Prophet Muhammad died and Arab tribes began to move out of the Arabian Peninsula into Iraq and Syria. Amr ibn al As, who led the Arab army into Egypt, was made a military commander by the Prophet himself.

Amr crossed into Egypt on December 12, 639, at Al Arish with an army of about 4,000 men on horseback, armed with lances, swords, and bows. The army's objective was the fortress of Babylon (Bab al Yun) opposite the island of Rawdah in the Nile at the apex of the Delta. The fortress was the key to the conquest of Egypt because an advance up the Delta to Alexandria could not be risked until the fortress was taken.

Great Pyramid and Sphinx at Giza, Fourth Dynasty, ca. 2540 B.C.
Courtesy Boris Boguslavsky

In June 640, reinforcements for the Arab army arrived, increasing Amr's forces to between 8,000 and 12,000 men. In July the Arab and Byzantine armies met on the plains of Heliopolis. Although the Byzantine army was routed, the results were inconclusive because the Byzantine troops fled to Babylon. Finally, after a six-month siege, the fortress fell to the Arabs on April 9, 641.

The Arab army then marched to Alexandria, which was not prepared to resist despite its well fortified condition. Consequently, the governor of Alexandria agreed to surrender, and a treaty was signed in November 641. The following year, the Byzantines broke the treaty and attempted unsuccessfully to retake the city.

Muslim conquerors habitually gave the people they defeated three alternatives: converting to Islam, retaining their religion with freedom of worship in return for the payment of the poll tax, or war. In surrendering to the Arab armies, the Byzantines agreed to the second option. The Arab conquerors treated the Egyptian Copts well. During the battle for Egypt, the Copts had either remained neutral or had actively supported the Arabs. After the surrender, the Coptic patriarch was reinstated, exiled bishops were called home, and churches that had been forcibly turned over to the Byzantines were returned to the Copts. Amr allowed Copts who held office to retain their positions and appointed Copts to other offices.

Amr moved the capital south to a new city called Al Fustat (present-day Old Cairo). The mosque he built there bears his name and still stands, although it has been much rebuilt.

For two centuries after the conquest, Egypt was a province ruled by a line of governors appointed by the caliphs in the east. Egypt provided abundant grain and tax revenue. In time most of the people accepted the Muslim faith, and the Arabic language became the language of government, culture, and commerce. The Arabization of the country was aided by the continued settlement of Arab tribes in Egypt.

From the time of the conquest onward, Egypt's history was intertwined with the history of the Arab world. Thus, in the eighth century, Egypt felt the effects of the Arab civil war that resulted in the defeat of the Umayyad Dynasty, the establishment of the Abbasid caliphate, and the transfer of the capital of the empire from Damascus to Baghdad. For Egypt, the transfer of the capital farther east meant a weakening of control by the central government. When the Abbasid caliphate began to decline in the ninth century, local autonomous dynasties arose to control the political, economic, social, and cultural life of the country.

The Tulinids, Ikhshidids, Fatimids, and Ayyubids, 868–1260

A new era began in Egypt with the arrival in Al Fustat in 868 of Ahmad ibn Tulun as governor on behalf of his stepfather, Bayakbah, a chamberlain in Baghdad to whom Caliph Al Mutazz had granted Egypt as a fief. Ahmad ibn Tulun inaugurated the autonomy of Egypt and, with the succession of his son, Khumarawayh, to power, established the principle of locally based hereditary rule. Autonomy greatly benefited Egypt because the local dynasty halted or reduced the drain of revenue from the country to Baghdad. The Tulinid state ended in 905 when imperial troops entered Al Fustat. For the next thirty years, Egypt was again under the direct control of the central government in Baghdad.

The next autonomous dynasty in Egypt, the Ikhshidid, was founded by Muhammad ibn Tughj, who arrived as governor in 935. The dynasty's name comes from the title of Ikhshid given to Tughj by the caliph. This dynasty ruled Egypt until the Fatimid conquest of 969.

The Tulinids and the Ikhshidids brought Egypt peace and prosperity by pursuing wise agrarian policies that increased yields, by eliminating tax abuses, and by reforming the administration. Neither the Tulinids nor the Ikhshidids sought to withdraw Egypt from the Islamic empire headed by the caliph in Baghdad. Ahmad ibn Tulun and his successors were orthodox Sunni Muslims, loyal to the principle of Islamic unity. Their purpose was to carve out an autonomous and hereditary principality under loose caliphal authority.

The Fatimids, the next dynasty to rule Egypt, unlike the Tulinids and the Ikhshidids, wanted independence, not autonomy, from Baghdad. In addition, as heads of a great religious movement, Ismaili Shia Islam (see Glossary), they also challenged the Sunni Abbasids for the caliphate itself. The name of the dynasty is derived from Fatima, the daughter of the Prophet Muhammad and the wife of Ali, the fourth caliph and the founder of Shia Islam. The leader of the movement, who first established the dynasty in Tunisia in 906, claimed descent from Fatima.

Under the Fatimids, Egypt became the center of a vast empire, which at its peak comprised North Africa, Sicily, Palestine, Syria, the Red Sea coast of Africa, Yemen, and the Hijaz in Arabia, including the holy cities of Mecca and Medina. Control of the holy cities conferred enormous prestige on a Muslim sovereign and the power to use the yearly pilgrimage to Mecca to his advantage. Cairo was the seat of the Shia caliph, who was the head of a religion as well as the sovereign of an empire. The Fatimids established Al

Azhar in Cairo as an intellectual center where scholars and teachers elaborated the doctrines of the Ismaili Shia faith.

The first century of Fatimid rule represents a high point for medieval Egypt. The administration were reorganized and expanded. It functioned with admirable efficiency: tax farming was abolished, and strict probity and regularity in the assessment and collection of taxes were enforced. The revenues of Egypt were high and were then augmented by the tribute of subject provinces.

This period was also an age of great commercial expansion and industrial production. The Fatimids fostered both agriculture and industry and developed an important export trade. Realizing the importance of trade both for the prosperity of Egypt and for the extension of Fatimid influence, the Fatimids developed a wide network of commercial relations, notably with Europe and India, two areas with which Egypt had previously had almost no contact.

Egyptian ships sailed to Sicily and Spain. Egyptian fleets controlled the eastern Mediterranean, and the Fatimids established close relations with the Italian city states, particularly Amalfi and Pisa. The two great harbors of Alexandria in Egypt and Tripoli in present-day Lebanon became centers of world trade. In the east, the Fatimids gradually extended their sovereignty over the ports and outlets of the Red Sea for trade with India and Southeast Asia and tried to win influence on the shores of the Indian Ocean. In lands far beyond the reach of Fatimid arms, the Ismaili missionary and the Egyptian merchant went side by side.

In the end, however, the Fatimid bid for world power failed. A weakened and shrunken empire was unable to resist the crusaders, who in July 1099 captured Jerusalem from the Fatimid garrison after a siege of five weeks.

The crusaders were driven from Jerusalem and most of Palestine by the great Kurdish general Salah ad Din ibn Ayyub, known in the West as Saladin. Saladin came to Egypt in 1168 in the entourage of his uncle, the Kurdish general Shirkuh, who became the *wazir,* or senior minister, of the last Fatimid caliph. After the death of his uncle, Saladin became the master of Egypt. The dynasty he founded in Egypt, called the Ayyubid, ruled until 1260.

Saladin abolished the Fatimid caliphate, which by this time was dead as a religious force, and returned Egypt to Sunni orthodoxy. He restored and tightened the bonds that tied Egypt to eastern Islam and reincorporated Egypt into the Sunni fold represented by the Abbasid caliphate in Baghdad. At the same time, Egypt was opened to the new social changes and intellectual movements that had been emerging in the East. Saladin introduced into Egypt the *madrasah,* a mosque-college, which was the intellectual heart of the

Sunni religious revival. Even Al Azhar, founded by the Fatimids, became in time *the* center of Islamic orthodoxy.

In 1193 Saladin died peacefully in Damascus. After his death, his dominions split up into a loose dynastic empire controlled by members of his family, the Ayyubids. Within this empire, the Ayyubid sultans of Egypt were paramount because their control of a rich, well-defined territory gave them a secure basis of power.

Economically, the Ayyubid period was one of growth and prosperity. Italian, French, and Catalan merchants operated in ports under Ayyubid control. Egyptian products, including alum, for which there was a great demand, were exported to Europe. Egypt also profited from the transit trade from the East. Like the Fatimids before him, Saladin brought Yemen under his control, thus securing both ends of the Red Sea and an important commercial and strategic advantage.

Culturally, too, the Ayyubid period was one of great activity. Egypt became a center of Arab scholarship and literature and, along with Syria, acquired a cultural primacy that it has retained through the modern period. The prosperity of the cities, the patronage of the Ayyubid princes, and the Sunni revival made the Ayyubid period a cultural high point in Egyptian and Arab history.

The Mamluks, 1250–1517

To understand the history of Egypt during the later Middle Ages, it is necessary to consider two major events in the eastern Arab world: the migration of Turkish tribes during the Abbasid caliphate and their eventual domination of it, and the Mongol invasion. Turkish tribes began moving west from the Eurasian steppes in the sixth century. As the Abbasid Empire weakened, Turkish tribes began to cross the frontier in search of pasturage. The Turks converted to Islam within a few decades after entering the Middle East. The Turks also entered the Middle East as mamluks (slaves) employed in the armies of Arab rulers. Mamluks, although slaves, were usually paid, sometimes handsomely, for their services. Indeed, a mamluk's service as a soldier and member of an elite unit or as an imperial guard was an enviable first step in a career that opened to him the possibility of occupying the highest offices in the state. Mamluk training was not restricted to military matters and often included languages and literary and administrative skills to enable the mamluks to occupy administrative posts.

In the late tenth century, a new wave of Turks entered the empire as free warriors and conquerors. One group occupied Baghdad, took control of the central government, and reduced the

Abbasid caliphs to puppets. The other moved west into Anatolia, which it conquered from a weakened Byzantine Empire.

The Mamluks had already established themselves in Egypt and were able to establish their own empire because the Mongols destroyed the Abbasid caliphate. In 1258 the Mongol invaders put to death the last Abbasid caliph in Baghdad. The following year, a Mongol army of as many as 120,000 men commanded by Hulagu Khan crossed the Euphrates and entered Syria. Meanwhile, in Egypt the last Ayyubid sultan had died in 1250, and political control of the state had passed to the Mamluk guards whose generals seized the sultanate. In 1258, soon after the news of the Mongol entry into Syria had reached Egypt, the Turkish Mamluk Qutuz declared himself sultan and organized the successful military resistance to the Mongol advance. The decisive battle was fought in 1260 at Ayn Jalut in Palestine, where Qutuz's forces defeated the Mongol army.

An important role in the fighting was played by Baybars I, who shortly afterwards assassinated Qutuz and was chosen sultan. Baybars I (1260–77) was the real founder of the Mamluk Empire. He came from the elite corps of Turkish Mamluks, the Bahriyyah, so-called because they were garrisoned on the island of Rawdah on the Nile River. Baybars I established his rule firmly in Syria, forcing the Mongols back to their Iraqi territories.

At the end of the fourteenth century, power passed from the original Turkish elite, the Bahriyyah Mamluks, to Circassians, whom the Turkish Mamluk sultans had in their turn recruited as slave soldiers. Between 1260 and 1517, Mamluk sultans of Turco-Circassian origin ruled an empire that stretched from Egypt to Syria and included the holy cities of Mecca and Medina. As "shadow caliphs," the Mamluk sultans organized the yearly pilgrimages to Mecca. Because of Mamluk power, the western Islamic world was shielded from the threat of the Mongols. The great cities, especially Cairo, the Mamluk capital, grew in prestige. By the fourteenth century, Cairo had become the preeminent religious center of the Muslim world.

Egypt under the Ottoman Empire

In 1517 the Ottoman sultan Selim I (1512–20), known as Selim the Grim, conquered Egypt, defeating the Mamluk forces at Ar Raydaniyah, immediately outside Cairo. The origins of the Ottoman Empire go back to the Turkish-speaking tribes who crossed the frontier into Arab lands beginning in the tenth century. These Turkish tribes established themselves in Baghdad and Anatolia, but they were destroyed by the Mongols in the thirteenth century.

In the wake of the Mongol invasion, petty Turkish dynasties called amirates were formed in Anatolia. The leader of one of those dynasties was Osman (1280–1324), the founder of the Ottoman Empire. In the thirteenth century, his amirate was one of many; by the sixteenth century, the amirate had become an empire, one of the largest and longest lived in world history. By the fourteenth century, the Ottomans already had a substantial empire in Eastern Europe. In 1453 they conquered Constantinople, the Byzantine capital, which became the Ottoman capital and was renamed Istanbul. Between 1512 and 1520, the Ottomans added the Arab provinces, including Egypt, to their empire.

In Egypt the victorious Selim I left behind one of his most trusted collaborators, Khair Bey, as the ruler of Egypt. Khair Bey ruled as the sultan's vassal, not as a provincial governor. He kept his court in the citadel, the ancient residence of the rulers of Egypt. Although Selim I did away with the Mamluk sultanate, neither he nor his successors succeeded in extinguishing Mamluk power and influence in Egypt.

Only in the first century of Ottoman rule was the governor of Egypt able to perform his tasks without the interference of the Mamluk beys (bey was the highest rank among the Mamluks). During the latter decades of the sixteenth century and the early seventeenth century, a series of revolts by various elements of the garrison troops occurred. During these years, there was also a revival within the Mamluk military structure. By the middle of the seventeenth century, political supremacy had passed to the beys. As the historian Daniel Crecelius has written, from that point on the history of Ottoman Egypt can be explained as the struggle between the Ottomans and the Mamluks for control of the administration and, hence, the revenues of Egypt, and the competition among rival Mamluk houses for control of the beylicate. This struggle affected Egyptian history until the late eighteenth century when one Mamluk bey gained an unprecedented control over the military and political structures and ousted the Ottoman governor.

Modern Egypt
The Neo-Mamluk Beylicate, 1760–98

Most scholars of Egyptian history now agree that the political and economic changes that occurred in the early nineteenth century had their origins not in the French invasion of 1798 but rather in events that occurred in Egypt itself in the latter half of the eighteenth century. At that time, political and military power was consolidated in the hands of the Mamluk Ali Bey al Kabir (1760–66)

25

and his successor, Muhammad Bey Abu adh Dhahab (1772-75). Before 1760 a balance of power and separate spheres of influence were maintained by the Mamluk beylicate, which controlled the civil administration and derived its revenues from the rural tax farms, and by the Mamluks, who dominated the military and derived their revenues from the urban tax farms and the customs house.

In 1760 Ali Bey gained control of the military and drove the sultan's governor from the country. He issued *firmans* (decrees) in his own name, redirected the state revenues to his own use, and attempted to recreate the medieval Mamluk empire by invading Syria. In addition, Ali Bey tried to strengthen commercial ties with Europe by encouraging trade and attempting to open the port of Suez to European shipping.

Ali Bey ruled only briefly, but his successors, especially Muhammad Bey, continued his policies. These two beys effectively eliminated Ottoman control and repositioned Egypt at the center of a newly emerging network of international relationships that embraced the lands of the eastern Mediterranean, the Red Sea coasts, and Europe. Thus, Napoleon Bonaparte did not ''open'' an isolated Egypt to the West, nor was Muhammad Ali Pasha in the nineteenth century the originator of the policies responsible for Egypt's transformation. Only Ali Bey's dramatic expulsion from the country and Muhammad Bey's premature death of a fever prevented them from using the authority they acquired to carry on those policies that are associated with Egypt's revival in the nineteenth century.

The French Invasion and Occupation, 1798-1801

After the death of Muhammad Bey, there was a decade-long struggle for dominance among the beys. Eventually Ibrahim Bey and Murad Bey succeeded in asserting their authority and shared power in Egypt. Their dominance in the country survived an unsuccessful attempt by the Ottomans to reestablish the empire's control (1786-91). The two continued in power until the French invasion in 1798.

In addition to the upheavals caused by the Ottoman-Mamluk clashes, waves of famine and plague hit Egypt between 1784 and 1792. Thus, Cairo was a devastated city and Egypt an impoverished country when the French arrived in 1798.

On July 1, 1798, a French invasion force under the command of Napoleon disembarked near Alexandria. The invasion force, which had sailed from Toulon on May 19, was accompanied by a commission of scholars and scientists whose function was to investigate every aspect of life in ancient and contemporary Egypt.

France wanted control of Egypt for two major reasons—its commercial and agricultural potential and its strategic importance to the Anglo-French rivalry. During the eighteenth century, the principal share of European trade with Egypt was handled by French merchants. The French also looked to Egypt as a source of grain and raw materials. In strategic terms, French control of Egypt could be used to threaten British commercial interests in the region and to block Britain's overland route to India.

The French forces took Alexandria without difficulty, defeated the Mamluk army at Shubra Khit and Imbabah, and entered Cairo on July 25. Murad Bey fled to Upper Egypt while Ibrahim Bey and the Ottoman viceroy went to Syria. Mamluk rule in Egypt collapsed.

Nevertheless, Napoleon's position in Egypt was precarious. The French controlled only the Delta and Cairo; Upper Egypt was the preserve of the Mamluks and the beduins. In addition, Britain and the Ottoman government joined forces in an attempt to defeat Napoleon and drive him out of Egypt. On August 1, 1798, the British fleet under Lord Nelson annihilated the French ships as they lay at anchor at Abu Qir, thus isolating Napoleon's forces in Egypt. On September 11, Sultan Selim III declared war on France.

On October 21, the people of Cairo rioted against the French, whom they regarded as occupying strangers, not as liberators. The rebellion had a religious as well as a national character and centered around Al Azhar mosque. Its leaders were the ulama, religiously trained scholars, whom Napoleon had tried to woo to the French side. During this period, the populace began to regard the ulama not only as moral but also as political leaders.

To forestall an Ottoman invasion, Napoleon invaded Syria, but, unable to take Acre in Palestine, his forces retreated on May 20, 1799. On August 22, Napoleon, with a very small company, secretly left Egypt for France, leaving his troops behind and General Jean-Baptiste Kléber as his successor. Kléber found himself the unwilling commander in chief of a dispirited army with a bankrupt treasury. His main preoccupation was to secure the evacuation of his troops to France. When Britain rejected the evacuation plan, Kléber was forced to fight.

After Kléber's assassination by a Syrian, his command was taken over by General Abdullah Jacques Menou, a French convert to Islam. The occupation was finally terminated by an Anglo-Ottoman invasion force. The French forces in Cairo surrendered on June 18, 1801, and Menou himself surrendered at Alexandria on September 3. By the end of September, the last French forces had left the country.

As historian Afaf Lutfi al-Sayyid Marsot has written, the three-year French occupation was too short to exert any lasting effects on Egypt, despite claims to the contrary. Its most important effect on Egypt internally was the rapid decline in the power of the Mamluks.

The major impact of the French invasion was the effect it had on Europe. Napoleon's invasion revealed the Middle East as an area of immense strategic importance to the European powers, thus inaugurating the Anglo-French rivalry for influence in the region and bringing the British into the Mediterranean. The French invasion of Egypt also had an important effect on France because of the publication of *Description de l'Egypte,* which detailed the findings of the scholars and scientists who had accompanied Napoleon to Egypt. This publication became the foundation of modern research into the history, society, and economics of Egypt.

Muhammad Ali, 1805–48

After the French left Egypt, an Ottoman army remained in the country. The Ottoman government was determined to prevent a revival of Mamluk power and autonomy and to bring Egypt under the control of the central government. The Ottomans appointed Khusraw Pasha as viceroy. Hostilities occasionally broke out between his forces and those of the Mamluks who had established themselves in Upper Egypt.

By 1803 it was apparent that a third party had emerged in the struggle for power in Egypt. This was the Albanian contingent of Ottoman forces that had come in 1801 to fight against the French. Muhammad Ali, who had arrived in Egypt as a junior commander in the Albanian forces, had by 1803 risen to commander. In just two short years, he would become the Ottoman viceroy in Egypt.

Muhammad Ali, who has been called the "father of modern Egypt," was able to attain control of Egypt because of his own leadership abilities and political shrewdness but also because the country seemed to be slipping into anarchy. The urban notables and the ulama believed that Muhammad Ali was the only leader capable of bringing order and security to the country. The Ottoman government, however, aware of the threat Muhammad Ali represented to the central authority, attempted to get rid of him by making him governor of the Hijaz. Eventually, the Ottomans capitulated to Egyptian pressure, and in June 1805, they appointed Muhammad Ali governor of Egypt.

Between 1805 and 1811, Muhammad Ali consolidated his position in Egypt by defeating the Mamluks and bringing Upper Egypt under his control. Finally, in March 1811, Muhammad Ali had

Temple of Queen Hatshepsut at Dayr al Bahri, ca. 1500 B.C.
Courtesy Martha Hopkins

sixty-four Mamluks, including twenty-four beys, assassinated in the citadel. From then on, Muhammad Ali was the sole ruler of Egypt. Muhammad Ali represented the successful continuation of policies begun by the Mamluk Ali Bey al Kabir. Like Ali Bey, Muhammad Ali had great ambitions. He, too, wanted to detach Egypt from the Ottoman Empire, and he realized that to do so Egypt had to be strong economically and militarily.

Muhammad Ali's development strategy was based on agriculture. He expanded the area under cultivation and planted crops specifically for export, such as long-staple cotton, rice, indigo, and sugarcane. The surplus income from agricultural production was used for public works, such as irrigation, canals, dams, and barrages, and to finance industrial development and the military. The development plans hinged on the state's gaining a monopoly over the country's agricultural resources. In practical terms, this meant the peasants were told what crops to plant, in what quantity, and over what area. The government bought directly from the peasants and sold directly to the buyer, cutting out the intermediaries or merchants.

Muhammad Ali was also committed to the industrial development of Egypt. The government set up modern factories for weaving cotton, jute, silk, and wool. Workers were drafted into factories

29

to weave on government looms. Factories for sugar, indigo, glass, and tanning were set up with the assistance of foreign advisers and imported machinery. Industries employed about 4 percent of the population, or between 180,000 and 200,000 persons fifteen years of age and over. The textile industry was protected by embargoes imposed by the government to prohibit the import of the cheap British textiles that had flooded the Egyptian market. Commercial activities were geared toward the establishment of foreign trade monopolies and an attempt to acquire a favorable balance of trade.

The historian Marsot has argued that Britain became determined to check Muhammad Ali because a strong Egypt represented a threat to Britain's economic and strategic interests. Economically, British interests would be served as long as Egypt continued to produce raw cotton for the textile mills of Lancashire and to import finished goods from Britain. Thus, the British and also the French were particularly angered by the Egyptian monopolies even though Britain and France engaged in such trade practices as high tariffs and embargoes to protect their own economies. Strategically, Britain wanted to maintain access to the overland route through Egypt to India, a vital link in the line of imperial communications. Britain was worried not only about the establishment of a united, militarily strong state straddling the eastern Mediterranean but also about Muhammad Ali's close ties to France.

It was at this time that Lord Palmerston, the British minister of foreign affairs, established the British policy, which lasted until the outbreak of World War I, of preserving the integrity of the Ottoman Empire. Britain preferred a weakened but intact Ottoman Empire that would grant it the strategic and commercial advantages it needed to maintain its influence in the region. Thus, Muhammad Ali's invasion of Syria in 1831 and his attempt to break away from the Ottoman Empire jeopardized British policy and its military and commercial interests in the Middle East and India. The Egyptian invasion of Syria was provoked ostensibly by the sultan's refusal to give Syria and Morea (Peloponnesus) to Muhammad Ali in return for his assistance in opposing the Greek war for independence in the late 1820s. This resulted in Turkey and Egypt being forced out of the eastern Mediterranean by the destruction of their combined naval strength at Navarino on the southern coast of Greece.

When Egyptian forces invaded and occupied Syria and came within sight of Istanbul, the great powers (Britain, France, Austria, Russia, and Prussia) allied themselves with the Ottoman government to drive the Egyptian forces out of Syria. A British fleet bombarded Beirut in September 1840, and an Anglo-Turkish force landed, causing uprisings against the Egyptian forces. Acre fell in November, and a British naval force anchored off Alexandria. The Egyptian army was forced to retreat to Egypt, and Muhammad Ali was obliged to accede to British demands. According to the Treaty of 1841, Muhammad Ali was stripped of all the conquered territory except Sudan but was granted the hereditary governorship of Egypt for life, with succession going to the eldest male in the family. Muhammad Ali was also compelled to agree to the Anglo-Ottoman Convention of 1838, which established "free trade" in Egypt. This meant that Muhammad Ali was forced to abandon his monopolies and establish new tariffs that were favorable to imports. Thus, Egypt was unable to control the flood of cheap manufactured imports that decimated local industries.

Muhammad Ali continued to rule Egypt after his defeat in Syria. He became increasingly senile toward the end of his rule and his eldest son, Ibrahim, petitioned the Ottoman government to be appointed governor because of his father's inability to rule. Ibrahim was gravely ill of tuberculosis, however, and ruled for only six months, from July to November 1848. Muhammad Ali died in August 1849.

Abbas Hilmi I, 1848-54 and Said, 1854-63

Ibrahim was succeeded by Abbas Hilmi I, a genuine traditionalist with no interest in continuing the development plans of his grandfather, Muhammad Ali. Abbas disliked Europeans, but he allowed a railroad line to be built between Alexandria and Cairo that facilitated British imperial communications with India. Regular steamship services already linked Britain to India via Alexandria, Suez, and Bombay. This partially overland route to India took thirty-one days, compared to three months for the journey around the Cape of Good Hope.

Abbas's successor was Said, the fourth son of Muhammad Ali. He revived the works in agriculture, irrigation, and education begun by his father. Under his rule, the first land law governing private landed property in Egypt was passed in 1858. Said abolished the agricultural monopolies of his father by granting landowners the right to dispose freely of their produce as well as the freedom to choose what crops to cultivate. He also introduced uniform military service and the first organized pension plan for public servants.

Said was a friend of the French engineer Ferdinand de Lesseps, to whom he granted a concession in 1854 to construct a canal from the Red Sea to the Mediterranean. The Suez Canal Company was organized to undertake the construction, and the concession to the company included two items that proved costly for Egypt. First,

31

the company was granted a strip of land linking the Nile with the canal site. There a freshwater canal was constructed, and the strip of land was decreed tax free, allowing the company to enjoy the benefits of its cultivation. Second, the viceroy undertook to supply labor for the canal's construction, in what amounted to a system of forced labor (see Suez Canal, ch. 3).

Social Change in the Nineteenth Century

During the nineteenth century, the socioeconomic and political foundations of the modern Egyptian state were laid. The transformation of Egypt began with the integration of the economy into the world capitalist system with the result that by the end of the century Egypt had become an exporter of raw materials to Europe and an importer of European manufactured goods. The transformation of Egypt led to the emergence of a ruling elite composed of large landowners of Turco-Circassian origin and the creation of a class of medium-sized landowners of Egyptian origin who played an increasingly important role in the political and economic life of the country. In the countryside, peasants were dispossessed because of debt, and many landless peasants migrated to the cities where they joined the swelling ranks of the under- and unemployed. In the cities, a professional middle class emerged composed of civil servants, lawyers, teachers, and technicians. Finally, Western ideas and cultural forms were introduced into the country.

Rural Society

Muhammad Ali had attempted to take Egypt directly from a subsistence agricultural economy to a complex industrial one. He failed because of internal weaknesses and European pressures. Ironically, Muhammad Ali, whose goal was to make Egypt economically and politically independent of Europe, set the country on the path to economic dependence and foreign domination.

In the industrial sector, Muhammad Ali's factories did not last past his death. In the agricultural sector, Egypt's long-staple cotton became increasingly attractive to British textile manufacturers. Between 1840 and 1860, the export of cotton increased 300 percent. During the American Civil War, the area devoted to cotton cultivation in Egypt increased almost fourfold and cotton prices rose along with cotton production.

The transformation of the rural economy from subsistence to cash-crop agriculture caused dramatic changes, including the privatization of land in fewer hands and the dispossession of peasants. The privatization of land began during the reign of Muhammad Ali, who in the 1840s distributed half the agricultural land to royal family members, Turco-Circassian officials, and Egyptian notables or village headmen. Although many land grants were rescinded during the reign of Abbas, consolidation of landholdings proceeded during the reigns of Said and Ismail at the expense of small and middle-sized peasant proprietors. By the 1870s, the royal family owned one-fifth of all the cultivated land in the country. The largest royal estates could be as large as 10,000 *feddans* (a *feddan* is slightly more than an acre—see Glossary). By the 1890s, 42.5 percent of all registered land was held in tracts of more than fifty *feddans*. The largest landowners included members of the royal family, and the Turco-Circassian elite of officers and officials. Their estates were worked by sharecroppers or agricultural laborers. By the time of Ismail, these landowners had developed into a landed aristocracy. Another group of landholding elite originated with Muhammad Ali's appointment of Egyptians as village headmen (*umada;* sing., *umdah*), the state's agents in the countryside. This was Muhammad Ali's attempt to reduce the power of the Turco-Circassians. With the privatization of land, the Egyptian notables became substantial landowners with considerable political influence.

Historian Judith Tucker has described the nineteenth century as a time when the peasants were transformed from independent producers with rights to use the land to landless peasants forced to work as wage-laborers or to migrate to the cities where they became part of the urban dispossessed. The development of capitalist agriculture and a monetized rural economy spelled disaster for many peasants. Despite land laws like those of Said in 1855 and 1858, which gave peasants legal ownership of their plots, peasant land loss occurred at an unprecedented rate, chiefly because of indebtedness. Forced to borrow at high rates of interest to get the seed and animals necessary for sowing and to pay monthly installments on their taxes, the peasants had to repay these loans at harvest time when the prices were lowest.

The American Civil War put a premium on Egyptian cotton, and the price increased. When the war ended, the inflated prices suddenly dropped. For the first time in Egypt, a serious problem of peasant indebtedness appeared with its inevitable consequences: mortgages, foreclosures, and usurious loans. The village headmen and the owners of great estates profited from the crisis by purchasing abandoned land. The headmen also profited as moneylenders.

Peasants also lost land because taxes on peasant land were higher than on estate land. Large landholders sometimes paid as little as one-fourth of the taxes paid by the peasantry. In addition, peasants fled the countryside to escape corvée (forced labor) on the state's public works projects and military conscription.

At the turn of the century, the population of Egypt was about 10 million. Of this total, between 10 and 20 percent were landless peasants. In 1906 less than 20 percent of the privately held and *waqf* (religiously endowed) land was held by 80 percent of the population while 1 percent owned more than 40 percent. Most landowners owned between one and five *feddans*, with three *feddans* being necessary for subsistence.

Towns and Cities

Of the 10 million people in Egypt at the turn of the century, approximately 2 million lived in towns and cities, and of those, 500,000 lived in cities with a population of more than 20,000. The population of Alexandria grew as it became the financial and commercial center of the cotton industry. New towns like Az Zaqaziq and Port Said (Bur Said) on the Suez Canal were established.

Most of the increase in Egypt's urban population was the result of the migration of peasants from the countryside. Although some became workers or petty traders, most joined the ranks of the under- or unemployed. By the turn of the century, a working class had emerged. It was composed mainly of transport and building workers and of workers in the few industries that had been established— sugar refineries, ginning mills, and cigarette factories. However, a large proportion of the new urban lower class consisted of a fluctuating mass of people without any fixed employment.

The old lower class of the cities and towns, particularly the artisans, suffered from the influx of cheaply made European imports. Whereas some crafts, like basketry, pottery, and rug weaving, survived, others such as textiles and glass blowing were virtually eliminated. The urban guilds declined and eventually disappeared because Europeans replaced Egyptians in production and commerce.

The old, or traditional, middle class also declined in status and wealth. This middle class included the ulama, religiously educated elite who staffed the religious institutions and courts, and the merchants. The ulama and the merchants were closely tied to each other because of family and business connections. Furthermore, these categories overlapped; the ulama were also merchants and tax-farmers. The decline of the ulama began during the reign of Muhammad Ali who considered the ulama an intolerable alternative power center. He abolished tax farms, which were a major source of ulama wealth, thus weakening their position.

The decline of the ulama and the merchants was accelerated by the socioeconomic transformation of Egypt that led to the emergence of secular education, to secularly trained civil servants staffing the government bureaucracy, and to the reorientation of Egyptian trade. Secular education and the establishment of schools influenced by Western ideas and methods occurred throughout the century but were particularly widespread during the reign of Khedive (see Glossary) Ismail. Secular education became identified with entrance into government employment. Moreover, once government employment was opened to Egyptians, it became the goal of the educated because of the power and social status it conferred. Between 1882 and 1907, the number of persons employed in public administration grew by 83.7 percent. The rise of this new urban middle class, called the *effendiyah,* parallelled the rise of the rural notables or *umada.* In fact, during the nineteenth century, the *effendiyah* tended to be first-generation urbanites from rural notable families who took advantage of expanded education and employment opportunities in the cities.

Whereas the Egyptian *effendiyah* and *umada* were rising, the traditional merchant class declined because the lucrative import-export trade was dominated by resident foreigners, and Egyptian merchants were confined to internal trade. During the nineteenth century, foreign trade was completely reoriented. In the past, it had dealt mainly in Sudanese, Arabian, and oriental goods. Cairo was one of the most important centers of trade, and Egyptian, Syrian, and Turkish merchants engaged in it. During the nineteenth century, Greeks and other Europeans resident in Egypt monopolized the export of cotton to Europe and the import of European industrial goods.

The change was reflected in the increase of foreigners in Egypt— from between 8,000 and 10,000 in 1838 to 90,000 in 1881. The majority was engaged in cotton production, import-export trade, banking, and finance. The European community occupied a privileged position as a result of the capitulations, the treaties governing the status of foreigners within the Ottoman Empire. These treaties put Europeans virtually beyond the reach of Egyptian law until the establishment of the mixed courts (with jurisdiction over Egyptians and foreigners) in 1876. Like the artisans, Egyptian merchants suffered from a large variety of oppressive taxes and duties from which foreign merchants were exempt. With the support of their consuls, foreigners in Egypt became an increasingly powerful pressure group committed to defending their own interests.

From Autonomy to Occupation: Ismail, Tawfiq, and the Urabi Revolt

Khedive Ismail, 1863–79

No ruler of Egypt, except Gamal Abdul Nasser, has provoked such controversy in the West as Ismail. At the time, the anti-Ismail view was held mainly by British administrators like Evelyn Baring (Lord Cromer) and Lord Alfred Milner, who depicted him as squeezing the peasants for money by oppressive taxation and the whip, and "ruining Egypt" by his lavish spending and despotic ways. Journalists and the American consuls in Egypt such as Edwin de Leon held a more balanced view, arguing that Ismail inherited an unfavorable Suez Canal agreement and a significant public and private debt from his uncle, Said. They noted that although Ismail spent lavishly, much of the money he borrowed from European bankers was used for building or repairing the country's infrastructure. They also pointed out that European bankers and financiers loaned money to Egypt at usurious interest rates and, when it seemed Egypt would be unable to repay the loans, urged their governments to intervene to protect their interests.

Ismail's goals for Egypt were similar to those of his grandfather, Muhammad Ali. He wanted Egypt to become virtually independent of the Ottoman Empire, a political and military power in the eastern Mediterranean and an economic partner of Europe. Ismail achieved a considerable degree of independence from the Porte (from Sublime Porte, the term for the High Gate that came to be synonymous with the Ottoman government) by making large payments to the Ottoman treasury. For example, in return for increasing Egypt's annual payment to the Ottoman treasury from £175,000 to £400,000, Sultan Abdul Aziz allowed Ismail to change the rule of succession from the oldest surviving male heir of Muhammad Ali to direct male primogeniture in his family. The sultan also granted Ismail the formal title of khedive, which elevated his standing to a position closer to royalty.

Ismail's attempt to make Egypt independent foundered eventually because of the gap between the revenues the country could produce and the expenses necessary to achieve his goals. He attempted to generate more income by increasing agricultural productivity, chiefly by bringing more land into cultivation through expensive irrigation projects such as the construction of canals and dams. During his reign, an additional 506,000 hectares were brought under cultivation, representing a sizeable increase in both production and income.

To service the cotton crop, which was the basis of Egypt's prosperity, roads, bridges, railways, harbors, and telegraph lines had to be constructed. During Ismail's reign, 112 canals, 13,440 kilometers long, were dug; 400 bridges were built; 480 kilometers of railroad lines were laid; and 8,000 kilometers of telegraph lines were erected. Towns and cities were modernized by the expansion of public services such as water distribution, transport, street lighting, and gas supply. Public education was reorganized and expanded, and a postal service was established. The army and bureaucracy were expanded and modernized. In short, Ismail undertook the construction of the infrastructure of a modern state.

Ismail greatly expanded Egypt's revenues and exports during his reign. But the country's prosperity was tied to the export of cotton, whose price was set on a fluctuating world market, making income uncertain. Moreover, Ismail's infrastructure development entailed more expenditure than Egypt's income could provide, with the result that he was obliged to contract foreign loans. These loans, added to the expensive concessions that Said had made concerning the Suez Canal, meant that by 1875 Egypt was £100 million in debt. In that year, Ismail sold his shares in the Suez Canal Company, making the British government overnight the single largest shareholder in the company. The sale of Ismail's shares did not solve the country's financial problems, however, but merely staved off the crisis for another year.

From Intervention to Occupation, 1876–82

Seriously concerned with the country's financial situation, Ismail asked for British help in fiscal reform. Britain responded by sending Steven Cave, a member of Parliament, to investigate. Cave judged Egypt to be solvent on the basis of its resources and said that all the country needed to get back on its feet was time and the proper servicing of the debts. Cave recommended the establishment of a control commission over Egypt's finances to approve all future loans.

European creditors, however, would not allow Egypt time. When Ismail suspended payment of interest on the loans in 1875, his creditors in Britain and France appointed two men to represent their interests and negotiate new arrangements with the khedive. The Goschen-Joubert Mission achieved three things: the consolidation of the debt; the appointment of two European controllers, one British and one French; and the establishment of the Caisse de la Dette Publique, a special department with representatives from the various European creditor states to ensure the service of the debt. Revenue from the most productive provinces went straight to the department, and by 1877 more than 60 percent of all Egyptian revenue went to service the national debt.

Although Egypt serviced the debt faithfully, European intervention increased. At the insistence of the French, a commission of inquiry was appointed in 1878 to examine all sources of revenue and expenditure. The commission had the right to ask any Egyptian official or government deputy to testify before it and to subpoena all records. Such powers implied the dilution of Egyptian sovereignty by Europeans.

The commission report indicted the khedival government and suggested limiting Ismail's power as a first step in solving the country's financial problems. The khedive accepted the commission's conditions, including a cabinet containing Europeans and the principle of ministerial responsibility. He appointed Nubar Pasha as prime minister and asked him to form a government containing two Europeans. Many Europeans were appointed at high salaries in various government departments; thirty British officers were appointed to the Land Survey Department alone. Ismail was also forced to delegate governmental responsibility to his cabinet, which was made independent of the khedive and responsible for the administration of the country.

Opposition to European intervention in Egypt's internal affairs emerged from the Assembly of Delegates, which Ismail had created in 1866, and from the Egyptian army officers. The assembly, composed mainly of Egyptian notables, had no legislative power. It was Ismail's attempt to associate the Egyptian notables with his financial policies, and thus, to demonstrate support for his taxes and foreign loans. The presence of Egyptian officers in the army resulted from the 1854 decree of Said, who ordered the sons of village notables to join the army. Said allowed them to be trained as officers and to rise to the rank of colonel, but the top posts in the army continued to be held by members of the Turco-Circassian elite.

The Assembly of Delegates, meeting between January and July 1879, demanded more control over financial matters and accountability of the European ministers to the assembly. At the same time, a group of Egyptian army officers who opposed the mixed cabinet protested the placing of 2,500 officers on half-pay. A group of army officers marched on the Ministry of Finance and occupied the building. Only the personal intervention of the khedive, who was suspected of instigating the incident, saved the situation. At this point, Ismail realized that he could use both the assembly and the army officers to rid himself of foreign control.

In April 1879, Ismail's opportunity came. Under foreign pressure, Ismail ordered the assembly to dissolve. Its members refused, saying they represented the nation and would not relinquish their mandate at the order of the khedive, influenced and pressured as he was by foreign powers. On March 29, they presented a manifesto to the khedive protesting the Council of Ministers' attempts to usurp their power and authority. They also stated their determination to reject the European ministers' demand that Egypt declare itself bankrupt.

The leader of the delegates was the constitutionally minded Muhammad Sharif Pasha, who was among the members of a secret society called the National Society (later the Hulwan Society). The society had drawn up a plan for national reform (Laiha Wataniyah) that proposed constitutional and financial reforms to increase the power of the assembly and resolve Egypt's financial problems without foreign advisers or control.

In a shrewd political move, Ismail summoned the European consuls and confronted them with the discontent of the delegates, the disaffection in the army, and the general public uneasiness. He informed them that he had decided to act in accordance with the resolutions of the assembly. Therefore, he rejected the proposal to declare Egypt bankrupt and stated his intent to meet all obligations to Egypt's creditors. He also invited Sharif Pasha to form a government. Sharif Pasha and his Egyptian cabinet dismissed the European ministers.

Although these actions made Ismail popular at home, they threatened continued European control over Egypt's finances. The European powers, particularly Britain and France, decided Ismail had to go. Since he refused to abdicate, the European powers put pressure on the Ottoman sultan to dismiss him in favor of his son Tawfiq. On June 26, 1879, he received a telegram from the grand vizier addressed to "the ex-khedive Ismail." Ismail left Egypt for exile in Naples and subsequently in Istanbul, where he died in 1895.

Tawfiq proved to be a more pliable instrument in the hands of the European powers. The dual control of Egypt's finances was reinstituted. An international commission of liquidation was appointed with British, French, Austrian, and Italian members. In July 1880, the Law of Liquidation was promulgated, limiting Egypt to 50 percent of its total revenues. The rest went to the Caisse de la Dette Publique to service the debt. The Assembly of Delegates remained dissolved.

The direct interference of Europeans in Egypt's affairs and the deposition of Khedive Ismail forged a nationalist movement composed of Egyptian landowners and merchants, especially former members of the assembly, Egyptian army officers, and the intelligentsia, including the ulama and Muslim reformers. A secret society of Egyptian army officers had also come into existence in 1876, comparable to the secret society of Egyptian notables. The army society included Colonel Ahmad Urabi, who would become the leader of the nationalist movement, and colonels Ali Fahmi and Abd al Al Hilmi. In 1881 a link, if not a merger, was formed between the Urabists and the National Society. This expanded group took the name Al Hizb al Watani al Ahli, the National Popular Party.

Beginning in 1881, the army officers demonstrated their strength and their ability to intimidate the khedive. They began with a mutiny provoked by the anti-Urabist minister of war. Not only were they able to force the appointment of a more sympathetic minister but by January 1882, Urabi joined the government as undersecretary for war.

These developments alarmed the European powers, particularly Britain and France. Britain was especially concerned about protecting the Suez Canal and the British lifeline to India. In January 1882, Britain and France sent a joint note declaring their support for the khedive. The note had the opposite effect from that intended, producing an upsurge in anti-European feeling, a shift in leadership of the nationalist movement from the moderates in the assembly to the military, and the formation of a new government with Urabi as minister of war. At this point, the goal of Urabi and his followers became not only the removal of all European influence from Egypt but also the overthrow of the khedive.

In another attempt to break Urabi's power, the British and French agreed on a joint show of naval strength. They also issued a series of demands including the resignation of the government, the temporary exile of Urabi, and the internal exile of his two closest associates, Ali Fahmi and Abd al Al Hilmi. As a result, violent anti-European riots broke out in Alexandria with considerable loss of life on both sides.

During the summer, an international conference of the European powers met in Istanbul, but no agreement was reached. The Ottoman sultan Abdul Hamid boycotted the conference and refused to send troops to Egypt. Eventually, Britain decided to act alone. The French withdrew their naval squadron from Alexandria, and in July 1882, the British fleet began bombarding Alexandria.

Following the burning of Alexandria and its occupation by British marines, the British installed the khedive in the Ras at Tin Palace. The khedive obligingly declared Urabi a rebel and deprived him of his political rights. Urabi in turn obtained a religious ruling, a *fatwa,* signed by three Al Azhar shaykhs, deposing Tawfiq as a traitor who brought about the foreign occupation of his country and betrayed his religion. Urabi also ordered general conscription and declared war on Britain. Thus, as the British army was about to land in August, Egypt had two leaders: the khedive, whose authority was confined to British-controlled Alexandria, and Urabi, who was in full control of Cairo and the provinces.

Gold mask of Tutankhamen, bearing symbols of Upper and Lower Egypt
Courtesy Boris Boguslavsky

In August Sir Garnet Wolsley and an army of 20,000 invaded the Suez Canal Zone. Wolsley was authorized to crush the Urabi forces and clear the country of rebels. The decisive battle was fought at Tall al Kabir on September 13, 1882. The Urabi forces were routed and the capital captured. The nominal authority of the khedive was restored, and the British occupation of Egypt, which was to last for seventy-two years, had begun.

Urabi was captured, and he and his associates were put on trial. An Egyptian court sentenced Urabi to death, but through British intervention the sentence was commuted to banishment to Ceylon. Britain's military intervention in 1882 and its extended, if attenuated, occupation of the country left a legacy of bitterness among the Egyptians that would not be expunged until 1956 when British troops were finally removed from the country.

From Occupation to Nominal Independence, 1882–1923
The Occupiers

With the occupation of 1882, Egypt became a part of the British Empire but never officially a colony. The khedival government provided the facade of autonomy, but behind it lay the real power in the country, specifically, the British agent and consul general, backed by British troops.

At the outset of the occupation, the British government declared its intention to withdraw its troops as soon as possible. This could not be done, however, until the authority of the khedive was restored. Eventually, the British realized that these two aims were incompatible because the military intervention, which Khedive Tawfiq supported and which prevented his overthrow, had undermined the authority of the ruler. Without the British presence, the khedival government would probably have collapsed.

In addition, the British government realized that the most effective way to protect its interests was from its position in Egypt. This represented a change in the policy that had existed since the time of Muhammad Ali, when the British were committed to preserving the Ottoman Empire. The change in British policy occurred for several reasons. Sultan Abdul Hamid had refused Britain's request to intervene in Egypt against Urabi and to preserve the khedival government. Also, Britain's influence in Istanbul was declining while that of Germany was rising. Finally, Britain's unilateral invasion of Egypt gave Britain the opportunity to supplant French influence in the country. Moreover, Britain was determined to preserve its control over the Suez Canal and to safeguard the vital route to India.

Between 1883 and the outbreak of World War I in 1914, there were three British agents and consuls general in Egypt: Lord Cromer (1883–1907), Sir John Eldon Gorst (1907–11), and Lord Herbert Kitchener (1911–14). Cromer was an autocrat whose control over Egypt was more absolute than that of any Mamluk or khedive. Cromer believed his first task was to achieve financial solvency for Egypt. He serviced the debt, balanced the budget, and spent what money remained after debt payments on agriculture, irrigation, and railroads. He neglected industry and education, a policy that became a political issue in the country. He brought in British officials to staff the bureaucracy. This policy, too, was controversial because it prevented Egyptian civil servants from rising to the top of their fields.

Gorst, who was less autocratic than Cromer, had to face a growing Egyptian nationalism that demanded British evacuation from the country. Gorst's attempt to create a "moderate" nationalism ultimately failed because the nationalists refused to make any compromises over independence and because Britain considered any concession to the nationalists a sign of weakness.

When Kitchener arrived in Egypt in 1911, he was already famous as the man who had avenged the death of General Charles Gordon in Khartoum in 1885 during the Mahdist uprising. In 1913 Kitchener introduced a new constitution that gave the country some representative institutions locally and nationally. When the British occupation began, the Assembly of Delegates had ceased to exist. It was superseded by an assembly and legislative council that were consultative bodies whose advice was not binding on the government. The Organic Law of 1913 provided for a legislative assembly with an increased number of elected members and expanded powers.

On October 29, 1914, the Ottoman Empire entered World War I on the side of the Central Powers. Martial law was declared in Egypt on November 2. On November 3, the British government unilaterally declared Egypt a protectorate, severing the country from the Ottoman Empire. Britain deposed Khedive Abbas, who had succeeded Khedive Tawfiq upon the latter's death in 1892, because Abbas, who was in Istanbul when the war broke out, was suspected of pro-German sympathies. Kitchener was recalled to London to serve as minister of war.

Economy and Society under Occupation

By 1914 cotton constituted 90 percent of Egypt's exports. To the British, who controlled Egypt's financial and economic life, ensuring Egypt's prosperity and its ability to service its debt meant expanding Egypt's reliance on cotton production. Some British officials had more personal reasons for their interest in the production and export of cotton. Some were landowners; some were involved in the marketing of the crop; and some, like Lord Cromer, made huge fortunes from cotton speculation.

Trade policy was based on free trade, which favored the more industrialized nations whose products undersold those produced locally. Lord Cromer himself described the effects of the import of European manufactures on local craft production. He noted that quarters of the city that had been "hives of busy workmen" had shrunk or been eliminated entirely. Cafés and small stores selling European goods replaced productive workshops. Egyptian industrialization would have required protective tariffs that the British would not allow. Thus, although Egypt had a solid infrastructure, a sizeable local market, and an indigenous supply of capital, industrial development was stymied by a British trade policy that sought to protect the Egyptian market for British products and to maintain Britain's near monopoly on Egyptian cotton.

In spite of these formidable obstacles, a small industrial sector did develop, devoted primarily to processing raw materials and producing perishable or bulky goods. Industrialization gave rise to a modern working class engaged in factory labor. By 1916 there were 30,000 to 35,000 workers employed in modern factories.

Pay in the industrial sector was low and working conditions sometimes unsafe. Just as it maintained a hands-off policy concerning trade, the state refused to intervene to regulate working conditions. Between 1899 and 1907, at least seven workers' associations were formed, focusing on conditions and pay. Strikes were organized among cigarette wrappers; warehouse, port, and railroad workers; and spinners in factories. The working-class movement received considerable support from Mustafa Kamil's National Party (Al Hizb al Watani), which set up schools in working-class areas and assisted unions with publicity and legal counsel during strikes. The unions, like the nationalist movement, were severely repressed by the government.

In 1906 the Dinshawi Incident occurred, which intensified nationalist and anti-British sentiments. A fight broke out between the villagers of Dinshawi, near Tanta in the Delta, and a group of British officers who were shooting pigeons nearby. In the course of the shooting, the wife of the local imam (religious leader) was shot and wounded. Villagers surrounded the officers, and in the ensuing fracas, two British officers were wounded. The officers in turn panicked and opened fire on the villagers. One of the British officers died of his wounds as he attempted to march back to camp a few miles away. British soldiers who found the dead officer beat a peasant to death. Fifty-two Egyptians were arrested and brought before a special court convened in Shibin al Kawm. Four peasants were sentenced to death, many to terms of imprisonment at hard labor, and others to public flogging. The sentences were executed swiftly, publicly, and brutally. This event heightened Egyptian political consciousness and led to the organization of political parties.

In 1907 two political parties were formed, which served as vehicles for expressing nationalist ideas and actions. They were Kamil's National Party (also seen as the Watani Party) and the People's Party (Al Hizb al Umma or Umma Party). The Umma Party was founded by Mahmud Sulayman Pasha, a former leader of the assembly and ally of Colonel Urabi, and Hasan Abd ar Raziq, among others. The most prominent member of the Umma Party was Ahmad Lutfi as Sayyid, editor of the party's newspaper, *Al Jaridah* (The Newspaper). The National Party's newspaper was *Al Liwa* (The Standard). Kamil and Lutfi as Sayyid were Egyptian rather than Turco-Circassian in origin and represented the increasing political strength of Egyptians in national life. Kamil's party called for the British to evacuate Egypt immediately. Although Kamil agreed that Egypt needed reform, he argued that the British presence was not necessary to achieve it. Because Islam played a larger role in his thought and in the party ideology than in the Umma Party, Kamil and the National Party attracted to it anti-European conservatives and religious traditionalists.

The leaders of the Umma Party had been disciples of the influential Islamic reformer Muhammad Abduh. Unlike Abduh, however, who was concerned with the reform of Islam to accommodate it to the modern world, Lutfi as Sayyid was concerned with progress and the reform of society. The aim of the Umma Party was independence. Lutfi as Sayyid believed, however, that Egypt would attain self-rule not by attacking the British or the khedive but through reform of Egyptian laws and institutions and the participation of Egyptians in public life.

Lutfi as Sayyid believed Egypt should cooperate in any measures that would limit the autocracy of the khedive and expand constitutional government, which could only strengthen the nation. Implicit in the Umma program was the idea of tactical cooperation and eventual negotiation with the British on the future of Egypt, an idea that Kamil and the National Party rejected. The National Party was described as "extremist" because of its demand for the immediate withdrawal of the British, while the Umma Party was called "moderate" because of its gradualist approach to independence from British domination.

Kamil died in 1908; the party never recovered from his death although it continued to play a role in national political life until 1952. It was the only political group that refused to take part in negotiations for the Anglo-Egyptian Treaty of 1936. The Umma Party participated in Egyptian party politics until World War I, and its newspaper ceased publication in 1915. The party's influence was long-lasting, however, because Saad Zaghlul, who emerged as leader of the nationalist movement after the war, was part of the Umma/*Al Jaridah* circle.

Egypt under the Protectorate and the 1919 Revolution

Opposition to European interference in Egypt's affairs resulted in the emergence of a nationalist movement that coalesced and spread after the British military intervention and occupation of 1882. The immediate causes of what is known to Egyptians as the 1919 Revolution, however, were British actions during the war that caused widespread hardship and resentment. Specifically, these included Britain's purchase of cotton and requisitioning of fodder at below market prices, Britain's forcible recruitment of about 500,000 peasants into the Labor and Camel Transport Corps in the Egyptian Expeditionary Force, and its use of the country as a base and a garrison populated by British, Australian, and other troops. After the war, Egypt felt the adverse effects of soaring prices and unemployment.

When the war ended, the nationalists began to press the British again for independence. In addition to their other reasons, the Egyptians were influenced by American president Woodrow Wilson, who was preaching self-determination for all nations. In September 1918, Egypt made the first moves toward the formation of a *wafd*, or delegation, to voice its demands for independence at the Paris Peace Conference. The idea for a *wafd* had originated among prominent members of the Umma Party, including Lutfi as Sayyid, Saad Zaghlul, Muhammad Mahmud, Ali Sharawi, and Abd al Aziz Fahmi.

On November 13, 1918, thereafter celebrated in Egypt as Yawm al Jihad (Day of Struggle), Zaghlul, Fahmi, and Sharawi had an audience with Sir Reginald Wingate, the British high commissioner. They demanded complete independence with the proviso that Britain be allowed to supervise the Suez Canal and the public debt. They also asked permission to go to London to put their case before the British government. On the same day, the Egyptians formed a delegation for this purpose, Al Wafd al Misri (known as the Wafd), headed by Saad Zaghlul. The British refused to allow the Wafd to proceed to London. On March 8, Zaghlul and three other members of the Wafd were arrested and thrown into Qasr an Nil prison. The next day, they were deported to Malta, an action that sparked the popular uprising of March-April 1919 in which Egyptians of all social classes participated. There were violent clashes in Cairo and the provincial cities of Lower Egypt, especially Tanta, and the uprising spread to the south, culminating in violent confrontations in Asyut Province in Upper Egypt.

The deportation of the Wafdists also triggered student demonstrations and escalated into massive strikes by students, government officials, professionals, women, and transport workers. Within a week, all of Egypt was paralyzed by general strikes and rioting. Railroad and telegraph lines were cut, taxi drivers refused to work, lawyers failed to appear for court cases, and demonstrators marched through the streets shouting pro-Wafdist slogans and demanding independence. Violence resulted, with many Egyptians and Europeans being killed or injured when the British attempted to crush the demonstrations with force.

On March 16, between 150 and 300 upper-class Egyptian women in veils staged a demonstration against the British occupation, an event that marked the entrance of Egyptian women into public life. The women were led by Safia Zaghlul, wife of Wafd leader Saad Zaghlul; Huda Sharawi, wife of one of the original members of the Wafd and organizer of the Egyptian Feminist Union; and Muna Fahmi Wissa. Women of the lower classes demonstrated in the streets alongside the men. In the countryside, women engaged in activities like cutting rail lines.

The upper-class women participating in politics for the first time assumed key roles in the movement when the male leaders were exiled or detained. They organized strikes, demonstrations, and boycotts of British goods and wrote petitions, which they circulated to foreign embassies protesting British actions in Egypt.

The women's march of March 16 preceded by one day the largest demonstration of the 1919 Revolution. More than 10,000 teachers, students, workers, lawyers, and government employees started marching at Al Azhar and wound their way to Abdin Palace where they were joined by thousands more, who ignored British roadblocks and bans. Soon, similar demonstrations broke out in Alexandria, Tanta, Damanhur, Al Mansurah, and Al Fayyum. By the summer of 1919, more than 800 Egyptians had been killed, as well as 31 Europeans and 29 British soldiers.

Wingate, the British high commissioner, understood the strength of the nationalist forces and the threat the Wafd represented to British dominance and had tried to persuade the British government to allow the Wafd to travel to Paris. However, the British government remained hostile to Zaghlul and the nationalists and adamant in rejecting Egyptian demands for independence. Wingate was recalled to London for talks on the Egyptian situation, and Milne Cheetham became acting high commissioner in January 1919. When the 1919 Revolution began, Cheetham soon realized that he was powerless to stop the demonstrations and admitted that matters were completely out of his control. Nevertheless, the government in London ordered him not to give in to the Wafd and to restore order, a task that he was unable to accomplish.

London decided to replace Wingate with a strong military figure, General Edmund Allenby, the greatest British hero of World War I. He was named special high commissioner and arrived in Egypt on March 25. The next day, he met with a group of Egyptian nationalists and ulama. After persuading Allenby to release the Wafd leaders and to permit them to travel to Paris, the Egyptian group agreed to sign a statement urging the people to stop demonstrating. Allenby, who was convinced that this was the only way to stop the revolt, then had to persuade the British government to agree. On April 7, Zaghlul and his colleagues were released and set out for Paris.

In May 1919, Lord Milner was appointed to head a mission to investigate how Egypt could be granted "self-governing institutions" while maintaining the protectorate and safeguarding British interests. The mission arrived in Egypt in December 1919 but was boycotted by the nationalists, who opposed the continuation of the protectorate. The arrival of the Milner Mission was followed by strikes in which students, lawyers, professionals, and workers participated. Merchants closed their shops, and organizers distributed leaflets urging the Egyptians not to cooperate with the mission.

Milner realized that a direct approach to Zaghlul was necessary, and in the summer of 1920 private talks between the two men took place in London. As a result of the so-called Milner-Zaghlul Agreement, the British government announced in February 1921 that it would accept the abolition of the protectorate as the basis for negotiation of a treaty with Egypt.

On April 4, 1921, Zaghlul's return to Egypt was met by an unprecedented welcome, showing that the vast majority of Egyptians supported him. Allenby, however, was determined to break Zaghlul's political power and to build up a pro-British group to whom Britain could safely commit Egyptian independence. On December 23, Zaghlul was deported to the Seychelles via Aden. His deportation was followed by demonstrations, violent clashes with the police, and strikes by students and government employees that affected Cairo, Alexandria, Port Said, Suez, and provincial towns like Tanta, Zifta, Az Zaqaziq, and Jirja.

On February 28, 1922, Britain unilaterally declared Egyptian independence without any negotiations with Egypt. Four matters were "absolutely reserved to the discretion" of the British government until agreements concerning them could be negotiated: the security of communications of the British Empire in Egypt; the defense of Egypt against all foreign aggressors or interference, direct or indirect; the protection of foreign interests in Egypt and the protection of minorities; and Sudan. Sultan Ahmad Fuad became King Fuad I, and his son, Faruk, was named as his heir. On April 19, a new constitution was approved. Also that month, an electoral law was issued that ushered in a new phase in Egypt's political development—parliamentary elections.

The Era of Liberal Constitutionalism and Party Politics
The Rise and Decline of the Wafd, 1924–39

Political life in Egypt during this period has been described as basically triangular, consisting of the king, the Wafd, and the British. The basis of British power was its army of occupation as well as British officials in the administration, police, and army. The king's power rested on the rights he could exercise in accordance with the 1923 constitution and partly on the permanence of his position. The king's rights included selecting and appointing the prime minister, dismissing the cabinet, and dissolving Parliament. The Wafd's power was based on its popular support and its command of a vast majority in Parliament.

These three forces in Egyptian politics were of unequal strength. The British had overwhelming power, and if their interests were at stake, their power prevailed over the other two. The king was in a stronger position than the Wafd because his power was difficult to curb while the Wafd could easily be removed from power. The Wafd embodied parliamentary democracy in Egypt; thus, by its very existence, it constituted a threat to both the king and the British. To the king, any democratic system was a threat to his autocratic rule. To the British, a democratic system meant that in any free election the Wafd would be voted into power. The British believed that the Wafd in power was a threat to their own power in the country. Thus, the British attempted to destroy the power of the Wafd and to use the king as a counter to the Wafd.

In the parliamentary election of January 12, 1924, the Wafd won 179 of 211 parliamentary seats. Two seats each went to the Wafd's opponents, the National Party and the Liberal Constitutionalist

Party, a party founded in 1922 and considered excessively cooperative with the British. The Wafd felt it had a mandate to conclude a treaty with Britain that would assure Egypt complete independence. As prime minister, Zaghlul carefully selected a cross-section of Egyptian society for his cabinet, which he called the "People's Ministry." On March 15, 1924, the king opened the first Egyptian constitutional parliament amid national rejoicing. The Wafdist government did not last long, however.

On November 19, 1924, Sir Lee Stack, the British governor general of Sudan and commander of the Egyptian army, was assassinated in Cairo. The assassination was one of a series of killings of British officials that had begun in 1920. Allenby, who considered Stack an old and trusted friend, was determined to avenge the crime and in the process humiliate the Wafd and destroy its credibility in Egypt. Allenby demanded that Egypt apologize, prosecute the assailants, pay a £500,000 indemnity, withdraw all troops from Sudan, consent to an unlimited increase of irrigation in Sudan and end all opposition to the capitulations (Britain's demand of the right to protect foreign interests in the country). Zaghlul wanted to resign rather than accept the ultimatum, but Allenby presented it to him before Zaghlul could offer his resignation to the king. Zaghlul and his cabinet decided to accept the first four terms but to reject the last two. On November 24, after ordering the Ministry of Finance to pay the indemnity, Zaghlul resigned. He died three years later.

During the 1930s, Ismail Sidqi emerged as the "strong man" of Egyptian politics and an ardent opponent of the Wafd. It was he who abolished the constitution in 1930 and drafted another that enhanced the power of the monarch. He formed his own party, Al Hizb ash Shaab, which merged with the Ittihad Party in 1938. Also in 1938, dissident members of the Wafd formed the Saadist Party, named after Saad Zaghlul.

On April 28, 1936, King Fuad died and was succeeded by his son, Faruk. In the May elections, the Wafd won 89 percent of the vote and 157 seats in Parliament.

Negotiations with the British for a treaty to resolve matters that had been left outstanding since 1922 had resumed. The British delegation was led by its high commissioner, Miles Lampson, and the Egyptian delegation by Wafdist leader and prime minister, Mustafa Nahhas. On August 26, a draft treaty that came to be known as the Anglo-Egyptian Treaty of 1936 was signed.

The treaty provided for an Anglo-Egyptian military and defense alliance that allowed Britain to maintain a garrison of 10,000 men in the Suez Canal Zone. In addition, Britain was left in virtual control of Sudan. This contradicted the Anglo-Egyptian Condominium Agreement of 1899 that provided that Sudan be governed by Egypt and Britain jointly. In spite of the agreement, however, real power was in British hands. Egyptian army units had been withdrawn from Sudan in the aftermath of the Stack assassination, and the governor general was British. Nevertheless, Egyptian nationalists, and the Wafd particularly, continued to demand full Egyptian control of Sudan.

The treaty did provide for the end of the capitulations and the phasing out of the mixed courts. The British high commissioner was redesignated ambassador to Egypt, and when the British inspector general of the Egyptian army retired, an Egyptian officer was appointed to replace him.

In spite of these advances, the treaty did not give Egypt full independence, and its signing produced a wave of anti-Wafdist and anti-British demonstrations. To many of its followers, in negotiating and signing the treaty the Wafd had betrayed the nationalist cause. Because of this perception and also because it had failed to develop and implement a program for social and economic reform, the Wafd declined in power and influence. Although it considered itself the representative of the nation, the Wafd failed to offer meaningful domestic programs to deal with the problems of under- and unemployment, high living costs, lack of industrial development, and unequal distribution of land. Thus, during the 1930s, support for the Wafd, particularly among students and urban middle-class professionals and civil servants, was eroded by more militant, paramilitary organizations like the Muslim Brotherhood (Al Ikhwan al Muslimun, also known as the Brotherhood) and Young Egypt (Misr al Fatat).

The Muslim Brotherhood was founded in 1928 by religious leader Hasan al Banna who established himself as the supreme guide leading his followers in a purified Islamic state. The Brotherhood represented a trend in the Islamic reform movement that attributed the difficulties in Islamic society to a deviation from the ideals and practices of early Islam during the period of the first four caliphs. The aim, therefore, was to return society to a state of purity by reforming it from within and purging it of foreign domination and influence. The Brotherhood consisted of nationwide cells, battalions, youth groups, and a secret apparatus for underground activities.

Young Egypt was founded in 1933 by a lawyer, Ahmad Husayn. It was a radical nationalist organization with religious elements. Its aim was to make Egypt a great empire, which would consist of Egypt and Sudan. The empire would act as an ally to

Arab countries and serve as the leader of Islam. It was also a militaristic organization whose young members were organized in a paramilitary movement called the Green Shirts. The organization had fascist overtones and openly admired Nazi achievements. As German power grew, Young Egypt's anti-British tone increased.

Both of these organizations presented clearly defined programs for political, economic, and social reform. Both also represented a new political movement whose ideology was not the liberal constitutionalism of the nationalist movement, which was regarded as having failed.

Egypt During the War, 1939–45

With the beginning of World War II, Egypt again became vital to Britain's defense. Britain had to assure, if not the wholehearted support of Egypt, at least its acquiescence in British military and political policies during the crisis. For its part, Egypt considered the war a European conflict and hoped to avoid being entangled in it. As one Axis victory succeeded another, Egyptians grew increasingly convinced that Germany would win the war. Some were pleased at the prospect of a German victory, not because they were attracted to the Nazi ideology, but because they viewed any enemy of their enemy, Britain, as a friend. Meanwhile, the British were determined to prevent an Egyptian-German alliance.

The war gave the Wafd the opportunity to return to power. The Wafd set out to convince the British that they would not lead an anti-British insurrection during the wartime crisis. Uncertain of the loyalty of Prime Minister Ali Mahir and convinced that the king was intriguing against them, the British decided to entrust the Egyptian government to the Wafd. On February 2, 1942, with the German army under General Erwin Rommel advancing toward Egypt, Lampson, the British ambassador, ordered the king to ask Mustafa Nahhas, the Wafdist leader, to form a government. The incident clearly demonstrated that real power in Egypt resided in British hands and that the king and the political parties existed only so long as Britain was prepared to tolerate them. It also eroded popular support for the Wafd because it showed that the Wafd would make an alliance with the British for purely political reasons. The Wafd's credibility was eroded further in 1943 when a disaffected former Wafd member, Makram Ubayd, published his *Black Book*. The book contained details of Nahhas's corrupt dealings over the years and seriously damaged his reputation.

The Wafdist government fell in 1944, and the Wafd boycotted the elections of 1945, which brought a government of Liberal Constitutionalists and Saadists to power. As World War II ended, the

Temple of Abu Simbel (Abu Sunbul) with figures of Ramesses II, 1304–1237 B.C.
Courtesy Boris Boguslavsky

Wafd was splintered into several competing camps. The political initiative and popular support swung toward the militant organizations on the right, such as the Muslim Brotherhood and Young Egypt.

On the Threshold of Revolution, 1945–52

In 1945 a Labour Party government with anti-imperialist leanings was elected in Britain. This election encouraged Egyptians to believe that Britain would change its policy. The end of the war in Europe and the Pacific, however, saw the beginning of a new kind of global war, the Cold War, in which Egypt found itself embroiled against its will. Concerned by the possibility of expansion by the Soviet Union, the West would come to see the Middle East as a vital element in its postwar strategy of "containment." In addition, pro-imperialist British Conservatives like Winston Churchill spoke of Britain's "rightful position" in the Suez Canal Zone. He and Anthony Eden, the Conservative Party spokesman on foreign affairs, stressed the vital importance of the Suez Canal as an imperial lifeline and claimed international security would be threatened by British withdrawal.

In December 1945, Egyptian prime minister Mahmud Nuqrashi, sent a note to the British demanding that they renegotiate the 1936 treaty and evacuate British troops from the country. Britain refused. Riots and demonstrations by students and workers broke out in Cairo and Alexandria, accompanied by attacks on British property and personnel.

The new Egyptian prime minister, Ismail Sidqi, a driving force behind Egyptian politics in the 1930s and now seventy-one and in poor health, took over negotiations with the British. The British Labour Party prime minister, Clement Atlee, agreed to remove British troops from Egyptian cities and bases by September 1949. The British had withdrawn their troops to the Suez Canal Zone when negotiations foundered over the issue of Sudan. Britain said Sudan was ready for self-government while Egyptian nationalists were proclaiming "the unity of the Nile Valley," that is, that Sudan should be part of Egypt. Sidqi resigned in December 1946 and was succeeded by Nuqrashi, who referred the question of Sudan to the newly created United Nations (UN) during the following year. The Brotherhood called for strikes and a jihad (holy war) against the British, and newspapers called for a guerrilla war.

In 1948 another event strengthened the Egyptian desire to rid the country of imperial domination. This event was the Declaration of the Establishment of the State of Israel by David Ben-Gurion in Tel Aviv. The Egyptians, like most Arabs, considered the State of Israel a creation of Western, specifically British, imperialism and an alien entity in the Arab homeland. In September 1947, the League of Arab States (Arab League) had decided to resist by force the UN plan for partition of Palestine into an Arab and a Jewish state. Thus, when Israel announced its independence in 1948, the armies of the various Arab states, including Egypt, entered Palestine to save the country for the Arabs against what they considered Zionist aggression. The Arabs were defeated by Israel, although the Arab Legion of Transjordan held onto the Old City of Jerusalem and the West Bank (see Glossary), and Egypt saved a strip of territory around Gaza that became known as the Gaza Strip.

When the war began, the Egyptian army was poorly prepared and had no plan for coordination with the other Arab states. Although there were individual heroic acts of resistance, the army did not perform well, and nothing could disguise the defeat or mitigate the intense feeling of shame. After the war, there were scandals over the inferior equipment issued to the military, and the king and government were blamed for treacherously abandoning the army. One of the men who served in the war was Gamal Abdul Nasser, who commanded an army unit in Palestine and was wounded in the chest. Nasser was dismayed by the inefficiency and lack of preparation of the army. In the battle for the Negev Desert in October 1948, Nasser and his unit were trapped at Falluja, near

Beersheba. The unit held out and was eventually able to counter-attack. This event assumed great importance for Nasser, who saw it as a symbol of his country's determination to free Egypt from all forms of oppression, internal and external.

Nasser organized a clandestine group inside the army called the Free Officers. After the war against Israel, the Free Officers began to plan for a revolutionary overthrow of the government. In 1949 nine of the Free Officers formed the Committee of the Free Officers' Movement; in 1950 Nasser was elected chairman.

The Muslim Brotherhood, whose volunteer squads had fought well against Israel, gained in popularity and membership. Before the war, the Brotherhood was responsible for numerous attacks on British personnel and property. With the outbreak of the war against Israel, martial law was declared in Egypt, and the Brotherhood was ordered to dissolve. In retaliation, a member of the Brotherhood murdered Nuqrashi, the prime minister. His successor, Ibrahim Abdul Hadi, detained in concentration camps thousands of Brotherhood members as well as members of Young Egypt and communists. In February 1949, Brotherhood founder Hassan al Banna was assassinated, probably by agents of the security branch of the government.

In January 1950, the Wafd returned to power with Nahhas as prime minister. In October 1951, Nahhas introduced, and Parliament approved, decrees abrogating unilaterally the Anglo-Egyptian Treaty of 1936 and proclaiming Faruk king of Egypt and Sudan. Egypt exulted, with newspapers proclaiming that Egypt had broken "the fetters of British imperialism." The Wafd government gave way to pressure from the Brotherhood and leftist groups for militant opposition to the British. "Liberation battalions" were formed, and the Brotherhood and auxiliary police were armed. Food supplies to the Suez Canal Zone were blocked, and Egyptian workers were withdrawn from the base. A guerrilla war against the British in the Suez Canal Zone was undertaken by students and the Brotherhood.

In December British bulldozers and Centurion tanks demolished fifty Egyptian mud houses to open a road to a water supply for the British army. This incident and one that followed on January 25 provoked intense Egyptian anger. On January 25, 1952, the British attacked an Egyptian police barracks at Ismailiya (Al Ismailiyah) when its occupants refused to surrender to British troops. Fifty Egyptians were killed and 100 wounded.

The January incident led directly to "Black Saturday," January 26, 1952, which began with a mutiny by police in Cairo in protest against the death of their colleagues. Concurrently, groups of people in Cairo went on a rampage. British property and other symbols of the Western presence were attacked. By the end of the day, 750 establishments valued at £50 million had been burned or destroyed. Thirty persons were killed, including eleven British and other foreigners; hundreds were injured.

The British believed there was official connivance in the rioting. Wafdist interior minister Fuad Siraj ad Din (also seen as Serag al Din) was accused of negligence by an Egyptian government report and dismissed. The king dismissed Nahhas, and four prime ministers held office in the next six months. It became clear that the Egyptian ruling class had become unable to rule, and none of the radical nationalist groups was strong enough to take power. This power vacuum gave the Free Officers their opportunity.

On July 22, the Free Officers realized that the king might be preparing to move against them. They decided to strike and seize power the next morning. On July 26, King Faruk, forced to abdicate in favor of his infant son, sailed into exile on the same yacht on which his grandfather, Ismail, had left for exile about seventy years earlier.

The Revolution and the Early Years of the New Government, 1952–56

The nine men who had constituted themselves as the Committee of the Free Officers' Movement and led the 1952 Revolution were Lieutenant Colonel Gamal Abdul Nasser, Major Abd al Hakim Amir, Lieutenant Colonel Anwar as Sadat, Major Salah Salim, Major Kamal ad Din Husayn, Wing Commander Gamal Salim, Squadron Leader Hasan Ibrahim, Major Khalid Muhi ad Din, and Wing Commander Abd al Latif al Baghdadi. Major Husayn ash Shafii and Lieutenant Colonel Zakariyya Muhi ad Din joined the committee later.

After the coup, the Free Officers asked Ali Mahir, a previous prime minister, to head the government. The Free Officers formed the Revolutionary Command Council (RCC), which dictated policy to the civilian cabinet, abolished all civil titles such as pasha and bey, and ordered all political parties to purify their ranks and reconstitute their executive committees.

The RCC elected Muhammad Naguib president and commander in chief. He was chosen because he was a popular hero of the 1948 Arab-Israeli War and an officer trusted by the army. In 1951 the Free Officers had elected him as president of the Egyptian Army Officers Club over the candidate chosen by Faruk. It was extremely important for the Free Officers to ensure the loyalty of the army if the coup were to succeed. Naguib was fifty-one years old; the average age of the other Free Officers was thirty-three.

The decision made by the Wafd government after the Anglo-Egyptian Treaty of 1936 to allow sons of nonaristocratic families into the Military Academy had proved an important one for the future of Egypt. It meant that men such as Nasser and Sadat were able to become officers in the army and thus be in a position to shape events in Egypt. The decision had been made, not to create a more egalitarian officer corps, but rather to meet a desperate need for more officers. As it turned out, most members of the Free Officers' group and all of the original members of the RCC had entered the Military Academy during the period between 1937 and 1940. The men who profited from this new policy were not from the poorest families; their families had to have enough money to send their children to secondary schools. For the most part, they were from families of moderately prosperous landholders and minor government officials, who constituted the class of rural notables.

Nasser himself came from a rural notable family. His father was from a small village in Upper Egypt and worked as a postal clerk. In 1915 the senior Nasser moved to Alexandria, where on January 15, 1918, his first son, Gamal, was born. At the age of seven, Gamal was sent to Cairo to live with his uncle and to attend school. He went to a school in Khan al Khalili, the old quarter of the city near Al Azhar mosque, where he experienced firsthand the bustling, crowded quarters of Cairo and the poverty of many in the city. Between 1933 and 1938, he attended An Nahda (the Awakening) School in Cairo, where he combined studying with demonstrating against British and Egyptian politicians. In November 1935, he marched in demonstrations against the British and was wounded by a bullet fired by British troops. Identified as an agitator by the police, he was asked to leave his school. After a few months in law school, he joined the army.

Nasser desired vehemently to change his country; he believed that the British and the British-controlled king and politicians would continue to harm the interests of the majority of the population. Nasser and the other Free Officers had no particular desire for a military career, but Nasser had perceived that military life offered upward mobility and a chance to participate in shaping the country's future. The Free Officers were united by their desire to see Egypt freed of British control and a more equitable government established. Nasser and many of the others seemed to be attached to no particular political ideology, although some, such as Khalid Muhi ad Din, were Marxists and a few sympathized with the Muslim Brotherhood. The lack of a coherent ideology would cause difficulties in the future when these men set about the task of governing Egypt.

Although Naguib headed the RCC and Mahir the civilian government, Nasser was the real power behind the RCC. The years between 1952 and 1954 witnessed a struggle for control of the government that Nasser ultimately won. The first crisis to face the new government came in August 1952 with a violent strike involving more than 10,000 workers at the Misr Company textile factories at Kafr ad Dawwar in the Delta. Workers attacked and set fire to part of the premises, destroyed machinery, and clashed with the police. The army was called in to put down the strike; several workers lost their lives, and scores were injured. The RCC set up a special military court that tried the arrested textile workers. Two were convicted and executed, and many others were given prison sentences. The regime reacted quickly and ruthlessly because it had no intention of encouraging a popular revolution that it could not control. It then arrested about thirty persons charged with belonging to the outlawed Communist Party of Egypt (CPE). The Democratic Movement for National Liberation, a faction of the CPE, reacted by denouncing the regime as a military dictatorship.

On September 7, Ali Mahir resigned, and Naguib became prime minister, minister of war, commander in chief, and president of the RCC. That same month, the RCC passed its first major domestic measure, the Agrarian Reform Law of 1952. The law was intended to abolish the power of the absentee landlord class, to encourage investment in industry, and to build support for the regime. The law limited landholdings to 200 *feddans* with the right to transfer another 100 to wives and children. The owners of the land requisitioned by the government received about half the market value of the land at 1951 prices in the form of government bonds. The land was sold in lots of two to five *feddans* to tenants and small farmers owning less than five *feddans*. The small farmers had to buy the lots at a price equal to the compensation paid to the former owner.

The RCC also dealt with labor legislation and education. Initial legislation raised minimum wages, reduced working hours, and created more jobs to reduce unemployment. Enforcement of these measures was lax until the early 1960s, however. In another effort to reduce unemployment, the RCC instituted a policy of providing employment in government service for all university graduates, a practice that swelled the ranks of the bureaucracy and left many skilled people underused. The government increased its spending on education with the goal of educating all citizens. Rent control was established, and the government undertook construction of housing for workers. These programs were expanded in the 1960s.

On January 17, 1953, all political parties were dissolved and banned. A three-year transition period was proclaimed during which the RCC would rule. On February 10, the Liberation Rally headed by Nasser was launched to serve as an organization for the mobilization of popular support for the new government. On June 18, Egypt was declared a republic, and the monarchy was abolished, ending the rule of Muhammad Ali's dynasty. Naguib became the first president and also prime minister. Nasser became deputy prime minister and minister of interior. Other officers took over other ministries.

Between 1952 and 1954, there was a struggle between Naguib and Nasser and his colleagues on the RCC for control of the government and over the future form of the government. Naguib was to have one vote on the council and was responsible for carrying out council decisions. He enjoyed considerable popularity, and he developed his own following after conflicts involving policies arose between him and the RCC. The conflicts came to a head on February 23, 1954 when Naguib resigned. The RCC may have been relieved at this decision, but the popular outcry was so great that Naguib was reinstated as president of the republic. Nasser, however, took the position of prime minister, previously held by Naguib, and remained president of the RCC.

As soon as the Free Officers came to power, their immediate and major concern was the evacuation of Britain from Egypt. At first, the Free Officers feared that the British from their garrison in the Suez Canal Zone might try to intervene on behalf of the king. However, the British made it clear that they would not interfere on behalf of the king nor take any action unless British lives were threatened. Achieving the evacuation of the British, however, involved two contentious issues—Sudan and the Suez Canal. Sudan proved to be the easier to resolve. In February 1953, the Egyptian government agreed to a plan for self-determination for Sudan to be implemented over a three-year period. The Sudanese opted for independence rather than union with Egypt.

The issue of the Suez Canal was more complex and linked to Britain's desire to involve Egypt in the West's Cold War with the Soviet Union. As early as September 1952, the British government announced that there was no strategic alternative to the maintenance of the British base in the canal area. In the opinion of Anthony Eden, British foreign secretary, Egypt had to fit into a regional defense system, the Baghdad Pact, and agreement on this point would have to precede any withdrawal from the canal.

This was the period of pacts directed against the Soviet Union. The North Atlantic Treaty Organization and Southeast Asia Treaty Organization were supposed to contain the Soviet Union in the west and east. The Baghdad Pact, bringing into alliance Britain, Turkey, Iran, Pakistan, and Iraq, was supposed to do the same on the Soviet Union's southern borders. The British government was attempting to force Egypt to join the alliance by refusing to discuss evacuation of the Suez Canal base until Egypt agreed.

Egypt, however, would discuss only evacuation and eventual administration of the base, and the British slowly realized the drawbacks of holding the base without Egyptian acquiescence. By October 1954, Nasser signed an agreement providing for the withdrawal of all British troops from the base within twenty months, with the provision that the British base could be reactivated in the event of an attack on Egypt by an outside power or an Arab League state or an attack on Turkey.

The agreement gained a mixed reception among Egyptians. Despite the enthusiasm for ending imperialism, there were those who criticized Nasser for rewriting the old treaty. Nasser's chief critics were the communists and the Brotherhood. It was while Nasser was justifying the canal agreement to a crowd in Alexandria on October 26, 1954 that a member of the Brotherhood attempted to kill him. The following day, in a show of courage, Nasser deliberately appeared before crowds in Alexandria, at stations en route to Cairo, and in the capital. In Cairo he was met by an estimated 200,000 people, his popularity having been enormously strengthened by this incident.

Although the Muslim Brotherhood had a long history of anti-British and antiregime activities, its leaders stipulated that they would work with the Free Officers only if the officers would agree to Brotherhood objectives. Because the Brotherhood would not refrain from opposing the RCC, Nasser had outlawed the organization in February 1954. Naguib had always had a certain sympathy for the Brotherhood, and its leaders implicated him in the attack on Nasser. It is doubtful that he had any connection with the attack, but it gave Nasser the pretext he needed to remove Naguib from the presidency, and he did so in November.

In February 1955, Eden visited Cairo seeking again to persuade Nasser to join the Baghdad Pact. Nasser again refused. Many Egyptians were skeptical of Britain's intentions and believed that membership in the pact would amount to trading one form of British domination for another. In addition, however, Nasser was increasingly attracted to the Nonaligned Movement that eschewed membership in either the Western or the Soviet camp. Nasser was no particular friend of the Soviet Union, and the Communist Party remained outlawed in Egypt. It was Western imperialism and colonialism, however, that Egypt had been struggling against.

Nasser also had become an admirer and friend of President Marshal Josip Broz Tito of Yugoslavia and Prime Minister Jawaharlal Nehru of India. Tito had survived by aligning himself neither with the West nor with the Soviet Union. Together, he and Nasser developed the concept of nonalignment, which entailed avoiding both pro- and anti-Soviet pacts but did not prevent them from purchasing arms or receiving aid from either bloc. Nevertheless, the West, particularly the United States, expected Third World countries to support the West in return for both arms and aid, as Nasser was soon to learn.

A turning point for Nasser was the Conference of the Nonaligned Movement in Bandung, Indonesia in April 1955. There he found himself the center of attention as a Third World leader, accepted as a colleague by Chinese premier Zhou Enlai, and greeted by crowds in the streets. Egyptian participation in the conference, along with other former colonies such as India, symbolized not only the new postcolonial world order but also Egypt's own independence.

Another turning point for Nasser came in February 1955 when he became convinced that Egypt had to arm to defend itself against Israel. This decision put him on a collision course with the West that ended on the battlefields of Suez a year later. In February 1955, the Israeli army attacked Egyptian military outposts in Gaza. Thirty-nine Egyptians were killed. Until then, this had been Israel's least troublesome frontier. Since the end of the 1948 Arab-Israeli War, Egypt's leaders, from King Faruk to Nasser, had avoided militant attitudes on the grounds that Israel should not distract Egypt from domestic problems. Nasser made no serious attempt to narrow Israel's rapidly widening armaments lead. He preferred to spend Egypt's meager hard currency reserves on development.

Israel's raid on Gaza changed Nasser's mind, however. At first he sought Western aid, but he was rebuffed by the United States, France, and Britain. The United States government, especially the passionately anticommunist Secretary of State John Foster Dulles, clearly disapproved of Egypt's nonalignment and would make it difficult for Egypt to purchase arms. The French demanded that Egypt cease aiding the Algerian national movement, which was fighting for independence from France. The British warned Nasser that if he accepted Soviet weapons, none would be forthcoming from Britain.

Rejected in this shortsighted way by the West, Nasser negotiated the famous arms agreement with Czechoslovakia in September

1955. This agreement marked the Soviet Union's first great break-through in its effort to undermine Western influence in the Middle East. Egypt received no arms from the West and eventually became dependent on arms from the Soviet Union.

Relations between Nasser and the West reached a crisis over plans to finance the Aswan High Dam. Construction of the dam was one of the earliest decisions of the Free Officers. It would increase both electrical generating power and irrigated land area. It would serve industry and agriculture and symbolize the new Egypt. The United States agreed to give Egypt an unconditional loan of US$56 million, and Britain agreed to lend Egypt US$14. The British loan was contingent on the American loan. The World Bank (see Glossary) also agreed to lend Egypt an additional US$200 million. The World Bank loan stipulated that Egypt's budget be supervised by World Bank officials. To Nasser these conditions were insulting and were reminiscent of Europe's control over Egypt's finances in the 1870s.

While Nasser admitted to doubts about the West's sincerity, the United States became incensed over Egypt's decision to recognize communist China. Meanwhile, the Soviet Union was offering aid to Egypt in several forms, including a loan to finance the Aswan High Dam. Then, on July 19, the United States withdrew its loan offer, and Britain and the World Bank followed suit. Nasser was returning to Cairo from a meeting with President Tito and Prime Minister Nehru when he heard the news. He was furious and decided to retaliate with an action that shocked the West and made him the hero of the Arabs.

On July 26, 1956, the fourth anniversary of King Faruk's exile, Nasser appeared in Muhammad Ali Square in Alexandria where twenty months earlier an assassin had attempted to kill him. An immense crowd gathered, and he began a three-hour speech from a few notes jotted on the back of an envelope. When Nasser said the code word, "de Lesseps," it was the signal for engineer Mahmud Yunis to begin the takeover of the Suez Canal.

The canal's owner was the Suez Canal Company, an international company with headquarters in Paris. Anthony Eden, then British prime minister, called the nationalization of the canal "theft," and United States secretary of state Dulles said Nasser would have to be made to "disgorge" it. The French and British depended heavily on the canal for transporting oil supplies, and they felt that Nasser had become a threat to their remaining interests in the Middle East and Africa. Eden wanted to launch a military action immediately but was informed that Britain was not in a position to do so. Both France and Britain froze Egyptian assets in their countries and increased their military preparedness in the eastern Mediterranean.

Egypt promised to compensate the stockholders of the Suez Canal Company and to guarantee right of access to all ships, so it was difficult for the French and British to rally international support to regain the canal by force. The Soviet Union, its East European allies, and Third World countries generally supported Egypt. The United States moved farther away from Britain and stated that while it opposed the nationalization of the canal, it was against the use of force.

What followed was the invasion of Egypt by Britain, France, and Israel, an action known as the Tripartite Invasion or the 1956 War. Whereas the truth about the invasion eventually became known, at the time the Conservative government in London denied that it used Israel as an excuse for attacking Egypt. Eden, who had an intense personal dislike for Nasser, concealed the cooperation with Israel from his colleagues, British diplomats, and the United States.

The plan, which was supposed to enable Britain and France to gain physical control of the canal, called for Israel to attack across the Sinai Desert. When Israel neared the canal, Britain and France would issue an ultimatum for an Egyptian and Israeli withdrawal from both sides of the canal. An Anglo-French force would then occupy the canal to prevent further fighting and to keep it open to shipping. Israeli prime minister David Ben-Gurion agreed to the plan but informed Britain that Israel would not attack unless Britain and France first destroyed the Egyptian air force.

On October 28, Israeli troops crossed the frontier into the Sinai Peninsula (also seen as Sinai), allegedly to destroy the bases of Egyptian commandos. The first sign of collusion between Israel and Britain and France came on the same day when the Anglo-French ultimatum was handed to Egypt and Israel before Israel had even reached the canal. British bombing destroyed the Egyptian air force, and British and French paratroopers were dropped over Port Said and Port Fuad. The Egyptians put up fierce resistance. Ships were sunk in the canal to prevent transit. In the battle for Port Said, about 2,700 Egyptian civilians and soldiers were killed or wounded (see The 1956 War, ch. 5).

Although it was invaded and occupied for a time, Egypt can claim to have emerged the victor. There was almost universal condemnation of the Tripartite Invasion. The Soviet Union threatened Britain and France with a rocket attack if they did not withdraw. The United States, angered because it had not been informed by its allies of the invasion, realized it could not allow the Soviet

Union to appear as the champion of the Third World against Western imperialism. Thus, the United States put pressure on the British and French to withdraw. Faced with almost total opposition to the invasion, the anger of the United States, and the threat of the collapse of the pound sterling, the British agreed to withdraw. Severely condemned, Britain and France accepted a ceasefire on November 6, as their troops were poised to advance the length of the canal. The final evacuation took place on December 22.

Israel, which occupied all of Sinai, was reluctant to withdraw. President Dwight D. Eisenhower of the United States placed great pressure on Israel to give up all its territorial acquisitions and even threatened sanctions. The Israelis did withdraw from Sinai, but they carried out a scorched earth policy, destroying roads, railroads, and military installations as they went.

A United Nations Emergency Force (UNEF) was established and began arriving in Egypt on November 21. The troops were stationed on the Egyptian side of the Egyptian-Israeli border as well as along the eastern coast of Sinai. Israel refused to allow UN troops on its territory. The UN troops were stationed on the Gulf of Aqaba to ensure the free passage of Israeli shipping to Elat. The troops remained in Egypt until 1967, when their removal contributed to the outbreak of the June 1967 War.

Egypt reopened the canal to shipping in April and ran it smoothly. It was open to all ships except those of Israel, and it remained open until the June 1967 War (Arab-Israeli war, also known as the Six-Day War). Diplomatic relations between Egypt and Britain were not restored until 1969.

Nasser had won a significant victory. The immediate effect was that Britain and France were finally out of Egypt. Nasser went on to nationalize all other British and French assets in Egypt. The Egyptians now had full control of the canal and its revenues. The Suez crisis also made Nasser the hero of the Arab world, a man who had stood up to Western imperialism and had prevailed.

In response to his increased prestige, Nasser emphasized the Arab character of Egypt and its leadership role in the Arab world. He had always had a concern for Arab causes, as shown by his volunteering to fight in Palestine in 1948, but now this tendency was amplified. His Egyptian nationalism became Arab nationalism when he decided that if the Arab countries worked together, they would have the resources to solve their individual problems. In addition, the move toward nationalization, which started with French and British assets, continued in Egypt and became a cornerstone of Nasser's administration.

Temple of Hathor, Dendera (Dandarah), Ptolemaic period, 305–30 B.C.
Courtesy Boris Boguslavsky

Another result of the 1956 events was the increased Soviet influence in Egypt stemming from the Soviet financing of the Aswan High Dam construction and Soviet arms sales to Egypt. Thus, Egypt became the cornerstone of the Soviet Union's Middle East policy.

Egypt and the Arab World

For a variety of conflicting reasons, the political leaders of Syria in January 1958 asked Nasser for a union between their two countries. Nasser was skeptical at first and then insisted on strict conditions for union, including a complete union rather than a federal state and the abolition of the Baath (Arab Socialist Resurrection) Party, then in power, and all other Syrian political parties. Because the Syrians believed that Nasser's ideas represented their own goals and that they would play a large role in the union, they agreed to the conditions. A plebiscite was held in both countries in 1958, and Nasser was elected president. Cairo was designated the capital of the United Arab Republic. Nasser then visited Damascus, where he received a tumultuous welcome. Arabs everywhere felt a new sense of pride.

Several Arab governments viewed Nasser with less enthusiasm, however. The conservative monarchies of Saudi Arabia and Jordan saw his ideas as a potential threat to their own power. Nasser regarded these monarchs as reactionaries and as obstacles to Arab unity. The United States moved to strengthen these regimes as well as the government of Lebanon in an effort to offset the influence of Egypt.

The hastily conceived union of Syria and Egypt did not last long. There were too many problems to overcome: the two countries were not contiguous, their economies and populations were different, and the Syrian elite deeply resented being made subservient to Egyptian dictates. The deciding factor for the Syrian upper and middle classes came in July 1961 when Nasser issued the so-called "socialist decrees" that called for widespread nationalizations. This was followed by the elimination of local autonomy and a plan for the unification of Egyptian and Syrian currencies, a move that would deal the final blow to Syrian economic independence.

There was also resentment in the army that paralleled the resentment in civilian circles. On September 28, a group of army officers called the High Arab Revolutionary Command staged a successful coup and proclaimed the separation of Syria from Egypt. Nasser decided not to resist and ordered his troops to surrender. He blamed Syria's defection on "reactionaries" and "agents of imperialism."

During the same period, Egypt attempted a separate union with Yemen. This federation, called the United Arab States, fared no better than the Syrian one. In December 1961, Nasser formally ended it. In 1962 a military coup overthrew the royalist government in Yemen. Nasser intervened to support the new republican government against the Saudi Arabia-backed royalists, who were attempting to regain control. This undertaking proved to be a great drain on Egypt's financial and military resources. At the height of its involvement, Egypt had 75,000 troops in Yemen. Egypt's intervention also increased inter-Arab tensions, especially between Saudi Arabia and Egypt. Egypt's defeat at the hands of Israel in the June 1967 War obliged it to withdraw its forces from Yemen and to seek peace. A settlement was achieved at a conference in Khartoum in 1967.

Nasser and Arab Socialism

Nasser concentrated on implementing his doctrine of Arab socialism internally, especially after the break with Syria. The National Charter, essentially drawn up by Nasser, was promulgated in 1962. It established the basis of authority for the new constitution that was to follow. It showed a change in orientation from the nationalist goals of the original revolution and emphasized that Egypt was an Arab nation based on Islamic principles. In addition, the Arab Socialist Union (ASU) was created to be the sole political party and a means of gathering the support of the masses.

In July on the ninth anniversary of the 1952 coup, Nasser announced a list of nationalizations that cut more deeply into the private sector than had occurred in any country outside of Eastern Europe. The decrees nationalized all private banks, all insurance companies, and fifty shipping companies and firms in heavy and basic industries. Eighty-three companies were obliged to sell 50 percent or more of their shares to public agencies. A second agrarian reform law lowered the limit for an individual owner from 200 to 100 *feddans*. The nationalization program continued in successive waves through 1962 and 1963 and involved shipping companies, cotton-ginning factories, cotton-exporting companies, pharmaceutical producers, ocean and river transport companies, trucking companies, glass factories, and the largest book-publishing company in Egypt. Between 1952 and 1966, £E7 billion (for value of the Egyptian pound, see Glossary) in shared and public assets were transferred to public ownership (see The Role of Government, ch. 3).

The decrees also included legislation such as taxing gross incomes over £E5,000 at the rate of 90 percent, limiting base salaries of public sector directors to £E5,000, and limiting membership on all boards of directors to seven persons, two of whom must be workers. All joint-stock companies were required to place 5 percent of all profits in government bonds and to allot 10 percent to workers in cash and 15 percent to worker housing and community infrastructure. The work week was reduced to forty-two hours, and the minimum wage was raised. Half of all seats in Parliament and on all elective bodies and worker-management boards were reserved for peasants and workers.

Elections were held in March 1964 for a new National Assembly from a list of candidates drawn up by the ASU. Immediately after the election, Nasser released a draft constitution that functioned until 1971. The constitution was based on the National Charter and emphasized freedom, socialism, and unity.

The position of some minority groups changed during this period. Most Jews left Egypt, the last large group being several thousand who did not have Egyptian citizenship and who were expelled during the Suez crisis. The Greek community also decreased considerably because many Greeks who did not like socialism returned to Greece.

Egypt, the Arabs, and Israel

During the late 1950s and early 1960s, the question of Israel became more vexing for the Arab states. In 1964, in spite of the problems that existed among the various Arab states, Nasser initiated Arab summit meetings that were held in January, March, and September in Cairo and Casablanca. The immediate reason for the summits was to find a way to block Israel's plan to divert the waters of the Jordan River to irrigate the Negev Desert, a plan that would deprive the lower Jordan River valley of water. The Arab states drew up a plan that called for diverting the Jordan River in Syria and Lebanon but did not implement it.

The Arab summit meetings also took up other matters. League members agreed to created a unified military command, the United Arab Command, with headquarters in Cairo, but this plan, like that of diverting the Jordan River, remained on paper. The Arab leaders did implement a plan to create the Palestine Liberation Organization (PLO) to be the primary organization of Palestinians. The Arab governments, especially Egypt, were becoming increasingly uneasy about the growing activities of Palestinian guerrillas, and they wanted to create an organization through which they could control such operations. They created the Palestine Liberation Army, whose units would be stationed and controlled by Egypt, Syria, and Iraq. Egypt exercised control of the PLO until 1969 when Yasir Arafat, the leader of the guerrilla organization called Al Fatah, took control of the organization from Ahmad Shukairy, the choice of the Arab League governments.

The War with Israel, 1967

During the mid-1960s, tensions between the Arab states and Israel increased. In November 1966, Egypt and Syria signed a five-year defense pact. In the same month, Israeli forces crossed into the West Bank of Jordan to destroy the village of As Samu in retaliation for increasing Palestinian guerrilla raids. In 1967 Israeli leaders repeatedly threatened to invade Syria and overthrow the Syrian government if guerrilla raids across the Syrian border did not stop. In April 1967, there were serious Israeli-Syrian air clashes over Syrian air space. Israeli prime minister Levi Eshkol warned that Damascus could be occupied if necessary.

The Soviet Union warned Egypt that they had information that the Israelis had mobilized two brigades on the frontier. Nasser reacted by sending troops to the Israeli border, and Syria followed suit. The claim has been made that Nasser believed that the presence of Egyptian troops would deter the Israelis from attacking Syria. Israel responded by deploying its own forces. It was clear that it would be difficult for Egypt to come to Syria's aid according to the terms of their agreement because of an obstacle—the presence of UNEF troops, stationed on the Egyptian side of the Egyptian-Israeli border since the 1956 War. A great deal of pressure to remove the troops had been put on Nasser by Arab critics such as King Hussein of Jordan and Crown Prince Faisal (Faisal ibn Abdul Aziz Al Saud) of Saudi Arabia, who accused him of not living up to his responsibilities as an Arab leader. He was accused of failing to match words with deeds and of hiding behind the UN shield rather than thinking about liberating the Palestinian homeland.

On May 16, Nasser made the move that led inexorably to war. He asked the UN to remove the UNEF from the Egyptian-Israeli frontier in Sinai. Once the UNEF was withdrawn, Nasser declared he was closing the Strait of Tiran, which connects the Gulf of Aqaba and the Red Sea, to Israeli shipping—a threat he never carried out. Israel, for its part, regarded the withdrawal of the UNEF troops as a hostile act and the closing of the strait as a casus belli. Meanwhile, Jordan and Iraq signed defense agreements with Egypt.

Field Marshal Amir, deputy supreme commander of the armed forces, and Shams ad Din Badran, the minister of defense, urged Nasser to strike first, saying the Egyptian army was strong enough to win. The Soviet Union and the United States urged Nasser not to go to war. Nasser publicly denied that Egypt would strike first and spoke of a negotiated peace if the Palestinians were allowed to return to their homeland and of a possible compromise over the Strait of Tiran.

On the morning of June 5, Israel launched a full-scale attack on Egypt, Jordan, and Syria. In three hours, at least 300 of Egypt's 430 combat aircraft were destroyed, many on the ground as the pilots did not have time to take off. Israeli ground forces started a lightning strike into Sinai and by June 8 had reached the Suez Canal (see The June 1967 War, ch. 5). On that day, both sides accepted a UN Security Council call for a cease-fire. By June 11, the Arab defeat was total; Israel now held all of historic Palestine, including the Old City of Jerusalem, the West Bank, and the Gaza Strip, as well as Sinai and part of the Golan Heights of Syria.

The Aftermath of the War
Internal Relations

Egypt's losses in the war were enormous: approximately 10,000 soldiers and 1,500 officers killed, 5,000 soldiers and 500 officers captured, 80 percent of military equipment destroyed. Sinai was under Israeli control, and the Suez Canal was blocked and closed to shipping.

On June 9, Nasser spoke on television and took full responsibility for the debacle. He resigned as president, but the Egyptian people poured into the streets to demonstrate their support for him. The cabinet and the National Assembly voted not to accept the resignation, and Nasser withdrew it.

Soon after the cease-fire, there was a broad shake-up in the military and the government. Field Marshal Amir and Minister of Defense Badran, who had been chosen for the post by Amir, were forced to resign. General Muhammad Fawzi became commander in chief, and Nasser retained the position of supreme commander. On June 19, Nasser enlarged his political powers by assuming the role of prime minister. He named a twenty-eight-member cabinet and took control of the ASU as secretary general. Ali Sabri, the vice president and secretary general of the ASU until that time, was named deputy prime minister in the new cabinet.

On August 25, 1967, Amir and fifty other high-ranking military and civilian officials were arrested and accused of plotting to overthrow Nasser. Approximately two weeks later, the government announced that Amir, who was once considered Nasser's closest associate among the Free Officers, had committed suicide by taking poison while under house arrest.

In March 1968, widespread demonstrations by students and workers broke out in Cairo, Alexandria, and the industrial town of Hulwan. The demonstrations were provoked by the decision of a military tribunal that convicted two air force commanders of negligence in the June 1967 War and acquitted two others. The demonstrators demanded stiffer sentences for the four officers. A sit-in by students at Cairo University ended only when the government promised to retry the officers and released arrested demonstrators.

Although the decision of the military tribunal was the immediate cause of the demonstrations, the underlying cause was popular frustration with the government repression over the preceding sixteen years and the lack of popular participation in the government. Nasser declared his desire to satisfy popular demands and promised to present a plan of action. The new plan, approved by a referendum in May, called for a new constitution that would reform the ASU, grant Parliament control over the government, and allow greater personal and press freedom. Popular elections were to be held for the National Assembly.

Nasser's reform of the existing political system was instituted through the formulation of new laws and the election of new members to all of the organs of the ASU. This initial phase of his plan was completed during October 1968, with the election of the reorganized Supreme Executive Committee (SEC) of the ASU. Only eight people received the required majority of votes, and the election of the remaining two members was postponed. The SEC organized itself into five permanent committees: political affairs, chaired by Anwar as Sadat; administration, chaired by Ali Sabri; internal affairs, chaired by Abdul Muhsin Abu an Nur; economic development, chaired by Muhammad Labib Shuqayr; and culture and information, chaired by Diya Muhammad Daud. Nasser headed the SEC, and its three remaining members were Husayn ash Shafii, General Muhammad Fawzi, and Kamal Ramzi Stinu.

This reorganization proved unsatisfactory to those who had hoped for an expansion of freedom and democracy. Thus, in November, demonstrations broke out again with cries of "Nasser resign" reported. Several demonstrators were killed or wounded in clashes with the police. Universities and secondary schools were again closed. The demonstrators were expressing popular frustration over the failure of the government to implement the program approved by the referendum. Nasser apparently was unwilling or unable to widen popular participation in the government.

External Relations

The first move of the Arabs after the June 1967 War was to hold a summit conference in Khartoum in September 1967. At that meeting, Nasser and Faisal came to an agreement: Nasser would stop his attempts to destabilize the Saudi regime, and in return Saudi Arabia would give Egypt the financial aid needed to rebuild its army and retake the territory lost to Israel. At the conference, the Arab leaders were united in their opposition to Israel and proclaimed what became known as "the three no's" of the Khartoum summit: no peace with Israel, no negotiations, no recognition.

At the UN in November, the Security Council unanimously adopted Resolution 242, which provided a framework for settlement of the June 1967 War. This resolution, still not implemented in 1990, declared that the acquisition of territory by force was unacceptable. The resolution called for Israel to withdraw "from territories occupied in the recent conflict," for the termination of the state of belligerency, and for the right of all states in the area "to live in peace within secure and recognized boundaries." Freedom of navigation through international waterways in the area was to be guaranteed, and a just settlement of the "refugee" problem was to be attained.

Gunnar Jarring, a Swedish diplomat at the UN, started a series of journeys in the Middle East in an attempt to bring both sides together. In May 1968, Egypt agreed to accept the resolution if Israel agreed to evacuate all occupied areas. By accepting the resolution, Egypt for the first time implicitly recognized the existence—and the right to continued existence—of Israel. In return Egypt gained a UN commitment to the restoration of Sinai. The PLO rejected the resolution because it referred to the Palestinians only as "refugees" and thus appeared to dismiss Palestinian demands for self-determination and national rights. Syria characterized the plan as a "sellout" of Arafat and the PLO. The disagreement on that issue was compounded when, throughout 1969, tensions grew between the Lebanese government and Palestinian groups within Lebanon's borders, and serious clashes broke out. Syria condemned Lebanese action. Nasser invited both parties to Cairo, and an agreement was negotiated in November 1969 to end the hostilities.

Israel rejected Jarring's mission as meaningless, insisting that negotiations should precede any evacuation. Israel also objected to Nasser's support for the PLO, whose objective at the time was the establishment of a secular state in all "liberated" Palestinian territory. Nasser replied that if Israel refused to support Resolution 242 while Egypt accepted it, he had no choice "but to support courageous resistance fighters who want to liberate their land."

The mutual frustration led to the outbreak of the so-called War of Attrition from March 1969 to August 1970. Hoping to use Egypt's superiority in artillery to cause unacceptable casualties to Israeli forces dug in along the canal, Nasser ordered Egyptian guns to begin a steady pounding of the Israeli positions. Israel responded by constructing the Bar-Lev Line, a series of fortifications along the canal, and by using the one weapon in which it had absolute superiority, its air force, to silence the Egyptian artillery. Having accomplished this with minimal aircraft losses, Israel embarked on a series of deep penetration raids into the heartland of Egypt with its newly acquired American-made Phantom bombers. By January 1970, Israeli planes were flying at will over eastern Egypt.

To remedy this politically intolerable situation, Nasser flew to Moscow and asked the Soviet Union to establish an air defense system manned by Soviet pilots and antiaircraft forces protected by Soviet troops. To obtain Soviet aid, Nasser had to grant the Soviet Union control over a number of Egyptian airfields as well as operational control over a large portion of the Egyptian army. The Soviet Union sent between 10,000 and 15,000 Soviet troops and advisers to Egypt, and Soviet pilots flew combat missions. A screen of surface-to-air missiles (SAMs) was set up, and Soviet pilots joined Egyptian ones in patrolling Egyptian air space.

After the June 1967 War, the Soviet Union poured aid into Egypt to replace lost military equipment and rebuild the armed forces. However, by sending troops and advisers to Egypt and pilots to fly combat missions, the Soviet Union took a calculated risk of possible superpower confrontation over the Middle East. This added risk occurred because the United States under the Nixon administration was supplying Israel with military aid and regarded Israel as a bulwark against Soviet expansion in the area.

Many plans for peace were formulated and rejected, but on June 25, 1970, the Rogers Plan, put forth by United States secretary of state William Rogers, started a dialogue that eventually led to the long-awaited cease-fire in the War of Attrition along the Suez Canal. Basically, the plan was a modification of Resolution 242. Shortly after the plan was announced, from June 29 to July 17, Nasser visited Moscow. Discussions were held on the Rogers Plan, a newly formed Moscow peace plan, and the future of Soviet-Egyptian relations.

After his return to Egypt, Nasser declared a major policy shift based on his assertion that Egypt must be respected for doing what it could on its own because the other Arab states were not prepared to wage war with Israel. This policy shift set the stage for Egypt's acceptance of the Rogers Plan in July, to the surprise of Israel and the consternation of many Arab states that feared Egypt would sign a separate peace agreement with Israel. Jordan, however, followed Egypt's lead and accepted the plan. Israel accepted the plan in August.

Egyptian-Israeli fighting halted along the Suez Canal on August 7, 1970, in accordance with the first phase of the plan, and a ninety-day truce began. Palestinian guerrilla groups in opposition to the cease-fire continued to engage in small-scale actions on the Jordanian-Syrian-Lebanese fronts.

PLO leader Arafat's open criticism of the parties accepting the truce led Nasser to close down the Voice of Palestine radio station in Cairo and to terminate most of the material support Egypt provided to the PLO. In addition, many PLO activists were expelled from Egypt. Within a month, the guerrillas had effectively undermined progress on the Rogers Plan by a series of acts, including the hijacking of five international airplanes in early September 1970, thus triggering the Jordanian civil war that month.

King Hussein launched a major Jordanian military drive against the Jordan-based Palestinian guerrilla groups on September 14, partly out of fear that their attacks on Israel would sabotage the truce, but primarily because the guerrillas were becoming powerful enough to challenge his government. Nasser's position on these events, as in the preceding year when hostilities broke out between the Palestinians and Lebanese, was based on a desire to stop any form of intra-Arab conflict. He was extremely angry when Syria sent an armored force into Jordan to support the guerrillas. The United States and Israel offered assistance to the beleaguered King Hussein.

Nasser called for a meeting in Cairo to stop the civil war. The Arab summit finally came about on September 26 after bloody military engagements in which Jordan decisively repulsed the Syrians and seemed to be defeating the PLO, although PLO forces were not pushed out of Jordan until July 1971. On September 27, 1970, Hussein and Arafat agreed to a fourteen-point cease-fire under Nasser's mediation, officially ending the war.

The effort by Nasser to bring about this unlikely reconciliation between two bitter enemies was enormous. He was by then a tired and sick man. He had been suffering from diabetes since 1958 and from arteriosclerosis of the leg. He had treatment in the Soviet Union, and his doctors had warned him to avoid physical and emotional strain. He had ignored their advice and suffered a heart attack in September 1969. The strain of the summit was too much. He felt ill at the airport on September 28 when bidding good-bye to Arab leaders and returned home to bed. He had another heart attack and died that afternoon.

Nasser's Legacy

When news of Nasser's death was announced, Egyptians took to the streets by the tens of thousands to express shock and grief at the death of their leader. In spite of the doubts that many Egyptians may have felt about the path on which Nasser had taken Egypt, the sense of loss was overwhelming, and there was great uncertainty about the future. It has been argued that Nasser's rule was not a great success; that there were almost as many landless peasants in 1970 as when the Free Officers took over in 1952 because it was the wealthier peasants who had profited and still controlled the villages; that the army had done no better in 1967 after fifteen years of the revolution than it had done in 1948 or 1956; that nationalization had caused inefficiency and corruption; and, finally, that repression was so pervasive that Egyptians were less free than they had been in the past.

It was under Nasser that Egypt finally succeeded in ridding itself of the last vestiges of British imperialism; that Egypt attempted to steer a middle course between the Western countries and the Soviet Union and its allies and in so doing became a founder of the Nonaligned Movement that exists to this day; that Egypt moved out of the isolation the British had imposed on the country and assumed a leadership position in the Arab world; and that Egypt

Archaeological expedition of American Museum of Natural History, 1908
Courtesy American Museum of Natural History

became the "beating heart" of pan-Arabism and the symbol of renewed Arab pride.

Internally, Nasser destroyed the political and economic power of the old feudal landowning class. Education and employment opportunities were made available to all Egyptians regardless of class or sex. Women were encouraged to get an education and go to work as part of the national struggle for economic progress and development. After the revolution, women were at last granted the right to vote. Nasser emphasized social programs to improve the living and working conditions of the peasants and workers, such as the electrification of villages, worker housing, minimum wage laws, decreased working hours, and worker participation in management. Industrialization intensified, and the country became less dependent on the export of cotton. The economy grew at acceptable rates in spite of some problems. After the June 1967 War, however, the military expenditures began to absorb about 25 percent of Egypt's gross national product (GNP—see Glossary). Also, the population increase that had begun in the 1940s began to overtake the economic advances.

It is true that Nasser never really opened up his rule to popular participation. He once admitted that he had become so used to conspiracy, by necessity, that he tended to see a conspiracy in everything, a view that prevented him from conducting an open rule. He wanted to establish a basis of support for his regime but one that would not require the regime to give significant power to the public (see The Presidency, ch. 4). He felt that an ideology such as socialism might accomplish this, but at the same time he feared that the commitment would be to the ideology and not to him. Thus, when Nasser died in 1970 he left behind an imperfect and unfinished revolution.

Sadat Takes Over, 1970–73

When Nasser died, it became apparent that his successor, Anwar as Sadat, did not intend to be another Nasser. As Sadat's rule progressed, it became clear that his priority was solving Egypt's pressing economic problems by encouraging Western financial investment. Sadat realized, however, that Western investment would not be forthcoming until there was peace between Egypt and Israel, Soviet influence was eliminated, and the climate became more favorable to Western capitalism.

Sadat was a Free Officer who had served as secretary of the Islamic Congress and of the National Union and as speaker of the National Assembly. In 1969 he was appointed vice president and so became acting president on Nasser's death. On October 3, 1970, the ASU recommended that Sadat be nominated to succeed Nasser as president. An election was held on October 15, and Sadat won more than 90 percent of the vote. Almost no one expected that Sadat would be able to hold power for long. Sadat was considered a rather weak and colorless figure who would last only as long as it would take for the political maneuvering to result in the emergence of Nasser's true successor. Sadat surprised everyone with a series of astute political moves by which he was able to retain the presidency and emerge as a leader in his own right.

Sadat moved very cautiously at first and pledged to continue Nasser's policies. On May 2, 1971, however, Sadat dismissed Ali Sabri, the vice president and head of the ASU. On May 15, Sadat announced that Sabri and more than 100 others had been arrested and charged with plotting a coup against the government. Also charged in the plot were Sharawy Jumaa, minister of interior and head of internal security, and Muhammad Fawzi, minister of war. These men were considered to be left-leaning and pro-Soviet. They were arrested with other important figures of the Nasser era. They had all resigned their positions on May 13, apparently in preparation for a takeover. But anticipating their moves, Sadat outflanked them and was then able to assert himself and appoint his own followers, rather than Free Officer colleagues, to leadership positions.

This action, which became known as the Corrective Revolution, began Sadat's move away from Nasser's policies. He announced new elections and a complete reorganization of the ASU. The armed forces pledged their support for Sadat on May 15. There were also some popular demonstrations in the streets in support of Sadat's moves.

Sadat signed the first Soviet-Egyptian Treaty of Friendship and Cooperation on May 27, 1971. He later explained that he did it to allay Soviet fears provoked by his ouster of Ali Sabri and the others and to speed up deliveries of Soviet military supplies. Even as he was preparing to break the stalemate with Israel, however, he was already thinking of expelling the Soviet advisers.

October 1973 War

On February 4, 1971, Sadat announced a new peace initiative that contained a significant concession: he was willing to accept an interim agreement with Israel in return for a partial Israeli withdrawal from Sinai. A timetable would then be set for Israel's withdrawal from the rest of the occupied territories in accordance with UN Resolution 242. Egypt would reopen the canal, restore diplomatic relations with the United States, which had been broken after the June 1967 War, and sign a peace agreement with Israel through Jarring. Sadat's initiative fell on deaf ears in Tel Aviv and in Washington, which was not disposed to assisting the Soviet Union's major client in the region. Disillusioned by Israel's failure to respond to his initiative, Sadat rejected the Rogers Plan and the cease-fire.

In May 1972, President Nixon met Soviet president Leonid Brezhnev, and Sadat was convinced that the two superpowers would try to prevent a new war in the Middle East and that a position of stalemate—no peace, no war—had been reached. For Sadat this position was intolerable. The June 1967 War had been a humiliating defeat for the Arabs. Without a military victory, any Arab leader who agreed to negotiate directly with Israel would do so from a position of extreme weakness. At the same time, the United States and the Soviet Union were urging restraint and caution. However, the United States refused to put pressure on Israel to make concessions, and the Soviet Union, which had broken off diplomatic relations with Israel as a result of the June 1967 War, had no influence over Israel. Internally, the Egyptian economy was being steadily drained by the confrontation with Israel. Economic problems were becoming more serious because of the tremendous amount of resources directed toward building up the military since the June 1967 War, and it was clear that Sadat would have to demonstrate some results from this policy. In the last half of 1972, there were large-scale student riots, and some journalists came out publicly in support of the students. Thus, Sadat felt under increasing pressure to go to war against Israel as the only way to regain the lost territories.

In retrospect, there were indications that Egypt was preparing for war. On July 17, 1972, Sadat expelled the 15,000 Soviet advisers from Egypt. Sadat later explained that the expulsion freed him to pursue his preparations for war. On December 28, 1972, Sadat created "permanent war committees." On March 26, 1973, Sadat assumed the additional title of prime minister and formed a new government designed to continue preparations for a confrontation with Israel.

Then on October 6, 1973, Egyptian forces launched a successful surprise attack across the Suez Canal (see War of Attrition and the October 1973 War, ch. 5). The Syrians carried out an attack on Israel at the same time. For the Arabs, it was the fasting month of Ramadan, and for Israel it was Yom Kippur. The crossing of the canal, an astounding feat of technology and military acumen, took only four hours to complete. The crossing was code-named Operation Badr after the first victory of the Prophet Muhammad, which culminated in his entry into Mecca in 630.

On October 17 the Arab oil producers announced a program of reprisals against the Western backers of Israel: a 5 percent cutback in output, followed by further such reductions every month until Israel had withdrawn from all the occupied territories and the rights of the Palestinians had been restored. The next day, President Nixon formally asked Congress for US$2.2 billion in emergency funds to finance the massive airlift of arms to Israel that was already under way. The following day, King Faisal of Saudi Arabia decreed an immediate 10 percent cutback in Saudi oil and, five days after that, the complete suspension of all shipments to the United States.

Israel was shocked and unprepared for the war. After the initial confusion and near panic in Israel followed by the infusion of United States weaponry, Israel was able to counterattack and succeeded in crossing to the west bank of the canal and surrounding the Egyptian Third Army. With the Third Army surrounded, Sadat appealed to the Soviet Union for help. Soviet prime minister Alexei Kosygin believed he had obtained the American acceptance of a cease-fire through Henry Kissinger, United States secretary of state. On October 22, the UN Security Council passed Resolution 338, calling for a cease-fire by all parties within twelve hours in the positions they occupied. Egypt accepted the cease-fire, but Israel, alleging Egyptian violations of the cease-fire, completed the encirclement of the Third Army to the east of the canal. By nightfall on October 23, the road to Suez, the Third Army's only supply line, was in Israeli hands, cutting off two divisions and 45,000 men.

The Soviet Union were furious, believing it had been doublecrossed by the United States. On October 24, the Soviet ambassador handed Kissinger a note from Brezhnev threatening that if the United States were not prepared to join in sending forces to impose the cease-fire, the Soviet Union would act alone. The United States took the threat very seriously and responded by ordering a grade-three nuclear alert, the first of its kind since President John F. Kennedy's order during the Cuban missile crisis of 1962. The threat came to naught, however, because a UN emergency force arrived in the battle zone to police the cease-fire.

Meanwhile, Syria felt betrayed by Egypt because Sadat did not inform his ally of his decision to accept the cease-fire. Two days after Sadat, President Hafiz al Assad of Syria accepted the cease-fire as well.

Neither side had won a clear-cut victory, but for the Egyptians, it was a victory nonetheless. The Arabs had taken the initiative in attacking the Israelis and had shown that Israel was not invincible. The stinging defeats of 1948, 1956, and 1967 seemed to be avenged.

The Israelis, however, paid a heavy price for merely holding their attackers to an inconclusive draw. In three weeks, they lost 2,523 personnel, two and a half times as many, proportionally speaking, as the United States lost in the ten years of the Vietnam war. The war had a devastating effect on Israel's economy and was followed by savage austerity measures and drastically reduced living standards. For the first time, Israelis witnessed the humiliating spectacle of Israeli prisoners, heads bowed, paraded on Arab television. Also, for the first time captured Israeli hardware was exhibited in Cairo.

In Egypt the casualties included about 8,000 killed. The effect of the war on the morale of the Egyptian population, however, was immense. Sadat's prestige grew tremendously. The war, along with the political moves Sadat had made previously, meant that he was totally in control and able to implement the programs he wanted. He was the hero of the day.

Negotiations toward a permanent cease-fire began in December 1973. In January 1974, Kissinger began his shuttle diplomacy between Egypt and Israel. On January 18, the first disengagement agreement was signed separately by Sadat and Golda Meir. A second disengagement agreement was signed on September 1, 1975.

The agreement provided for a partial Israeli withdrawal in Sinai and limited the number of troops and kinds of weapons Egypt could have on the eastern side of the canal. Israel agreed to withdraw from the Abu Rudays oil fields in western Sinai, which produced small but important revenue for Egypt. Egypt also agreed not to use force to achieve its aims, a concession that in effect made Egypt a nonbelligerent in the Arab-Israeli conflict. As the price for its agreement, Israel extracted important concessions from the United States. Kissinger's secret promises to Israel included meeting Israel's military needs in any emergency, preserving Israel's arms superiority by providing the most advanced and sophisticated weaponry, and pledging not to recognize or to negotiate with the PLO.

On June 5, 1975, the Suez Canal was reopened. This was a great moment for Sadat, not only politically but economically, because the canal provided Egypt with considerable revenues (see Suez Canal, ch. 3).

Political Developments, 1971–78

On September 11, 1971, a new constitution was presented by Sadat and approved by the electorate. The previous constitution had been issued as "provisional" in 1964. The Constitution of 1971 provides additional guarantees against arbitrary arrest, seizure of property, and other Nasser-era abuses. The responsibility of the People's Assembly, which replaced the National Assembly, was widened, but the president clearly retained dominant authority. Sadat dissolved the old legislature on September 8, 1971, and on September 19, he formed a new cabinet.

The Constitution provides that the president may issue binding decrees, which was essentially the way Sadat ruled the country. After ridding himself of Ali Sabri and his allies, Sadat conducted his presidency without the constraints that Nasser had faced. Sadat's government came to be composed of his own handpicked followers, not of colleagues whose opinions he had to consider. Especially during the euphoria following the October 1973 War, Sadat was able to consolidate the power of the presidency in a way that Nasser never had (see The Presidency, ch. 4).

Nevertheless, Sadat attempted to allow a certain degree of political expression. Competitive, but not totally free, elections were held for the People's Assembly on October 27, 1971. In 1975 Sadat permitted the establishment of three groupings in the ASU to express the opinions of the left, the right, and the center of the regime. By 1976 the three platforms were permitted, within established guidelines, to act as separate political entities, but each group needed to elect a minimum of twelve deputies to the People's Assembly to be recognized. The leftist group was originally known as the National Progressive Unionist Organization (NPUO—later NPUP when it was allowed to become a party) led by Khalid Muhi ad Din, a Free Officer and a Marxist. The right-wing group was the Socialist Liberal Organization (SLO—later the Liberal or Ahrar Party) led by Mustafa Kamil Murad. The center group was known as the Egyptian Arab Socialist Organization. The country's main political forces, the Wafd, the Muslim Brotherhood, the Nasserites, and the communists, were not allowed representation.

In the October 1976 election, not unexpectedly, the progovernment center platform of the ASU won an overwhelming majority, 280 seats; the SLP won 12 and the NPUP only 2. Independent candidates won forty-eight seats. When he opened the new assembly, Sadat announced that the platforms would become political parties.

In July 1977, Sadat announced that he would establish his own party, the National Democratic Party (NDP), signaling the end of the Arab Socialist Union, which was merged with the NDP. Sadat also wanted a more pliable left-wing opposition party, so the Socialist Labor Party (Amal) was founded with Sadat's brother-in-law as vice president.

Sadat also allowed comparative freedom of action to the Muslim Brotherhood. Sadat felt he could use the Islamic fundamentalists to counter the growing influence of the left. The leaders of the Muslim Brotherhood were freed in 1974 along with other political prisoners. They were not allowed to become a legal organization, but they were allowed to operate openly and to publish their magazine, *Al Awd* (The Return) as long as they did not criticize the regime too sharply. This policy seemed to work until the peace treaty with Israel, and then the Brotherhood became a severe critic of the regime (see The "Dominant Party" System, ch. 4).

The movement away from a one-party system matched Egypt's turn away from the Soviet Union and toward the United States. Sadat hoped that his new political and economic policies would attract large sums of private American investment. He also felt that the United States was the only country that could pressure Israel into a final peace settlement. To enhance relations with the United States and to respond to the Soviet Union's refusal to reschedule repayments of Egypt's debt, Sadat unilaterally renounced the Soviet-Egyptian Treaty of Friendship and Cooperation on March 15, 1976.

Egypt's New Direction

In April 1974, Sadat presented what he called the October Working Paper, which described his vision of Egypt's future. The paper committed Egypt to building a strong country, continuing the confrontation with Israel, working toward Arab unity, and playing a leading role in world politics. Perhaps the most important part of Sadat's paper was the announcement of a new economic policy that came to be called *infitah,* (opening or open door; see Glossary and The Role of Government, ch. 3).

This new economic policy allowed increased foreign investment in Egypt, greater participation by the private sector in the Egyptian economy, more freedom for individuals to develop their own wealth and property, and relaxed currency regulations so that Egyptians could have access to foreign currency. The new direction gradually changed Egypt in many ways: the shops filled with foreign consumer goods; foreign companies built huge modern hotels; and new wealth was displayed in a way that had not been seen in Egypt since before the 1952 Revolution. Doubts began to be expressed, however, about how much all this was actually doing for the Egyptian people since foreign investment in long-term agricultural or industrial projects was lacking.

In January 1977, Egyptians took to the streets in antigovernment riots that demonstrated their disillusionment with *infitah* and the nepotism and corruption it spawned. The cause of the riots went back to late 1976 when Sadat, in an effort to solve the country's economic problems, asked the World Bank for loans. In response to the bank's criticisms of public subsidies, the government announced in January 1977 that it was ending subsidies on flour, rice, and cooking oil and canceling bonuses and pay increases.

The result was immediate and shocking. On January 18 and 19, there was rioting in towns from Aswan to Alexandria, variously described as the biggest upheaval since the 1919 riots against the British, or a second Black Saturday. It was the first time the army had been brought into the streets since 1952. For thirty-six hours, the rioters unleashed their pent-up fury on targets that symbolized the yawning gap between the haves and have-nots, the frivolity and corruption of the ruling class, and the incompetence and insensitivity of the administration. The rioters shouted slogans like, "Hero of the crossing, where is our breakfast?" and "Thieves of the *infitah,* the people are famished." There were also shouts of "Nasser, Nasser." In the clashes between demonstrators and police, 800 persons were killed, and several thousands were wounded, according to unofficial estimates. The rioting ended when the government canceled the price increases while retaining 10 percent wage increases and other benefits for public sector employees.

Peace with Israel

In 1977 the outlook for peace between Israel and Egypt was not good. Israel still held most of Sinai, and negotiations had been at a stalemate since the second disengagement agreement in 1975. Israeli prime minister Menachem Begin was a hard-liner and a supporter of Israeli expansion. He approved the development of settlements on the occupied West Bank and reprisal raids into southern Lebanon. He also refused to approve any negotiation with the PLO. After the food riots of January 1977, Sadat decided that something dramatic had to be done, and so on November 19, 1977, in response to an invitation from Begin, Sadat journeyed to Jerusalem.

The world was amazed by this courageous move. The reaction in Egypt was generally favorable. Many Egyptians accepted peace with Israel if it meant regaining Egyptian territories. They were tired of bearing the major burden of the confrontation and, considering the sacrifices Egypt had already made, felt that the Palestinians were ungrateful. Of the Arab countries, only Sudan, Oman, and Morocco were favorable to Sadat's trip. In the other Arab states, there was shock and dismay. The Arabs felt that Sadat had betrayed the cause of Arab solidarity and the Palestinians. In spite of Sadat's denials, the Arabs believed that he intended to go it alone and make a separate peace with Israel.

In fact, that is what happened. In December 1977, Egypt and Israel began peace negotiations in Cairo. These negotiations continued on and off over the next several months, but by September 1978 it was clear that they were deadlocked. President Jimmy Carter had become closely involved in the negotiations. In an effort to break the deadlock, Carter invited Sadat and Begin to Camp David. The negotiations were tense and almost broke down several times. On September 17, however, Carter announced that the Camp David Accords had been reached. They consisted of two parts, the Framework for Peace in the Middle East and the Framework for the Conclusion of a Peace Treaty between Israel and Egypt. The Egyptian-Israeli peace treaty was signed on March 26, 1979. Israel agreed to withdraw from Sinai within three years of the treaty; normal diplomatic and trade relations were to be established, and Israeli ships would pass unhindered through the canal. Egypt, however, would not have full sovereignty over Sinai. A multinational observer force would be stationed in Sinai, and the United States would monitor events there.

The Framework for Peace in the Middle East was an elaboration of the ''autonomy'' plan that Begin had put forward nine months before. A ''self-governing authority'' was to be established for a five-year transitional period, by the third year of which negotiations would begin to determine the final status of the West Bank and the Gaza Strip and to conclude a peace treaty between Israel and Jordan. Within one month of the ratification of the treaty, Egypt and Israel were supposed to begin negotiations for the establishment of the ''elected self-governing authority'' in the West Bank and the Gaza Strip. They set themselves the goal of completing the negotiations within one year so that elections could be held ''as expeditiously as possible.'' These deadlines came and went, and by 1990 the Framework for Peace had become a virtual dead letter. Begin made his position perfectly clear: Jerusalem would remain undivided; settlement would continue, and autonomy would never become sovereignty. There would be no Palestinian state. On May 12, 1979, shortly before the autonomy talks were supposed to begin, deputy Geula Cohen, a Zionist extremist, introduced a bill, adopted by the Knesset, that declared Jerusalem to be Israel's united and indivisible capital.

The Camp David Accords made Sadat a hero in Europe and the United States. The reaction in Egypt was generally favorable, but there was opposition from the left and from the Muslim Brotherhood. In the Arab world, Sadat was almost universally condemned. Only Sudan issued an ambivalent statement of support. The Arab states suspended all official aid and severed diplomatic relations. Egypt was expelled from the Arab League, which it was instrumental in founding, and from other Arab institutions. Saudi Arabia withdrew the funds it had promised for Egypt's purchase of American fighter aircraft.

In the West, where Sadat was extolled as a hero and a champion of peace, the Arab rejection of the Camp David Accords is often confused with the rejection of peace. The basis for Arab rejection was opposition to Egypt's separate peace with Israel. Although Sadat insisted that the treaty provided for a comprehensive settlement of the Arab-Israeli conflict, the Arab states and the PLO saw it as a separate peace, which Sadat had vowed he would not sign. The Arabs believed that only a unified Arab stance and the threat of force would persuade Israel to negotiate a settlement of the Palestinian issue that would satisfy Palestinian demands for a homeland. Without Egypt's military power, the threat of force evaporated because no single Arab state was strong enough militarily to confront Israel alone. Thus, the Arabs felt betrayed and dismayed that the Palestinian issue, the core of the Arab-Israeli conflict, would remain an unresolved, destabilizing force in the region.

The Aftermath of Camp David and the Assassination of Sadat

The Camp David Accords brought peace to Egypt but not prosperity. With no real improvement in the economy, Sadat became increasingly unpopular. His isolation in the Arab world was matched by his increasing remoteness from the mass of Egyptians. While Sadat's critics in the Arab world remained beyond his reach, increasingly he reacted to criticism at home by expanding censorship and jailing his opponents. In addition, Sadat subjected the Egyptians to a series of referenda on his actions and proposals that he invariably won by more than 99 percent of the vote. For example, in May 1979 the Egyptian people approved the Egyptian-Israeli peace treaty by 99.9 percent of those voting.

One of Sadat's most remarkable acts during this period was the so-called Law of Shame, which was drafted at Sadat's express instructions. Among the shameful crimes punishable under this law were "advocating any doctrine that implies negation of divine teaching," "allowing children or youth to go astray by advocating the repudiation of popular, religious, moral, or national values or by setting a bad example in a public place," and "broadcasting or publishing gross or scurrilous words or pictures that could offend public sensibilities or undermine the dignity of the state." Offenders could be barred from public life or from engaging in economic activity or managing their own property; they could be condemned to internal exile or prohibited from leaving the country. The Law of Shame was approved in a referendum by more than 98 percent of the electorate. This was remarkable since there was widespread opposition to the law, which was denounced as "an act of shame."

In May 1980, an impressive, nonpartisan body of citizens charged Sadat with superseding his own constitution. Their manifesto declared, "The style in which Egypt is governed today is not based on any specific form of government. While it is not dictatorship, Nazism, or fascism, neither is it democracy or pseudodemocracy."

In September 1981, Sadat ordered the biggest roundup of his opponents since he came to power, at least 1,500 people according to the official figure but more according to unofficial reports. The Muslim Brotherhood bore the brunt of the arrests. The supreme guide of the Brotherhood, Umar Tilmasani, and other religious militants were arrested. Sadat also withdrew his "recognition" of the Coptic pope Shenudah III, banished him to a desert monastery, and arrested several bishops and priests. Also arrested were such prominent figures as journalist Mohamed Heikal, and Wafd leader

Fuad Siraj ad Din. Sadat ordered the arrest of several SLP leaders and the closing of *Ash Shaab* (The People) newspaper. A referendum on his purge showed nearly 99.5 percent of the electorate approved.

On October 6, while observing a military parade commemorating the eighth anniversary of the October 1973 War, Sadat was assassinated by members of Al Jihad movement, a group of religious extremists. Sadat's assassin was Lieutenant Colonel Khalid al Islambuli. The conspirators were arrested and tried. In April 1982, two of the conspirators were shot and three hanged.

Whereas a number of Western leaders, including three former United States presidents, attended Sadat's funeral, only one member of the Arab League was represented by a head of state, Sudan. Only two, Oman and Somalia, sent representatives. In Egypt 43 million people went on with the celebration of Id al Adha, the Feast of Sacrifice, as if nothing had happened. There were no throngs in the streets, grieving and lamenting, as there were when Nasser died. In the Arab world, Sadat's death was greeted with jubilation.

Mubarak and the Middle Way

Sadat's handpicked successor, Husni Mubarak, was overwhelmingly approved in a national referendum on October 24, 1981. Sadat appointed Mubarak vice president of the state in 1975 and of the NDP in 1978. Mubarak, who was born in 1928 in Lower Egypt and had spent his career in the armed forces, was not a member of the Free Officers' movement. He had trained as a pilot in the Soviet Union and became air force chief of staff in 1969 and deputy minister of war in 1972.

In a speech to the People's Assembly in November 1981, Mubarak outlined the principles of his government's policy and spoke about the future he wanted for Egypt. *Infitah* would continue, and there would be no return to the restrictive days of Nasser. Mubarak called for an *infitah* of production, however, rather than of consumption, that would benefit all of society and not just the wealthy few. Food subsidies would remain, and imports of unnecessary luxury goods would be curtailed. Opposition parties would be allowed. The peace treaty with Israel would be observed. Thus, Mubarak sought to chart a middle course between the conflicting legacies of Nasser and Sadat.

Since 1981 Mubarak has allowed more overt political activity. Slowly, parties and newspapers began to function again, and political opponents jailed by Sadat were released. At the time of the 1984 election, five parties were allowed to function in addition to the ruling NDP. The left-wing opposition consisted of the National

Progressive Unionist Party, a grouping of socialists led by Khalid Muhi ad Din, and the Socialist Labor Party. The Wafd resurfaced and won a court case against its prohibition. One religious party was licensed, the Umma. Not officially represented were the communists, the Muslim Brotherhood, and avowed Nasserites, although all three tendencies were represented in other parties (see The "Dominant Party System," ch. 4).

In the 1984 election, a party had to win at least 8 percent of the vote to be represented in the Assembly. The NDP received more than 70 percent of the vote (391 seats). The Wafd, the only other party to gain any seats, won fifty-seven. The NPUP received only 7 percent of the votes and consequently lost them all to the NDP. There were some complaints that the election was rigged, but no serious challenge was mounted against the results.

In addition to domestic programs, Mubarak was concerned to regain the Sinai Peninsula for Egypt and to return his country to the Arab fold. One of Mubarak's first acts was to pledge to honor the peace treaty with Israel. In April 1982, the Israeli withdrawal from Sinai took place as scheduled. A multinational force of observers took up positions in Sinai to monitor the peace. Egypt was allowed to station only one army division in Sinai.

In 1983 Egypt's isolation in the Arab world began to end. In that year, Arafat met Mubarak in Cairo after the PLO leader had been expelled from Lebanon under Syrian pressure. In January 1984, Egypt was readmitted unconditionally to the Islamic Conference Organization. In November 1987, an Arab summit resolution allowed the Arab countries to resume diplomatic relations with Egypt. This action was taken largely as a result of the Iran-Iraq War and Arab alarm over the Iranian offensive on Iraqi territories at the end of 1986 and throughout January and February 1987. On Egypt's side, its economic crisis worsened, and it needed economic assistance from the Arab oil states. Thus, the summit resolution amounted to an exchange of Egyptian security assistance in the Persian Gulf crisis for Arab aid to Egypt's economy. The summit indicated that Mubarak, in attempting to steer a middle course between the imposing legacies of Nasser and Sadat, had brought Egypt back into the Arab fold and into the center of Middle East peace making.

* * *

The literature on Egypt from ancient to modern times is extensive. Good basic works on ancient Egypt are *Egypt before the Pharaohs* by Michael H. Hoffman and *Ancient Egypt,* edited by B.G. Trigger,

B.J. Kemp, D. O'Connor, and A.B. Lloyd. Also recommended are Cyril Aldred's *The Egyptians* and *Egypt to the End of the Old Kingdom*. Two readable, popular histories are Jill Kamil's *The Ancient Egyptians* and Robert A. Armour's *Gods and Myths of Ancient Egypt*. Egyptian art is covered in W. Stevenson Smith's *The Art and Architecture of Ancient Egypt*.

The Arab Conquest of Egypt by Alfred Butler and *Egypt During the Middle Ages* by Stanley Lane-Poole are classics that should be read for the periods they cover. For Egypt during the medieval period, there are also Robert Irwin's *The Middle East in the Middle Ages* and Bernard Lewis's article, "Egypt and Syria," in *The Cambridge History of Islam*. Egypt during the Ottoman period is covered in P.M. Holt's *Egypt and the Fertile Crescent, 1516-1922*.

For the late Ottoman period and the transition to modernity, two important historical works are *The Roots of Modern Egypt* by Daniel Crecelius and *Islamic Roots of Capitalism* by Peter Gran. Valuable French works are André Raymond's *Artisans et commerçants au Caire au XVIIIe siècle* and the collection of articles in *L'Egypte au XIXe siècle*.

For the modern period, there are several good general histories, including P.M. Holt's *Egypt and the Fertile Crescent, 1516-1922*, which ends with World War I and Egyptian independence, and P.J. Vatikiotis's *The History of Egypt from Muhammad Ali to Sadat*. Roger Owen's *The Middle East in the World Economy* has informative chapters on Egypt. Also important for an understanding of the transformation that took place in Egypt in the nineteenth century are Holt's *Political and Social Change in Modern Egypt* and Gabriel Baer's *Studies in the Social History of Modern Egypt*.

Other important studies on particular aspects of this period include Afaf Lutfi al-Sayyid Marsot's *Egypt in the Reign of Muhmmad Ali;* Robert Hunter's *Egypt under the Khedives, 1805-1879;* Albert Hourani's intellectual history, *Arabic Thought in the Liberal Age, 1798-1939*; Timothy Mitchell's *Colonizing Egypt;* and Eric Davis's *Challenging Colonialism*. The definitive study of the Urabi Revolt and the British invasion of 1882 remains Alexander Scholch's *Egypt for the Egyptians*. Also important are the first book-length history of Egyptian women in English, *Women in Nineteenth-Century Egypt* by Judith Tucker, and two studies of the development of the working class, *Workers on the Nile* by Joel Beinin and Zachary Lockman, and *Tinker, Tailor, and Textile Worker* by Ellis Goldberg.

The period of parliamentary democracy is well covered in *Party Politics in Egypt* by Marius Deeb and *The Wafd* by Janice Terry. For the revolutionary and postrevolutionary periods, there are Anthony McDermott's *Egypt from Nasser to Mubarak: A Flawed Revolution* and Derek Hopwood's *Egypt: Politics and Society, 1945–1984.* Also important are Anouar Abdel-Malek's *Egypt: Military Society,* John Waterbury's *The Egypt of Nasser and Sadat,* and Raymond A. Hinnebusch, Jr.'s *Egyptian Politics under Sadat.* Egypt's most recent history is covered in David Hirst's and Irene Beeson's biography of Anwar Sadat entitled *Sadat,* Muhammed Hassanain Haikal's attempt to explain Sadat's assassination in *Autumn of Fury,* and Robert Springborg's *Mubarak's Egypt.* (For further information and complete citations, see Bibliography.)

Chapter 2. The Society and Its Environment

Queen Nefertiti

EGYPTIAN SOCIETY IN 1990 reflected both ancient roots and the profound changes that have occurred since Napoleon Bonaparte invaded the country in 1798. Land tenure, crops, and cultivation patterns had all been transformed during the nineteenth and twentieth centuries, and the country had become increasingly urbanized and industrialized. Nevertheless, approximately half the population still lived in rural areas where settlement patterns remained defined, as they had been since pharaonic times, by the Nile River and irrigated agriculture. Villages were clustered along both banks of the Nile and along myriad irrigation canals in the Delta.

The rise of commercial agriculture in the nineteenth century set in motion a transformation of rural society. Land that was previously held in common by a village and granted in usufruct to individual families was transferred to private ownership. The transfers created a small class of wealthy absentee landowners, a somewhat larger class of relatively prosperous farmers who owned medium-sized parcels of land, and an enormous class of small farmers, sharecroppers, and landless casual laborers.

The land-reform measures implemented by the government in the 1950s and 1960s led to the redistribution of nearly 15 percent of the arable land to about 10 percent of the rural population. Land reform limited individual landownership to twenty-one hectares, thus forcing the wealthiest landed families to sell most of their holdings. Small peasant proprietors were the main beneficiaries of the redistribution. By the early 1980s, however, continued population growth and rising production costs had eroded many of the accomplishments of land reform. Inheritance tended to fragment already small holdings, and the number of landless people increased.

Land reform was only one of several social programs initiated by the Free Officers who led the 1952 Revolution (see The Revolution and the Early Years of the New Government, 1952–56, ch. 1). The majority of these officers, who came mostly from the middle class, was determined to broaden opportunities in a society that had been dominated by a narrow elite. They perceived education as a critical force for change. Beginning in the nineteenth century, secular education provided the country with the foundation for a civil bureaucracy. Access to a university education and government employment, however, was generally limited to the urban upper classes until the mid-1930s, when sons of urban and rural middle-class families were accepted into the military or civil administration. Following the 1952 Revolution, educational opportunities from primary school through university increased substantially. Through the 1980s, university enrollments swelled as increasing numbers of middle- and lower-class youth pursued higher education in the hope of obtaining prestigious employment.

By the 1980s, overstaffing in the state bureaucracy had become a major problem. Periodic discussion by the mass media on the need to reform the government's hiring and promotion systems, which gave preference to university graduates, caused anxiety among students, many of whom had migrated from rural areas and faced limited employment prospects in agriculture. Most of these students perceived higher education and government employment as means for achieving upward mobility. They therefore showed little support for the proposed reforms, which would reduce their opportunities.

Massive urbanization beginning after World War II has had a pervasive and accelerating impact on the nation's cities, especially Cairo and Alexandria. These cities, which were once the enclaves of the relatively prosperous and privileged, have attracted millions of rural migrants, including landowning families' children who wanted to pursue an education and illiterate sons and daughters of poor, landless peasants who were willing to work as unskilled laborers. The migrants have adapted to urban life by attempting to replicate the social organization found in villages. Residential patterns, employment practices, and socializing have tended to reflect and to reinforce relationships formed in the countryside.

Religion, mainly Islam, is an integral aspect of social life. Although most Egyptian Muslims respect and agree on the basic tenets of Islam, their religious perspectives differ. Trained theologians, for example, practice orthodox Islam while villagers practice a simple form of the religion. Since the 1970s, there has been a resurgence of Islamic political groups. Activists ranged from persons fervent in religious practice to individuals who favor the adoption of the Muslim legal code as the basis of Egyptian law to others who espouse the violent overthrow of the government to achieve an Islamic social order. Some leaders of the Islamic political groups are former university students or recent graduates whose families migrated from rural areas. Many Muslims have responded favorably to these leaders, who are likely to remain a potent political force in the 1990s.

Geography

Physical Size and Borders

Egypt, covering 1,001,449 square kilometers of la
the same size as Texas and New Mexico combined. Tl   ..y s
greatest distance from north to south is 1,024 kilometers, and from
east to west, 1,240 kilometers. The country is located in northeastern
Africa and includes the Sinai Peninsula (also seen as Sinai), which
is often considered part of Asia. Egypt's natural boundaries consist of more than 2,900 kilometers of coastline along the Mediterranean Sea, the Gulf of Suez, the Gulf of Aqaba, and the Red Sea
(see fig. 1).

Egypt has land boundaries with Israel, Libya, Sudan, and the
Gaza Strip, a Palestinian area formerly administered by Egypt and
occupied by Israel since 1967. The land boundaries are generally
straight lines that do not conform to geographic features such as
rivers. Egypt shares its longest boundary, which extends 1,273
kilometers, with Sudan. In accordance with the Anglo-Egyptian
Condominium Agreement of 1899, this boundary runs westward
from the Red Sea along the twenty-second parallel, includes the
Sudanese Nile salient (Wadi Halfa salient), and continues along
the twenty-second parallel until it meets the twenty-fifth meridi-
an. The Sudanese Nile salient, a finger-shaped area along the Nile
River (Nahr an Nil) north of the twenty-second parallel, is nearly
covered by Lake Nasser, which was created when the Aswan High
Dam was constructed in the 1960s. An "administrative" boundary, which supplements the main Egyptian-Sudanese boundary permits nomadic tribes to gain access to water holes at the eastern end
of Egypt's southern frontier. The administrative boundary departs
from the international boundary in two places; Egypt administers
the area south of the twenty-second parallel, and Sudan administers
the area north of it.

Egypt shares all 1,150 kilometers of the western border with
Libya. This border was defined in 1925 under an agreement with
Italy, which had colonized Libya. Before and after World War II,
the northern border was adjusted, resulting in the return of the
village of As Sallum to Egyptian sovereignty. Egypt shares 255
kilometers of its eastern border in Sinai with Israel and 11 kilometers with the Gaza Strip.

Egypt is divided into twenty-six governorates (sometimes called
provinces), which include four city governorates: Alexandria (Al
Iskandariyah), Cairo (Al Qahirah), Port Said (Bur Said) and Suez;
the nine governorates of Lower Egypt in the Nile Delta region;
the eight governorates of Upper Egypt along the Nile River south

from Cairo to Aswan; and the five frontier governorates covering Sinai and the deserts that lie west and east of the Nile. All governorates, except the frontier ones, are in the Nile Delta or along the Nile Valley and Suez Canal.

Natural Regions

Egypt is predominantly desert. Only 35,000 square kilometers—3.5 percent of the total land area—are cultivated and permanently settled. Most of the country lies within the wide band of desert that stretches from Africa's Atlantic Coast across the continent and into southwest Asia. Egypt's geological history has produced four major physical regions: the Nile Valley and Delta, the Western Desert (also known as the Libyan Desert), the Eastern Desert (also known as the Arabian Desert), and the Sinai Peninsula (see fig. 3). The Nile Valley and Delta is the most important region because it supports 99 percent of the population on the country's only cultivable land.

Nile Valley and Delta

The Nile Valley and Delta, the most extensive oasis on earth, was created by the world's second-longest river and its seemingly inexhaustible sources. Without the topographic channel that permits the Nile to flow across the Sahara, Egypt would be entirely desert; the Nile River traverses about 1,600 kilometers through Egypt and flows northward from the Egyptian-Sudanese border to the Mediterranean Sea. The Nile is a combination of three long rivers whose sources are in central Africa: the White Nile, the Blue Nile, and the Atbarah.

The White Nile, which begins at Lake Victoria in Uganda, supplies about 28 percent of the Nile's waters in Egypt. In its course from Lake Victoria to Juba in southern Sudan, the elevation of the White Nile's channel drops more than 600 meters. In its 1,600-kilometer course from Juba to Khartoum, Sudan's capital, the river descends only 75 meters. In southern and central Sudan, the White Nile passes through a wide, flat plain covered with swamp vegetation and slows almost to stagnation.

The Blue Nile, which originates at Lake Tana in Ethiopia, provides an average of 58 percent of the Nile's waters in Egypt. It has a steeper gradient and flows more swiftly than the White Nile, which it joins at Khartoum. Unlike the White Nile, the Blue Nile carries a considerable amount of sediment; for several kilometers north of Khartoum, water closer to the eastern bank of the river is visibly muddy and comes from the Blue Nile, while the water closer to the western bank is clearer and comes from the White Nile.

The much shorter Atbarah River, which also originates in Ethiopia, joins the main Nile north of Khartoum between the fifth and sixth cataracts (areas of steep rapids) and provides about 14 percent of the Nile's waters in Egypt. During the low-water season, which runs from January to June, the Atbarah shrinks to a number of pools. But in late summer, when torrential rains fall on the Ethiopian plateau, the Atbarah provides 22 percent of the Nile's flow.

The Blue Nile has a similar pattern. It contributes 17 percent of the Nile's waters in the low-water season and 68 percent during the high-water season. In contrast, the White Nile provides only 10 percent of the Nile's waters during the high-water season but contributes more than 80 percent during the low-water period. Thus, before the Aswan High Dam was completed in 1971, the White Nile watered the Egyptian stretch of the river throughout the year, whereas the Blue Nile, carrying seasonal rain from Ethiopia, caused the Nile to overflow its banks and deposit a layer of fertile mud over adjacent fields. The great flood of the main Nile usually occurred in Egypt during August, September, and October, but it sometimes began as early as June at Aswan and often did not completely wane until January.

The Nile enters Egypt a few kilometers north of Wadi Halfa, a Sudanese town that was completely rebuilt on high ground when its original site was submerged in the reservoir created by the Aswan High Dam. As a result of the dam's construction, the Nile actually begins its flow into Egypt as Lake Nasser, which extends south from the dam 320 kilometers to the border and an additional 158 kilometers into Sudan. Lake Nasser's waters fill the area through Lower Nubia (Upper Egypt and northern Sudan) within the narrow gorge between the cliffs of sandstone and granite created by the flow of the river over many centuries. Below Aswan the cultivated floodplain strip widens to as much as twenty kilometers. North of Isna (160 kilometers north of Aswan), the plateau on both sides of the valley rises as high as 550 meters above sea level; at Qina (about 90 kilometers north of Isna) the 300-meter limestone cliffs force the Nile to change course to the southwest for about 60 kilometers before turning northwest for about 160 kilometers to Asyut. Northward from Asyut, the escarpments on both sides diminish, and the valley widens to a maximum of twenty-two kilometers. The Nile reaches the Delta at Cairo.

At Cairo the Nile spreads out over what was once a broad estuary that has been filled by silt deposits to form a fertile, fan-shaped delta about 250 kilometers wide at the seaward base and about 160 kilometers from north to south. The Nile Delta extends over approximately 22,000 square kilometers (roughly equivalent in area to Massachusetts). According to historical accounts from the first century A.D., seven branches of the Nile once ran through the Delta. According to later accounts, the Nile had only six branches by around the twelfth century. Since then, nature and man have closed all but two main outlets: the east branch, Damietta (also seen as Dumyat; 240 kilometers long), and the west branch, Rosetta (235 kilometers long). Both outlets are named after the ports located at their mouths. A network of drainage and irrigation canals supplements these remaining outlets. In the north near the coast, the Delta embraces a series of salt marshes and lakes; most notable among them are Idku, Al Burullus, and Manzilah.

The fertility and productivity of the land adjacent to the Nile depends largely on the silt deposited by floodwaters. Archaeological research indicates that people once lived at a much higher elevation along the river than they do today, probably because the river was higher or the floods more severe. The timing and the amount of annual flow were always unpredictable. Measurements of annual flows as low as 1.2 billion cubic meters and as high as 4.25 billion cubic meters have been recorded. For centuries Egyptians attempted to predict and take advantage of the flows and moderate the severity of floods.

The construction of dams on the Nile, particularly the Aswan High Dam, transformed the mighty river into a large and predictable irrigation ditch. Lake Nasser, the world's largest artificial lake, has enabled planned use of the Nile regardless of the amount of rainfall in Central Africa and East Africa. The dams have also affected the Nile Valley's fertility, which was dependent for centuries not only on the water brought to the arable land but also on the materials left by the water. Researchers have estimated that beneficial silt deposits in the valley began about 10,000 years ago. The average annual deposit of arable soil through the course of the river valley was about nine meters. Analysis of the flow revealed that 10.7 million tons of solid matter passed Cairo each year. Today the Aswan High Dam obstructs most of this sediment, which is now retained in Lake Nasser. The reduction in annual silt deposits has contributed to rising water tables and increasing soil salinity in the Delta, the erosion of the river's banks in Upper Egypt, and the erosion of the alluvial fan along the shore of the Mediterranean Sea.

Western Desert

The Western Desert covers about 700,000 square kilometers (equivalent in size to Texas) and accounts for about two-thirds of

Egypt's land area. This immense desert to the west of the Nile spans the area from the Mediterranean Sea south to the Sudanese border. The desert's Jilf al Kabir Plateau has an altitude of about 1,000 meters, an exception to the uninterrupted territory of basement rocks covered by layers of horizontally bedded sediments forming a massive plain or low plateau. The Great Sand Sea lies within the desert's plain and extends from the Siwah Oasis to Jilf al Kabir. Scarps (ridges) and deep depressions (basins) exist in several parts of the Western Desert, and no rivers or streams drain into or out of the area.

The government has considered the Western Desert a frontier region and has divided it into two governorates at about the twenty-eighth parallel: Matruh to the north and New Valley (Al Wadi al Jadid) to the south. There are seven important depressions in the Western Desert, and all are considered oases except the largest, Qattara, the water of which is salty. The Qattara Depression is approximately 15,000 square kilometers (about the size of Connecticut and Rhode Island) and is largely below sea level (its lowest point is 133 meters below sea level). Badlands, salt marshes, and salt lakes cover the sparsely inhabited Qattara Depression.

Limited agricultural production, the presence of some natural resources, and permanent settlements are found in the other six depressions, all of which have fresh water provided by the Nile or by local groundwater. The Siwah Oasis, close to the Libyan border and west of Qattara, is isolated from the rest of Egypt but has sustained life since ancient times. Siwah's cliff-hung Temple of Amun was renowned for its oracles for more than 1,000 years. Herodotus and Alexander the Great were among the many illustrious people who visited the temple in the pre-Christian era.

The other major oases form a topographic chain of basins extending from the Al Fayyum Oasis (sometimes called the Fayyum Depression) which lies sixty kilometers southwest of Cairo, south to the Bahriyah, Farafirah, and Dakhilah oases before reaching the country's largest oasis, Kharijah. A brackish lake, Birkat Qarun, at the northern reaches of Al Fayyum Oasis, drained into the Nile in ancient times. For centuries sweetwater artesian wells in the Fayyum Oasis have permitted extensive cultivation in an irrigated area that extends over 1,800 square kilometers.

Eastern Desert

The topographic features of the region east of the Nile are very different from those of the Western Desert. The relatively mountainous Eastern Desert rises abruptly from the Nile and extends over an area of approximately 220,000 square kilometers (roughly equivalent in size to Utah). The upward-sloping plateau of sand gives way within 100 kilometers to arid, defoliated, rocky hills running north and south between the Sudan border and the Delta. The hills reach elevations of more than 1,900 meters. The region's most prominent feature is the easterly chain of rugged mountains, the Red Sea Hills, which extend from the Nile Valley eastward to the Gulf of Suez and the Red Sea. This elevated region has a natural drainage pattern that rarely functions because of insufficient rainfall. It also has a complex of irregular, sharply cut wadis that extend westward toward the Nile.

The Eastern Desert is generally isolated from the rest of the country. There is no oasis cultivation in the region because of the difficulty in sustaining any form of agriculture. Except for a few villages on the Red Sea coast, there are no permanent settlements. The importance of the Eastern Desert lies in its natural resources, especially oil (see Energy, ch. 3). A single governorate, the capital of which is at Al Ghardaqah, administers the entire region.

Sinai Peninsula

This triangular area covers about 61,100 square kilometers (slightly smaller than West Virginia). Similar to the desert, the peninsula contains mountains in its southern sector that are a geological extension of the Red Sea Hills, the low range along the Red Sea coast that includes Mount Catherine (Jabal Katrinah), the country's highest point—2,642 meters. The Red Sea is named after these mountains, which are red.

The southern side of the peninsula has a sharp escarpment that subsides after a narrow coastal shelf that slopes into the Red Sea and the Gulf of Aqaba. The elevation of Sinai's southern rim is about 1,000 meters. Moving northward, the elevation of this limestone plateau decreases. The northern third of Sinai is a flat, sandy coastal plain, which extends from the Suez Canal into the Gaza Strip and Israel.

Before the Israeli military occupied Sinai during the June 1967 War (Arab-Israeli war, also known as the Six-Day War), a single Egyptian governorate administered the whole peninsula. By 1982 after all of Sinai was returned to Egypt, the central government divided the peninsula into two governorates. North Sinai has its capital at Al Arish and the South Sinai has its capital in At Tur.

Climate

Throughout Egypt, days are commonly warm or hot, and nights are cool. Egypt has only two seasons: a mild winter from November to April and a hot summer from May to October. The only differences between the seasons are variations in daytime temperatures and changes in prevailing winds. In the coastal regions, temperatures range between an average minimum of 14°C in winter and an average maximum of 30°C in summer.

Temperatures vary widely in the inland desert areas, especially in summer, when they may range from 7°C at night to 43°C during the day. During winter, temperatures in the desert fluctuate less dramatically, but they can be as low as 0°C at night and as high as 18°C during the day.

The average annual temperature increases moving southward from the Delta to the Sudanese border, where temperatures are similar to those of the open deserts to the east and west. In the north, the cooler temperatures of Alexandria during the summer have made the city a popular resort. Throughout the Delta and the northern Nile Valley, there are occasional winter cold spells accompanied by light frost and even snow. At Aswan, in the south, June temperatures can be as low as 10°C at night and as high as 41°C during the day when the sky is clear.

Egypt receives fewer than eighty millimeters of precipitation annually in most areas. Most rain falls along the coast, but even the wettest area, around Alexandria, receives only about 200 millimeters of precipitation per year. Alexandria has relatively high humidity, but sea breezes help keep the moisture down to a comfortable level. Moving southward, the amount of precipitation decreases suddenly. Cairo receives a little more than one centimeter of precipitation each year. The city, however, reports humidity as high as 77 percent during the summer. But during the rest of the year, humidity is low. The areas south of Cairo receive only traces of rainfall. Some areas will go years without rain and then experience sudden downpours that result in flash floods. Sinai receives somewhat more rainfall (about twelve centimeters annually in the north) than the other desert areas, and the region is dotted by numerous wells and oases, which support small population centers that formerly were focal points on trade routes. Water drainage toward the Mediterranean Sea from the main plateau supplies sufficient moisture to permit some agriculture in the coastal area, particularly near Al Arish.

A phenomenon of Egypt's climate is the hot spring wind that blows across the country. The winds, known to Europeans as the sirocco and to Egyptians as the *khamsin,* usually arrive in April but occasionally occur in March and May. The winds form in small but vigorous low-pressure areas in the Isthmus of Suez and sweep across the northern coast of Africa. Unobstructed by geographical features, the winds reach high velocities and carry great quantities of sand

and dust from the deserts. These sandstorms, often accompanied by winds of up to 140 kilometers per hour, can cause temperatures to rise as much as 20°C in two hours. The winds blow intermittently and may continue for days, cause illness in people and animals, harm crops, and occasionally damage houses and infrastructure.

Population

Egypt's population, estimated at 3 million when Napoleon invaded the country in 1798, has increased at varying rates. The population grew gradually and steadily throughout the nineteenth century, doubling in size over the course of eighty years. Beginning in the 1880s, the growth rate accelerated, and the population increased more than 600 percent in 100 years. The growth rate was especially high after World War II. In 1947 a census indicated that Egypt's population was 19 million. A census in 1976 revealed that the population had ballooned to 36.6 million. After 1976 the population grew at an annual rate of 2.9 percent and in 1986 reached a total of 50.4 million, including about 2.3 million Egyptians working in other countries. Projections indicated the population would reach 60 million by 1996.

Egypt's population in mid-1990 was estimated at 52.5 million, about an 8 percent increase over the 1986 figure. The increase meant that the annual population growth rate had slowed slightly to 2.6 percent. Although Egypt's overall population density in 1990 was only about fifty-four people per square kilometer, close to 99 percent of all Egyptians lived along the banks of the Nile River in 3.5 percent of the country's total area. Average population densities in the Nile Valley exceeded 1,500 per square kilometer— one of the world's highest densities (see fig. 4).

According to the 1986 census, 51.1 percent of Egypt's population was male and 48.9 percent female. More than 34 percent of the population was twelve years old or younger, and 68 percent was under age thirty. Fewer than 3 percent of Egyptians were sixty-five years or older. In 1989 average life expectancy at birth was fifty-nine years for men and sixty years for women. The infant mortality rate was 94 deaths per 1,000 births. Although the urban population has been increasing at a higher rate than the rural population since the 1947 census, approximately 51 percent of people still lived in villages in 1986. By the end of 1989, however, demographers estimated the urban-rural distribution to be equal.

Population Control Policies

Egypt's population is very large in relation to the country's natural resources. Although it is not a perfect measure of the impact of high population growth rates, the amount of land cultivated by the average farmer provides a glimpse at the extent of the problem. In slightly more than 150 years (1821–1976), the per capita cultivated area dropped from 0.8 *feddan* (see Glossary) to 0.27 *feddan* among the rural population. If the urban population is included, the per capita cultivated area in 1976 amounted to only 0.15 *feddan*. The decline has meant that the same amount of cultivated land must feed a continuously increasing population. In 1974 Egypt, which had been a net exporter of cereals for centuries, became a net importer of food, especially grains.

As early as 1959, government economists expressed concern about the negative impact of high population growth rates on the country's development efforts. In 1966 the government initiated a nationwide birth control program aimed at reducing the annual population growth rate to 2.5 percent or less. Since then state-run family planning clinics have distributed birth control information and contraceptives. These programs were somewhat successful in reducing the population growth rate, but in 1973 the rate began to increase again. Population control policies tended to be ineffective because most Egyptians, especially in rural areas, valued large families.

Major Cities

Although Egypt's urban history is lengthy, modern urbanization, characterized by massive and continuing rural-to-urban migration, is largely a post-World War II phenomenon. Since 1947, urban growth rates have averaged about one percentage point higher than the rates for rural areas. Thus, for forty years, the urban population has been expanding at the rate of 4 percent annually. Cairo, the country's capital and largest city, has been affected the most by this urbanization. Between 1947 and 1986, the city's population grew from 1.5 million to more than 6 million (within the city's corporate limits). During the same period, the population of Giza (Al Jizah), across the Nile from Cairo, grew even more dramatically, from 18,000 to 1.6 million. In 1989 an estimated 10.5 million people, or 20 percent of all Egyptians, lived in the urban agglomeration known as Greater Cairo, which extended along both banks of the Nile from Shubra al Khaymah in the north to Hulwan in the south. Within the city's boundaries, the population density averaged 26,000 people per square kilometer. In some of the more crowded quarters of the city, such as Rawd al Faraj, densities were as high as 135,000 per square kilometer.

Cairo is an ancient city, occupying a site that has been continuously inhabited for more than 3,500 years. Over the centuries,

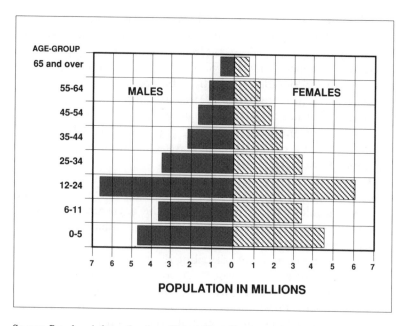

Source: Based on information from United States Bureau of the Census; and *Population, Housing, and Establishment Census,* Cairo, 1986, 13, 17.

Figure 4. Estimated Population Distribution by Age and Sex, 1986

there have been nine distinct cities where Cairo is located. The "modern" city was founded in 969 near the site of ancient Egypt's Khere-ohe, better known in the West by its Greek name of Heliopolis. In Arabic, "Cairo" means "victorious" and is the same name used for the planet Mars. Cairo has consistently been a city of preeminence in the Arab world for more than 1,000 years, but its political and economic influence within and beyond Egypt has varied. One of its more illustrious periods ran from 1170 to 1345, when Cairo became one of the world's largest cities with a population of about 500,000. The layout of central Cairo remains similar to what it was during that time. Many of the city's renowned mosques—there are more than 600 Islamic monuments in Cairo— also date back to the medieval period. Cairo's importance derived from its role as a center for the production and export of textiles and refined sugar and for goods manufactured from cotton, flax, and sugarcane. Cairo was also a transshipment center for overland trade from India and Africa to Europe.

The plague known as the Black Death devastated Cairo and the rest of Egypt between 1347 and 1350. The plague killed about 40 percent of the country's population.

Cairo quickly lost its preeminent role as a transshipment center when the Europeans discovered a maritime route to India and China around the Cape of Good Hope. Cairo remained Egypt's administrative and commercial center, but it experienced relative economic stagnation for the next three centuries. By the time Napoleon conquered the city in 1798, its population had declined to approximately 200,000.

During the nineteenth century, the rise of the cotton export trade, government sponsorship of industrial development, and the completion of the construction of the Suez Canal in 1869 revitalized Cairo, and the city began to grow again. During the last half of the nineteenth century, the French approach to urban planning changed Cairo's layout. Egypt's ruler, Ismail (1863–79), had been educated in France and aspired to have his capital rival Paris. To coincide with the ceremonies for the opening of the Suez Canal, Ismail proposed a design for "modern" Cairo. The proposal included a wooden replica of La Scala opera house in Milan. The structure was to host the premier of Giuseppe Verdi's opera *Aida*. Ismail's efforts to build a modern Cairo resulted in a separation— still apparent today—between the western part of the city, called Al Izbakiya Gardens (which is European) and the eastern part (which is Arabic).

Cairo has continued to grow rapidly since 1850, when its population was approximately 250,000. By 1930 the population had reached 1 million. Throughout the twentieth century, it has been the most populous city in Africa and the Arab world. Cairo's development has been most intense since World War II, and has resulted in a variety of problems. The city's population, growing about 300,000 per year in the 1980s, has strained urban services to the breaking point. Public transportation was woefully inadequate in the late 1980s, with about one of every four buses out of commission at any given time. Public water supplies, sewer facilities, and trash collection were all overburdened (see Urban Society, this ch.). Housing was perhaps the most pressing problem because persistent shortages of skilled labor and construction materials hampered efforts to build residential units quickly enough to meet demand. The demand for moderately priced housing was especially high. Some people resorted to clandestine and semilegal housing arrangements; as many as 200,000 wooden, cardboard, and metal huts were constructed on the roofs of apartment buildings. An estimated 500,000 people were living in the mausoleums in the city's cemeteries.

Alexandria is Egypt's second largest city. Located on the coastline of the Mediterranean Sea, it has been an important port ever since it was founded by Alexander the Great more than 2,300 years ago. The city declined dramatically during the sixteenth to eighteenth centuries when its maritime trade with Europe virtually ceased as a result of new sea routes around Africa to India. When the French landed at Alexandria in 1798, barely 10,000 people lived in the city. Alexandria grew substantially in the nineteenth century because of industrialization and Egypt's emergence as an exporter of agricultural commodities to Europe. Between 1821 and 1846, Alexandria's population grew from 12,500 to 164,000. By the end of the century, its population had almost doubled to 320,000. Between 1947 and 1986, Alexandria's population grew from 700,000 to 2.7 million.

In 1990 Alexandria was a major industrial center that included two large oil refineries; chemical, cement, and metal plants; textile mills; and food processing operations. Alexandria is also the country's most important harbor for exports and imports.

Egypt's third and fourth largest cities, Giza and Shubra al Khaymah, are part of Greater Cairo. The rapid growth of these cities since 1947 is directly related to the growth of Cairo. Giza (1986 population 1.6 million), opposite the Nile River island of Ar Rawdah, is the location of Cairo University and the famed Pyramids of Giza. Shubra al Khaymah (1986 population 500,000), on the Nile north of Cairo's Bulaq quarter, is a manufacturing suburb with a heavy concentration of textile factories.

As of 1989, Egypt had nine other cities with populations greater than 200,000. In the Delta were Al Mahallah al Kubra with a population of 375,000, Tanta with 365,000, Al Mansurah with 335,000, Az Zaqaziq with 260,000, and Damanhur with 215,000. These five cities were local administrative, commercial, and manufacturing centers. At the northern and southern termini of the Suez Canal were Port Said with a population of 358,000 and Suez with 271,000. In Upper Egypt were Asyut on the Nile with a population of 250,000 and Al Fayyum, an oasis with a population of 215,000. Five other cities had populations ranging between 150,00 and 200,000. These included Al Minya, Aswan, and Bani Suwayf in Upper Egypt; Kafr ad Dawwar in the Delta; and Ismailia (Al Ismailiyah) on the Suez Canal.

Emigration

The 1986 census estimated that 2.25 million Egyptian nationals were working outside the country. Only small numbers of Egyptians, primarily professionals, had left the country in search of employment before 1974. Then, in that year, the government lifted all restrictions on labor migration. The move came at a time when oil-rich Arab states of the Persian Gulf and neighboring Libya were implementing major development programs with funds generated by the quadrupling of oil revenues in 1973. By 1975 an estimated 500,000 Egyptians, mostly single, unskilled men, were working on construction sites in Libya, Saudi Arabia, Kuwait, and the United Arab Emirates. At least 50,000 others were employed elsewhere in the Middle East. By 1980 more than 1 million Egyptians were working abroad. That number doubled by 1982. The emergence of foreign job opportunities alleviated some of the pressure on domestic employment. Many of these workers sent a significant portion of their earnings to their families in Egypt. As early as 1979, these remittances amounted to US$2 billion, a sum equivalent to the country's combined earnings from cotton exports, Suez Canal transit fees, and tourism (see Remittances, ch. 3).

The foreign demand for Egyptian labor peaked in 1983, at which time an estimated 3.28 million Egyptians workers were employed abroad. After that year, political and economic developments in the Arab oil-producing countries caused a retrenchment in employment opportunities. The Iran-Iraq War and the decline in oil prices forced the Persian Gulf oil industry into a recession, which caused many Egyptians to lose their jobs. Up to 1 million workers returned home. Most of the expatriate workforce remained abroad but new labor migration from Egypt slowed considerably. In late 1989, the number of Egyptian workers abroad still exceeded 2.2 million.

The majority of Egyptian labor migrants expected to return home eventually, but thousands left their country each year with the intention of permanently resettling in various Arab countries, Europe, or North America. These emigrants tended to be highly educated professionals, mostly doctors, engineers, and teachers. Their departure caused a serious ''brain drain'' for Egypt. Iraq and, to a lesser extent, Kuwait were the Arab countries most likely to accept skilled Egyptians as permanent residents. Iraq, which sought agriculturists trained in irrigation techniques, encouraged Egyptian farmers to move to the sparsely populated but fertile lands in the south. Outside of the Arab countries, the United States was a preferred destination. Between 1970 and 1985, about 45,000 Egyptians immigrated to the United States.

In 1989 there were several thousand Americans, Europeans, and other non-Arabs in Egypt working on projects sponsored by foreign governments, international agencies, and private charitable groups. The United States stationed more than 2,000 diplomatic personnel in the country. The majority of these personnel worked for the United States Agency for International Development (AID), which managed the largest of the many economic aid programs in

Egypt. Projects financed by AID during the 1980s included irrigation networks, rural sanitation systems, pest control, family planning, and communications development.

Since 1948 Egypt has been a haven for Arab refugees and political dissidents. The number of exiles has fluctuated in response to political developments in other Arab countries and to Egypt's relations with the different regimes. In 1989 Egypt was host to several thousand Palestinian refugees and hundreds of exiles from Libya, Sudan, and various countries of the Arabian Peninsula, especially the Yemen Arab Republic (North Yemen) and the People's Democratic Republic of Yemen (South Yemen). Egyptian accusations that Libya had sponsored terrorist acts against Libyan exiles in Egypt fueled tension between the two countries in the late 1970s and 1980s.

Minorities

Although the ancestors of the Egyptian people include many races and ethnic groups, among them Africans, Arabs, Berbers, Greeks, Persians, Romans, and Turks, the population today is relatively homogeneous linguistically and culturally. Nevertheless, approximately 3 percent of Egyptians belong to minority groups. Linguistic minorities include small communities of Armenians and Greeks, principally in the cities of Cairo and Alexandria; groups of Berber origin in the oases of the Western Desert; and Nubians living in cities in Lower Egypt and in villages clustered along the Nile in Upper Egypt. The Arabic-speaking beduins (nomads) in the Western and Eastern Deserts and the Sinai Peninsula constitute the principal cultural minority. Several hundred Europeans, mostly Italians and French, also lived in Egypt.

In 1989 an estimated 350,000 Greeks constituted Egypt's largest non-Arab minority. Greeks have lived in Egypt since before the time of Alexander the Great. For centuries they have remained culturally, linguistically, and religiously separate from the Egyptians. In 1990 the majority of Greeks lived in Alexandria, although many resided in Cairo.

Armenians have also lived in Egypt for several centuries, although their numbers have declined as a result of heavy emigration since the 1952 Revolution. In 1989 the Armenian community in Egypt was estimated at 12,000. Cairo was traditionally the center of Armenian culture in Egypt, but many Armenians also lived in Alexandria.

An estimated 6,000 Egyptians of Berber origin lived in the Western Desert near the border with Libya. They were ethnically related to the Berber peoples of North Africa. The largest Berber community lived in Siwah Oasis. The Berbers are Muslims, but they have their own language, which is not related to Arabic, and certain unique cultural practices.

About 160,000 Nubians, also Muslims, lived in Egypt in 1990. Most Nubians lived in cities, especially Cairo, Alexandria, and urban areas along the Suez Canal. In the past, Nubians had lived in villages along the Nile from Aswan southward to about 500 kilometers inside Sudan. Before the construction of the Aswan High Dam forced their resettlement, three linguistically separate groups of Nubians lived in this region—the Kenuzi in northern Nubia; the beduin-descended Arabs in central Nubia; and the Fadija-speaking people in southern Nubia near Abu Simbel (Abu Sunbul). Isolated geographically and politically for centuries, the Nubian Valley was only rarely under the control of any central government. Until Egypt's 1952 Revolution, Nubia lacked strong political links with Lower Egypt. Nevertheless, Nubia had persistent economic ties to the rest of Egypt. Since at least the nineteenth century, Nubian men have migrated to the cities of Lower Egypt, where they typically worked for several years at a time as merchants and wage laborers. Nubian society adapted to the migrants' prolonged absences. Complex kinship and property relations enabled men to leave and still take care of their families, guard their wives, and ensure protection of their herds and crops.

After 1952 the central government increased its involvement in Nubia, mostly by building schools and public health services. With the construction of the Aswan High Dam, the government's policies in the area destroyed Nubia, as water inundated the Nubian Valley. In 1963 and 1964 the government resettled approximately 50,000 Nubians to thirty-three villages around Kawm Umbu, about fifty kilometers north of the city of Aswan. As compensation, the government gave the Nubians new land and homes and provided them with some financial support until their new holdings were productive.

Nubians were dissatisfied with their resettlement for several reasons. They did not like their government-built, cement-block houses, which were uncomfortable and vastly different in design from their old homes. Further, their resettlement at Kawm Umbu disrupted family ties and ignored historical rivalries among the three Nubian ethnic groups. The government also required the Nubian farmers to join agricultural cooperatives and pressured them to cultivate sugarcane, a crop that had not been part of their traditional culture. Dissatisfaction with the resettlement program led many to migrate to cities. A large number of migrants rented their land to sharecroppers and tenants from Upper Egypt. After the Aswan

111

High Dam was completed in 1971, a handful of Nubians left the resettlement area and returned to Nubia, where they established farming villages along the shores of Lake Nasser. By the early 1980s, Nubians had constructed at least four villages, complete with traditional homes.

Egypt's largest minority group consisted of several tribes of beduins who traditionally lived in the Eastern and Western Deserts and the Sinai Peninsula. Because the beduins spoke Arabic dialects, the government did not consider them ethnic minorities. Nevertheless, almost everyone in Egypt—including the beduins—considered these people as culturally distinct. The beduins have historically been nomads, but since the nineteenth century, most tribes have adopted sedentary agricultural life-styles, in response to various government incentives (see Social Organization, this ch.). Among the beduins, traditional tribal social structure comprised lineage segments linked to specific territories, water, and pasture. Descent was patrilineal, and most beduins sought patterns of kinship and marriage that would strengthen the bonds between patrilineally related males. A patrilineage acted as a corporate group that shared the home territory's resources and lived together for most of the year. In the event of a feud, the group would collectively seek revenge, either through the death of the other group's males or through collective payment of compensation. A family's livelihood depended on its sheep, goats, and camels. Inheritance customs usually kept the family herds in the hands of fathers, sons, brothers, and cousins related through the male line.

In 1990 the total number of beduins in Egypt ranged between 500,000 and 1 million—less than 1 percent of the country's population. Over the centuries, their numbers fluctuated as governments alternately ignored and persecuted them. In the 1890s, beduins comprised as much as 10 percent of the total population. During the twentieth century, sedentarization and urban migration have caused many beduins to become assimilated into Egypt's dominant culture.

Since the 1952 Revolution, Egypt has intensified its efforts to persuade beduins to abandon their nomadic life-style. The beduins of the Western Desert generally resisted pressure to become farmers. Some beduins engaged in the profitable trade of smuggling goods across the Libyan border into Egypt while others became involved in the hotel and restaurant business in the summer tourist town of Marsa Matruh. The beduins in the Eastern Desert continued to maintain close ties with nomads on the Arabian Peninsula and profited from the high demand for meat and livestock in Saudi Arabia. The Aswan High Dam submerged some summer pasture and disrupted some migratory routes along the Red Sea coast that beduins customarily used in bringing their herds to Nubia during that season. Beduin settlements tended to be overcrowded, a situation that exacerbated feuding among various lineages. And, as beduin herds encroached on cropland, friction between agriculturists and pastoralists intensified. An increasing number of beduin families began to emulate tribal leaders by sending sons to college to prepare them for civil service careers in local government.

Social Organization

In 1990 Egypt remained under the social, political, and cultural dominance of an elite, a pattern it has retained since pharaonic (see Glossary) times. Although the personal, ideological orientation, and cultural values of the ruling class changed drastically after the 1952 Revolution, the gulf between the urban elite and the popular masses remained large. A group called the Free Officers came to power in 1952. The group, which included people such as Gamal Abdul Nasser (former president of Egypt), Anwar as Sadat (also former president of Egypt), and Husni Mubarak (current president of Egypt), played an instrumental role in carrying out the 1952 Revolution. The Free Officers, along with their civilian allies, comprised a strongly nationalistic cadre who believed the former ruling class had betrayed the country's welfare to foreign interests. The Free Officers, many of whom were not from the top social classes, altered the country's structure of wealth and power. But according to some scholars, the Free Officers' policies merely changed the membership of the elite rather than causing its demise.

The prerevolutionary elite rose to their position of power through the country's entry into the world agricultural commodity market in the nineteenth century (see Rural Society, this ch.). The upper classes consisted of the royal family, absentee landlords, professionals, and business people (merchants, financiers, and a few industrialists). A disproportionately large number of foreigners belonged to the elite groups in Cairo and Alexandria. Opportunities for social mobility changed in response to the transformation of the country's economy. A prosperous landowning family, for example, might choose to secure its status by sending one son to Al Azhar University for a career in religion and another to one of the newly established secular universities while encouraging still another to manage the family's estates.

The civil bureaucracy established by Muhammad Ali (1805–49) and elaborated under British hegemony provided a career for sons of middle- and upper middle-class families. It gave employment to the growing number of Egyptian professionals (mostly lawyers, doctors, and engineers) and fueled the expansion of secular education. The government bureaucracy employed the sons of landlords, of prosperous farmers, and of civil servants themselves.

Despite the major social changes in Egypt between 1800 and 1950, the upper-class elite continued to dominate politics in the country. The educated middle class increasingly resented the elite's control of government. This resentment was particularly strong among military officers because their middle-class origins impeded their advancement to the top decision-making ranks. Among these military officers were the Free Officers.

Egypt's new political elite pledged to rid the country of foreign influences and to broaden economic opportunities for the general population. Nasser implemented numerous socialist policies designed to alter the pattern of class stratification. The June 1967 War, however, halted government initiatives for redistributing wealth. Beginning in 1974, the government introduced a series of laws intended to restore and promote private ownership of previously socialized sectors of the economy. These new policies, known as *infitah* (opening or open door; see Glossary), helped consolidate the class structure. In 1990 Egypt continued to be a country with a skewed distribution of wealth; about 2,000 families had annual incomes in excess of £E35,000 (for the value of the Egyptian pound—see Glossary) while more than 4 million people earned less than £E200.

Urban Society

Although the majority of Egyptians lived in villages as recently as 1988, cities, which have been important in Egypt for more than 2,000 years, continued to be important. Traditional urban society was more heterogeneous than in most other areas of the Middle East. Quarters, segregated along religious and occupational lines, were effectively self-governing in their internal affairs. As in villages, kinship relations provided a basis for solidarity, and relationships among families frequently overrode differences in wealth and social position. Prosperous families assumed leadership roles and took responsibility for their less fortunate kin and neighbors. The rapid urbanization that began in the nineteenth century created large residential and industrial suburbs and led to the emergence of a professional middle class and a working class. Nevertheless, elite wealthy families that had ruled Egypt for generations, and in some cases for centuries, continued to dominate the cities until the early 1950s.

The postrevolutionary ruling elite was believed by many to have come from rural backgrounds. In reality most of the elite came from the urban middle class and were sons of mid- and low-ranking bureaucrats. A few members of the new elite came from the ranks of the old elite, although most influential members of the new elite were military officers. Most of these officers held positions in the government agencies that were in charge of national security, but others also held important positions in local government and the diplomatic service. Below the top echelons of government, however, the military played a less important role. This situation was reflected in the fact that since 1952, only about 6 percent of individuals in lower-level administrative posts had attended a military college. Educated bureaucrats from the middle and upper-middle classes continued to fill the bulk of civil service posts. Since 1952 three of every four bureaucrats have come from cities, with one of every two coming from Cairo. About a third had fathers who were civil servants. Although the military's formal presence in the bureaucracy was limited, officers clearly made the most important decisions. The emergence of a military elite led to a new kind of civil servant, the officer-technocrat. Politically ambitious professionals had a significant incentive to join the officers corps, and officers were motivated to acquire professional training (see Training and Education, ch. 5).

Although the prerevolutionary elite lost its status as the ruling class, it was not eliminated. The land redistribution program of the 1950s and socialist policies of the 1960s compelled many old elite families to sell agricultural and industrial properties that had been important sources of their wealth. Nevertheless, most of these families were able to maintain their social and economic positions through their domination of the prestigious professions. The old elite had highly valued education before the revolution, and many families had sent at least one son abroad for professional training. Thus, the old elite had lost its political influence after the 1952 Revolution, but its investments in education enabled its offspring to emerge as the doctors, engineers, and top-level administrators of the new regime.

After 1974 the government encouraged the growth of private enterprise through *infitah* policies, and a large number of people from old elite families emerged as part of a new class of wealthy contractors, financiers, and industrialists. Many of these people, who had held senior-level civil service positions, switched to private practice, industry, or commerce because their government salaries had been relatively low. A person holding a ministerial-level position in government could earn up to 1,000 percent more by taking a post in the private sector. Joint ventures between Egyptian and foreign firms, partnerships for Egyptians in foreign firms, and commissions for Egyptians dealing with private companies all contributed to the formation of a new entrepreneurial class. By 1990 prerevolutionary elite families remained financially secure and socially prominent and had regained some political influence.

The middle class, emulating the old elite, recognized the link between higher education and prestigious civil service jobs. The government, which had initiated the development of secular education as part of the effort to staff the civil bureaucracy with trained personnel, has provided a secure, well-paid position to virtually every college-educated applicant since the 1920s. Prior to the 1952 Revolution, postsecondary education was costly, and middle-class families who were determined to send at least one son to college usually endured considerable financial hardship. Most middle-class youth could not afford to attend college, but they could still gain entry into the less prestigious, lower civil-service ranks by obtaining a high school diploma. Before 1950 secondary schools were not free, but middle-class families could generally afford the fees. As an increasing number of middle-class high school graduates sought government employment, the bureaucracy became overstaffed with poorly paid, white-collar workers who had little prospect of advancement into top administrative positions, most of which were held by university graduates. Frustration among low-ranking civil servants was an important factor leading to the 1952 Revolution.

After the 1952 Revolution, the Free Officers increased career-advancement opportunities in government, improved pay scales in the civil service, and expanded public education opportunities at all levels. To meet middle-class demands for equitable access to higher education, the government abolished college and university fees and introduced competitive admission based on special entrance examinations. The state continued to be the principal employer of college graduates. A government decree in 1964 required the civil service to offer jobs to all Egyptians holding degrees from postsecondary colleges and institutes. During the early and mid-1960s, when Egypt's economy was socialized, the public sector employed thousands of new mid- and upper-rank administrators, as well as tens of thousands of high school graduates. The annual increase in the number of university graduates soon greatly exceeded the number of positions available in the civil service. By the mid-1970s, the civil service employed more than 1.3 million people, and overstaffing became a serious problem in all government ministries. After the government introduced the *infitah* in 1974, it no longer felt obliged to hire every college graduate. Individual ministries determined the number of new positions that needed to be filled each year; once the quota was met, the names of other applicants were placed on waiting lists. During the 1980s, an average of 250,000 college graduates were waiting at any given time to be called for government jobs; the typical applicant remained on the waiting list for more than three years. This situation caused unrest among middle- and lower-middle-income students who had hoped that higher education would be their ticket to upward mobility.

Whereas the middle class was preoccupied with education and civil service careers, most urban Egyptians, who belonged to the lower class, were concerned about earning a livelihood in an economy characterized by persistent and extensive unemployment and underemployment (see Employment, ch. 3). In terms of occupations and incomes, the lower class was very heterogeneous and comprised three main groups: service providers, skilled workers, and unskilled laborers. The first group included artisans, bakers, barbers, butchers, carpenters, office and sales clerks, cobblers, drivers, household and hotel domestic workers, janitors, small shopkeepers, tailors, street vendors, waiters, and numerous other providers of urban services. The majority of service workers were involved in the large informal sector of the economy; they were not covered by minimum wage laws and did not participate in the social security program. A few service workers, primarily talented artisans and enterprising shopkeepers, earned sufficient money to support a family without the assistance of a second income; the more successful among them actually merged into the lower middle class. The majority of service workers, however, were generally unable to provide adequate food and shelter for a family on the income from one job.

The second lower-class group consisted of skilled workers who were usually employed in private or public factories. Many also worked in the construction industry as electricians, masons, mechanics, painters, and plumbers. Workers in this group tended to prefer jobs in the public sector, which employed approximately 42 percent of the industrial labor force in the 1980s, because government-owned manufacturing enterprises guaranteed job security, paid salaries that were at or above the legal minimum wage, and provided benefits such as routine promotions, raises, paid holidays, and sick leave. Most skilled workers were generally more financially secure than most service workers. Nevertheless, the typical working male who headed a household found it difficult to support a family on one income. To supplement family incomes, most workers held two jobs, permitted their wives or unmarried daughters to work, or received remittances from family members working abroad. Many skilled workers also migrated to other Arab countries where they received higher salaries.

Unskilled laborers comprised the poorest stratum of urban society. Most of them either lacked permanent jobs or were employed in low-wage, menial jobs such as street sweeping, trash collection, sewage-system maintenance, and grave digging. Males with no skills frequently found temporary work on construction sites, especially in Greater Cairo. Intermittent work was also available on the docks of Alexandria and the cities along the Suez Canal. During the 1980s, unskilled workers headed most of the estimated 35 percent of urban households with incomes below the poverty line. According to a study by AID, about half of Egypt's urban population lived in absolute poverty, and most of these lived in households headed by unskilled workers.

The *infitah* generally had an adverse impact on the lower class. Despite the substantial rise in wages after the mid-1970s, real incomes failed to keep pace with the rampant inflation. Although extensive government subsidies on basic necessities alleviated the worst effects of inflation, most lower-class families spent up to 75 percent of their budgets on food. When the government announced in January 1977 that it would eliminate subsidies on selected "luxury" items, including beer, French bread, refined flour, and granulated sugar, the poor rioted in cities throughout the Delta and Nile Valley. In Cairo the police were unable to control the violence, and the government called in the army to restore order. The government canceled its plan to abolish certain subsidies, and since 1977, it has periodically expanded the whole subsidy program.

In addition to the food subsidies, some members of the lower-class benefited from remittances sent to them from family members who were working abroad. About nine of every ten Egyptians working in other countries were from the lower class. At least 1 million poor families received remittances from fathers or sons who were working in Libya or the Arab countries of the Persian Gulf. The remittances raised household incomes by between 100 percent and 700 percent, resulting in significantly higher living standards. The absence of so many workers had also created a general shortage of trained personnel, a situation that permitted skilled workers to bargain for increasingly higher wages. In the early 1980s, for example, a free-lance tile-setter could earn about as much in one week as a government minister could earn in a month.

Although the living standards of poor families receiving remittances improved after 1974, the lower class, like the middle class, was generally skeptical of the *infitah*. Both classes benefited from Nasser's policies, which expanded access to education and employment opportunities, but they generally believed that reduced government spending on social programs, pared public sector employment, and increased incentives for private enterprise would undermine gains achieved in the 1950s and 1960s. The upper class, which accounted for less than 10 percent of the total population, supported the *infitah* because they benefited from policies aimed at easing import-export restrictions and from programs designed to attract foreign investment.

Rural Society

Until the time of Napoleon's invasion, Mamluk fief holders, large landowners, and the chiefs of nomadic tribes controlled rural Egypt. This rural elite—a small fraction of the populace—derived its wealth from land, livestock, and the collection of taxes on commission. Beduin shaykhs lived among and were related to the tribal people over whom they exercised jurisdiction. The large landowners lived in villages and were usually related to some of the other families. The fief holders, predominantly Turkish and Circassian in origin, had the most tenuous links to the villages because they tended to reside in cities and often brutalized the peasants on their estates. Most fellahin (sing., fellah; peasant, from the Arabic verb, *falaha*, to till the soil), were socioeconomically similar. Village headmen allocated families usufruct right to village land, but the village as a whole was responsible for tax payments.

Rural society changed during the nineteenth century. Rulers made it easier for individuals to own land, and they held individuals responsible for tax payments. Large land grants to court favorites and extensive land registration frauds resulted in concentrated landholdings and an increased number of people who owned large pieces of land. During this period, the government gave tribal shaykhs substantial land grants but required that they permanently farm and occupy their parcels. The move caused many beduins to give up their nomadic way of life. Settled beduins gradually became liable for the same taxes imposed on the fellahin.

Granting land (and government administrative posts) only to shaykhs undermined tribal loyalty and solidarity. The process created a class of wealthy landholders within tribes, and the landlord-tenant relationship proved inimical to the strongly egalitarian traditions of beduin society. As tribal loyalties weakened, shaykhs began marrying prosperous settled Egyptian women, while poorer nomads married within the masses of peasants. Many of the beduin and nontribal owners of large amounts of land pursued economic opportunities in the growing cities and became absentee landlords. Many absentee landlords specialized in commodity trading and controlled Egypt's expanding agricultural exports. They also became involved in the urban credit market. The fellahin sharecroppers who tilled the land of absentee owners became increasingly indebted to the local, usually usurious, moneylenders because their share of crops generally provided insufficient income to support a family for the entire period between harvests.

Private ownership of land and increased production of export crops, especially cotton, also resulted in the emergence of landholders, who owned mid-sized plots of five to fifty *feddans*. This group competed only marginally with the landed elite but was prosperous by rural standards. In 1990 these mid-sized landowners continued to play an integral role in rural society.

Class differentiation increased among the fellahin throughout the nineteenth century. Small landholders with one to five *feddans* became poorer but were better off than tenants and sharecroppers. The tenants and sharecroppers were better off than a growing class of landless villagers who earned their livelihoods from casual agricultural labor. (By the end of the nineteenth century, one of every four people in rural areas owned no land.) Landowners who became indebted or fell into tax arrears easily lost their holdings. Until 1926 the government could expropriate land if its owner owed as little as £E2 in back taxes.

From the mid-nineteenth to the mid-twentieth century, large estates continued to consolidate their holdings while small farms fragmented further with each passing generation. From 1896 to the eve of the first land-reform legislation in 1952, the number of landowners with parcels of fewer than five *feddans* had nearly tripled. The number of large landowners with holdings of at least fifty *feddans* declined gradually in the same period. Large landowners controlled 33 percent of all cultivated land by 1952 (only 0.5 percent of all landowners were large landowners). In contrast, about 75 percent of all rural property owners were peasants with holdings of less than one *feddan*. This group owned only 13 percent of the land. The average-sized holding in the under-five-*feddan* range dropped by 50 percent. The number of mid-sized holders (owning six to fifty *feddans*) dropped from about 12 percent to 5 percent of all landowners, although their share of cultivated land remained nearly constant at 30 percent.

Frequent incidents of peasant unrest accompanied the changes in rural Egypt. Peasant uprisings, which were usually localized, were all sparked by complaints such as high taxes, intolerable landlord imposts, corvées, foreclosures, and rising rents. Some protests spread throughout a district or region and required extensive military intervention to restore control. Uprisings often took on religious or messianic overtones. By 1950 when an estimated 60 percent of the rural population was landless, it was not uncommon for groups of discontented sharecroppers and tenants to try to seize the land they cultivated.

The Free Officers made land reform a priority after the 1952 Revolution. Continuing into the 1960s, the Free Officers promulgated measures that distributed about 700,000 *feddans* of land to about 318,000 peasant households, i.e., 13 percent of the cultivated land to 10 percent of the country's rural families. A law in 1952 limited individual landownership to 200 *feddans*. The law also prevented owners from transferring more than 100 *feddans* to members of their immediate families; excess holdings had to be sold to small farmers or tenants. The law also limited the amount of cash rents and the percentage of the harvest that absentee owners could collect from tenants and sharecroppers. A law in 1961 limited individual ownership to 100 *feddans;* another law in 1969 limited it to 50 *feddans*. These land reforms failed to eliminate large landowners, but they did reduce the group's share of cultivated land from 33 percent of the total to 15 percent between 1952 and 1975.

Peasant smallholders (with fewer than five *feddans*) were the main beneficiaries of the reforms. In 1952 they owned about 35 percent (2.1 million *feddans*) of Egypt's cultivated land. By 1965 they owned 52 percent (3.2 million *feddans*). Although several thousand tenant and sharecropping families were able to purchase tiny parcels (none greater than five *feddans*) and join the ranks of smallholders, the majority of landless villagers did not benefit from the reforms. Landlords' creativity in exploiting the surplus rural labor market thwarted government efforts to assist these landless villagers. Landlords also learned how to circumvent legislation designed to guarantee sharecroppers half of the harvest. By the 1980s, the combination of rapid population growth, increasing production costs, and high rates of inflation had eroded the gains of the smallholders. An estimated 44 percent of all rural families lived below the officially defined poverty level.

Peasants who owned between eleven and fifty *feddans* were able to increase their landholdings by purchasing excess land from large landlords. This group of peasants comprised 2.5 percent of all landowners in 1952 and 3 percent in 1965. By the latter date, this group owned 24 percent of all cultivated land.

In 1990 rural society was just as stratified as it had been before the initiation of land reform in 1952. Approximately 11,000 large landowners (those owning more than fifty *feddans*—less than 0.3 percent of all owners) were still at the top of the social hierarchy. These large landowners were typically absentee landlords and renters who worked in urban areas as merchants, civil servants, professionals, or corporate managers. Although wealthy, they lacked the prerevolutionary landowning elite's influence in rural areas, and their impact on village social relations tended to be limited. Nevertheless, they continued to be influential in national politics and exercised indirect influence in rural areas through their diverse ties to large peasant owners.

The second stratum of rural landowners consisted of two peasant groups, medium holders owning six to ten *feddans* and large holders owning eleven to fifty *feddans*. Although this second stratum accounted for only 5.5 percent of all rural landowners, it owned one-third of all the cultivated land. Both groups' holdings were large enough to generate profits from agriculture, and the more prosperous individuals among the groups tended to fill the political role previously held by the large landlords. Large peasant owners in particular exercised significant influence in local and even regional politics. The large holders tended to be commercial farmers with extensive ties to domestic capital and were frequently involved in subsidiary marketing, livestock, and transport enterprises. In most villages, at least one of the peasant families with medium or large landholdings was descended from a lineage that most members of the community considered superior. Farmers in this second stratum have also experienced substantial occupational mobility since 1952. A typical family with several sons would send one or more of them to university to prepare for careers in the civil service, the military, or the professions.

Peasant smallholders (those owning fewer than five *feddans*) comprised 94 percent of all Egyptian landowners. In general, holdings of fewer than five *feddans* were too small for profitable agriculture. Consequently, smallholders had to supplement their incomes by working on the land of larger owners, by engaging in other agricultural activities such as raising livestock, or by finding seasonal work in urban areas. Many smallholders rented their plots for part or all of the year to other peasants, especially to those who owned between five and ten *feddans*. About one-quarter of all land owned by smallholders was leased to larger owners.

Since 1952 there have been no reliable statistics on the number of landless villagers. Although landlessness decreased between 1952 and 1965, it has been rising since the late 1960s. Throughout Egypt the landless constituted perhaps as much as 40 percent of the rural population; the majority lived in the villages of the Delta and Upper Egypt. Landless peasants supported their families by cultivating land for absentee owners as tenants and sharecroppers; by working as agricultural laborers for large peasant owners; by providing village services such as carpentry, blacksmithing, machinery maintenance, and livestock herding; and by migrating to cities and other Arab countries in search of short- and long-term employment. Remittances from adult males working away from home and a rise in rural wages (stimulated by labor shortages in agriculture) combined to outpace inflation and helped to alleviate poverty among the landless peasants—the poorest villagers—in the 1980s.

In 1990 approximately 50 percent of Egypt's population lived in villages. In the past, urban residents had little or no contact with the villagers who produced their food. Most peasants were suspicious of urban landlords and government officials whose presence in the villages coincided with the collection of rent and taxes. But in the twentieth century, extensive rural-urban contacts developed as a result of large-scale migration to the cities, the establishment of government services in villages, and the mass media. Nevertheless, a sharp distinction between rural and urban areas persisted. Wide disparities existed between cities and villages in amenities, services, and educational and health facilities. Mortality rates, especially for infants, and illiteracy rates were notably higher in rural areas (see Population; and Health and Welfare, this ch.).

In the 1980s, temporary migration in search of wage labor was particularly common among villagers in Upper Egypt; men left their families in the care of relatives during the slack agricultural seasons. In some Nubian villages, for example, all males between the ages of eighteen and forty-five were gone for much of the year. Migrants served as intermediaries between rural and urban Egypt and as agents of social change in the village. Because of the increasingly important role of nonagricultural work in the Delta, many villagers found new occupations that resulted in social cleavages. For example, the opportunity to earn a living independent of their fathers permitted men to exercise more freedom from traditional authority figures. Higher education provided upward mobility for substantial numbers of rural children and led to new social distinctions within villages.

The basic unit of village organization was the patrilineal lineage or clan. Composed of various families descended from a common male ancestor four to six generations in the past, a lineage inhabited a specific quarter of the village. Lineages, controlled by elder males, were an integral force in village life and politics. Families gained their identity not as autonomous entities but as part of their larger lineage.

Lineages had a corporate identity with a recognized leadership pattern. A man's closest social contacts were with his brothers and cousins. A guest house was used to entertain visitors at the lineage's expense. Various lineages vied for power and influence within the village. The interests of the lineage were frequently more important than the interests of individuals. Propinquity was crucial in settling disputes within a lineage. In conflicts with outsiders, individuals were expected to unite in the interests of their lineage. Propinquity was so important in rural society that to suggest a person had no kin was a profound insult.

Lineages and a general disapproval of the public display of wealth blunted many of the economic disparities within and among village clans. Still, religious feasts and rites of passage provided an opportunity for lineages to display their wealth. Lineages usually invited other lineages to extravagant weddings and other celebrations. Several religious festivals required wealthy people to distribute meat to the less fortunate. Return from the hajj (pilgrimage to Mecca) called for elaborate decorations in the pilgrim's house. In general, the socially acceptable means of displaying wealth helped integrate prosperous individuals into the community rather than separate them from it.

A number of changes in the 1980s limited the influence of lineages. In the past, lineage elders maintained their authority by controlling land. But the recent increase in pressure on land has meant that fewer young men would inherit large plots. Many of these young men, realizing they would never own a substantial piece of land, have migrated to cities and other countries and are no longer influenced by their elders. The prevalence of nuclear families in cities has also eroded lineage ties.

Family and Kinship
Importance of Kinship

The family remained the most significant unit of Egyptian society in 1990, and kinship played an important role in virtually all social relations. An individual's social identity was closely linked to his or her status in the network of kin relations. Socialization of children emphasized integration among their kin group. An important goal of marriage was to ensure the continuity of a family. A husband and wife were not considered a family until they produced their first child. After the child's birth, the parents were addressed as father and mother of Muhammad or Amal or whatever was the name of their child. The most deeply held values—honor, dignity, and security—were derived by an individual only as part of a larger kin group. Kinship as a first principle was evident from the most essential to the most trivial aspects of social organization.

Feluccas at bend in the Nile near Bani Hasan; Muslim tombs in foreground
Courtesy Boris Boguslavsky

Egyptians reckoned descent patrilineally, and the ideal family was an extended family consisting of a man, his wife (or wives), his single and married sons and their wives and children, as well as his unmarried daughters. Younger members of the family deferred to older members, and women deferred to men. The political and economic upheavals of the nineteenth and twentieth centuries had only limited impact on this family structure. The traditional Sunni religious code for Muslims (see Islam, this ch.) defined most Muslims' family matters (marriage, guardianship, and inheritance) while canon law defined these matters among Christians. The father controlled families' possessions and income. Even though adult male heads of household wielded immense authority within the family, traditional expectations of parental responsibilities prevented most fathers from exercising the full extent of their powers.

Although an extended family that lived together was considered the ideal, it was not common. A nuclear family consisting of parents and their unmarried children was the norm in cities. Even in rural areas, nuclear families accounted for approximately 80 to 90 percent of all households. Nevertheless, relations with in-laws, grandparents, nieces, and nephews continued to have an impact on the lives of most adults. Newly married couples typically set up their households near the homes of the groom's parents and married brothers. Tensions between wives and their mothers-in-law, as well as tensions among wives of brothers, often disrupted the extended family's harmony.

Both patrilineal descent and the patrilocal extended family functioned differently for men and women. Men were the preferred, valued members of the lineage. A son's birth was occasion to celebrate, whereas the birth of a daughter, especially if she were the first child, was generally greeted with ambivalence. Men were valued both as providers and as progenitors because descent was reckoned through males. Men remained with their consanguineous kin throughout their lives. Lineages commonly kept property in the hands of their males through marriages among cousins. If daughters married within their paternal lineage, then the property they might inherit and transfer to their children would remain within the lineage. For a beduin male or a villager, the ideal bride was the daughter of his father's brother. More than 50 percent of the marriages in rural areas and among the urban lower class were endogamous. Marriage between relatives has been declining among the urban middle and upper classes since the 1952 Revolution, and by the 1980s, most marriages in these social groups were exogamous.

For most men, marriage marked the transition to adulthood. Married men were expected to defer to their fathers, but they still had considerable autonomy because of their responsibility for their families' livelihoods and households. For most women, marriage meant leaving their families' homes and sometimes their home areas. In most cases, marriage merely substituted a woman's dependence on her husband for dependence on her father.

A woman retained membership in her patrilineage regardless of her marital status. Indeed, if members of her lineage were feuding with members of her husband's lineage, the wife was expected to side with her paternal family. A woman was entitled to make demands of her father and brothers, especially in case of marital difficulties, throughout her life. Most women generally preferred to live near home and thus tried to avoid marriages with men whose families lived in other cities or villages. Geographical proximity to patrilineal kin served as a source of emotional support in the early years of marriage when women were most vulnerable to divorce. Women in villages often asked their brothers to hold their inheritances for them. This move helped prevent mistreatment of the women by their in-laws. A divorced woman could have her brother return the inheritance to her as her children approached adulthood.

Attitudes Toward Women

Rural and lower-class Egyptians generally believed that women were morally inferior to men. Women were expected to defer to senior male relatives, to avoid contact with men who were not kin, and to veil themselves in public. As children women learned to accept dependency on their fathers and older brothers. After marriage women expected their husbands to make all decisions. Early married life could be a time of extreme subordination and insecurity. The new wife usually lived with or near her husband's family and was expected to help her mother-in-law with household chores. A young wife was under considerable pressure from her husband and his family until she bore a son. Barrenness was a woman's worst possible misfortune, and not giving birth to a son was almost as bad. Women who had only daughters were derogatorily called "mothers of brides." Most families continued having children until they had at least two sons. As the length of a woman's marriage increased, and her sons matured, her position in the family grew more secure. A woman was at the peak of her power when her sons were married because she could then exercise influence over her sons' children and wives.

Patrilineal families valued honor (*ird*). The sexual behavior and reputation of the women of a lineage were the most important components of a family's honor. A bad reputation for one woman meant a bad reputation for the whole lineage. Honor was essential to social life; without it even a minimal social standing in the community was impossible. Men were especially interested in maintaining honor. Women were always on their best behavior around men from other families because they were afraid of getting a bad reputation. A bad reputation could disgrace the men of her family. A disgraced husband could restore his status, however, through divorce. Most disgraced fathers and brothers in rural and lower-class urban families, however, believed that honor could only be restored by killing the daughter or sister suspected of sexual misconduct. Family members who murdered the women were prepared to accept legal penalties for their actions.

Women have traditionally been preoccupied with household tasks and child rearing and have rarely had opportunities for contact with men outside the family. But since the 1952 Revolution, social changes, especially in education, have caused many women to spend time in public places among men who were not related to them. To limit women's contact with these men, practices such as veiling and gender segregation at schools, work, and recreation have become commonplace. Furthermore, lower-class families, especially in Upper Egypt, have tended to withdraw girls from school as they reached puberty to minimize their interaction with men. Lower-class men frequently preferred marriage to women who had been secluded rather than to those who had worked or attended secondary school.

Egypt's laws pertaining to marriage and divorce favored the social position of men. Muslim husbands were traditionally allowed to have up to four wives at a time in accordance with Islamic religious custom, but a woman could have only one husband at a time. A Muslim man could divorce his wife with ease by saying "I divorce thee" on three separate occasions in the presence of witnesses. A woman wishing to dissolve a marriage had to instigate legal proceedings and prove to a court that her husband had failed to support her or that his behavior was having a harmful moral effect on the family. The laws required men to support their ex-wives for only one year after a divorce, and the fathers gained custody of the children. A man faced few or no penalties if he refused to provide equal support to his wives or if he refused to pay alimony to his divorced wife. Divorce was much more difficult for Copts than it was for Muslims. Canon law regulated the marriages and divorces of Copts.

After decades of debate, the government amended the laws relating to personal status in 1979. The amendments, which became known as the "women's rights law," were in the form of a presidential decree and subsequently approved by the People's Assembly. The leading orthodox Islamic clergy endorsed these amendments, but Islamist groups opposed them as state infringements of religious precepts and campaigned for their repeal. The amendments stated that polygyny was legally harmful to a first wife and entitled her to sue for divorce within a year after learning of her husband's second marriage. The amendments also entitled the first wife to compensation. A husband retained the right to divorce his wife without recourse to the courts, but he was required to file for his divorce before witnesses at a registrar's office and officially and immediately to inform his wife. The divorced wife was entitled to alimony equivalent to one year's maintenance in addition to compensation equivalent to two years' maintenance; a court could increase these amounts under extenuating circumstances such as the dissolution of a long marriage. The divorced wife automatically retained custody of sons under the age of ten and daughters under twelve; courts could extend the mother's custody of minors until their eighteenth birthdays.

In 1985 Egyptian authorities ruled that the amendments of 1979 were unconstitutional because they had been enacted through a presidential decree while the People's Assembly was not in session. A new law reversed many of the rights accorded to women in 1979 (see The Limits of Incorporation: The Rise of Political Islam and the Continuing Role of Repression, ch. 4). A woman lost her automatic right to divorce her husband if he married a second wife. She could still petition a court to consider her case, but a judge would grant a divorce only if it were in the interests of the family. If a divorce were granted, the judge would also determine what was an appropriate residence for the divorced woman and her children.

The changes in divorce legislation in 1979 and 1985 did not significantly alter the divorce rate, which has been relatively high since the early 1950s. About one in five marriages ended in divorce in the 1980s. Remarriage was common, and most divorced men and women expected to wed again. Seven out of ten divorces took place within the first five years of marriage, and one out of three in the first year. The divorce rate depended on residence and level of education. The highest divorce rates were among the urban lower class, the lowest rates among the villagers of Upper Egypt. Throughout the country, as much as 95 percent of all divorces occurred among couples who were illiterate.

Changing Status of Women

Since the early 1970s, women's status has been changing, mostly because an increasing number of women have joined the nonagricultural workforce. According to government estimates, the number of working women doubled from 500,000 to 1 million between 1978 and 1980. By 1982 women accounted for 14 percent of all wage-earning and salaried employees throughout the country. Although substantial numbers of women were in the professions, particularly education, engineering, and medicine, most women held low-paying jobs in factories, offices, and service industries. Half of all employed women held jobs such as street cleaners, janitors, hotel and domestic servants, and hospital aides. In 1990 women accounted for more than 12 percent of all industrial workers; most female factory workers were in textiles, food processing, and pharmaceuticals.

Religion

Religion has traditionally been a pervasive social force in Egypt. For more than 1,000 years, the country has been mostly Islamic. Still, there is an indigenous Christian minority, the Copts, which accounted for as much as 8.5 percent of the total population. Other Christians living in the country included approximately 750,000 adherents of various Latin and Eastern Catholic rites, Greek and Armenian Orthodox churches, and Protestant denominations; many of these Christians emigrated after the 1956 War. An estimated 1,000 Jews lived in Egypt as of 1990. These Jews were a fragment of a community of 80,000 who lived in the country before 1948. Egypt's Constitution of 1971 guarantees freedom of religion (see Islam, this ch.).

Religious fervor increased among all social classes after Egypt's defeat in the June 1967 War. Pious individuals commonly blamed Egypt's lack of faith for the country's setbacks. The resurgence in public worship and displays of devotion persisted in the late 1980s. A relaxation of press censorship in 1974 stimulated the growth of religious publications. Religiously inspired political activism and participation in Sufi orders intensified among the urban, educated, formerly secular-minded segments of the populace.

Islam

In 610 Muhammad (later known as the Prophet), a merchant member of the Hashimite branch of the Quraysh clan that ruled the Arabian town of Mecca, began to preach the first of a series of revelations that Muslims believe were given him by God through the angel Gabriel. A fervent monotheist, Muhammad denounced the polytheism of his fellow Meccans. His vigorous and continuing censure earned him the bitter enmity of Mecca's leaders, who feared the impact of Muhammad's ideas on Mecca's thriving business based on pilgrimages to numerous pagan religious sites.

In 622 Muhammad and a group of followers left for the town of Yathrib, which became known as Medina (the city). Their move, or *hijra* (Hegira), marks the beginning of the Muslim calendar, which is based on the lunar year and is several days shorter than the solar year. Muhammad continued to preach in Medina, defeated his detractors in Mecca in battle, and consolidated both temporal and spiritual leadership of all Arabia by 632, the year of his death.

Muhammad's followers compiled the Quran (also seen as Koran), a book containing the words that had come directly to the prophet from God. The Quran serves as the holy scriptures of Islam. Muhammad's sayings and teachings were compiled separately and referred to as the *hadith*. The Quran and the *hadith* form the sunna, a comprehensive guide to the spiritual, ethical, and social life of the orthodox Sunni Muslim.

The *shahada* (profession of faith) succinctly states the central belief of Islam: "There is no god but God (Allah), and Muhammad is His Prophet." Muslims repeat this profession of faith during many rituals. Reciting the phrase with unquestioning sincerity designates one a Muslim. The God about whom Muhammad preached was known to Christians and Jews living in Arabia at the time. Most Arabs, however, worshipped many gods and spirits whose existence was denied by Muhammad. Muhammad urged the people to worship the monotheistic God as the omnipotent and unique creator. Muhammad explained that his God was omnipresent and invisible. Therefore, representing God through symbols would have been a sin. Muhammad said God determined world events, and resisting God would have been futile and sinful.

Islam means submission (to God). One who submits is a Muslim. Muslims believe that Muhammad is the "seal of the prophets" and that his revelations complete the series of biblical revelations received by Jews and Christians. They also believe that God is one and the same throughout time, but his true teachings had been forgotten until Muhammad arrived. Muslims recognized biblical prophets and sages such as Abraham, Moses, and Jesus (known in Arabic as Ibrahim, Musa, and Isa, respectively) as inspired vehicles of God's will. Islam, however, reveres only their messages as sacred. Islam rejects the Christian belief that Jesus is the son of God. Islam accepts the concepts of guardian angels, the Day of Judgment (or the last day), general resurrection, heaven and hell, and eternal life of the soul.

The duties of the Muslim form the five pillars of the faith. These are the recitation of the *shahada*; daily prayer (*salat*); almsgiving (*zakat*); fasting (*sawm*); and hajj, or pilgrimage. The believer prays in a prescribed manner after purification through ritual ablutions each day at dawn, midday, midafternoon, sunset, and nightfall. Prescribed genuflections and prostrations accompany the prayers, which the worshipper recites facing Mecca. Whenever possible men pray in congregation at the mosque with an imam (see Glossary), or prayer leader. On Fridays corporate prayer is obligatory. The Friday noon prayers provide the occasion for weekly sermons by religious leaders. Women may also attend public worship at the mosque, but they are segregated from the men. Most women who pray, however, do it at home. A special functionary, the muezzin, intones a call to prayer to the entire community at the appropriate hour; people in outlying areas determine the proper time from the sun. Public prayer is a conspicuous and widely practiced aspect of Islam in Egypt.

Early Islamic authorities imposed a tax on personal property proportionate to one's wealth and distributed the revenues to the mosques and to the needy. In addition, many believers made voluntary donations. Although almsgiving is still a duty of the believer, it is no longer enforced by the state and has become a more private matter. Many properties contributed by pious individuals to support religious and charitable activities or institutions were traditionally administered as inalienable *waqfs*.

Ramadan, the ninth month of the Muslim calendar, is a period of obligatory fasting in commemoration of Muhammad's receipt of God's revelation, the Quran. Throughout the month, everyone except the sick, the weak, pregnant or nursing women, soldiers on duty, travelers on necessary journeys, and young children are enjoined from eating and drinking during daylight hours. Adults excused from the fasting are obliged to observe an equivalent fast at their earliest opportunity. A meal breaks each daily fast and inaugurates a night of feasting and celebration. Wealthy individuals usually do little work for all or part of the day.

Because the months of the lunar calendar are shorter than the months of the solar year, Ramadan falls at different times each year. For example, when Ramadan occurs in summer, it imposes special hardship on farmers who do heavy physical labor in the fields in the daytime.

At least once in their lifetimes, all Muslims who are financially and physically capable are expected to make a pilgrimage to the holy city of Mecca to participate in special rites held there during the twelfth month of the lunar calendar. Muhammad instituted this requirement, modifying pre-Islamic custom, to emphasize sites associated with Allah and Abraham, whom Arabs believe founded monotheism and is the ancestor of Arabs through his son Ishmael (Ismail). More than 20,000 Egyptians made pilgrimages to Mecca each year in the late 1980s. Traditionally the departure of Egypt's pilgrims climaxed in the ceremony of *mahmal,* during which the national gift of carpets and shrouds for the Kaaba shrine and the tomb of Muhammad at Medina were presented. The pilgrims would later deliver the gifts.

Once in Mecca, pilgrims, dressed in the white, seamless *ihram,* refrain from activities considered unclean. Highlights of the pilgrimage include kissing the sacred black stone; circumambulating the Kaaba, the sacred structure reputedly built by Abraham that houses the stone; running seven times between the hills of As Safa and Al Marwa in reenactment of Hagar's desperate search for water after Abraham had cast her and her son Ismail out into the desert; and standing in prayer on Mount Arafat. Id al Adha, a major Islamic festival celebrated worldwide, marks the end of the hajj. Each family, if it has the financial means, slaughters a lamb on Id al Adha to commemorate an ancient Arab sacrificial custom. The returning pilgrim is accorded the honorific *hajj* or *hajji* before his or her name.

Early Developments

During his lifetime, Muhammad was the spiritual and temporal leader of the Muslim community. He established the concept of Islam as a complete, all-encompassing way of life for individuals and society. Islam teaches that Allah revealed to Muhammad the immutable principles of correct behavior. Islam therefore obliged Muslims to live according to these principles. It also obliged the community to perfect human society on earth according to holy injunctions. Islam generally made no distinction between religion and state; it merged religious and secular life, as well as religious and secular law. Muslims have traditionally been subject to the sharia (Islamic jurisprudence, but in a larger sense meaning the Islamic way). A comprehensive legal system, the sharia developed gradually during the first four centuries of Islam, primarily through the accretion of precedent and interpretation by various judges and scholars. During the tenth century, legal opinion hardened into authoritative doctrine, and the figurative *bab al ijtihad* (gate of interpretation) gradually closed. Thereafter, Islamic law has tended to follow precedent rather than to interpret law according to circumstances.

In 632, after Muhammad's death the leaders of the Muslim community consensually chose Abu Bakr, the Prophet's father-in-law and one of his earliest followers, to succeed him. At that time, some people favored Ali, the Prophet's cousin and husband of his favorite daughter Fatima, but Ali and his supporters (the Shiat Ali, or party of Ali, commonly known as Shia) eventually accepted the community's choice. The next two caliphs (from *khalifa,* literally successor)—Umar, who succeeded in 634, and Uthman, who took power in 644—enjoyed the recognition of the entire community. When Ali finally succeeded to the caliphate in 656, Muawiyah, governor of Syria, rebelled in the name of his murdered kinsman, Uthman. After the ensuing civil war, Ali moved his capital to Mesopotamia (present-day Iraq), where in a short time he, too, was murdered.

Ali was the last of the so-called four orthodox caliphs. His death marked the end of the period in which all Muslims recognized a single caliph. Muawiyah then proclaimed himself caliph from Damascus. The Shia, however, refusing to recognize Muawiyah or his line of Umayyad caliphs, withdrew, causing Islam's first great schism. The Shia supported the claims of Ali's sons and grandsons to a presumptive right to the caliphate based on descent from the Prophet through Fatima and Ali. The larger faction of Islam, the Sunni, claimed to follow the orthodox teaching and example of the Prophet as embodied in the sunna.

Early Islam was intensely expansionist. Fervor for the new religion, as well as economic and social factors, fueled this expansionism. Conquering armies and migrating tribes swept out of Arabia and spread Islam. By the end of Islam's first century, Islamic armies had reached far into North Africa and eastward and northward into Asia. Among the first countries to come under their control was Egypt, which Arab forces invaded in 640. The following year, Amr ibn al As conquered Cairo (then known as Babylon) and renamed the city Al Fustat. By 647, after the surrender of Alexandria, the whole country was under Muslim rule (see The Arab Conquest, 639–41, ch. 1). Amr, Egypt's first Muslim ruler, was influenced by the Prophet's advice that Muslims should be kind to the Egyptians because of their kinship ties to Arabs. According to Islamic tradition, Ismail's mother, Hagar, was of Egyptian origin.

Amr allowed the Copts to choose between converting to Islam or retaining their beliefs as a protected people. Amr gave them this choice because the Prophet had recognized the special status of the "People of the Book" (Jews and Christians), whose scriptures he considered perversions of God's true word but nevertheless contributory to Islam. Amr believed that Jews and Christians were people who had approached but not yet achieved the perfection of Islam, so he did not treat them like pagans who would be forced into choosing between Islam and death. Jews and Christians in Muslim territories could live according to their own religious laws and in their own communities if they accepted the position of *dhimmis,* or tolerated subject peoples. *Dhimmis* were required to recognize Muslim authority, pay additional taxes, avoid proselytism among Muslims, and give up certain political rights. By the ninth century A.D., most Egyptians had converted to Islam.

Amr had chosen Al Fustat as the capital of Islamic Egypt because a canal connected the city to the Red Sea, which provided easy access to the Muslim heartland in the Arabian Peninsula. He initiated construction of Cairo's oldest extant mosque, the Amr ibn al As Mosque, which was completed in 711, several years after his death. Successive rulers also built mosques and other religious buildings as monuments to their faith and accomplishments. Egypt's first Turkish ruler, Ahmad ibn Tulun, built one of Cairo's most renowned mosques, the Ibn Tulun Mosque, in 876.

A Shia dynasty, the Fatimids, conquered Egypt in 969 and ruled the country for 200 years (see The Tulinids, Ikhshidids, Fatimids, and Ayyubids, 868–1260, ch. 1). Although the Fatimids endowed numerous mosques, shrines, and theological schools, they did not firmly establish their faith (known today as Ismaili Shia Islam— see Glossary) in Egypt. Numerous sectarian conflicts among Fatimid Ismailis after 1050 may have been a factor in Egyptian Muslim acceptance of Saladin's (Salah ad Din ibn Ayyub) reestablishment of Sunni Islam as the state religion in 1171. Al Azhar theological school, endowed by the Fatimids, changed quickly from a center of Shia learning to a bastion of Sunni orthodoxy. There were virtually no Ismailis in Egypt in 1990, although large numbers lived in India and Pakistan and smaller communities were in Afghanistan, Iran, Syria, and several countries in East Africa.

Contemporary Islam

Prior to Napoleon's invasion, almost all of Egypt's educational, legal, public health, and social welfare issues were in the hands of religious functionaries. Ottoman rule reinforced the public and political roles of the ulama (religious scholars) because Islam was the state religion and because political divisions in the country were based on religious divisions. During the nineteenth and twentieth centuries, successive governments made extensive efforts to limit the role of the ulama in public life and to bring religious institutions under closer state control. The secular transformation of public life in Egypt depended on the development of a civil bureaucracy that would absorb many of the ulama's responsibilities in the country.

After the 1952 Revolution, the government assumed responsibility for appointing officials to mosques and religious schools. The government mandated reform of Al Azhar University beginning in 1961. These reforms permitted department heads to be drawn from outside the ranks of the traditionally trained orthodox ulama. At the same time, the government established a number of modern faculties, including medicine, engineering, and commerce. The media periodically campaigned against the ulama as old-fashioned members of a "priestly caste."

As of 1990, Egyptian Islam was a complex and diverse religion. Although Muslims agreed on the faith's basic tenets, the country's various social groups and classes applied Islam differently in their daily lives. The literate theologians of Al Azhar University generally rejected the version of Islam practiced by illiterate religious preachers and peasants in the countryside. Most upper- and middle-class Muslims believed either that religious expression was a private matter for each individual or that Islam should play a more dominant role in public life. Islamic religious revival movements, whose appeal cut across class lines, were present in most cities and in many villages.

Today devout Muslims believe that Islam defines one's relationship to God, to other Muslims, and to non-Muslims. They also believe that there can be no dichotomy between the sacred and the secular. Many devout Muslims say that Egypt's governments have been secularist and even antireligious since the early 1920s. Politically organized Muslims who seek to purge the country of its secular policies are referred to as "Islamists." Orthodox ulama found themselves in a difficult position during the wave of Islamic activism that swept through Egypt in the 1970s and 1980s. Radical Islamists viewed the ulama as puppets of the status quo. To maintain their influence in the country, the ulama espoused more conservative stances. After 1974, for example, many Al Azhar ulama, who had acquiesced to family planning initiatives in the 1960s, openly criticized government efforts at population control. The ulama also supported moves to reform the country's legal code to conform to Islamic teaching. They remained, nonetheless, comparatively moderate; they were largely loyal to the government and condemned the violence of radical Islamist groups.

Egypt's largely uneducated urban and rural lower classes were intensely devoted to Islam, but they lacked a thorough knowledge of the religion. Even village religious leaders had only a rudimentary knowledge of Islam. The typical village imam or prayer leader had at most a few years of schooling; his scholarly work was limited to reading prayers and sermons prepared by others and to learning passages from the Quran. Popular religion included a variety of unorthodox practices, such as veneration of saints, recourse to charms and amulets, and belief in the influence of evil spirits.

Popular Islam is based mostly on oral tradition. Imams with virtually no formal education commonly memorize the entire Quran and recite appropriate verses on religious occasions. They also tell religious stories at village festivals and commemorations marking an individual's rites of passage. Predestination plays an important role in popular Islam. This concept includes the belief that everything that happens in life is the will of God and the belief that trying to avoid misfortune is useless and invites worse affliction. Monotheism merges with a belief in magic and spirits (jinns) who are believed to inhabit the mountains.

Popular Islam ranges from informal prayer sessions or Quran study to organized cults or orders. Because of the pervasive sexual segregation of Egypt's Islamic society, men and women often practice their religion in different ways. A specifically female religious custom is the *zar*, a ceremony for helping women placate spirits who are believed to have possessed them. Women specially trained by their mothers or other women in *zar* lore organize the ceremonies. A *zar* organizer holds weekly meetings and employs music and dance to induce ecstatic trances in possessed women. Wealthy women sometimes pay to have private *zars* conducted in their homes; these *zars* are more elaborate than public ones, last for several days, and sometimes involve efforts to exorcise spirits.

A primarily male spiritual manifestation is Sufism, an Islamic mystical tradition. Sufism has existed since the early days of Islam and is found in all Islamic countries. The name derives from the Arabic word *suf* (wool), referring to the rough garb of the early mystics. Sufism exists in a number of forms, most of which represent an original *tariqa* (discipline or way; pl., *turuq*) developed by an inspired founder, or shaykh. These shaykhs gradually gathered about themselves *murids,* or disciples, whom they initiated into the *tariqa.* Gradually the *murids* formed orders, also known as *turuq,* which were loyal to the shaykh or his successors. The devotions of many Sufi orders center on various forms of the *dhikr,* a ceremony at which music, body movements, and chants induce a state of ecstatic trance in the disciples. Since the early 1970s, there has been a revival of interest in Sufism. Egypt's contemporary Sufis tend to be young, college-educated men in professional careers.

Islamic Political Movements

Islamic political activism has a lengthy history in Egypt. Several Islamic political groups started soon after World War I ended. The most well-known Islamic political organization is the Muslim Brotherhood (Al Ikhwan al Muslimun, also known as the Brotherhood), founded in 1928 by Hasan al Banna. After World War II, the Muslim Brotherhood acquired a reputation as a radical group prepared to use violence to achieve its religious goals. The group was implicated in several assassinations, including the murder of one prime minister. The Brotherhood had contacts with the Free Officers before the 1952 Revolution and supported most of their initial policies. The Brotherhood, however, soon came into conflict with Nasser. The government accused the Brotherhood of complicity in an alleged 1954 plot to assassinate the president and imprisoned many of the group's leaders. In the 1970s, Anwar as Sadat amnestied the leaders and permitted them to resume some of their activities. But by that time, the Brotherhood was divided into at least three factions. The more militant faction was committed to a policy of political opposition to the government. A second faction advocated peaceful withdrawal from society and the creation, to the extent possible, of a separate, parallel society based upon Islamic values and law. The dominant moderate group advocated cooperation with the regime (see Controlling the Mass Political Arena, ch. 4; and Muslim Extremism, ch. 5).

The Muslim Brotherhood's reemergence as a political force coincided with the proliferation of Islamic groups. Some of these groups espoused the violent overthrow of the government while others espoused living a devout life of rigorous observance of religious practices. It is impossible to list all the Islamic groups that emerged in the late 1970s because many of them had diffuse structures and some of the more militant groups were underground. Egypt's defeat and loss of territory in the June 1967 War was the main cause for the growth of religiously inspired political activism. Muslims tended to view the humiliating experience as the culmination of 150 years of foreign intrusion and an affront to their vision of a true Islamic community. Islamic tradition rejected the idea of non-Muslims dominating Muslim society. Such a state of affairs discredited Muslim rulers who permitted it to persist. It was, therefore, incumbent on believers to end the domination and restore the true supremacy of Islam. As part of their Sunni creed, the most radical activists adopted jihad (holy war—the Shia sixth pillar of faith) and committed themselves to battling unbelievers and impious Muslims. During the 1970s and 1980s, Islamists perpetrated a number of violent acts, including the assassination of Sadat in October 1981.

Disruptive social changes and Sadat's relative tolerance toward political parties contributed to the rapid growth of Islamic groups in the 1970s. On university campuses, for example, Sadat initially viewed the rise of Islamic associations (Jamaat al Islamiyah) as a counterbalance to leftist influence among students. The Jamaat al Islamiyah spread quite rapidly on campuses and won up to one-third of all student union elections. These victories provided a platform from which the associations campaigned for Islamic dress, the veiling of women, and the segregation of classes by gender. Secular university administrators opposed these goals. In 1979 Sadat sought to diminish the influence of the associations through a law that transferred most of the authority of the student unions to professors and administrators. During the 1980s, however, Islamists gradually penetrated college faculties. At Asyut University, which was the scene of some of the most intense clashes between Islamists and their opponents (including security forces, secularists, and Copts), the president and other top administrators—who were Islamists—supported Jamaat al Islamiyah demands to end mixed-sex classes and to reduce total female enrollment.

As of 1990, the Islamists sought to make Egypt a community of the faithful based on their vision of an Islamic social order. They rejected conventional, secularist social analyses of Egypt's socioeconomic problems. They maintained, for example, that the causes of poverty were not overpopulation or high defense expenditures but the populace's spiritual failures—laxness, secularism, and corruption. The solution was a return to the simplicity, hard work, and self-reliance of earlier Muslim life. The Islamists created their own alternative network of social and economic institutions through which members could work, study, and receive medical treatment in an Islamic environment.

Islamists rejected Marxism and Western capitalism. Indeed, they viewed atheistic communism, Jewish Zionism, and Western "Crusader-minded" Christianity as their main enemies, which were responsible for the decadence that led to foreign domination and defeat by Zionists. They were intolerant of people who did not share their world view. Islamists tended to be hostile toward the orthodox ulama, especially the scholars at Al Azhar who frequently criticized the Islamists' extreme religious interpretations. Islamists believed that the established social and political order had tainted the ulama, who had come to represent stumbling blocks to the new Islamic order. In addition, Islamists condemned the orthodox as "pulpit parrots" committed to a formalist practice of Islam but not to its spirit.

The social origins of Islamists changed after the 1952 Revolution. In the 1940s and early 1950s, the Muslim Brotherhood had appealed primarily to urban civil servants and white-and blue-collar workers. After the early 1970s, the Islamic revival attracted followers from a broad spectrum of social classes. Most activists were university students or recent graduates; they included rural-urban migrants and urban middle-class youth whose fathers were middle-level government employees or professionals. Their fields of study—medicine, engineering, military science, and pharmacy—were among the most highly competitive and prestigious disciplines in the university system. The rank-and-file members of Islamist groups have come from the middle class, the lower-middle class, and the urban working class.

Various Islamist groups espoused different means for achieving their political agenda. All Islamists, however, were concerned with Islam's role in the complex and changing society of Egypt in the late twentieth century. A common focus of their political efforts has been to incorporate the sharia into the country's legal code. In deference to their increasing influence, the Ministry of Justice in 1977 published a draft law making apostasy by a Muslim a capital offense and proposing traditional Islamic punishments for crimes, such as stoning for adultery and amputation of a hand for theft. In 1980 Egypt supported a referendum that proposed a constitutional amendment to make the sharia "the sole source of law." The influence of the Islamists temporarily waned in the aftermath of Sadat's assassination in 1981, but the election of nine members of the Muslim Brotherhood to the People's Assembly in 1984 revived Islamists' prospects. In 1985 the People's Assembly voted to initiate a procedure for the gradual application of the sharia, beginning with an indefinite education period to prepare the population for the legal changes; the next step would be to amend all existing laws to exclude any provisions that conflict with the sharia. Moves to reform the legal code received support from many Muslims who wanted to purify society and reject Western legal codes forced on Egypt in the nineteenth and twentieth centuries.

Coptic Church

The Copts have remained a significant minority throughout the medieval and modern periods. After the Turks incorporated Egypt into the Ottoman Empire in the sixteenth century, they organized the government around a system of millets, or religious communities. The Copts were one of the communities. Each organized religious minority lived according to its own canon law under the leadership of recognized religious authorities who represented the millet to the outside world and supervised the millet's internal communal life. This form of organization preserved and nourished the religious differences among these peoples. Most historians believe that the millet system prevented the full integration of non-Muslims into Muslim life. The system, which the Ottomans applied throughout their empire, had an enduring influence on the social structure of all countries in the Middle East.

The Copts, an indigenous Christian sect, constituted Egypt's largest religious minority. Estimates of their numbers in 1990 ranged between 3 million to 7 million. The Copts claimed descent from the ancient Egyptians; the word *copt* is derived from the Arabic word *qubt* (Egyptian). Egypt was Christianized during the first century A.D., when the country was part of the Roman Empire. The Coptic Church claims to hold an unbroken line of patriarchal succession to the See of Alexandria founded by Saint Mark, a disciple of Christ. Egyptian Christianity developed distinct dogmas and practices during the more than two centuries that the religion was illegal. By the fourth century, when Constantine made Christianity the official religion of the Roman Empire, Coptic traditions were sufficiently different from those in Rome and Constantinople (formerly Byzantium; present-day Istanbul) to cause major religious conflicts. Dissension persisted for 150 years until most Copts seceded from the main body of Christianity because they rejected the decision of the Council of Chalcedon that Christ had a dual nature, both human and divine, believing instead in Christ's single, divine nature.

The Coptic Church developed separately from other Eastern churches. The Coptic Church's clerical hierarchy had evolved by the sixth century. A patriarch, referred to as the pope, heads the church. A synod or council of senior priests (people who have attained the status of bishops) is responsible for electing or removing popes. Members of the Coptic Church worldwide (about 1 million Copts lived outside of Egypt as of 1990) recognize the pope as their spiritual leader. The pope, traditionally based in Alexandria, also serves as the chief administrator of the church. The administrator's functionaries include hundreds of priests serving urban and rural parishes, friars in monasteries, and nuns in convents.

Following Islam's spread through Egypt, Muslims alternately tolerated and persecuted the Copts. Heavy taxation of Christians encouraged mass conversions to Islam, and within two centuries, Copts had become a distinct minority. By the tenth century, Arabic

141

had replaced Coptic as the primary spoken language, and Coptic was relegated to a liturgical language.

The Ottoman millet system of drawing administrative divisions along religious lines reinforced Coptic solidarity. The dismantling of the millet system during the nineteenth century helped open new career opportunities for the Copts. Egypt's Muslim rulers had traditionally used minority members as administrators, and the Copts were initially the main beneficiaries of the burgeoning civil service. During the early twentieth century, however, the British purged many Copts from the bureaucracy. The Copts resented this policy, but it accelerated their entry into professional careers.

In the twentieth century, Copts have been disproportionately represented among the ranks of prosperous city dwellers. Urban Copts tended to favor careers in commerce and the professions, whereas the livelihoods of rural Copts were virtually indistinguishable from their Muslim counterparts. Urban Copts were stratified into groups of long-time residents and groups of recent migrants from the countryside. The latter group was often impoverished and fell outside the traditional urban Coptic community. The former group included many university professors, lawyers, doctors, a few prominent public officials, and a substantial middle echelon of factory workers and service sector employees.

Anti-Coptic sentiment has accompanied the resurgence of Islamic activism in Egypt. Since 1972 several Coptic churches have been burned, including the historic Qasriyat ar Rihan Church in Cairo. Islamist groups frequently and explicitly denounced Copts in their pamphlets and prayer meetings. The increasing tensions between Copts and Muslims inevitably led to clashes in Upper Egypt in 1977 and 1978 and later in the cities and villages of the Delta. Three days of religious riots in Cairo in 1981 left at least 17 Copts and Muslims dead and more than 100 injured. Isolated incidents of Muslim-Coptic violence continued throughout the 1980s and during 1990.

Coptic Pope Shenudah III (elected in 1971) blamed government silence for the increasing violence. He also expressed alarm at official actions that he said encouraged anti-Coptic feelings. In 1977, to protest a Ministry of Justice proposal to apply sharia legal penalties to any Muslim who converted from Islam, the pope called on the Coptic community to fast for five days. As harassment of Copts increased, Pope Shenudah III canceled official Easter celebrations for 1980 and fled to a desert convent with his bishops. Sadat accused the pope of inciting the Coptic-Muslim strife and banished him in September 1981 to internal exile. The government then appointed a committee of five bishops to administer the church. The following year, the government called upon the church synod to elect a new pope, but the Coptic clergy rejected this state intervention. In 1985 Husni Mubarak released Pope Shenudah III from internal exile and permitted him to resume his religious duties.

Other Religious Minorities

Egypt's other religious minorities in 1990 included approximately 350,000 adherents of the Greek Orthodox Church, 175,000 Eastern and Latin Rite Catholics, 200,000 Protestants, and fewer than 1,000 Jews. The Greek Orthodox Church was headquartered in Alexandria, where most of its members lived. Most members of the Greek Orthodox were of Greek origin, but followers also included Arabs, Armenians, and the affiliated Coptic Orthodox Church. The Catholics embraced seven distinct rites that Rome historically authorized to use languages other than Latin as integral parts of their liturgies. Approximately 85 percent of all Catholics in Egypt belonged to the Coptic Catholic Church. Other Catholics included followers of the Armenian, Chaldean, Greek, Latin, Maronite, and Syrian rites. There were also numerous Protestant churches. The government suspended the Anglican Church in 1958 after the Anglo-French occupation of the Suez Canal but permitted it to resume functioning in 1974. The Anglican Church in Egypt was part of the Episcopal Church in Jerusalem and the Middle East. Other Protestant churches included the Armenian Apostolic Church, the Union of Armenian Evangelical Churches in the Near East, and the Coptic Evangelical Church.

Education

Prior to the nineteenth century, the ulama and Coptic clergy controlled Egypt's traditional education. The country's most important institutes were theological seminaries, but most mosques and churches—even in villages—operated basic schools where boys could learn to read and write Arabic, to do simple arithmetic, and to memorize passages from the Quran or Bible. Muhammad Ali established the system of modern secular education in the early nineteenth century to provide technically trained cadres for his civil administration and military. His grandson, Ismail, greatly expanded the system by creating a network of public schools at the primary, secondary, and higher levels. Ismail's wife set up the first school for girls in 1873. Between 1882 and 1922, when the country was under British administration, state education did not expand. However, numerous private schools, including Egypt's first secular university, were established. After direct British rule ended, Egypt adopted a new constitution that proclaimed the state's responsibility to ensure adequate primary schools for all Egyptians. Nevertheless, education generally remained accessible only to the elite. At the time of the 1952 Revolution, fewer than 50 percent of all primary-school-age children attended school, and the majority of the children who were enrolled were boys. Nearly 75 percent of the population over ten years of age was illiterate. More than 90 percent of the females in this age group were illiterate.

The Free Officers dramatically expanded educational opportunities. They pledged to provide free education for all citizens and abolished all fees for public schools. They doubled the Ministry of Education's budget in one decade; government spending on education grew from less than 3 percent of the gross domestic product (GDP—see Glossary) in 1952–53 to more than 5 percent by 1978. Expenditures on school construction increased 1,000 percent between 1952 and 1976, and the total number of primary schools doubled to 10,000. By the mid-1970s, the educational budget represented more than 25 percent of the government's total current budget expenses. Since the mid-1970s, however, the government has virtually abandoned the country's earlier educational goals. Consequently, public investment in new educational infrastructure has declined in relation to total educational expenditures; about 85 percent of the Ministry of Education's budget has been designated for salaries.

From academic year 1953–54 through 1965–66, overall enrollments more than doubled. They almost doubled again from 1965–66 through 1975–76. Since 1975 primary-school enrollments have continued to grow at an average of 4.1 percent annually, and intermediate school (grades seven through nine) at an average of 6.9 percent annually (for 1985–86 enrollments, see table 2, Appendix). The proportion of the population with some secondary education more than doubled between 1960 and 1976; the number of people with some university education nearly tripled. Women made great educational gains: the percentage of women with preuniversity education grew more than 300 percent while women with university education grew more than 600 percent. By academic year 1985–86, about 84 percent of the primary-school-age population (more than 6 million of the 7.2 million children between the ages of seven and twelve) were enrolled in primary school. Less than 30 percent of eligible youth, however, attended intermediate and secondary schools. Because as many as 16 percent of Egyptian children were receiving no education in the 1980s, the literacy rate lagged behind the expansion in enrollments; in 1990 only 45 percent of the population could read and write.

*Literacy class for girls at women's
vocational training center
Courtesy UNICEF (Sean Sprague)*

*Students in an engineering
class at Cairo University
Courtesy Embassy of Egypt,
Washington*

Law Number 139 of 1981, which defined the structure of pre-university public education, made the nine-year basic cycle compulsory. Regardless of this law, most parents removed their children from school before they completed ninth grade. The basic cycle included six years of primary school and three years of intermediate school. Promotion from primary to intermediate school was contingent upon obtaining passing scores on special examinations. Admission to the three-year secondary cycle (grades ten through twelve) also was determined by examination scores. Secondary students chose between a general (college preparatory) curriculum and a technical curriculum. During the eleventh and twelfth grades, students in the general curriculum concentrated their studies on the humanities, mathematics, or the sciences. Students in the technical curriculum studied agriculture, communications, or industry. Students could advance between grades only after they received satisfactory scores on standardized tests. The Ministry of Education, however, strictly limited the number of times a student could retake an examination.

Various government ministries also operated training institutes that accepted students who had completed the basic cycle. Training-institute programs, which incorporated both secondary and post-secondary vocational education, varied in length and provided certificates to students who successfully completed the prescribed curricula. Teacher-training institutes, for example, offered a five-year program. In the academic year 1985–86, approximately 85,000 students were enrolled in all training programs; 60 percent of the enrollees were women.

As of 1990, problems persisted in Egypt's education system. For example, the government did not enforce laws requiring primary-school-age children to attend school. In some areas, as many as 50 percent of the formally enrolled children did not regularly attend classes. There were also significant regional differences in the primary-school enrollment rate. In urban areas, nearly 90 percent of the school-age children attended. In some rural areas of Upper Egypt, only 50 percent attended. Overall, only half of the students enrolled in primary school completed all six grades.

The enrollment rate for girls continued to be significantly lower than for boys. Although increases in the number of girls enrolled in school were greater than they were for boys in the 1960s and 1970s, boys still outnumbered girls at every educational level. In 1985–86, for example, only 45 percent of all primary students were girls. An estimated 75 percent of girls between the ages of six and twelve were enrolled in primary school compared with 94 percent of boys in the same age-group. Girls' primary-school enrollment was lowest in Upper Egypt, where less than 30 percent of all students were girls. Girls also dropped out of primary school more frequently than boys. About 66 percent of the boys beginning primary school completed the primary cycle, while only 57 percent of the girls completed all six grades. Girls accounted for about 41 percent of total intermediate school enrollment and 39 percent of secondary school enrollment. Among all girls aged twelve to eighteen in 1985–86, only 46 percent were enrolled in school.

The shortage of teachers was a chronic problem, especially in rural primary schools. Under British rule, educated Egyptians had perceived teaching as a career that lacked prestige. Young people chose this career only when there was no other option or when it would serve as a stepping-stone to a more lucrative career in law. Despite improvements in training and salaries, teaching—especially at the primary level—remained a low-status career. In 1985–86, Egypt's primary and secondary schools employed only 155,000 teachers to serve 9.6 million pupils—a ratio of about 62 students per teacher. Some city schools were so crowded that they operated two shifts daily. Many Egyptian teachers preferred to go abroad, where salaries were higher and classroom conditions better. During the 1980s, the government granted 30,000 exit visas a year to teachers who had contracts to teach in Arab countries.

Higher education expanded even more dramatically than the preuniversity system. In the first ten years following the 1952 Revolution, spending on higher education increased 400 percent. Between academic years 1951–52 and 1978–79, student enrollment in public universities grew nearly 1,400 percent. In 1989–90 there were fourteen public universities with a total enrollment of 700,000. More than half of these institutions were established as autonomous universities after 1952, four in the 1970s and five in the 1980s. The total number of female college students had doubled; by 1985–86 women accounted for 32 percent of all students. In the 1980s, public universities—accounting for roughly 7 percent of total student enrollment—received more than one-fourth of all current education-budget spending.

Since the late 1970s, government policies have attempted to reorient postsecondary education. The state expanded technical training programs in agriculture, commerce, and a variety of other fields. Student subsidies were partially responsible for a 15 percent annual increase in enrollments in the country's five-year technical institutes. The technical institutes were set up to provide the growing private sector with trained personnel and to alleviate the shortage of skilled labor. Universities, however, permitted graduates of secondary schools and technical institutes to enroll as "external students," which meant they could not attend classes but were allowed to sit for examinations and to earn degrees. The policy resulted in a flourishing clandestine trade in class notes and overburdened professors with additional examinations. Further, widespread desire for a university degree led many students in technical institutes to view their curricula as simply a stepping-stone to a university degree.

Health and Welfare

Since the 1952 Revolution, the government has striven to improve the general health of the population. The National Charter of 1962 stipulated that "the right of health welfare is foremost among the rights of every citizen." Per capita public spending for health increased almost 500 percent between 1952 and 1976. As a result of this spending, the average Egyptian in 1990 was healthier and lived longer than the typical Egyptian of the early 1950s. For example, life expectancy at birth, only thirty-nine years in 1952, had climbed to fifty-nine years for men and sixty years for women by 1989. The crude death rate, which was 23.9 in 1952, had declined to 10.3 by 1990. Its main component, the infant mortality rate, declined more dramatically in the same period, from 193 infant deaths per 1,000 live births to 85 per 1,000. Nevertheless, major disparities remained in the mortality rates of cities and villages as well as in those of Upper and Lower Egypt. Although mortality and morbidity data were adequate for establishing general trends, they were not reliable for precise measurements. Egypt's official infant mortality rate, for example, was probably understated because parents tended not to report infants who died in the first few weeks of life. Corrected estimates of the infant mortality rate for 1990 ranged as high as 113 per 1,000 live births.

Although mortality rates have declined since 1952, the main causes of death (respiratory ailments and diseases of the digestive tract) have remained unchanged for much of the twentieth century. Death rates for infants and children ages one to five dropped, but children remained the largest contributors to the mortality rate. Nearly seventeen infants and four children under five years of age died for each death of an individual between age five and thirty-four. Children younger than five years of age accounted for about half of all mortality—one of the world's highest rates. During the 1980s, diarrhea and associated dehydration accounted for 67 percent of the deaths among infants and children. Concern about this health problem prompted the government to establish the National Control of Diarrheal Diseases Project (NCDDP) in 1982. With funds provided by the United States Agency for International Development, NCDDP initiated a program to educate health care workers

Children's immunization campaign promoted by health centers nationwide
Dayas (traditional birth attendants), with the medical kits
received upon completing their training
Courtesy UNICEF (Sean Sprague)

and families about oral-rehydration therapy. NCDDP's efforts helped reduce diarrhea-related deaths by 60 percent between 1983 and 1988. The highest rates of infant mortality were in Upper Egypt, followed by Cairo, Alexandria, and other urban areas; the lowest rates were in Lower Egypt.

The average Egyptian's nutritional status compared favorably with that of people in most middle- and low-income countries. Bread, rice, legumes, seasonal fresh fruits, and vegetables such as onions and tomatoes constituted the daily diet of a majority of the population. Middle- and upper-income families also regularly consumed red meat, poultry, or fish. Caloric intake was adequate, although there were indications of widespread vitamin deficiencies. The most recent surveys of nutrition, undertaken in the late 1970s, revealed that approximately 25 percent of public-school children were either malnourished or anemic. The incidence of poor nutrition was highest in rural areas, where nearly 33 percent of surveyed children were malnourished, compared with only 17 percent in the cities; among low-income families, about 50 percent of all children showed indications of inadequate nutrition.

The major endemic diseases in 1990 were tuberculosis, trachoma, schistosomiasis, and malaria. Schistosomiasis, carried by blood flukes and spread to humans by water-dwelling snails, was a major parasitic affliction. Historically, the disease was most prevalent in the Delta, where standing water in irrigation ditches provided an ideal environment for the snails and other parasites. Those working in agriculture were particularly susceptible; their prevalence rate was nearly three times that of nonagriculturists. Debility owing to schistosomiasis could not be calculated accurately; its severity generally varied depending on the infected organs, commonly the bladder, genitals, liver, and lungs. Treatments for the disease are not always effective, and the main medicines have toxic side effects. The government tried to control the spread of the disease by educating the population about the dangers of using stagnant water. According to Ministry of Health statistics, the incidence of schistosomiasis dropped by half between 1935 and 1966. One of the negative health consequences of the Aswan High Dam, however, was an increase in the incidence of schistosomiasis in Upper Egypt, where the dam has permitted a change from basin to perennial agriculture with its continuous presence of standing water.

The Ministry of Health provided free, basic health care at hundreds of public medical facilities. General health centers offered routine medical care, maternal and child care, family planning services, and screening for hospital admittance. These clinics were usually associated with the 1,300 social service units or the 5,000 social care cooperatives that served both urban and rural areas. In addition, in 1990 the Ministry of Health maintained 344 general hospitals, 280 specialized health care units for the treatment of endemic diseases, respiratory ailments, cancer and other diseases, and dental centers. There were about 45,000 beds in all government hospitals, plus an additional 40,000 beds available in private health institutes. The number of trained medical personnel was high relative to most middle-income countries. In 1990 there were more than 73,300 doctors in the country, approximately 1 physician per 715 inhabitants. There were also about 70,000 certified nurses. Medical personnel tended to be concentrated in the cities, and most preferred private practice to employment in public facilities. Fewer than 30 percent of all doctors and scarcely 10 percent of nurses served in villages.

Although public health clinics were distributed relatively evenly throughout the country, their services were generally inadequate because of the shortage of doctors and nurses and the lack of modern equipment. In both cities and villages, patients using the free or low-cost government facilities expected a lengthy journey and a long wait to see a physician; service was usually impersonal and perfunctory. Dissatisfaction with public clinics forced even low-income patients to patronize the expensive private clinics. In rural areas, village midwives assisted between 50 percent and 80 percent of all births. Even when women used the maternal care available, prenatal care was minimal, and most births occurred before trained personnel arrived.

Further improvements in the health of Egyptians required increasing the effectiveness of the primary health-care system and improving public sanitation and health education. In 1990 approximately 25 percent of the total population, including 36 percent of all villagers, did not have access to safe water for drinking and food preparation. Use of unhygienic water was the major cause of diarrheal diseases. In addition, more than 50 percent of all families lived in homes that lacked plumbing. Sewage facilities throughout the country were inadequate. Increasing the level of women's education would probably help to decrease the infant mortality rate. Studies have found that infant mortality decreases as mothers increase their level of education, even when age and family income are held constant. Surveys undertaken in the 1970s indicated that 78 percent of the infants born to illiterate women survived early childhood. That figure increased to 84 percent for infants born to women who finished primary school and to 90 percent for infants born to women with secondary or higher education.

The government also had established 1,300 social service centers and 5,100 social care cooperatives by 1990. The social service centers provided instruction in adult literacy, health education, vocational training, and family planning. The social care cooperatives had similar services and also provided child care centers for working mothers, aid for the handicapped, and transportation for the elderly and infirm. About 65 percent of the social service centers were in villages; 65 percent of social care cooperatives were in cities. In many villages, the social service centers were associated with the local public health clinic and supplemented the primary health care services. The overall impact of the centers and cooperatives has been limited by the lack of funding since the late 1970s.

The government instituted a social security program in the early 1960s to provide pensions, through forced savings, for employees. Coverage also included unemployment, disability, and death benefits. In 1990 less than half of the work force participated in the program. Self-employed individuals and most private sector workers (including domestics, farm workers, and casual laborers) were not covered by the program. The overwhelming majority of participants were civil servants and employees of government enterprises. Workers in private factories could only participate in social security if their employers chose to make regular contributions to the program.

* * *

Although there is extensive English-language literature on Egypt, few studies treat Egyptian society comprehensively. The most detailed discussion of Egypt's geography is in W.B. Fisher's *The Middle East.* This research has been updated in the article, ''Egypt: Physical and Social Geography,'' in *The Middle East and North Africa, 1989.*

A useful overview of contemporary Egyptian society is Anthony McDermott's *Egypt From Nasser to Mubarak.* Although primarily political science books, Raymond A. Hinnebusch, Jr.'s *Egyptian Politics under Sadat*, Robert Springborg's *Mubarak's Egypt,* and John Waterbury's *The Egypt of Nasser and Sadat* all contain valuable detail about social groups and the impact of the government's social and economic policies on class structure.

Several scholars have written insightful studies of rural society. The classic study of traditional village life, first published in French in the 1930s, is Henry Habib Ayrout's *The Egyptian Peasant.* Although Ayrout's data are outdated, his descriptions of customs, kinship, and farming techniques still have contemporary relevance. A recent book, Lila Abu-Lughod's *Veiled Sentiments,* presents equally thorough descriptions of customs and kinship patterns among the beduins. Egypt's land redistribution policies of the 1950s and 1960s have attracted considerable interest from scholars who have reached very different conclusions about the impact of the policies. Iliya Harik's *The Political Mobilization of Peasants* suggests that the small peasant owners and the landless benefited most from redistribution. However, in *In a Moment of Enthusiasm* Leonard Binder argues that the land redistribution primarily benefited and helped to consolidate the class of middle peasants. Hamied Ansari challenges the theses of Harik and Binder in *Egypt: The Stalled Society.* In *Family, Power and Politics in Egypt,* Robert Springborg argues that the old landlord class retained substantial influence and continued to control substantial land despite official limits on individual holdings.

There are many studies about life in urban Egypt. Among the most interesting is Unni Wikan's *Life Among the Poor of Cairo.* This book, a case study of the family and friends of one lower-class woman, provides valuable insights into the strength of family ties in the midst of poverty and adversity. Andrea B. Rugh's *Family in Contemporary Egypt* analyzes the various family adaptation patterns to the social and economic changes that have been occurring since the 1960s.

Articles in many periodicals address the role of religion in contemporary Egyptian society. The most useful studies generally are published in current issues of quarterlies such as the *International Journal of Middle East Studies, Middle East Report,* and *Middle East Journal.* Giles Keppel's *Muslim Extremism in Egypt* is a penetrating study of the role of Islamic political groups in the late 1970s and early 1980s.

Finally, one of the most valuable ways of gaining insight into Egyptian society is through the novels, plays, and short stories of several contemporary writers whose works have been translated into English. The best-known novelist is Naguib Mahfouz, who won the Nobel Prize for Literature in 1988. His novels, including *Midaq Alley, The Fountain and Tomb, Mirrors,* and *The Trilogy,* deal with the lives of the poor and the middle class and provide glimpses into the impact of social, political, and economic changes on individuals and families. (For further information and complete citations, see Bibliography.)

Senwosret (Kheperkare) and god Min; sunken relief on limestone with hieroglyphs

FROM THE 1850s UNTIL the 1930s, Egypt's economy exhibited a classic Third World dependency syndrome, the essence of which was reliance on the export of a single, usually primary, commodity. In the case of Egypt, the commodity was long-staple cotton, introduced in the mid-1820s during the reign of Muhammad Ali (1805–49), and made possible by the switch from basin to perennial, modern irrigation. Cotton cultivation was a key ingredient in an ambitious program that the Egyptian ruler undertook to diversify and develop the economy.

Another such ingredient was industrialization. Industrialization, however, proved for various domestic and external reasons to be less than successful, and until the 1930s, virtually no industrial build-up occurred. The failure of industrialization resulted largely from tariff restrictions that Britain imposed on Egypt through the 1838 commercial treaty, which allowed only minuscule tariffs, if any. The isolated industrial ventures initiated by members of Egypt's landed aristocracy, who otherwise channeled their investment into land acquisition and speculation, were nipped in the bud by foreign competition. The few surviving enterprises were owned by the foreign community. These enterprises either enjoyed natural protection as in the case of sugar and cotton processing, or benefited from the special skills that the foreign owners had acquired, as in the case of cigarette making by Greeks and Turks.

The beginnings of industrialization awaited the depression of the late 1920s and 1930s and World War II. The depression sent cotton prices tumbling, and Britain acceded to Egyptian demands to raise tariffs. Moreover, World War II, by substantially reducing the flow of foreign goods into the country, gave further impetus to the establishment of import-substitution industries. A distinguishing feature of the factories built at this time was that they were owned by Egyptian entrepreneurs.

In spite of the lack of industrialization, the economy grew rapidly throughout the nineteenth century. Growth, however, was confined to the cotton sector and the supporting transportation, financial, and other facilities. Little of the cotton revenues was invested in economic development. The revenues were largely drained out of the country as repatriated profits or repayments of debts that the state had incurred to pay for irrigation works and the extravagance of the khedives.

Rapid economic growth ended in the early 1900s. The supply of readily available land had been largely exhausted and multiple cropping, concentration on cotton, and perennial irrigation had lessened the fertility of the soil. Cotton yields dropped in the early 1900s and recovered to their former level only in the 1940s, through investments in modern inputs such as fertilizers and drainage.

The fall in agricultural productivity and terms of trade led to a stagnation in the per capita gross national product (GNP—see Glossary) between the end of World War I and the 1952 Revolution: the GNP averaged £E43.0 (for value of the Egyptian pound—see Glossary), in 1954 prices, at both ends of the period. By 1952 Egypt was in the throes of both economic and political crises, which culminated in the assumption of power by the Free Officers.

Structure, Growth, and Development of the Economy

By necessity if not by design, the revolutionary regime gave considerably greater priority to economic development than did the monarchy, and the economy has been a central government concern since then. While the economy grew steadily, it sometimes exhibited sharp fluctuations. Analysis of economic growth is further complicated by the difficulty in obtaining reliable statistics. Growth figures are often disputed, and economists contend that growth estimates may be grossly inaccurate because of the informal economy and workers' remittances, which may contribute as much as one-fourth of GNP (see Remittances, this ch.). According to one estimate, the gross domestic product (GDP—see Glossary), at 1965 constant prices, grew at an annual compound rate of about 4.2 percent between 1955 and 1975. This was about 1.7 times larger than the annual population growth rate of 2.5 percent in the same period. The period between 1967 and 1974, the final years of Gamal Abdul Nasser's presidency and the early part of Anwar as Sadat's, however, were lean years, with growth rates of only about 3.3 percent. The slowdown was caused by many factors, including agricultural and industrial stagnation and the costs of the June 1967 War. Investments, which were a crucial factor for the preceding growth, also nose-dived and recovered only in 1975 after the dramatic 1973 increase in oil prices.

Like most countries in the Middle East, Egypt partook of the oil boom and suffered the subsequent slump. Available figures suggest that between 1975 and 1980 the GDP (at 1980 prices) grew at an annual rate of more than 11 percent. This impressive achievement resulted, not from the contribution of manufacturing or agriculture, but from oil exports, remittances, foreign aid, and grants (see Balance of Payments and Main Sources of Foreign

Exchange, this ch.). From the mid-1980s, the GDP growth slowed as a result of the 1985–86 crash in oil prices. In the two succeeding years, the GDP grew at no more than an annual rate of 2.9 percent. Of concern for the future was the decline of the fixed investment ratio from around 30 percent during most of the 1975–85 decade to 22 percent in 1987.

The post-World War II growth was accompanied by a certain degree of diversification of the economic structure, although not without serious flaws in the diversification (see table 3, Appendix). By 1952 agriculture's share of GDP at fiscal year (FY—see Glossary) 1959 market prices was 33 percent, industry's (including mining and electricity) share reached 13 percent, and the service sectors' share amounted to 54 percent. The diversification resulted from the decline of agriculture's contribution to the GDP and the ascendancy of industry and, particularly, of government services. Agriculture's share in the GDP dropped by more than half from 1952, stabilizing near 15 percent through most of the 1980s. Industry's share moved in the opposite direction: from only 13 percent in 1952, it hovered around 35 percent in the 1980s.

Although the industrial sector's contribution to the GNP rose during this period, that growth was due to the increase in energy-related activity, especially oil-drilling. Manufacturing stagnated and may even have declined. In 1974 (when data for the subsector became available), manufacturing accounted for 15 percent of GNP, but its share fell to 12 percent in 1986 and remained there in early 1990. The lackluster performance of manufacturing was one of the main reasons for the Egyptian economy's inability to become self-sustaining, and for its dependence on oil and external financing.

The services (including construction) held relatively steady, comprising around one-half of GDP, a figure that included the contributions of the various subsectors. An important subsector from a developmental viewpoint was the one entitled "other services"—mostly government services. These averaged 14.2 percent of the growth in GDP in the years from 1952 to 1959 and 32.7 percent of the growth in the years from 1959 to 1969. The increase resulted primarily from the expansion in the bureaucracy that followed the 1961 decree guaranteeing government jobs for all university graduates. The trend continued under Anwar as Sadat (1970–79), and slowed, or may have reversed under Husni Mubarak as the state became financially incapable of hiring the many new job-seeking graduates (see The Role of Government, this ch.). Although government employment may have encouraged economic growth temporarily, it impeded it over the long run, competing for scarce investment funds and exacerbating the trade deficit.

Infrastructure

In spite of progress in the 1980s, by the end of the decade Egypt still had a long way to go in expanding and improving existing services such as housing, transportation, telecommunications, and water supply. Housing remained inadequate; urban dwellings were often very crowded, and residents lived in makeshift accommodations. Housing was essentially a private activity, and the government tended to underinvest in the sector. The electric grid reached essentially all villages in Egypt by the early 1980s, but blackouts in Cairo and other cities were not uncommon. A major sewage project was under way. It aimed at revamping and expanding the overflowing, antiquated network of sewers, pumping stations, and treatment plants. Some of the work was scheduled for completion by 1991. With help from the United States Agency for International Development (AID), telephone lines doubled at the end of the FY 1982–86 Five-Year Plan.

Because infrastructural improvements and additions were costly and required a long lead time, no relief was anticipated before the mid-1990s. The FY 1987–91 Five-Year Plan allocated more than £E4.1 billion for infrastructure. The problem that faced the government was how to balance the badly needed improvement of the infrastructure against the fact that such investments created only temporary employment and had small impact on industries that served or were served by the infrastructure.

Transportation

Egypt's road and rail network was developed primarily to transport population and was most extensive in the densely populated areas near the Nile River (Nahr an Nil) and in the Nile Delta. Areas along the Mediterranean coast were generally served by a few paved roads or rail lines, but large areas of the Western Desert, Sinai Peninsula (Sinai), and the mountains in the east were inaccessible except by air (see fig. 5). The Nile and a system of canals in the Delta were the traditional means of transporting goods, although freight was increasingly carried by truck or rail. The entire system was unable to keep up with rapid population growth, particularly in the large urban areas, and expansion and modernization of all forms of transportation were under way.

In early 1990, Egypt had more than 49,000 kilometers of roads, of which about 15,000 kilometers were paved, 2,500 kilometers were gravel, and the remaining 31,500 kilometers were earthen. The highway system was concentrated in the Nile Valley north of Aswan and throughout the Delta; paved roads also extended along the

Mediterranean coast from the Libyan border in the west to the border with Israel. In the east, a surfaced road ran south from Suez along the Red Sea, and another connected areas along the southern coast of Sinai from Suez to the Israeli town of Elat. A well maintained route circled through several western oases and tied into the main Nile corridor of highways at Cairo in the north and Asyut in the south. Large areas of the Western Desert, the mountainous areas near the Red Sea, and the interior of the Sinai Peninsula remained without any permanent-surface roads, however.

The state-owned Egyptian Railways had more than 4,800 kilometers of track running through the populated areas of the Nile Valley and the coastal regions. Most of the track was 1.435-meter standard gauge, although 347 kilometers were 0.750-meter narrow gauge. Portions of the main route connecting Luxor with Cairo and Alexandria were double tracked and a commuter line linking Cairo with the suburb of Hulwan was electrified. Built primarily to transport people, the passenger service along the Nile was heavily used.

Less heavily traveled routes provided connections to outlying areas. A coastal route west from Alexandria to the Libyan border was being upgraded to allow for increased passenger travel. Tracks along the Mediterranean coast of Sinai, destroyed during the June 1967 War, had been repaired, and service was restored between Al Qantarah on the Suez Canal and the Israeli railroad system in the Gaza Strip. New ferry boats allowed passengers at Aswan, the southern terminus of the Egyptian Railways, to connect with the Sudanese system. A new line intended to export phosphates was under construction from Al Kharijah in the Western Desert to the port of Bur Safajah.

The southern leg of the forty-two-kilometer Cairo Metro, the first subway system in Africa or the Middle East, opened in 1987. This line, built with the cooperation of France, linked Hulwan in the south with three main downtown stations, named Sadat, Nasser, and Mubarak. In 1989 the northeast line opened, extending from downtown to the suburbs. The city planned to build an east-west route across the Nile to Giza (Al Jizah). The government hoped that the subway construction would relieve the extremely jammed streets, buses, streetcars, and trains.

Although Egypt had sixty-six airfields with paved runways, only the airports at Cairo and Alexandria handled international traffic. EgyptAir, the principal government airline, maintained an extensive international network and had domestic flights from Cairo and Alexandria to Luxor, Aswan, Abu Simbel (Abu Sunbul), and Al Ghardaqah on the Red Sea. In 1983 EgyptAir carried 1.6 million passengers. A smaller, state-owned airline, Air Sinai, provided service from Cairo to points in the Sinai Peninsula. Zas Passenger Service, the newest airline and the only one that was privately owned, had daily flights from Cairo to Aswan, Luxor, Al Gharda-qah, and points in Sinai.

Alexandria was Egypt's principal port and in the early 1990s was capable of handling 13 million metric tons of cargo yearly. Egypt's two other main ports, Port Said (Bur Said) and Suez, re-opened in 1975, after an eight-year hiatus following the June 1967 War. Realizing the importance of shipping to the economy, the government embarked on an ambitious plan in the late 1980s to build new ports and increase capacity at existing facilities, includ-ing constructing a facility capable of handling up to 20 million metric tons of cargo just west of Alexandria. Bur Safajah on the Red Sea was being developed to handle phosphate exports, and the first stage of a new port at the mouth of the Nile's eastern Damietta (Dumyat) tributary opened in 1986.

Egypt had about 3,500 kilometers of inland waterways. The Nile constituted about half of this system, and the rest was canals. Several canals in the Delta accommodated ocean-going vessels, and a canal from the Nile just north of Cairo to the Suez Canal at Ismailia (Al Ismailiyah) permitted ships to pass from the Nile to the Red Sea without entering the Mediterranean Sea. Extensive boat and ferry service on Lake Nasser moved cargo and passengers between Aswan and Sudan.

The Suez Canal was Egypt's most important waterway and one of the world's strategic links, being the shortest maritime route be-tween Europe and the Middle East, South Asia, and the Orient. Serious proposals for a canal between the Mediterranean and the Red Sea had been made as early as the fifteenth century by the Venetians, and Napoleon ordered the first survey of the region to assess a canal's feasibility in 1799. After several subsequent studies in the early nineteenth century, construction began in 1859. After ten years of construction and numerous unforeseen difficulties, the canal finally opened in 1869 (see Suez Canal, this ch.).

The canal extends 160 kilometers from Port Said on the Mediter-ranean to a point just south of Suez on the Red Sea. It can handle ships with up to sixteen meters draught; transit times through the length of the canal averaged fifteen hours. Passing occurs in con-voys with large passing bays every twenty-five kilometers to ac-commodate traffic from opposite directions. Traffic patterns have changed considerably over the last century, reflecting different global priorities: passenger transit has dropped while the move-ment of goods, especially petroleum, has increased dramatically.

Cairo metro train, the first underground system in the Middle East and in Africa
Courtesy Embassy of Egypt, Washington

It was estimated that before the 1967 Arab-Israeli War, 15 percent of the world's total sea traffic passed through the canal.

Communications

In addition to its radio and television facilities, which were well developed, Egypt had a domestic telephone system that in 1984 counted approximately 600,000 telephones, most of them located in Cairo or Alexandria (see The Political Role of the Media, ch. 4). Although improvement to the system was under way in the early 1990s, domestic service was still unreliable. The quality of international service was better, as international calls traveled over a variety of high-quality links: submarine cables to Lebanon and to southern Europe; radio-relay links with Libya and Sudan; and a ground satellite station just south of Cairo with two antennas for worldwide telephone, television, and data transmissions. Egypt was to be a focal part of the Arab Satellite (Arabsat) communications network linking the various Arab states, scheduled to be inaugurated in 1991.

The Role of Government

Muhammad Ali's era saw strong state intervention in the economy; the subsequent century witnessed a passive state and the dominance

165

of private foreign and domestic investors. Yet both failed to achieve economic development or to lift Egypt from poverty and dependence. The Gamal Abdul Nasser regime (1952–70) inherited an underdeveloped economy with great inequalities. A few rich foreigners and nationals controlled the country's wealth, from large landed estates to manufacturing and commercial firms, while the bulk of the population was poor and disenfranchised. The new regime, borrowing from the debates and programs put forward by various political parties and interests during the 1930s and World War II, undertook the task of economic restructuring (see Nasser and Arab Socialism, ch. 1).

The process transformed the state into the dominant economic agent in the country and culminated in a new economic system labeled "Arab socialism" in the National Charter issued in 1962. The government implemented a land reform program that aimed at eliminating what it referred to as a "feudalist" stratification of landholding and instead distributing land to small peasants and the landless. By 1964 a huge public sector had evolved, including all utilities, communications, and finance as well as large manufacturing enterprises, transportation, wholesale and foreign trade, some big retail stores, and construction firms. By 1973 the ratio of public to private in the composition of GDP was 58 to 42 in contrast to 15 to 85 in 1953. The government fixed the exchange rate of the Egyptian pound, began development planning, and controlled foreign trade. Nasser nationalized the Suez Canal in 1956 and in the early 1960s nationalized about 300 key enterprises owned by Egyptian nationals and foreigners. The private sector came under extensive regulation.

Because of the economic difficulties in the second half of the 1960s, which were exacerbated by the June 1967 War with Israel, the regime began to reconsider aspects of state controls and its attitude toward the private sector. A pronounced shift in orientation, however, awaited Sadat's takeover at the end of 1970.

A combination of economic problems, political considerations, and his own predilections led Sadat after the October 1973 War, to declare a new policy he dubbed *infitah* (opening or open door). The main ingredients of the policy were to relax existing government controls over the economy and bureaucratic procedures, to encourage the private sector, and to stimulate a large inflow of foreign funds.

The open-door policy succeeded in generating a large inflow of foreign funds in the form of remittances, foreign grants, and aid, especially from the United States after the signing of the Camp David Accords with Israel. The economy also grew at impressive rates. But the negative side of the policy was that the country was flooded with imports, and the government was compelled several times in the 1980s to reimpose import restrictions (see Imports; Balance of Payments and Main Sources of Foreign Exchange, this ch.). The income gap between rich and poor widened, and conspicuous consumption reappeared (see Urban Society, ch. 2).

Despite the *infitah,* the government found itself even more deeply involved in the economy. Subsidies grew from 1 percent of GDP in 1970 to 11 percent in 1979. The state's contribution to fixed investment remained high, at 87 percent in 1977. In the same year, government employment accounted for 32 percent of the total, but the increased personnel did little to clear up the bureaucratic snarls that blocked development. Private domestic and international investment went primarily to housing and trading companies. Foreign investment remained meager because of the cumbersome regulations, the bureaucracy, the political uncertainty, and insufficient incentives.

Mubarak's Gradualism?

Whereas Nasser followed a statist approach to economics and Sadat, at least in theory, tried to break away from that model through *infitah,* analysts found it harder to label Mubarak's policy. It has variously been called "gradualism," "reform by stealth," and even "indecisiveness." The president himself seemed to indicate his commitment to privatization and at the same time to the public sector, which he once described as the only cushion for the poor. Analysts attributed this state of affairs to such reasons as the personality of the president, vested public and private interests, fragmentation of the elite, the government's long-standing commitment to providing a safety net for the broad mass of the population that was its main source of legitimacy, the questionable success of the *infitah,* and the sheer weight of the bureaucracy.

Available information seemed to indicate perceptible, albeit slow, changes in the relative weights of the state and private sectors in the economy that favored the latter. For example, between FY 1983 and FY 1986 the ratio of public investment to gross investment dropped from 83 percent to 70 percent. The FY 1987–91 Five-Year Plan envisioned private sector investment to rise to 39 percent of all investment compared with 23 percent in the previous plan. In September 1982, Mubarak introduced a new investment law that offered Egyptian investors most of the privileges foreign investors had enjoyed. The draft of another new investment law was being debated in early 1989 in the People's Assembly (Majlis ash Shaab, formerly the National Assembly), but as of early 1990 no action had been taken (see Direct Foreign Investment, this ch.). This latest proposal aimed at combining and amending all the investment laws passed in the preceding fifteen years to provide more incentives for the private sector.

Private-sector investment was largely confined to the service areas and agriculture, where land was privately owned, although the state retained considerable influence through a web of price and other controls. At the end of the FY 1982–86 Five-Year Plan, 57 percent of private investment was in housing and about 11 percent in agriculture. The private sector made some inroads into the tourist industry after the mid-1980s, when privatization was actively encouraged by the minister of tourism. As of 1990, private investment had not yet become a major player in the commodity-producing sectors, apart from agriculture. Foreign direct investment was not forthcoming, and what little there was went mainly into the oil industry.

The government's control of the economy was reinforced by various financial and administrative mechanisms. Prominent among these were price controls, setting the exchange rate of the Egyptian pound, collection of public revenues and allocation of expenditures, and development planning. Since 1987, reforms loosened the government's control over these areas.

Development Planning

Planning in Egypt remained essentially a blueprint for investment, and the balance between supply and demand was adjusted through quasi-market mechanisms and fiscal and monetary policies. The emergence of Egyptian economic planning could be traced to the creation in 1952 of the Permanent Council for National Production (PCNP). The PCNP initiated partial planning by surveying the country's basic economic resources and proposing investment projects and budgets. More comprehensive planning awaited the formulation of the First Five-Year Plan (1960–65). The plan was the work of the National Planning Committee, which absorbed the PCNP and other planning affiliates. It sought progress on all economic fronts, following what economists called a balanced growth model, which required heavy investments. It favored heavy industry, electricity, irrigation, and land reclamation—a persistent pattern since then.

Achievements were mixed: GDP grew at a rate close to the target of 7 percent per annum, but other goals were not met. The lack of macroeconomic coordination and implementation mechanisms, as well as the projection of unrealistic targets are cited as reasons for this failure. Furthermore, private-sector investment, which was expected to play a key role, did not materialize, especially after the wave of nationalization in the early 1960s.

A number of subsequent plans were never implemented. It is indicative of the long hiatus in planning that the next plan was also called the First Five-Year Plan (FY 1982–86). (To avoid confusion, this plan is referred to as the 1980s First Five-Year Plan, and the earlier one as the 1960s First Five-Year Plan). It was seen as part of a long-term plan extending to the year 2002. With this plan, the Ministry of Planning began to assume major responsibility for the economic process.

The plan itself had the same thrust as that of the 1960s, emphasizing heavy industry and electricity, and suffered similar problems. Apart from improving the infrastructure, especially in the metropolitan areas, its targets, including an annual GDP growth rate of 8 percent, were seldom accomplished. Before its conclusion, Egypt was feeling the heavy burden of external debt (see Debt and Restructuring, this ch.).

The latest plan, the Second Five-Year Plan (FY 1987–91), promised continuity and change. The most prominent investment areas were those of electricity and power, industry, public utilities, irrigation, and land reclamation. It anticipated a GDP growth rate of 5.8 percent per year, which in early 1990 it was already failing to meet. Most noticeably, the plan envisaged that private-sector investment would almost double to 39 percent of the total, from 23 percent in the previous plan. The increase was predicated upon an assessment of the sector's outlays in the preceding plan, which showed outlays as often surpassing targets, and upon the incentives the government would offer. The government specified other plan objectives, such as increased productivity, rather than added capacity; a shift to exports rather than import substitution; improvement of data gathering by spreading computer usage and training census personnel; and redressing regional disparities through investment in new and previously neglected regions.

Pricing and Subsidy

Beginning in 1952 the government initiated a program of price controls that included both indirect taxation and subsidies. The aim was to reallocate resources to serve various goals ranging from industrialization to social welfare, but the effects were mixed. In agriculture, for example, the state set the price of agricultural inputs, such as fertilizers and pesticides, and crops, especially cotton and sugar. Some basic consumer commodities, especially food and energy, and services, such as education, were subsidized to make them available for the bulk of the population. In industry, public enterprises paid subsidized rates for energy but had to sell their products to consumers at fixed, low prices.

Price distortions and subsidies were magnified over time, resulting in the misallocation of resources and straining the government budget. For example, in 1987 the ratio of consumer price per kilowatt-hour of electricity to production and distribution costs was less than 0.25. This shortfall, coupled with rising consumption, contributed to a growing government deficit, which compelled the government to reconsider its pricing policy (see also Energy; Manufacturing; Agriculture, this ch.).

Exchange Rates

In 1835 Muhammad Ali introduced as a monetary reform a bimetallic currency system. As a result of the decline of the price of silver and the inflation associated with it, in 1885 the government switched to the gold standard. Subsequently, and up to 1948, the country's currency was pegged to the British pound sterling, then the dominant world currency. In 1949 authorities fixed the Egyptian pound with the International Monetary Fund (IMF—see Glossary) at the rate of £E1 = US$2.87. In May 1962 a uniform premium was applied to most foreign exchange transactions that in effect made £E1 worth US$2.30.

From the mid-1960s onward, many experts were convinced that the Egyptian pound was overvalued, adversely affecting the balance of payments by making exports less competitive and imports artificially cheaper. Needing foreign currency in the late 1960s, the government applied a premium rate of £E1 = US$1.70, which became known as the parallel market, to a range of transactions. The rate lasted until 1975.

After 1975 a complex, multiple-rate exchange system emerged, a manifestation of the *infitah* and the tinkering of Mubarak's regime. It continued in 1990 to be a subject of negotiations between the government and the IMF (see Debt and Restructuring, this ch). Three major rates dominated the system: the rates of the Central Bank, the rates of the "free" commercial banks, and the rate on the free market, all of which tended to fluctuate. The three rates were converted into a weighted average to calculate such entities as GDP and GNP in United States dollars.

The Central Bank rate had been fixed at £E1 = US$1.43 since 1979. This rate was used for oil and cotton exports, Suez Canal fees, imports of essential foodstuffs and agrochemical inputs, and a large segment of public-sector capital transactions and bilateral payment agreements. The arrangement kept the subsidy bill nominally lower than its actual costs in world market prices. The parallel market rate was institutionalized in 1987, as part of an agreement with the IMF, into a private commercial bank rate. About forty banks set the rate on a daily basis to reflect the changing value of the currency in the free market; hence the rate was partly free and partly fixed. It covered part of workers' remittances and tourist receipts, some export items, and certain private- and public-sector imports that did not fall within the Central Bank rate. The free-market rate covered part of workers' remittances as well as tourist receipts and some export receipts. It was tacitly approved by the government but remained illegal. The presence of commercial bank rates and free-market rates reflected the weakening hold of the government on the exchange system.

Public Finance

Until 1952, budgets seemed to have been drafted as much to obscure as to reveal the country's finances. Muhammad Ali apparently felt no obligation to make public the condition of the treasury, and his private expenses were not separated from those of the government. The same arbitrariness was exercised by his successors, a practice that contributed to ruinous fiscal policy. A relatively sound fiscal system was first imposed on Egypt in the 1880s by Europeans whose primary motivation was to collect debts (see Debt and Restructuring, this ch.). Upon the termination of the British protectorate in 1922, Egyptian governments once more began to manipulate budgets so as to divert public funds to private pockets. The situation lasted until the Free Officers assumed power.

Among the charges that the new regime made against the monarchy were corruption and the abuse of public money. Gaining the confidence of the population entailed the sound management of public finance. Extensive budget data have subsequently been published, permitting public scrutiny.

Until 1980 the budgetary procedures involved a complex accounting system with several budgets and special funds. Budget formats took a long time to standardize, and the fiscal year was altered several times. In July 1980, budgetary procedures were simplified and the fiscal year was fixed between July 1 and June 30, instead of the previously used calendar year.

The new budget still contained a number of special-purpose funds, such as subsidies and support for the armed forces, which were outside the main budget. Public sector companies and authorities, such as that for the Suez Canal, had their separate budgets, although they were connected to the state budget through transfers to and from the latter. The primary agencies handling the budget were the Ministry of Finance and the National Investment Bank, founded in 1980. The ministry prepared the budgets and managed all transactions, except new investments, which were the responsibility of the investment bank.

The state budget included those of the central and local governments. The central government, however, exercised great control over the budget, as was apparent from the preponderance of its revenues and expenditures relative to those of the local government (see table 4, Appendix). Examination of the budget revealed a number of characteristics and trends. State revenues as a proportion of GDP tended to remain steady, staying around one-third. They consisted primarily of tax receipts. The largest revenue items were business, consumption, and import taxes (the latter two categories were also called indirect taxes). Personal and property taxes were minuscule by comparison. An IMF international tax comparison index ranked Egypt in 1978–80 as eleventh among forty-four developing countries in the ability to collect taxes.

In addition to generating revenues, taxes could be a vital instrument in redistributing income. The impact of taxes on income distribution was little studied in Egypt. Income taxes were progressive, but because collection was not systematic, it was difficult to judge their actual impact. Also, little was known about the equity effect of indirect taxes, which made up a large part of overall revenues. These taxes were usually regressive, but subsidies may have compensated for some of the unfavorable impact.

Another aspect of the revenues was the instability of foreign exchange income. For example, the contribution of petroleum—the major source of foreign currency in the state budget apart from foreign aid—dropped (at current prices) from nearly £E1.07 billion in 1983 to £E781 million in 1988. Translated into real prices, the drop would be more dramatic. Revenues from the import tax also were tied to the volume of foreign exchange, especially to that of remittances. Because this volume was not really known, however, the effect of its fluctuations could not be meaningfully estimated (see Remittances, this ch.).

Entries for expenditures illustrated the results of the steps taken by the Mubarak government to trim spending. Wages, the predominant expenditure item, were nearly halved as a percentage of GDP in the period from 1979 to 1988. While this was positive for the state budget, it could also mean that the income of public employees declined relative to overall per capita income. The subsidy bill also fell from the levels of the 1970s and early 1980s. These two factors, among others, led to the decline of expenditures and gross deficit as a proportion of GDP. Expenditures had risen from 50 percent of GDP in 1979 to 70 percent in 1983, then dropped to 49 percent in 1988. Trends similar to those for expenditures also characterized the budget deficit.

Banking, Credit, and Inflation

Like other economic sectors, banking fell under government control during the Nasser era. Banks were nationalized and amalgamated in 1963 into four big commercial banks: the National Bank of Egypt, the Bank of Alexandria, Bank Misr, and the Bank of Cairo. They were owned and regulated by the Central Bank. Numerous special-purpose banks were also created, including those for industrial and agricultural credit, mortgages, and social security funds. They held about 9 percent of total assets of the banking system.

When Law Number 43 (of 1974) for Arab and Foreign Capital Investment and Free Zones was extended to the domestic private sector, banking boomed and its structure was altered. The number of banks grew between 1974 and 1988 from 8 to more than 100. Furthermore, banking absorbed a big chunk of investment outlays. In 1983, for example, 54 percent of the £E2.1 billion capital investment went into banking and associated financial activities. The banking sector thrived because the Central Bank allowed a highly profitable mark-up of 6 percent over fund costs of banks, pushing banking investment returns to about 70 percent, probably a higher rate of return than in any other sector. The most important change in the banking structure was the emergence of three types of establishments: private, joint venture, and, after 1984, Islamic investment companies. Nevertheless, the big four banks, partly because they had branches throughout the country, continued to handle about 60 to 70 percent of total assets.

Banks were highly liquid throughout the 1980s. Time and foreign currency deposits increased from nearly £E3.6 billion to nearly £E34 billion between 1980 and 1988, or at an annual rate of 32.4 percent (see table 5, Appendix). Part of the increase came from the revaluation of foreign currency deposits against the depreciating pound (see Exchange Rates, this ch.). The largest shares of the increase were those of time deposits and foreign currency. It was difficult to determine the savings rate, because the Central Bank did not separate time deposits from foreign currency. Some estimates showed that Egypt had a savings rate of 17 percent of GNP, one of the highest in the world. This was mostly private savings; public savings fell considerably in the 1970s and 1980s because of military expenditures, the high cost of subsidies, and the growth of foreign debt.

The generally good performance of the banking sector was marred by corruption, embezzlement, smuggling of hard currency abroad, and a stormy confrontation between the government and the Islamic investment companies. In one case in 1984, a black marketer was able, through bribery, to obtain loans worth US$3 billion and then to smuggle the funds abroad. It was estimated that in 1981 about 54 percent of hard currency deposits in private banks were placed with overseas branches or corresponding banks. The government believed there were £E40 to £E70 billion abroad, which either had flowed out of, or never flowed into, the country (see Remittances, this ch.).

Islamic investment companies came into being in 1984 and were dominated by four or five major enterprises. They grew spectacularly and accumulated deposits totaling billions of dollars. Their practices differed from those of other banks in that they offered depositors risky open-ended mutual fund certificates instead of interest, which Islamic law forbade as usury. Initially, they were able to offer depositors returns of 20 percent. The government, and many observers, accused them of being able to do so through black-market money trading and by luring depositors with "pyramid" schemes, such as the establishment of fictitious corporations, by which dividends were paid from old investments. They were also charged with smuggling large sums of hard currency abroad and with defrauding many depositors. The government issued new regulations in 1988 that required the companies to reconstitute themselves as stockholding enterprises, issue share certificates, and place deposits under official scrutiny. Whether the companies would submit to such regulations remained unclear. It was feared that if they refused and liquidated themselves instead, they could cause havoc in the financial market.

The increase in bank liquidity was reflected in the growth of credit. Banks were permitted to lend only 60 percent to 65 percent of the value of their deposits, except to the government, which could borrow at will. The value of loans grew steadily in the 1980s, increasing as much as 20.7 percent per year. Part of the increase resulted from the depreciation of the pound. The highest loans were consistently to the government, which borrowed heavily to finance its chronic deficit. Government borrowing represented from 40 percent to 60 percent of the total. Public sector enterprises, although they received direct funds from the government budget, were the second-largest borrower until the mid-1980s.

After 1985 the private sector replaced the public sector as the second largest debtor after the government. By the second half of the 1980s, private borrowers were becoming less and less able to honor their obligations. As a result, banks, especially some foreign and joint venture banks that were not allowed to deal in local currency, faced a depressed business atmosphere.

Nominal interest rates remained essentially the same through most of the 1980s. They ranged from 5 to 13 percent for deposits and 11 to 17 percent for loans. That real interest rates were consistently negative because of higher inflation rates apparently did not lead to excessive borrowing by the public sector. In spite of IMF insistence on raising interest rates, the government was reluctant to increase them by more than 1 percent to 2 percent, for fear of slowing economic growth.

The increase in the money supply probably also contributed to the rise in inflation levels. Total money supply increased between 1980 and 1988 at an annual rate of 23 percent. Major sources of this increase were government borrowing, revaluation of foreign currency holdings, and private-sector borrowing. Double-digit inflation marked the economy in the 1980s. The consumer price index rose by 336 percent between 1980 and 1988, or at an annual rate of 16 percent, about 5 to 6 percentage points higher than the rate in the 1970s. Since 1987, annual inflation rates have risen between 20 percent and 30 percent. Economists spoke of "stagflation," the combination of low growth and high inflation, as characterizing the Egyptian economy in the second half of the 1980s.

Labor

Creating jobs for a rapidly growing population has been one of the most difficult tasks that faced successive Egyptian governments. After 1976 the population grew at an annual rate of 2.9 percent. Reliable information on the occupational structure was scarce, partly because of the fast pace at which this structure changed, of the rural-urban migration, and of the dearth of in-depth studies.

Employment

Official estimates differed on employment figures. According to the Ministry of Planning, employment in the formal sector increased at the rate of 2.6 percent per year between 1976 and 1986 (the census years). The number of workers in agriculture stayed steady, at around 4.2 to 4.5 million, during the same period. Agricultural workers represented 44 percent and 37 percent of total employment at the beginning and end of the period, respectively, indicating a decline in agriculture's share. The preceding data may exaggerate the participation of labor in agriculture, which in the 1980s became only a part-time occupation for many workers as employment patterns in the countryside began to resemble those of some urban areas. Overall, the 1986 census showed that employment in rural areas was about 6.19 million, compared with 5.48 million in urban areas.

In 1976 and 1986, industry absorbed about 13 percent and 16 percent, respectively, of total employment. The annual growth rate of employment in the sector was 4.5 percent over the same period. The number of people employed over the same period fell substantially in construction and rose steadily in the services, which absorbed about 31 percent of the labor force in 1986. Employment in trade grew significantly following the initiation of Sadat's open-door policy and the import boom after 1974, and leveled off subsequently (see table 6, Appendix).

The distribution of employment also shifted along gender lines. Female participation in the labor force grew steadily, although slowly. One estimate gave the female share of total employment as 8 percent and 9.5 percent in 1976 and 1988, respectively, representing a growth rate of 4.1 percent annually (see also Family and Kinship, ch. 2).

The breakdown of public versus private employment was difficult to ascertain because official statistics did not distinguish between the two. Employment in the private sector in 1977 was more than double (6.6 million to 3.1 million) that in the public sector and was concentrated in agriculture and the services. It has been estimated that the increase in private employment accounted for more than 65 percent of overall employment growth between 1973 and 1983, suggesting that the ratio of private to public employment increased. Considering that both overall employment and government employment stagnated after 1983, the ratio also probably remained unaltered thereafter (for employment of Egyptians abroad, see Remittances, this ch.).

Information on employment in the late 1980s in the informal sector, which included small-scale manufacturing, handicrafts, personal services, retailing, and other ill-defined activities, was not available. Activities of the sector were not registered, and participants changed their jobs frequently. Most of those considered unemployed probably engaged in one or another of these activities; hence, the size of the informal sector was most likely to expand as unemployment increased at the close of the decade. Mobility between the informal and the formal sectors was effectively nonexistent; those who joined the informal sector overwhelmingly remained there.

Employment grew at a slower rate than did the population and the labor force, resulting in a worsening unemployment situation. According to official accounts, the rate of unemployment increased

Traditional craft work:
copper engraving
Courtesy Embassy of Egypt,
Washington

Mashrabiyah *woodwork*
Courtesy Embassy of Egypt,
Washington

from 2.8 percent in the period from 1975 to 1977 to about 12 percent in 1986. The figures probably understated the problem, because other informed sources put the rates at 20 percent to 25 percent in 1987 and 1988. Analysts adduced a multitude of reasons for the rapid increase in unemployment, including high population and low economic growth rates, inability of industry to absorb larger numbers of workers, high capital intensity in new industrial enterprises, the focus of the 1980s Five-Year Plan on the infrastructure, and the return of Egyptians formerly working abroad.

In addition to unemployment, economists pointed to underemployment, or disguised unemployment. There was a consensus that underemployment was rampant in the government bureaucracy, because of overstaffing and low remuneration. In 1990 the government was considering paying private-sector employers a two-year salary for every new graduate they hired. It viewed the measure as a means of checking the expansion of the bureaucracy and ameliorating the unemployment problem.

Although Egypt had a high percentage of high-school and college graduates, the country continued to face shortages in skilled labor. Probably 35 percent of civil servants and 60 percent of persons in public-sector enterprises were unskilled or illiterate. The lack of skilled labor was blamed on, among other things, the cultural bias against manual work, the theoretical nature of courses in most higher education institutions, and the emigration of skilled personnel abroad, where they received higher wages. There were complaints that the implementation of development plans was hampered by the insufficient supply of skilled labor.

Wages

The wage structure did not exhibit major shifts, except perhaps between private and public employment. The real average wage per worker throughout the economy probably increased from £E257 in 1977 to £E1,210 in 1986, or at the rate of 18.8 percent per year. In the same period, the consumer price index rose at an annual rate of about 15 percent. Not all sectors, however, exhibited increases similar to the overall average.

The highest wages in 1986 were recorded in the oil industry and finance and insurance. Oil industry workers received 4.8 times the overall average wage, and workers in finance and insurance, 2.8 times. Agricultural wages remained the lowest, about 42 percent of the overall average, similar to their 1977 ratio. Unofficial studies, however, indicated that agricultural workers' wages did not exceed 20 percent to 29 percent of the overall average. The industrial and mining wage remained steady at about 1.3 times the overall average in 1986.

Average annual pay in the private sector was said to be three times that in the government. Government employees, who lived on fixed incomes and had been given the sobriquet "the new poor," probably suffered the most from inflation, in spite of ad hoc cost-of-living raises, including an 18 percent increment in the FY 1987 budget to offset the impact of the May 1987 austerity program. The government had a limited ability to raise salaries significantly, because wages constituted the largest item of its budget (see Public Finance, this ch.). Civil service remuneration was based on a grade system that left little room for merit allowances. Public-sector enterprises were given more leeway with respect to wage determination, although most raises were intended to compensate for cost-of-living increments. Workers in public-sector enterprises, especially in industry, were unionized and were able to bargain collectively. There was little unionization among private-sector employees.

Wages alone did not tell the whole story of workers' compensation. The Nasser regime introduced a set of fringe benefits, including pension, health insurance, and paid holidays that had been practically nonexistent before. Their costs as a whole in organized urban industry amounted to 20 percent of the wages in FY 1969. No such estimates were available for the 1980s.

Agriculture

Farming in Egypt was confined to less than 3 percent of the total land area, because the country falls within arid and hyper-arid zones. About 90 percent of the agricultural area was concentrated in the Delta, and the rest fell within a narrow ribbon along the Nile between Aswan and Cairo (Upper Egypt) and a strip along the Mediterranean. The arable land was estimated by the United Nations Food and Agriculture Organization as being about 6.02 million *feddans* (1 *feddan* = 1.038 acres = .42 hectare) in 1987. This was the equivalent of about 0.12 *feddan* per capita, one of the lowest in the world, and less than Bangladesh's 0.19. The warm weather, plentiful water, and exceptionally fertile soil, however, enabled Egyptian farmers to practice double and multiple cropping, which effectively doubled the arable area (see table 7, Appendix). Nevertheless, the relative scarcity of arable land, coupled with, among other things, high population growth, made Egypt depend on external sources for about half of its food supply in the late 1980s.

In spite of Egypt's dependence on foreign food supplies and agriculture's generally poor performance over the 1980s, agriculture remained a key sector of the Egyptian economy and its future development. In 1988 it contributed more than 20 percent of GDP and about 9 percent of exports and employed more than 4 million workers, or about one-third of total employment. Its significance would be even more pronounced if account were taken of the industries from which it purchased, such as fertilizers and machinery, and those to which it sold, such as food processing and textiles.

Agricultural development responded to the ecology, state policy, technology, and shifts in the international political economy. In the early nineteenth century under Muhammad Ali, Egypt introduced long-staple cotton, which in 1990 remained a prized commodity on the world market, and initiated the long-term process of upgrading the irrigation system. The ecological conditions of the Nile Valley proved eminently suitable for cotton cultivation. Helped by a world cotton shortage arising from the American Civil War in the 1860s, Egyptian agriculture expanded rapidly. By the early 1900s, the situation had changed: additions to new arable land were slow and increasingly costly as the quality of land to be added became poorer, expansion of irrigation was not coupled with expanded drainage, and the intensive cultivation of cotton exhausted the soil and reduced its fertility. During the first half of the twentieth century, agricultural growth may have averaged less than 1 percent a year.

In addition to agriculture's declining growth rate, a social crisis ensued in the countryside, manifested in great inequalities and sporadic peasant rebellions. Reforming the conditions of agriculture fell after 1952 to the Free Officers. The new regime sought to carry out the task through extensive intervention in the sector to the point where the state was described as the silent partner; examination of state policy vis-à-vis agriculture is, therefore, a prerequisite for understanding the evolution of the sector. The state implemented land-reform programs, extended and altered the irrigation system, reclaimed new land, and regulated input and output prices as well as land use. Carrying out agricultural controls was entrusted to the rural cooperatives. The controls continued and were modified under Sadat and were gradually being relaxed under Mubarak. The results of state intervention were often mixed, both economically and socially.

The Food Gap

In 1960 Egypt was self-sufficient in almost all basic food commodities, with the exception of wheat, of which the country had a self-sufficiency ratio (domestic production in relation to consumption) of 70 percent. The self-sufficiency ratio declined dramatically

Traditional pottery making near a site visited by tourists
Courtesy Susan Becker

for most products during the 1970s and 1980s, and economists began to speak of a serious food gap in Egypt (see table 8, Appendix). Food security, in the sense of adequate production and provision of food to consumers at relatively low prices, also became a linchpin of agricultural and development policies.

Food gap data were difficult to ascertain, especially because public-sector food imports often bypassed customs. By the end of the 1980s, the self-sufficiency ratio was only around 20 percent for wheat, lentils, and edible oil. The major basic staple for which Egypt did not rely on external supply sources was rice. The country also produced most of the poultry and eggs it consumed. On the whole, it imported more than one-half of the food consumed, and food imports made up about one-quarter of total imports. Meanwhile, agricultural exports, mainly cotton, were declining, and Egypt was transformed from a net agricultural exporter to a net importer (see Foreign Trade, this ch.). Most worrisome, both financially and politically, was the wheat gap: wheat was the basic staple of the Egyptian diet. Some of the external wheat supply came in the form of aid, especially from the United States, which donated about 10 percent to 20 percent of wheat consumed. But food aid was not a secure source because of the volatility of politics, and, in any case, the share of food aid dropped as the country's consumption grew.

Moreover, food subsidies to consumers imposed severe strains on the budget deficit. The debt-ridden government faced difficulties finding creditors to finance food imports, and rising world food commodity prices may have added as much as US$600 million to wheat imports alone in 1989. Food shortages were reported in 1988 and 1989, including such basic items as tea, sugar, and oil.

The drop in food self-sufficiency was attributed, on the demand side, to the rising demand caused by high rates of population growth, the rapid rise of incomes in the 1970s, and subsidized prices, and, on the supply side, to the slow growth of agricultural yields. Egyptians consumed annually less than 110 kilograms per capita of wheat in 1960. In the 1980s, the wheat supply was enough to provide 175 to 200 kilograms per capita, compared with a world average of less than 60 to 75 kilograms per capita. Some of this went to chicken and cattle feed because the low prices made it economical for farmers and households to substitute wheat for other fodder.

The silver lining of this cloudy picture was the marked improvement in the average Egyptian diet. Daily food consumption increased from 2,307 calories per capita in the period 1961 to 1963, to 3,313 calories per capita from 1984 to 1986, and from 62.5 grams per capita of protein to 81.1 grams per capita over the same period. These averages put the Egyptian diet directly below that of developed countries. But not all segments of the population benefited to the same extent. For example, a sample survey of 6,300 urban and rural families in 1981 found that the daily per capita caloric intake was 1,500 for the lowest 17 percent and more than 3,500 for the highest 18 percent; the distribution of protein intake was even more skewed. A 1986 study done for the United Nations International Labour Organisation recommended that, to avoid further deterioration of the diet of the poor, the prices of basic staples should not be raised.

Land Ownership and Reform

On the eve of the 1952 Revolution, ownership of land was heavily concentrated in a few hands, more so than in the twenty preceding years. About 0.1 percent of owners possessed one-fifth of the land and 0.4 percent controlled one-third, in contrast to the 95 percent of small owners with only 35 percent of the land. In addition, 44 percent of all rural inhabitants were landless. Egypt as a whole was experiencing political instability, which was manifested in the countryside in the growing insecurity of property and in peasant resistance and demand for land. Although several land reform bills were presented to the Egyptian parliament, for a variety of reasons none passed.

The task of mending conditions in the countryside thus passed to the new regime, which in 1952 initiated a phased land reform program that targeted the property of the upper class of landowners, dubbed "feudalists" by the government, for distribution. The 1952 land reform law limited individual ownerships to 200 *feddans*. The beneficiaries were to be tenants, estate workers, and the poorest villagers. The law also fixed rents, set tenancy duration at a minimum of three years, and established a minimum wage.

The 1952 law was followed by others in 1961 and 1969 that aimed at deepening the reform and further reducing the maximum size of landownership. The ceiling was reduced to 100 *feddans* in 1961 and to 50 in 1969. The land reform was implemented with a reasonable measure of success, perhaps because its aim was somewhat modest. More than 700,000 *feddans* were distributed (864,500 *feddans* according to official statistics), or about 12 percent to 14 percent of the cultivated area, and more than 341,000 families, primarily tenants who presumably were more skillful at farming than other workers, received land. The pyramid of landownership was truncated at the top and widened at the base: whereas large holdings were not entirely eliminated, the share of those owning fifty *feddans* or more dropped to 15 percent, and 95 percent of owners came to control 52 percent of the land instead of the 35 percent they had owned before the reform.

Official accounts indicated that this general picture remained relatively stable in 1984, with a slight reduction in the area owned by the upper stratum of those with fifty or more *feddans*. However, the number of small owners, those with fewer than five *feddans*, increased to nearly 3.29 million in 1984 from 2.92 million in 1961, while the area they owned dropped from 3.17 million *feddans* to 2.9 million *feddans*. This suggested that land fragmentation worsened, as a result of the continual division of land among heirs in accordance with Islamic inheritance laws. Land reform laws in Egypt never had a land consolidation component as they did, for example, in Jordan. The number of landless families also rose because of population growth. Students of agrarian Egypt had not resolved satisfactorily whether the middle strata, those who owned between eleven and fifty *feddans,* shrank after the reform.

Land tenure, however, rather than landownership reflected how land was actually operated in Egypt. Land was either operated by the owner with family and/or hired labor, rented for cash, or sharecropped. The system was complex in that the same person might be engaged in several arrangements at the same time. The operational unit was called the *hiyazah* (holding); cooperatives (see below) kept records of such holdings in allocating government crop quotas and amounts of subsidized inputs. The tendency was for the number of holdings to be smaller than that of ownerships, indicating that a measure of consolidation took place in practice. Nevertheless, the average size of a holding was probably less than two *feddans* by the end of the 1970s; no figures were available subsequently.

The rapid changes that occurred in Egypt after 1975 and the increasing mechanization and intensification of agriculture led some scholars to conclude that landownership might no longer be the sole instrument of land control or wealth. Land leasing and ownership of other assets, such as tractors, were also significant factors.

To implement its agricultural policy, the government at the outset established agricultural cooperatives in rural areas. Initially, only land recipients were obligated to join; by 1962 all farmers were required to do so. The cooperatives performed several functions. They consolidated resources through distribution of inputs; preserved private incentives, such as profits; determined responsibility for planting government quotas of particular crops, such as cotton; and bought the government share of procurement crops at prices fixed by the government. The cooperatives, on the one hand, enhanced agricultural growth by encouraging farmers to use fertilizers and other inputs and to adopt the three-year crop rotation that the Ministry of Agriculture considered ecologically superior to the traditional, two-year rotation (see Cropping Patterns, Production, and Yield, this ch.). On the other hand, the cooperatives came under the control of the well-to-do farmers. There was also evidence of widespread corruption among those who managed cooperatives. Their role was downgraded under Sadat, and more prominence was given to the Principal Bank for Development and Credit. The role of the cooperatives diminished further in the 1980s as the government relaxed its controls over agriculture.

Agriculture grew at respectable rates after the land reform and the universalization of cooperatives. It was difficult, however, to tell how much of the credit should go to these two factors and how much to investments in irrigation and other inputs.

Land Reclamation and Loss

The quest to bring new land under cultivation has been a cornerstone of Egyptian agricultural policy since the 1950s. Systematic land reclamation efforts, mostly by foreigners, had begun in 1902 with the completion of the Aswan Dam. The government joined in reclamation in the 1930s, but did not entirely take over the activity until the First Five-Year Plan (1960–65). According to official figures, the total area reclaimed amounted to nearly 1.92 million *feddans* between 1952 and 1987, of which 0.82 million *feddans* were reclaimed between 1952 and 1968. Reclamation activity slowed from 1966 to 1976, then picked up again. The Second Five-Year Plan (FY 1987–91) projected agricultural land to be expanded by 627,000 *feddans,* mostly in the Delta and to the east and west of it, and in Sinai. Total reclaimable land by the year 2002 was estimated at 2.8 million *feddans;* less than 3 percent of this was first-class land, 20 percent was second class, an insignificant percent was third class, and more than 33 percent was fourth and fifth class. Public-sector companies were expected to reclaim about 427,000 *feddans,* and private companies the rest. Two major schemes were under way in early 1990: one west of the Delta that was expected to yield 434,000 *feddans* by 1993, and the second in northern Sinai that would draw water from the Nile through a tunnel under the Suez Canal.

Bringing new land under cultivation required heavy investment. Reclamation outlays in most years represented the second largest agricultural investment after irrigation. In the first half of the mid-1980s, reclamation cost about £E600 million, or about 30 percent of public investments in agriculture, and the figure was expected to rise to 35 percent in the Second Five-Year Plan (FY 1987–91). The cost per *feddan* rose continually because reclamation began with better quality soil and because of the rising costs of labor and energy required for pumping the water. The cost was estimated to reach £E2,500 to £E5,000 per *feddan* for projects in the 1990s.

Land reclamation was time-consuming and involved planning, irrigation, planting, building new settlements, and establishing agro-industries. The process often encountered natural, financial, technical, and managerial difficulties. For example, because the soil was poor, fertilizers leached; building an adequate soil structure would require planting a crop such as alfalfa that fixed nitrogen. This process was unduly time-consuming for many farmers, who opted instead to truck soil from the old lands, which often was infested with pests. As a result of these problems, only one-third of the land reclaimed by 1980 was making a profit.

The difficulties led foreign donors in the 1970s to question the wisdom of the undertaking, and most of them refrained from participating. Egyptians, however, were not deterred and challenged the economic criteria and calculation methods by which donors judged the results. They also argued that land reclamation had external benefits, such as generating employment (the share of labor costs exceeded one-half of the total), relief of crowded areas, and defense (a presence in the Sinai Peninsula) that simple economic cost-benefit analysis did not reflect.

The main beneficiaries of land reclamation in the 1960s were small peasants; in the 1970s principal beneficiaries were army personnel, families of soldiers killed in the October 1973 War, and graduates of technical schools. Of more than 1.2 million *feddans* reclaimed between 1952 and 1982, small peasants probably obtained more than 400,000 *feddans,* graduates received more than 300,000 *feddans,* and the remainder was unaccounted for. Reclaimed areas at first were run as state farms; the experiment failed, however, and the areas were given into private hands. Public companies acted as the management, providing credit and inputs, determining crop patterns, and obtaining the government's crop quotas.

While land was being added to cultivation, other land was being lost to desertification and urban and infrastructural expansion. Desertification was caused by lack of drainage and the concomitant soil salinization and water clogging. Other causes were sand movement, intensive cultivation, removal of topsoil in the Delta for brick making, and lack of effective conservation measures (see Technology, this ch.). Information on soil degradation and desertification was sketchy. One estimate put the decrease of cropland at 6.6 percent annually between 1964 and 1985; another estimated the annual decrease at 8 percent. Of the reclaimed areas, about 40 percent probably reverted to desert conditions. In addition, other areas were probably losing soil nutrients because of the decreased use of organic fertilizers, the lack of annual alluvial deposits following the construction of the Aswan High Dam, and inadequate compensation for nutrients removed from the soil by intensive cultivation.

Pricing Policy

World War II led to shortages of food supplies as a result of increased demand by Allied troops. The government enforced a system of grain deliveries, a measure that was tantamount to nationalizing the grain trade. It also compelled farmers to increase the areas devoted to grains, and it subsidized fertilizers to appease small farmers. The revolutionary regime both deepened and broadened these policy measures in accordance with its objective of industrializing the country. The new policy sought to extract a surplus from agriculture to finance industry, an approach that was then favored by economists in both East and West, and to ensure food supply at relatively low prices to keep industrial wages down.

Specifically, the policy involved the allotment of areas for particular crops, compulsory sales by farmers to the government of a fraction of the output at fixed prices, and, at the same time, a subsidy on agricultural inputs and on basic food staples for consumers.

Farmers referred to controlled crops as "government crops." The policy varied by crop type and over time to serve changing economic, political, and social objectives. The level of control over crops ranged from total control, at least in theory, to total absence of control. The pricing system directly affected the area and output of controlled crops, including cotton, clover, rice, wheat, and sugarcane. Indirectly, however, pricing had a chain reaction on all crops.

The impact of the pricing system was difficult to evaluate because of the multiplicity of other factors—such as the ecology, crop rotation, land distribution, wages, and trade and other macroeconomic policies—that shaped agricultural operations. A 1989 study by the World Bank (see Glossary) concluded that there was virtually no connection between subsidized consumer prices and producer prices—prices paid to farmers; output was affected by the latter but not by the former.

The relative impact on the various strata of the population and on rural as opposed to urban dwellers changed over time. In the 1960s, policies were generally biased toward urban consumers: the low prices for their staples were made possible by the low prices that were paid to farmers. In other words, the countryside, not the government, subsidized the city. After 1974 the government, wishing to keep the social peace and not jeopardize the newly promulgated *infitah,* raised producer prices and input subsidies to disgruntled farmers and simultaneously underwrote the bill for the consumer price subsidy. Overall, the pricing policy seemed to have removed the bias against the rural regions.

In the 1980s, the government gradually dismantled procurement quotas for practically all crops. The two major exceptions were cotton and rice. The government still bought all cotton and one-half of the rice output as it did in the 1960s. Cotton remained on the quota system because it was an important source of foreign currency; the reason for rice exemption was less clear. Furthermore, by the end of the 1980s, the state offered prices for wheat higher than world market prices to encourage expansion of the wheat area. On the distribution side, the government gradually raised the prices of all subsidized food items, including sugar, rice, and cooking oil, and exempted wheat only. The policy changes in the 1980s probably favored rural over urban areas.

Within the countryside itself, the impact probably differed according to farm size, because of cropping pattern differences. Data on the topic were extremely sketchy and contradictory. It would seem that the upper stratum owning more than ten *feddans* was affected proportionally less than the lowest segment—those owning

ian one *feddan*—because its members were able to grow more
or the uncontrolled crops, such as fruit trees, and to bend the rules
more. The raising of food prices probably had a more adverse impact on the poorer segments of the population, irrespective of where
they lived, because they spent larger proportions of their incomes
on food.

Cropping Patterns, Production, and Yield

Egyptian farmers grew a rich variety of crops, including grains,
cotton, *barsim* (clover), legumes, fruits, and vegetables, thanks to
the warm climate, plentiful water along the Nile, and exceptionally fertile soil. The country essentially has two seasons, summer and
winter; spring and fall are quite short. The climatic differences
between north and south have some impact on the geographical
distribution of crops. For example, humidity in the Delta suits long-
staple cotton. The drier, hotter climate of the south favors the planting of sugarcane, onions, and lentils. Variations in climate are not
great, however, and major crops were grown in most of the climatic zones.

The single most important change in the cropping pattern in
Egypt's modern history was the introduction of cotton during the
reign of Muhammad Ali, because it led to the transformation of
irrigation methods. Cotton requires a good deal of water in summer when the Nile water is low, and it must be harvested before
the flood season. This necessitated the regulation of the Nile flow
and brought about a shift from basin (flood) to perennial (roughly, on demand) irrigation (see Technology, this ch.).

Perennial irrigation not only made cotton growing possible, it
also permitted double and even triple cropping on most of the arable land. Furthermore, it enabled farmers to switch the crop rotation from a three- to a two-year cycle. The original three-year cycle
included clover and cotton in the first year, beans and fallow in
the second, and wheat or barley and corn in the third. The two-
year rotation consisted of clover or fallow followed by cotton, and
the second year, crops of wheat or barley and beans followed by
clover and corn. By 1890 about 40 percent of the land was put on
a two-year rotation. The biennial rotation was believed to be harsh
on the land, and the government tried to eliminate it under Nasser; farmers resorted to both rotations flexibly.

Crop areas were regulated by the government according to
manifold economic, technical, and social criteria. Comprehensive
land use planning began only in 1966, and requirements were
relaxed in 1974. But farmers responded to other imperatives as well,
and the area occupied by various crops changed over time.

The major shift since 1952 was the significant reduction of the cotton area and the parallel increase in that of clover, horticulture, and rice. Originally, the government put a maximum limit on the cotton area to avoid excess production and lower prices on the world market; the Egyptian supply of long-staple cotton affected world prices because of its large share. As the cotton area shrank, however, the government began to set minimum limits, because cotton was needed in order to obtain foreign exchange. Cheap cotton has represented an important source of foreign currency for the government and has enabled it to subsidize consumer clothing. At the same time, cotton became less profitable for the farmer than other, noncontrolled crops. The cotton area was almost halved between 1952 and 1987, thanks to the government policy requiring farmers to sell all their cotton output to the government at fixed prices that were kept below world market prices. Cotton profitability was further reduced in the late 1970s and the 1980s by rising wages, because cotton is one of the most labor intensive major crops.

Cotton output also declined, but not in the same proportion as the decline in land area, because of the rise in yields. Yields increased over the long term, although they fluctuated annually. Overall, they increased by about 50 percent between 1952 and 1980 but stagnated or actually declined in the 1980s. The continuous breeding of new varieties and the pest-control program organized by the government helped increase the yield. The reduced labor input in the 1980s, however, may have caused yields to level off or drop.

Clover occupied by far the largest area of all crops, increasing by about 500,000 *feddans* between 1952 and 1987 and comprising about one-quarter of the cropped area in the latter year. The government policy vis-à-vis clover was diametrically opposite to its cotton policy. Clover was used as animal feed, and the government protected both the crop and meat by tariffs. This protection made clover a lucrative crop for many farmers, especially as demand for livestock grew during the oil boom. Farmers, especially small farmers, also had to grow sufficient amounts of clover to feed their draft animals. On the one hand, the expansion of animal-displacing mechanization could lead to a reduction of the clover area in the future. Such an outcome would leave more room for basic staples, especially wheat. On the other hand, clover fixes soil nitrogen, and a serious reduction in its area could have an adverse impact on soil fertility. Clover production increased mainly because of the expansion of the land area; little plant breeding was undertaken, and yields remained relatively stable. The slight increase may have been caused by the additional labor time, water, and fertilizers allocated to the crop and by the farmers' delay in planting cotton, which followed clover, so as to allow an extra cutting of clover.

The wheat area remained relatively stable. The stability may be explained by the fact that although the crop was partially controlled, the government procurement price was kept close to the domestic free market price. Wheat was also the basic staple; small and medium-size farmers retained large proportions of it for subsistence or animal feed. The straw also served as animal forage in the summer. Wheat production increased over the long run, because of rising yields. Yields rose steadily, especially between 1980 and 1987; the annual growth rate increased from 5 to 6 percent in the period from 1980 to 1987. The diffusion of high-yielding varieties (HYVs) encountered many problems, however, including susceptibility of the bred varieties to rust and the shortness of their straw-producing stem. Despite these difficulties, the diffusion of HYVs expanded steadily in the 1980s. The area of HYVs increased from about 1,300 *feddans* in 1978 to more than 128,000 *feddans* in 1983.

The area planted with corn, which was introduced in Egypt in the nineteenth century, remained relatively stable. Corn was consumed by both humans and animals. It was not a controlled crop; the government, moreover, subsidized yellow corn until 1987 when it raised the price considerably, effectively cutting the subsidy. The rise in production occurred as a result of the increase in yields. The yields rose by about 40 percent after the completion of the Aswan High Dam in 1964. Perennial irrigation enabled farmers to plant corn during May or June instead of July or August. The new timing afforded the crop cooler temperatures and escape from the summer corn borer. Yields were also bolstered by the application of more water and fertilizers. Plant breeding played virtually no role in yield increases until the 1980s, but HYVs probably accounted for most of the increase in yields in the 1980s.

Rice, grown in Egypt for 1,400 years, saw its area expand sharply by about 500,000 *feddans* promptly after the Aswan High Dam was built and has hovered around 1 million *feddans* since then. Rice was an important staple, and about one-third of it was probably consumed by small farm households. It was a partially controlled crop; the government procured one-half of the output and subsidized it to consumers, but procurement prices were close to the domestic free market price. The consumer subsidy was lowered after 1987. Production increased in proportion to yields. Yields exhibited a steady upward movement as water became more available and fertilizer use increased. Yield increase was also achieved by the breeding and diffusion of new varieties. An early maturing

Sprinkler irrigation used on large farms and newly reclaimed areas
Greenhouse growing pyrethrum, used for making insecticides, in As Salihiyah
Courtesy Embassy of Egypt, Washington

variety derived from Japanese rice was diffused through about 25 percent of the area in 1984, compared with 2 percent two years previously. New varieties were being developed by the end of the decade.

One of the most significant shifts in land use was the expansion of the horticultural area. Egyptian farmers cultivated a wide array of fruits and vegetables, including tomatoes, cucumbers, potatoes, lettuce, onions, citrus, and mangoes. Vegetables were planted on more than 1 million *feddans* by 1980, and the area has stabilized since then. The most prevalent crops were tomatoes and melons, which in 1987 occupied more than 400,000 and 125,000 *feddans,* respectively. Vegetables were not a controlled crop, and demand for them grew rapidly during the oil boom. Domestic demand leveled off subsequently, and no significant export outlets had been found by 1990. Further expansion would probably depend on establishing such markets, not a simple task considering the stiff regional competition. Yields rose, but it was difficult to determine the sources of overall growth; the combination of more water and fertilizers would be a factor.

The area planted with fruits also expanded steadily and reached about 616,000 *feddans* in 1987. Fruits, like vegetables, were not a controlled crop, and demand rose with the rise in incomes after 1974. Citrus fruits and grapes, the two dominant crops, were planted on more than 200,000 and 110,000 *feddans,* respectively. Overall, agricultural crop production increased at annual rates of 2.6 percent between 1964 and 1970 and 3.5 percent between 1970 and 1980, but it stagnated in the 1980s. Yields were relatively high by the standards of developing countries. Rice yields, for example, were higher than those of Asian countries using modern, capital-intensive farming systems, save for that of the Japanese. Wheat and cotton yields were among the highest in the world. Agronomists, however, believed that these yields could be considerably enhanced, given better cultivation practices, management, and pricing policies.

Cropping patterns and crop yields differed according to farm size. The Egyptian farmer grew a variety of crops; there was little single cropping in Egypt as there was, for example, in the United States or in Asia. It is difficult to describe farming patterns in more detail, however, because the scarce information available is inconclusive and sometimes contradictory. A survey of three Delta villages in 1984 found that farmers who cultivated one *feddan* or less were more likely to grow cotton than those with holdings greater than ten *feddans,* a conclusion that contradicted findings of an earlier study. It also revealed that yield levels of different-sized farms varied by crop. For instance, wheat yields were higher on small farms, while the opposite was true for rice. The reasons were not clear, and the findings contradicted a large body of evidence from other countries that showed yields were invariably greater on small farms. There was agreement, however, that larger farms produced proportionally more fruit crops, probably because the high capital investment and the long-term commitment required would be prohibitive to small farmers, who needed more flexibility.

In addition to crops, Egypt had a relatively significant stock of animals that yielded meat, milk, and power. The country had virtually no permanent pastureland, and animals were fed clover, corn, barley, and wheat, competing with humans for the scarce land resources. Livestock populations grew slowly, although steadily, after 1952 and stabilized or even declined in some years during the 1980s. The growth before the 1980s was stimulated by a 100-percent meat protection rate, rising demand, and cheap credit to farmers. The stagnation in the 1980s possibly reflected the limited availability of feed, as is further indicated in increasing yellow corn imports, probably in response to the demand for feed. The number of water buffalo, the primary source of milk on farms and of draft power before mechanization, almost doubled to 2.5 million between 1952 and 1978. The number declined slightly in succeeding years, then climbed again to the 1978 level in 1986. The cattle stock stood at about 1.8 million in the 1980s. The numbers of both sheep and camels continued a downward trend. The number of sheep fell from close to 2 million in 1937 to fewer than 1.2 million in 1986, and the number of camels dropped from 200,000 in 1947 to 68,000 in 1986. The increasing availability of vehicles was probably an important factor in the decline of camel herds, as the beasts were used for transport. The number of pigs remained stable at 15,000; only Egyptian Coptic Christians and Christian foreigners ate pork. Poultry became an important industry in the mid-1970s; the number of chickens approached 30 million in 1986, and the number of eggs approached 4 million.

Technology

Egyptian agriculture was transformed over the last century in large measure as a result of technological change. Technological changes included the switch from basin to perennial irrigation, mechanization, application of pesticides and chemical fertilizers, breeding new seed varieties, and, in the 1980s, the beginning of the use of drip irrigation and plastic greenhouses.

At the core of these changes lay the shift from basin to perennial irrigation. Basin irrigation depended on the annual Nile flooding, usually in August and September. The floodwaters soaked the low-lying land, providing moisture for a single crop after they receded. The silt borne by the river renewed and enriched the soil. The area irrigated by the river's high waters was extended with canals and dikes.

Perennial irrigation was more complex but more rewarding. It regulated the Nile flow through the building of canals, barrages, dams, and reservoirs, which made irrigation water available throughout the year, not just at flood time. In 1990 practically all of Egypt's cropped land was under perennial irrigation. Muhammad Ali was the first to conceive of perennial irrigation as a way of increasing cotton production. He initiated barrage construction at the head of the Delta, but the barrages were not completed until the 1860s. Meanwhile, temporary canals deeper than the Nile were built, and water was lifted by pumps. The British expanded the system after their occupation of Egypt in 1882. Under their auspices, the Asyut barrages and the Aswan Dam were completed in 1902. Perennial irrigation enabled Egyptian farmers to double and even triple crop the land. It also allowed them to add biennial crop rotation to the traditional triennial rotation.

Except for a few additions, the system remained unchanged until the Aswan High Dam was built in 1964 during Nasser's presidency. The dam created Lake Nasser, which extends about 480 kilometers south behind it, cost about £E850 million, and represented approximately one-third of Egypt's gross capital formation in the mid-1960s. This control of the Nile waters made possible the reclamation of about 650,000 *feddans* and brought about 880,000 *feddans* under perennial irrigation, in addition to generating a considerable portion of Egypt's electrical power (see Energy, this ch.). It effected a shift in the cropping pattern, particularly in the cases of rice and corn. By making water more available, the system encouraged investment in other inputs and augmented crop yields. Many Egyptians were glad to have the dam during the prolonged drought that struck the areas where most of the Nile originates in the early 1980s and lasted until 1988.

The Aswan High Dam turned out to be not just an irrigation project but also a political project; it became a symbol of Egyptian nationalism and of Nasser's era, as well as a legacy of the Cold War. The edifice was built with help from the Soviet Union after the United States and Britain, in protest against the arms agreement that Nasser struck with Czechoslovakia in late 1958, rescinded an earlier assistance agreement. In response, Nasser nationalized the Suez Canal and said the revenues from the canal would be used to finance the dam. Because of the political tensions surrounding the building of the Aswan High Dam and its irrigation system, subsequent criticism of the project has sometimes mixed political considerations with technical assessment.

The structure was not without difficulties. Some problems involved miscalculations, such as the underestimation of evaporation levels from the lake. Other problems were probably unanticipated, such as the impact the absence of silt in the canals would have. Under basin irrigation, the annual flood deposited large quantities of silt that revitalized the soil. The shift to perennial irrigation kept the silt in the canals, but because they were cleared regularly, the silt was added to the soil. After the dam was built, the silt was deposited in the lake behind it. The seriousness of the impact on the soil and the reasons for it remained controversial. Another unforeseen consequence of deposit retention in Lake Nasser was the use of topsoil from the Nile Valley to make bricks for construction; formerly these had been made of silt deposits. In addition, the dam's construction led to the relocation of the Nubians, an operation whose social and economic costs were not easy to estimate.

Whereas the government invested heavily in irrigation in the 1960s, it neglected irrigation's mirror image, drainage. The failure to invest in drainage was believed to have caused tremendous water clogging and soil salinization problems that reduced soil fertility and led to loss of arable land. More than 70 percent of the land was believed to be affected by these problems. Since 1974, however, the government with international assistance has earmarked considerable funds toward drainage in both the Delta and Upper Egypt. A major tile drainage scheme was under way in 1990 in cooperation with the World Bank. In the 1980s First Five-Year Plan, tile drainage covered 1.5 million *feddans,* in addition to 0.65 million *feddans* already tiled by 1983. General drainage covered about 1.7 million *feddans* by the end of the plan's period. In other words, from 50 to 60 percent of the arable land has been provided with drainage facilities. The Second Five-Year Plan (FY 1987–91) allocated about £E1.5 billion for irrigation and drainage (see table 9, Appendix), but the allocation of funds between the two was not specified.

Although agricultural mechanization accelerated in the 1980s, it remained limited. The main agricultural tasks to undergo mechanization were plowing, threshing, and water-pumping. Planting, transplanting, weeding, and harvesting were still performed manually. Most tractors were privately owned. Large owners, who benefited from economies of scale, were more likely to own tractors. There was a widespread private rental market, however, and mechanical plowing was practically universal. The number of water pumps, which were introduced in the 1930s, grew rapidly; as in the case of tractors, they were concentrated in the hands of larger owners. The traditional *saqiyah,* the waterwheel drawn by water buffalo, did not disappear, and small farmers still found its use economical. A survey of three Delta villages in 1984 found that more than 60 percent of the less-than-one-*feddan* farms adopted pumps. The ratio increased with increased farm size, and virtually all farms above five *feddans* used pumps. Similar trends were found in pest control. Mechanical threshing was also becoming universal by the early 1980s. The government was trying to persuade farmers to adopt mechanical rice transplanting by demonstrating its effectiveness. Overall, however, mechanization remained confined to tasks that were mechanized before the 1980s and was not being adopted for new tasks.

Both the government and international donors encouraged mechanization through subsidized credit, assuming that the labor market was getting tighter and that mechanization would enhance crop yields. There was no doubt that subsidized fuel prices helped spread mechanization by reducing its costs. In the early 1980s, the labor market was tightening, and labor costs were rising as a proportion of total costs, from 25 to 33 percent in the early 1970s to between 40 and 60 percent in the early 1980s for major crops. The rise in labor costs resulted from emigration, alternative job opportunities in rural areas, and higher educational levels. But labor was not scarce everywhere, as was indicated by the persistence of seasonal labor. Some economists in the late 1980s questioned the wisdom of pushing the labor-displacing mechanization process in light of the rise in unemployment, the narrowing possibilities of emigration, and the inability of other sectors to create needed employment opportunities (see Employment, this ch.). They pointed out that the assumption that mechanization augmented yields was not supported by investigations in Egypt or by other studies.

As part of its reform program, the government wanted to increase the use of fertilizers and pesticides. To do so, it controlled the distribution of fertilizers through the cooperatives and specified the amounts allocated by region and crop. Farmers received their rations from the cooperatives on credit and were obliged to buy the minimum amount set by the government. Subsidies on the prices for inputs increased in the 1970s, and prices for these items declined in real terms over time. The cost of inputs, including pesticides and seeds, fell from an average of 25 to 33 percent in 1972 to around 15 percent for major crops in 1984. As a result, fertilizer application increased, growing steadily from about 940,000 tons in 1960 to 3.7 million tons in 1978 and to 6.3 million tons in 1986. In 1986 fertilizer application stood at roughly 0.5 ton per *feddan* of cropped area. Consumption grew sufficiently to support the domestic fertilizer industry, and domestic production supplied a considerable share of nitrogen fertilizers, which were the primary type in use.

Egyptian agriculture was susceptible to pests, thanks to the year-round cultivation and water cover. The government assumed responsibility for the task of controlling these pests and sought to develop pest-resistant varieties of many crops. The cotton crop was the main consumer of pesticides, and the government did the spraying. In the latter half of the 1980s, the government increasingly used aerial spraying.

In the 1980s Egyptian farmers began to use drip irrigation and plastic greenhouses, which had been spreading in other Arab countries since the mid-1970s. The extent of their use was minuscule by 1990; about 3,000 greenhouses were installed in reclaimed areas. Although they could potentially transform Egyptian agriculture, the technologies were highly capital-intensive, especially for the greenhouses that were often combined with drip irrigation. The government in 1990 wanted the greenhouses used only in the reclaimed areas to conserve the old land for wheat and other staples.

Energy, Mining, and Manufacturing

The industrial sector, which included energy, mining, and manufacturing, constituted the backbone of the Egyptian economy in the early 1990s. Whereas its share of GDP did not exceed 15 percent in 1952, it stood at more than 33 percent of GDP throughout the 1980s. The sector, however, did not perform as well in other respects, especially in creation of employment. In 1986 it absorbed less than 2 million persons out of a total work force of more than 12 million. The sector faced many problems that hampered its growth. Reform was required in many policy areas within and outside industry if the sector were to lift Egypt from dependence on raw material exports and other exogenous resources that supplied the major portion of foreign currency (see Balance of Payments and Main Sources of Foreign Exchange, this ch.).

Energy

Egypt produced from domestic sources practically all the energy it consumed. Electricity was generated from oil-powered stations and hydro-powered turbines on the Nile, especially those of the Aswan High Dam. Oil and, increasingly, gas and their derivatives supplied other types of energy, and in 1990 Egypt was about to begin mining coal in Sinai. Solar energy, an abundant resource, had not been tapped because technology was not sufficiently developed to enable it to compete with other energy sources.

Oil increasingly dominated the energy sector after the mid-1970s. In 1986 petroleum constituted about 90 percent of production and about 75 percent of consumption, in addition to being one of the major foreign exchange earners. The first oil well was drilled in Egypt in 1886, but commercial production began only in 1913. Output remained minimal until the 1950s, when the government entered into joint ventures with foreign oil companies for exploration and development. Through the Egyptian General Petroleum Company (EGPC), which was established in 1962, the government pushed for production expansion after the 1974 oil price rise; by 1976 Egypt had an oil trade surplus. Production continued to grow in the 1980s, from nearly 29.4 million tons per year (1 ton = 6.6 to 8 barrels depending on density) in 1981 to an average of 42.7 million tons per year between 1984 and 1988. The average was lowered somewhat by the drop in output in 1986 when oil prices plummeted from US$22 per barrel in the previous year to US$12 per barrel. Egypt became an observer member in the Organization of Petroleum Exporting Countries (OPEC) in 1984, but its production policy was dictated less by OPEC's limits than by market conditions.

About 75 percent to 80 percent of oil output in the 1980s came from the Gulf of Suez fields, and the rest from scattered sites in the Western, Arabian (or Eastern), and Sinai deserts and the Delta. The major foreign oil company in Egypt was Amoco, which operated in Egypt through its subsidiary, the Gulf of Suez Petroleum Company (Gupco). The firm produced about one-half of the country's oil output. In 1987 it leased 19,000 square kilometers in Sinai for oil exploration. Other concessions were given to companies such as Shell and the Italian Azienda Generale Italiana dei Petroli (AGIP). The drop in oil prices in 1986 compelled the EGPC to agree to production sharing based on a sliding scale tied to the price of crude oil. Egypt's recoverable reserves were put at 4.5 billion barrels or the equivalent of less than fourteen years of production at the rate of the late 1980s. At the end of the decade, however, oil companies were confident that there was more oil to be discovered in the Western Desert and possibly in Sinai. If more oil should be found, it was likely that recovery costs would increase because of the greater depths at which deposits might be located, especially offshore.

In addition to oil, important natural gas discoveries were made during the 1970s and 1980s, and gas was projected to gain greater significance in the 1990s. Natural gas, condensates, and butagas output increased steadily between 1980 and 1988, from 1.8 million tons to 6.8 million tons (oil equivalent), or at an annual rate of 18 percent. Gas was expected to be used mostly domestically, as an oil substitute, thus extending the period during which oil would be available for export. Gas reserves were estimated at about 0.28 trillion cubic meters and could be as high as 1.12 trillion cubic meters. In the Second Five-Year Plan (FY 1987–91), gas output was projected to increase by more than 76 percent over the 1986 level.

In 1989 the government signed thirty-five contracts for gas exploration and development, mainly in the Western Desert. Many of these had awaited signature for some time. The government at first thought itself capable of producing gas on its own; however, the debt pressure, the fall of oil prices, and the large investment needed for the task forced it to reconsider its position. Moreover, the government offered contracting firms better terms than previously, including payment in cash and oil (which the companies preferred) at international market prices, with a 15 percent discount for the government as a compensation for building the pipeline network. The company investing the most was Shell.

Egypt's electric power capacity grew substantially between 1952 and 1969 and leveled off for the next ten years. It increased from 21,000 megawatts in FY 1981 to 35,200 megawatts in FY 1986. Nearly 20,000 megawatts of the latter was power supplied by the Aswan Dam and the Aswan High Dam; the rest was thermal power. The country was in near panic by 1988 because the long drought in Ethiopia, where most of the Nile water originates, lowered the water in the Aswan High Dam's Lake Nasser to levels that threatened complete stoppage of the turbines. Fortunately, the rains came before this happened, but the event pointed to the danger of heavy reliance on a single source of power. The government planned to increase power capacity to 40,500 megawatts by 1992.

A final source of energy in Egypt was coal from the Magharah mines in northeastern Sinai. The mines were thought to contain 25 million tons of recoverable reserves. They were closed in the 1960s but were expected to produce 600,000 tons per year from 1989 onward. The fuel would be earmarked mainly for the 2,500-megawatt Zaafaranah complex on the Gulf of Suez.

Overall energy consumption grew rapidly after the mid-1970s. The growth was estimated at 10 to 13 percent annually beginning in the mid-1970s and throughout the 1980s. Energy consumption per capita was estimated at 588 kilograms of oil equivalent in 1987, commensurate with Egypt's status as a low-middle-income country in World Bank classification. Industry was the largest energy consumer; its share, for example, stood at 55 percent of total consumption in the 1970s and probably higher in the 1980s. The electric grid reached practically all villages by 1984.

The high growth of energy consumption was attributed to rising incomes, the price subsidy, and the building of an aluminum smelting plant. The implicit subsidy was estimated at US$3 billion in FY 1983 and at double that amount in FY 1986. In spite of two price hikes, electricity prices in 1988 were put at about 23 percent of the cost of generation, transportation, and distribution. Fuel prices were set at about 25 percent of international market prices. Both private domestic consumers and public industries received the subsidized rates.

The price issue clouded negotiations between the government and its creditors. In 1988 the World Bank held up a US$800-million loan for building power stations because of the issue. The government did, however, raise prices more than once. In 1985 prices were raised by 40 percent, on a graduated basis so as to protect low-income consumers. They were also pushed up drastically in 1986: 276 percent for fuel oil, 67 percent for kerosene, and 73 percent for diesel. The capacity of the government to raise private consumer prices to anywhere near their economic prices in the near future was limited; the government said that in 1987 the energy bill constituted about one-quarter of the average civil servant's salary.

Mining

Egypt had adequate energy sources, but only a few other natural resources. The total real value of minerals mined was about £E102 million in 1986, up from £E60 million in 1981. The chief minerals in terms of volume output were iron ore, phosphates, and salt. The quantities produced in 1986 were estimated at 2,048, 1,310, and 1,233 tons, respectively, compared with 2,139, 691, and 883 tons in 1981. In addition, minor amounts of asbestos, 313 tons, and quartz, 19 tons, were mined in 1986. Preliminary exploration in Sinai indicated the presence of zinc, tin, lead, and copper deposits.

Manufacturing

The first systematic effort in modern Egyptian history to create a manufacturing sector was undertaken during Muhammad Ali's rule in the first half of the nineteenth century. Although that attempt failed to achieve the ambitious goals set for it, the rudiments of modern manufacturing were put in place. These consisted primarily of food processing, such as rice milling and sugar refining, and textile production, including cotton ginning and production of linen and woolen fabrics. Little was accomplished, however, for about ninety years afterward, and the economy remained essentially dependent on cotton exports.

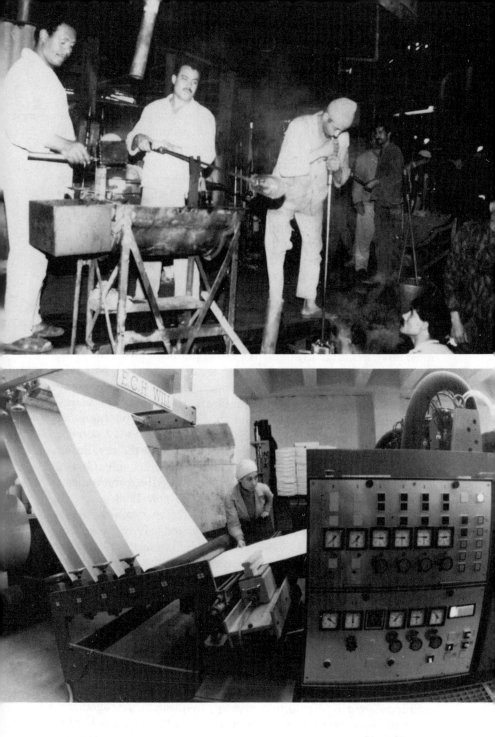

Glass blowers
Worker with textile machine
Courtesy Embassy of Egypt, Washington

The Great Depression and World War II opened up new opportunities for industrialization, and the interwar period witnessed the beginning of import-substitution industrialization. Industrial output, which rose more than 40 percent between 1939 and 1946, increased by nearly 63 percent between 1946 and 1951. A brief recession occurred between 1950 and 1953, after a post-World War II boom ended; recovery followed in 1954. The high growth rates before 1950 reflected the low base from which industrialization began; during this period, industry was still in its infancy. Industrial enterprises were overwhelmingly privately owned by Egyptian nationals, a situation that contrasted with the previous periods when foreigners dominated the sector.

Industrialization was given priority during Nasser's presidency. The government increased investment outlays and undertook a comprehensive planning effort to identify promising projects. Gradually, it took over industrial firms, and by the early 1960s, most large manufacturing firms were in public hands. From 1953 onward, growth of the manufacturing sector was uneven, with periods of high growth followed by recessions. Statistics in the manufacturing sector, as in others, were problematic and should be viewed with caution. In the ten years from FY 1953 to FY 1963, manufacturing output grew at an average rate of more than 10 percent. Whether this growth could have occurred without the revolutionary regime's drive and institutional changes is debatable. Growth slowed, however, in the late 1960s and early 1970s, even registering negative rates, especially between 1966 and 1968.

The situation shifted in the mid-1970s. The real value of manufacturing output at current prices was estimated to have grown from about £E2.1 billion in FY 1975 to £E5.3 billion in FY 1980, at an annual rate of 19.6 percent. The corresponding figures for the period from FY 1980 to FY 1985 showed an increase to £E10.1 billion, and an annual growth rate of 13.7 percent. By the end of the 1980s, however, the sector was facing difficulties and possibly experiencing a recession, thanks, among other things, to the plunge in oil prices in 1986 and to the country's accumulation of large debts.

The output increases of the 1970s resulted from investment in and improvement of the productivity of existing firms. The share of manufacturing (including mining) investment averaged from around one-fourth to one-third of total investment from 1954 up to 1989. For example, manufacturing investment was estimated at 31.3 percent in FY 1977 and 23.9 percent in FY 1986. The Second Five-Year Plan (FY 1987–91) projected that manufacturing would make up more than 26 percent of the total. It was not clear how financial difficulties would affect these projections, but the proportion of total investment to GDP was already falling by the end of the 1980s.

Manufacturing productivity improved after the slowdown between 1966 and 1974 as a result, among other factors, of capacity utilization made possible by the income-induced rise in demand. Idle capacity approximated 16 percent of output value in 1973. Subsequently, total-factor productivity of public-sector enterprises under the Ministry of Industry was calculated as having risen by 3.5 percent annually for textiles and by 8.7 percent annually for chemicals between 1973 and 1981. No similar information was readily available after that date. The growth rates of private-sector manufacturing productivity were lower, probably reflecting the higher prices the sector paid for inputs (see below). Yet in spite of the steady rise of productivity and output, the sector's share of GDP remained constant in the 1980s, because it was outperformed by other sectors.

The contribution of manufacturing to employment was also not commensurate with the funds that were allocated to it. The number of workers in manufacturing (including mining) was estimated at about 1.1 million in 1970, 1.4 million in 1980, and 1.8 million in 1986, or 12.3 percent, 12.6 percent, and 14.8 percent, respectively, of total employment. The sector's inability to increase employment substantially was usually attributed to the fact that manufacturing operations were highly capital intensive. Also, the increases in productivity and value added may have come largely from using previously underemployed labor, rather than from new hiring.

One of the central issues of Egyptian industry in the 1980s was governmental price regulation in both the production and distribution domains. In the production domain, public sector companies purchased inputs, such as energy, at subsidized prices. The private sector complained that it, in contrast, had to pay higher prices. The successive increases of energy prices and the lifting of controls on agricultural prices probably narrowed the gap between the costs of the two sectors, however.

In the distribution sphere, the government fixed the prices of a wide array of domestically manufactured consumer products, from beverages to soap to cars, at levels that many economists considered too low. Thus, the pricing system acted as a double-edged sword and affected companies differently; some benefited whereas others lost. After 1982 the government eased its price controls and permitted gradual increases so long as they did not threaten political stability. The companies themselves also resorted to various mechanisms to offset the restrictions. For example, private companies producing beverages reduced the bottle size but maintained the price, and the public car manufacturing company, An Nasr, required that buyers pay in dollars so as to have access to hard currency and avoid the continual decline of the value of the Egyptian pound. In spite of this, both private and public firms continued to lobby in 1990 for more flexibility in pricing their products.

Manufacturing exports grew slowly, falling in some years; exports started to make a strong showing only at the close of the 1980s. For example, the value of manufactured exports dropped from US$504 million in 1978 to US$373 million in 1979 and exceeded its former level only in 1983. Manufactured exports nearly doubled in value, however, between 1983 and 1987, from US$656 million to US$1.26 billion. The share of manufacturing in total exports was dwarfed by that of oil during the peak period of oil prices in the first half of the 1980s. It grew subsequently, amounting to more than 26 percent in 1988, and manufactured exports were becoming perhaps the fastest growing area of the economy in the late 1980s. The largest manufactured export item throughout was textiles because of the favorable reputation of Egyptian cotton. Textiles made up more than one-third of total manufacturing exports in the 1980s.

Industrialization was an inward-looking undertaking, intended in the first place to enhance self-reliance through import substitution. Industrial selection, therefore, often did not take into account comparative advantage. Some domestic-resource cost analyses indicated that steel and chemical industries, for example, did not enjoy comparative advantage. Comparative advantage changed over time, however, and domestic-resource costs for the steel industry, for instance, fell considerably between 1965 and 1985 as a result of experience, increasing skill of workers, discovery of better quality raw materials, and improving economies of scale. Manufacturing exports were also affected by macroeconomic factors, such as the overvalued currency and the level of domestic demand. The growth of exports in the late 1980s probably partially reflected the depreciation of the Egyptian pound that made Egyptian goods cheaper abroad. Developing a successful export market also required marketing skills and access to information that Egypt lacked after many years of bilateral trade. The Second Five-Year Plan (FY 1987–91) spoke of a shift to export-oriented rather than import-substitution industrialization.

Egyptian manufacturing was progressively diversified over the years through the introduction of new products, but food processing and textiles, which produced mostly consumer goods, remained the dominant categories. The share of food processing hovered around one-third of total manufacturing between 1975 and 1985. The share of textiles was close to that of food until 1981, when, because of the fall in cotton production, it began to shrink, reaching one-quarter in FY 1985. The proportion of engineering and electrical manufactured goods, which included such items as iron and steel, vehicles, and equipment, rose from 18 percent to nearly 24 percent between 1975 and 1985. The fourth largest category was chemicals and pharmaceuticals, with 12 to 14 percent of the total over the same period. The last two types of industry were those producing intermediate goods, that is, inputs for other industries, and capital goods; no data were available on the exact share of each of these.

Industries were located mainly in the urban governorates. Cairo and Giza accounted for about 37.5 percent of all industries and Alexandria for more than 23 percent. Industrial location was governed by factors such as population density, as in the case of food processing, and by the availability of skilled labor, as in the case of electronics in Cairo, Giza, and Alexandria, as well as in the case of furniture in Damietta and Al Qalyubiyah, north of Cairo. The concentration of industries both expressed and reinforced regional disparities as well as the skewed population distribution. In the 1980s, the government was offering tax and other incentives to investors who would locate their factories away from the metropolitan centers.

Manufacturing had become largely a public-sector activity by the early 1960s. Before 1952 the government owned a limited number of enterprises, including a petroleum refinery, the government press, and some military factories. By the late 1960s, the public sector's output value accounted for about two-thirds of the total, and it has remained more or less at that level since. The size of the public sector would be smaller if measured in terms of its share of employment, which ranged from 50 to 60 percent. The public sector was dominant in large-scale firms, especially those with more than 500 employees; its share declined in smaller-scale industries. Government firms tended to be large because investment favored such scale, the nationalized factories were selectively large, and government job guarantees in FY 1961 often led to overstaffing. The manufacturing categories in which the public sector dominated were the chemicals, pharmaceuticals, engineering, and electrical industries. The public sector also owned large textile and sugar refining factories.

The private sector dominated small-scale industries, especially those with ten workers or fewer. This group included industries devoted to food, beverages, dairy products, spinning and weaving, and various handicrafts. Some of the most profitable private-sector firms in the 1980s were those producing beverages, light tools, consumer electric products, printing, and apparel. Businesses with the highest productivity growth rates were food-processing operations, such as those producing sugar, oil, fodder, dairy products, and canned fruits and vegetables. Some analysts, therefore, anticipated that these manufacturing fields would attract private entrepreneurs in the near future, unless incentives in other areas were forthcoming.

The public-sector predominance occurred chiefly through investment. Public investment in manufacturing throughout the 1960s and 1970s ranged between 85 percent and 90 percent of total manufacturing investment. In the First Five-Year Plan (FY 1982–86), it constituted about 80 percent; in the Second Five-Year Plan (FY 1987–91), it was to be reduced to between 60 percent and 63 percent, mainly because of the government's dwindling financial resources. Public investment was to focus on finishing ongoing projects and upgrading industrial plants. Any new projects would be subject to greater technical and economic scrutiny than in the past.

Whether the private sector would be able to provide the estimated 40 percent of new investment remained to be seen. The sector faced a thicket of problems, including an unwieldy bureaucracy, a pricing system that was not based on market factors, a shortage of skilled labor, and the uncertainty of investment calculations because of the instability of the national currency. In addition, unregulated operations of investment companies drew investments from productive areas, and it was difficult to obtain foreign exchange as the pound depreciated, especially for schemes with a large import component.

The role and size of the public sector became a point of contention after the 1974 *infitah*. The struggle over the sector grew more heated as Egypt's creditors and aid donors, especially the United States through AID and the multilateral agencies, began to press the policy of privatization. Many interests were involved: business, labor, political parties, government, and the intelligentsia. The thrust of the argument for privatization was that the public sector was inefficient and that many firms were losing money and would have closed down had it not been for government "bail-out." Moreover, it was contended that by selling its companies the government could reduce its debt and its budget deficits. While admitting that some public firms had lost money, privatization opponents claimed that the number of losing firms had decreased substantially in recent years; that pricing policy was responsible for some of the losses; that profits as a whole substantially surpassed losses;

that the public sector invested in projects important for the country's welfare, in which the private sector would not be interested; that privatization would lead to the displacement of large numbers of workers; and that the public sector was the largest taxpayer in the country. Opponents of privatization argued that if the private sector wished to invest in manufacturing it could create new establishments rather than buy existing ones. They agreed, however, on the need for public-sector and other policy reforms. The proposed reforms revolved around giving the enterprises more flexibility to set their own production and price levels and employment policy, as well as introducing modern management procedures.

Foreign Trade

From 1840 to 1930, Egypt had a free trade system, based on the conventions that were imposed by the European powers. The conventions limited tariffs to 5 percent—later 8 percent—on most imported goods. This system constituted a serious obstacle to the country's industrialization. In 1930 Egyptian authorities, in their quest to establish an industrial base, were able to determine their own import duty levels, setting them at 6 to 8 percent for raw materials and up to 15 percent for manufactured goods. Another step toward more independent decision making in the foreign trade domain occurred in 1947 when the government decided to leave the sterling standard and move away from trade with Britain.

As with other aspects of the economy, foreign trade came under government control gradually in the 1950s and then decisively in 1961. From that year until Sadat's *infitah,* all exports, imports, prices, and payments were handled by public organizations and enterprises. The government, however, did not have an entirely free hand in running foreign trade. It had to operate within the constraints of domestic supply and demand and under the compromises reached with bilateral trading partners. The private sector also could still export fruit and vegetables and a few other items.

The state monopoly on trade was eased in the 1970s. Initially, private firms were permitted to import some commodities under particular conditions. Then, in 1976 the government holding company that had controlled foreign trade was abolished, and the private sector was able to trade in most goods, with a few exceptions, such as cotton. The government, especially under Mubarak, offered investment incentives that included fewer restrictions on imports and exports of commodities by the private sector. The government also extended the multirate exchange system, in part to facilitate foreign trade transactions. But the multiple exchange system created statistical difficulties, and foreign trade accounts could be more consistently examined if expressed in dollars or Special Drawing Rights (SDRs—see Glossary) of the IMF.

Exports

The composition of commodity (also called visible) exports shifted over time. Before World War II, raw cotton made up 90 percent of total export value, but by 1970 it had dropped to 45 percent. Cotton textiles, meanwhile, rose to represent 16 percent in 1970. In the 1970s and 1980s, oil and petroleum products dominated the export list, reaching about 79 percent of the total in 1985. This share, however, fell with the drop in oil prices in 1986 (see table 10, Appendix).

Non-oil exports stagnated and in some years decreased. For example, textile exports fell from US$267 million in 1979 to US$199 million in 1983. They increased after the government gave incentives to exporters, permitting them to retain their foreign-exchange earnings and to convert them at the free-market rate. The drop in the oil price in 1986, however, led to a serious decline of roughly 22 percent in the overall value of exports between 1985 and 1988. Economists advised that the country should strive to increase exports of textiles and other manufactured products in the long run, because of the volatility of raw material prices and the potential rapid depletion of some natural resources, especially oil.

Imports

Two major trends occurred in the composition of merchandise imports. The first trend was the decline in the late 1980s in the value of capital and intermediate goods (e.g., industrial and agricultural inputs). For example, the value of capital goods imports in 1988 was 14 percent less than it was in 1985. While capital goods and intermediate goods imports dropped in absolute value, however, their share of total imports grew. Nevertheless, the decline in the absolute value was likely to have an adverse impact on the development of such sectors as industry and agriculture.

The second trend was the continuous increase from 1979 to 1985 in the share of food and agriculture in the import bill. The increase began in the 1970s, as the result of a combination of population and income growth and the unsatisfactory performance of agriculture. The trend persisted through the 1980s, until food became the fourth largest item in the import bill. Not all the value of food coming into Egypt, however, appeared in foreign trade accounts, because a large proportion of the wheat came as grants, especially from the United States. Hence, the import figures seriously underestimated the value of imported foods.

Overall, merchandise imports rose rapidly after 1975, mainly because of the big rise in world oil prices, which gave Egypt more purchasing power, and because of the liberalization of import policy. In FY 1983, an election year, merchandise imports approached US$10 billion. The government subsequently reintroduced some restrictions on private-sector imports. These measures, together with the general scarcity of foreign exchange in commercial banks, led to a leveling off of imports and then to an actual decline.

The value of imports since World War II has consistently exceeded that of exports, and a chronic trade deficit has marked Egypt's foreign trade. The deficit nearly doubled between 1979 and 1985, growing at an annual rate of about 11.8 percent. The growth of the deficit slowed considerably after the 1985–86 collapse of oil prices and the concomitant drop in imports. In 1987 the deficit reached about US$4.4 billion, and it climbed again in 1988 to nearly US$5.9 billion.

Trade Partners

The revolutionary regime shifted Egypt not only politically but also economically toward the Soviet Union and Eastern Europe. Prior to 1952, Egypt's major trading partner was Britain. By 1970 the share of Egypt's exports to the Soviet Union and Eastern Europe had risen to about 60 percent of the total, climbing from about 20 percent in 1955. The share of imports from the Soviet Union and Eastern Europe during the same period increased from 7 percent to about 33 percent. Nevertheless, Western industrialized countries continued to be the major source of imports, especially of food, which Eastern Europe could not furnish. In general, trade with Eastern Europe showed a balance of payments surplus in favor of Egypt, but this surplus may have resulted partly from politically motivated subsidies.

Ending the concentration of trade with Eastern Europe was an integral element of Sadat's westward reorientation of the country. The consolidation of trade with the Organisation for Economic Cooperation and Development (OECD) continued apace under Mubarak. The United States emerged as Egypt's largest source of imports, in part because its aid to Egypt was conditioned on Egypt's purchasing American goods and services. Between 1982 and 1986, Egypt obtained from the United States an average of 16 percent of its total imports. On the average, OECD nations supplied 46 percent of imports and purchased 55 percent of Egypt's exports by 1986.

Put differently, Egyptian foreign trade was concentrated with the industrialized countries. Third World and Arab nations were minor trading partners. Some analysts argued, however, that if Egypt wished to attract foreign industrial investment it would need to obtain new markets, especially in the Arab region. The Arab market had been closed to Egypt because of Egypt's 1979 peace treaty with Israel, but the reentry of Egypt into the Arab fold in the mid-1980s might further trade with the Arab nations. A regional economic Arab Cooperation Council including Egypt, Iraq, Jordan, and the Yemen Arab Republic (North Yemen) was formed in February 1989. It set modest goals, and in the early 1990s it was unclear how this accord would fare, given the failed record of Arab integration schemes and the politicized nature of the bloc, which, for example, excluded Syria, a natural partner in regional economic cooperation.

Balance of Payments and Main Sources of Foreign Exchange

Balance of payments transactions are usually tabulated under two broad categories, current account and capital account. Current account includes visible (merchandise) trade as well as invisible items, such as tourism, shipping, and profits and other moneys earned overseas.

In Egypt the credit side of the current account balance was heavily influenced by four items: oil, the Suez Canal, tourism, and workers' remittances. Their share in total resources (GDP plus net imports) climbed to about 45 percent in the early 1980s, from 6 percent in 1974. It declined afterward but continued to be the backbone of the economy. These four items also contributed considerably more to Egypt's foreign exchange income than they did to the country's total resources. A common characteristic of these items was that they were "exogenous" resources, i.e., their productivity had little relationship to Egyptian labor, and their income was highly dependent on market and political forces beyond the control of the Egyptian government (see table 11, Appendix).

Petroleum

Petroleum played a major part in Egypt's balance of payments. For many years, it was the most important source of foreign exchange for the government and the second most important, after workers' remittances, for the economy as a whole. In addition, other exogenous sources, remittances, and Suez Canal revenues were directly and indirectly influenced by petroleum production. Its significance as a generator of foreign exchange first emerged in the 1970s. With the rise of oil prices in the world market in 1974, Egypt began to pump greater quantities of oil. Oil prices continued to increase between 1974 and 1980, when they reached about US$38 per barrel. They began to fall after 1980 until they crashed to about US$12 in 1986 but made a slight recovery after that date.

Crude oil production increased more than fivefold between 1974 and 1984, from 7.5 million tons to 38.5 million tons. Some of the increase was absorbed by domestic consumption, while the rest was exported. Crude oil exports tripled between 1976 and the first half of the 1980s. The index dropped to 70 in 1986 as the government sought to counter the decline in prices by reducing supply, hoping that the price would quickly rebound. Output was restored to previous levels in 1987. In 1988 the index fell once more to 68.

The export value of oil by domestic companies followed the trajectory of both prices and production. At current prices, it peaked in 1984 at about US$3 billion, dropped to about US$1.4 billion in 1986, and rose to about US$1.6 billion in 1988. These figures represented the Egyptian share, not that of foreign companies (the latter appeared on the credit side in export transactions, then as outflows on the debit side in net factor income entries, summing up to zero in the total current account balance).

Experts pointed out that not only were petroleum revenues unpredictable but oil was depletable. They predicted depletion could occur within twenty to thirty years or somewhat later if natural gas, which was in some respects an oil substitute, were taken into account. The exportable surplus of hydrocarbons, however, would end long before the supply was exhausted.

Suez Canal

The French played a significant role in the building of the Suez Canal, which links the Red Sea and the Mediterranean. French engineer Ferdinand de Lesseps designed and supervised the construction of the project. In addition, the French, who, like other European powers, sought to shorten the trip between Europe and Asia, funded most of the construction. Completion of the 160-kilometer long waterway, however, took ten years of excruciating and poorly compensated labor by Egyptian workers, who were drafted at the rate of 20,000 every ten months from the ranks of the peasantry.

The canal was opened to navigation in November 1869 under a concession to Britain and France scheduled to expire in 1968. Although the French were the force behind the project, Britain stood to gain the most because of its extensive possessions in Asia. In the 1870s it "bought" the shares of the Egyptian khedive. The canal remained under the control of both powers until Nasser nationalized it in 1956; it has since been operated by the Suez Canal Authority (see Abbas Hilmi, 1848–54 and Said, 1854–63, ch. 1).

The canal was closed to navigation twice in the contemporary period. The first closure was brief, coming after the Tripartite British-French-Israeli Invasion of Egypt in 1956, an invasion primarily motivated by the nationalization of the waterway. The canal was reopened in 1957. The second closure occurred after the June 1967 War with Israel and lasted until 1975, when Egypt and Israel signed the second disengagement accord.

The tonnage passing through the canal increased consistently except for a short interruption after 1985–86, when the Iran-Iraq War hampered oil production and navigation in the Persian Gulf. Between 1976 and 1983, net tonnage rose from 187 to 378, increasing at the rate of 10.5 percent annually. Traffic in the canal depended partially on oil shipments. Tanker tonnage made up more than 40 percent of total traffic in 1976, and about 36 percent of the total in 1983.

Revenues increased throughout the period, growing at an annual rate of 8.7 percent between 1979 and 1985. They were expected to reach US$1.3 billion in 1988. The canal thus emerged as the third major source of foreign exchange after workers' remittances and oil exports. Receipts from the canal continued to climb, in spite of the reduction in tonnage, partly because the canal toll was raised from 2 to 6.5 percent annually between 1981 and 1985. Also, because the toll was evaluated in SDRs of the IMF, revenues did not suffer in terms of the United States dollar value in 1986 although the dollar depreciated that year against the SDR.

Growth in canal revenues was likely to remain modest. The canal's size limited the volume of traffic that could pass through it, and if tolls were raised beyond certain limits, tankers and other vessels could opt for other routes. Economists accordingly estimated that future receipts would perhaps grow in line with world trade at the rate of 4 to 5 percent annually.

Remittances

The coincidence of the *infitah* and the upward jump in oil prices in the mid-1970s led to enormous labor emigration to the oil-producing Arab states, as well as to what became the largest source of foreign exchange: remittances. Egyptians had already been working in many of these countries but only in small numbers and usually as professionals and skilled workers. The sums they sent back home were modest; in 1970 recorded remittances were estimated at around US$30 million.

In 1986 the government estimated the number of Egyptians working abroad at 3 million. They included large numbers of unskilled workers, but there were also many skilled workers or professionals. Iraq hosted the largest number, sometimes estimated at 1 million. In part, the flow of Egyptian workers into Iraq was stimulated by its war with Iran, which required the drafting of large numbers of men of working age. The overall number of Egyptians working in Arab countries was thought to have decreased as a result of the drop in oil prices in the second half of the 1980s.

Analysts disagreed on both the amount and the actual impact of remittances on the economy. For instance, remittances were estimated in the early 1980s at between US$3 billion and US$18 billion. The reason for the discrepancy was that workers often remitted earnings to their families by hand, not through official banking channels. They were prompted to do so by the instability and official overvaluation of the Egyptian pound and by the fact that many workers were illiterate or had limited education and felt uneasy dealing with banks.

The avoidance of official routes gave rise to a hidden or invisible economy, controlled by intermediaries and money dealers who profited from exchange-rate differentials. Some analysts suggested that the presence of this economy, depending on its size, might invalidate calculations about such factors as the balance of payments, the GDP, and the government's ability to carry out particular exchange policies.

Recorded remittances fluctuated over time, not always reflecting the income of expatriate workers. According to some estimates, remittances fell to about US$1.94 billion in 1982, from about US$2.86 billion in 1981. The decline was probably caused by the uncertainty generated by the assassination of Sadat in 1981. Remittances recovered subsequently and in 1984 reached approximately US$3.93 billion, a record high. The combination of instability in the Persian Gulf and the collapse in oil prices caused remittances to fall again; in 1988 they stood at about US$3.39 billion.

Egyptian analysts and policy makers believed that a large pool of savings kept by migrant Egyptian workers and others either flowed abroad or never flowed home and that it vastly exceeded remittances. The sums they cited ranged from US$40 billion to US$70 billion. Attracting these funds to improve the balance of payments position might require improving the investment atmosphere and opportunities, raising interest rates, and simplifying exchange transactions. As one incentive, the government in 1986 offered tax exemptions on bonds it intended to sell in foreign exchange.

The future of remittances depended on many factors. In Iraq stirrings surfaced in late 1989 against the presence of large numbers of Egyptian workers. The events prompted high-level contacts between the two governments and the intervention of the Iraqi president to reassure the workers. In addition, because the construction boom in the Persian Gulf had ended, the Gulf countries, for social, political, and economic reasons, would hesitate to welcome many newcomers. According to one estimate, remittances could perhaps grow at a real annual rate of 1 to 2 percent after 1990.

Tourism

As the site of one of the oldest civilizations, Egypt held many unique attractions for tourists. In addition, the country has some of the finest beaches on the Mediterranean, modern cities, an attractive climate, moderate prices for services, and a reputation for hospitality to foreign visitors.

Whereas tourism was not an exogenous resource to the extent that oil or remittances were, it had been affected by politics and external developments in which Egypt had little say. The number of tourists reached a peak of 578,734 in 1966 before the June 1967 War. The number dropped sharply for several years afterward and then began to rebound. The figure in 1972 was 541,000, and it increased steadily thereafter. The only exception was in 1986 when the number fell to about 1.3 million from about 1.5 million in the preceding year. The decrease was attributed to the hijacking of the Italian liner, the *Achille Lauro,* toward the end of 1985; security police riots in Cairo in February 1986; and the United States air raid on Libya in April 1986. The growth rate in numbers of tourists arriving in Egypt between 1975 and 1985 was a respectable 6.7 percent per annum. In 1988 the minister of tourism anticipated that about 2 million tourists would visit Egypt that year.

The nationality composition of tourists fluctuated. The main groups were Arabs and OECD nationals. Between 1975 and 1980, the major increase came from OECD countries. Sadat's separate peace accord with Israel discouraged Arabs from spending time in Egypt. Between 1980 and 1984, the annual growth rate of tourists from both groups was approximately the same, 5.5 percent. Since 1978 the number of Arabs has averaged 80 percent of the number of OECD citizens.

Tourism earnings were difficult to trace because earnings fluctuated while the number of tourists kept rising. Economic and statistical reasons accounted for these difficulties. After 1982, income from EgyptAir, the national airline, was moved to nonfactor services, causing tourist receipts to seem lower in 1983 and 1985 than they were in 1979. Furthermore, the increase in the number of average tourist nights spent in the country did not necessarily correspond to the number of visitors. The value of the Egyptian pound also continued to depreciate, dropping by about 30 percent against the dollar in 1986 and adding another discrepancy to the accounts. Finally, tourists preferred to exchange their money in the free market, with its higher exchange rate, rather than in the official market. As a result, the records did not reflect actual income, which was believed to be much higher. Tourism income had risen fairly steadily, and was forecast to reach about £E1.17 billion in 1988, placing it next to the Suez Canal as a source of foreign exchange, or fourth among exogenous resources.

In the 1980s, the government initiated various measures to attract tourists and encourage them to use official exchange channels. It intensified marketing efforts and added tourist offices to its diplomatic missions in key countries. Tourist sites were developed in such places as the Sinai Desert. Since 1985 the minister of tourism had sought to privatize hotel management and to improve EgyptAir services. Encouraged by both the potential rise in tourism and privatization, several foreign companies won large contracts to build new and varied types of tourist centers. For example, in 1990 an Algerian investment group was completing a US$120-million development project on 1.2 million square meters at Al Ghardaqah on the Red Sea. In the late 1980s, applications for permits to establish floating hotels on the Nile surged.

To lure tourists into exchanging their foreign currency through its banks, the government lowered the official tourist value of the Egyptian pound vis-à-vis the United States dollar. For example, the tourist rate rose from £E0.83 = US$1 to £E1.12 to the United States dollar in March 1984. In January 1985 it went to a flexible rate that stood at £E1.25 to the United States dollar in the first half of 1986. Analysts generally thought that the tourist sector, given appropriate policies and incentives, could sustain rapid growth.

In sum, although petroleum, remittances, the Suez Canal, and tourism were crucial resources to Egypt's economy and balance of payments, their long-term potential was limited. Oil prices fluctuated, and Egypt could deplete its exportable oil within twenty to thirty years. The growth of remittances and Suez Canal revenues was likely to be moderate, and although tourism could achieve high growth rates, it had a ceiling. Economists, therefore, stressed that sustained economic growth and development required the expansion and increasing productivity of the country's own commodity-producing sectors, especially industry and agriculture.

Current Account Balance

The current account balance for more than forty years—except during the two depressions of 1968 and 1973 following war with Israel—was in the red, as was the merchandise trade balance, but the current account deficit was smaller. The accumulated deficit from 1950 through 1967 came to £E993 million. The first serious jump, however, took place in 1975, when the current deficit rose to US$1.56 billion from US$0.36 billion the previous year, reflecting an increase in imports because of the oil boom. Between 1982 and 1988, the current deficit averaged US$3.6 billion, or about 9 percent of GDP. This occurred in spite of the steady rise in income from exogenous resources. There were years in which the deficit was lowered because of the large inflow of foreign currency, such as in 1983 when it fell to about US$2.4 billion from US$3.1 the previous year, thanks to a rebound in remittances, but the overall trend was for it to rise. In 1985 the current account deficit soared to about US$4.7 billion or 14.3 percent of GDP. This deficit increase compelled the government to impose restrictions on imports by temporarily suspending the own-exchange (that is, foreign exchange supplied directly by the importer rather than through commercial banks; much foreign exchange in Egypt circulated outside formal channels) import system to ameliorate the deficit. In part as a result of policy and in part because of the lack of foreign exchange, imports were subsequently reduced, and the deficit improved. In 1988 it was slightly more than one-half of the 1985 deficit and the equivalent of 6.6 percent of GDP. Much pressure was being exerted on the government, especially because of the tremendous accumulated debt, to lower the annual deficit further, if not to shift to a positive balance of payments (see Debt and Restructuring, this ch.).

Capital Account and Capital Grants

The current account deficit was financed up to the late 1950s from previously accumulated reserves. As the reserves diminished, Egypt turned to external financing, which became the principal mechanism for covering the deficit. Some of the external financing sources were nondebt-creating, such as grants and foreign direct investment, whereas others, primarily loans, led eventually to heavy indebtedness. These items appeared in the capital account section of balance of payments transactions.

In the late 1950s and the 1960s, capital grants came primarily from Eastern Europe; no reliable estimates exist for the period, because grants were often in kind and the currencies of these countries were not convertible. After the October 1973 War, Egypt began to receive large grants, mainly from Arab countries, to help with reconstruction and to compensate for the drain on the economy caused by years of military preparedness. In 1974 the grants were estimated at US$1.4 billion, but they declined in succeeding years to less than US$100 million in 1979. Between 1973 and 1976, annual Arab grants averaged roughly US$900 million. Sources of capital grants altered after the signing of the peace accords with Israel in 1979, with OECD members, especially the United States, replacing Arab nations. Some data indicated that between 1982 and 1988 official capital grants averaged US$903 million per annum. Other estimates suggested larger amounts.

Military grants often supplemented economic grants. From the United States alone, military aid averaged US$1.28 billion per year in the period 1984 to 1988 (see Foreign Military Assistance, ch. 5). The United States probably granted Egypt over the same period US$953 million per year for civilian purposes, or about three-quarters as much as it gave for the military.

Capital grants were primary among nondebt-creating sources of external finance, but their future was unpredictable and would be influenced by political factors as well as by Egypt's economic performance. Whereas donor governments viewed grants as assistance, Egyptians tended to see them as mutual aid from which donor governments reaped political, strategic, and other dividends. It was unlikely, many experts believed, that the United States would increase its grants, given its own huge budget deficit, irrespective of political developments.

Direct Foreign Investment

Foreign investment in Egypt dated from the nineteenth century. Relatively large amounts were invested in the 1890s, with investment peaking in 1907. Between 1903 and 1907, for example, the cumulative private direct investment may have amounted to £E8.6 million. The two world wars and the depression interrupted the process, and little foreign direct investment occurred during the nationalist economic phase under Nasser. Whatever investments took place then were essentially in the oil sector. In 1974 they amounted to as little as US$87 million.

The picture changed in the following years, in part as a result of a new policy, embodied in Law Number 43 (of 1974) for Arab and Foreign Capital Investment and Free Zones. The law sought to provide incentives to investors in many sectors, including industry, land reclamation, tourism, and banking. It offered concessions on imports, profit transfers, and taxation, as well as guarantees against nationalization, to which foreign investors were particularly sensitive because of the sweeping nationalization that occurred under Nasser. The law gave priority to projects that promised to generate foreign exchange and had advanced technology components. A special body, the General Authority for Investment and Free Zones, was founded to supervise foreign investment.

Both Arab governments and private investors responded quickly. They initiated separate joint venture projects with Egypt, both in the military and civilian, especially banking, sectors. Arab and other foreign business concerns were located in the free zones near Alexandria, Cairo, Port Said, and Suez. Arab investments, however, declined severely after the 1979 Camp David Accords. Foreign investment continued to go mainly into oil production and exploration. By 1981 net foreign direct investment was estimated at about US$1.7 billion, a tenfold nominal increase from the US$0.17 billion of 1970.

The picture stayed basically the same in the 1980s. Oil and banking absorbed the bulk of investments. In the late 1980s, however, tourism attracted a number of foreign investment groups, and in 1989 a few major joint venture projects were under way with foreign firms, including a digital telephone exchange plant with Siemens, West Germany, a tire factory with Pielli, Italy, and a baby-food processing plant with Nestlé, Switzerland. According to some estimates, the average annual foreign direct investment amounted to about US$255 million between 1981 and 1988; according to others, it was considerably higher. The difference in estimates resulted from frequent lack of distinction in Egyptian official statistics between Egyptian and Arab investment.

As of early 1990, no action had resulted from parliamentary debate on a draft investment law that would synthesize and amend all previous laws. The new draft law also proposed modifications in profit transfers, making them use the highest exchange rate on the date of transfer. The draft law gave companies flexibility in distributing their capital between external and domestic sources and left it to the discretion of the prime minister to rule in specific situations. It also exempted foreign investors from administered prices and the setting of profit margins; the cabinet would have the right to intervene in special cases. In the view of some observers and business people, the new law of itself was insufficient to attract investments; a more significant factor would be the easing of bureaucratic hurdles.

Loans

Egypt's borrowing began on a modest scale in the early 1960s

Welder at work
Courtesy Embassy of Egypt, Washington

after the depletion of reserves. In 1970 long- and medium-term public loans (no figures were available for private loans) totaled US$397 million. Lending to Egypt rose rapidly after the mid-1970s. Up to 1978, loans came largely from Arab oil-producing states, which lent an average of more than US$950 million annually from 1975 to 1978. During this period, the government was also receiving loan commitments from OECD countries and multilateral organizations. These exceeded US$1 billion in 1976. By 1977 loans reached more than US$2.3 billion. (Unless otherwise stated, all loan figures in this section are equal to disbursements minus repayments and include public as well as private lending.) The figure fell to US$1.7 billion in 1979, because of the cessation of Arab aid. Since then most lending has been underwritten by OECD nations. Between 1979 and 1985, Egyptian borrowing ranged annually between less than US$1.4 billion and slightly more than US$1.8 billion, with an average of more than US$1.6 billion. Until 1985 external borrowing was thus the chief source for financing the current account deficit.

The situation was dramatically reversed in 1986, and annual loans in that year and in 1987 amounted to less than US$0.70 billion. This coincided with lower oil income, and was the opposite of what happened in the mid-1970s when oil prices as well as lending rose. By 1986 Egypt faced serious debt problems and was negotiating with the IMF and other creditors on debt payments and rescheduling as well as on economic restructuring. The creditors were reluctant to continue providing credit unless an agreement were reached with Egypt on these questions.

Interest rates on foreign economic loans fluctuated. The nominal rates for civilian loans ranged between 5 percent and 6.5 percent, averaging 5.6 between 1981 and 1988. The real rates were much lower, amounting to an average of 0.4 percent over the same period. Interest on military loans was, by agreement, fixed at 12 percent to 14 percent.

Repayments increased steadily. From US$764 million in 1977, they rose to their highest level of about US$1.54 billion in 1985 at the rate of 9.1 percent per annum. This meant that the actual amount of funds injected into the economy did not rise in proportion to the increase in loan commitments.

When all the preceding sources of external finance—grants, direct investment, and loans—began to fall to levels insufficient to cover the current deficit, Egypt resorted to incurring arrears in payments to official creditors. The arrears were difficult to document because of the lack of data. According to one estimate, the arrears may have risen from US$131 million in 1981 to US$739 million in 1986. They fell after the May 1987 IMF agreement and the subsequent arrangement with the Paris Club (the informal name for a consortium of eighteen Western creditor countries) to reschedule Egypt's debts.

In addition to loans, Egypt was also able to obtain short-term, high-interest credits from firms that supplied commodities and services. Egypt had resorted to these credits since the mid-1970s when imports soared. Disbursements rose steadily and between 1983 and 1985 averaged about US$1.86 billion annually, ranking higher than economic grants. Repayments, however, did not keep up with disbursements and in the late 1980s fell into arrears. Repayment delays of up to eighteen months and more for supplier credits were reported. Because of these delays and the mounting overall debt, until the signing of the agreement with the IMF in May 1987, Western credit agencies were hesitant to offer cover.

Debt and Restructuring

Ironically, in 1990 Egypt found itself heavily indebted as it had been more than a century previously. The practice of external borrowing began with Muhammad Ali, who sought funds to finance, among other things, his ambitious development schemes. Significant debt began to build up only in the second half of the nineteenth century, coinciding with the rise of the export economy. In the 1880s, Egypt was unable to repay its debts, and Britain, the main lender, used this an excuse to occupy Egypt for the next half century. The debt was economically disastrous for Egypt because it consumed all the surpluses accumulated during and after World War I, which could otherwise have been invested in economic development.

Egypt emerged from World II, as from World War I, with substantial reserves resulting from the goods and services it supplied to the Allies and its lower imports because of worldwide shortages. The reserves were kept under British control until the end of the 1940s, when Egypt started to use them to finance imports. They practically disappeared in the late 1950s, and Egypt again began external borrowing. Still, by the late 1960s debt was not substantial.

Only with the increased borrowing under Sadat and Mubarak did debt become the nagging problem it was in 1990. Debt information was incomplete, and estimates of it varied. Variations resulted from the multiplicity of creditors, the private nature of some arrangements, and the exclusion of debt data from official statistics or the showing of lower figures in government budgets. Publicly guaranteed, long-term debt climbed from more than US$3 billion in 1974 to about US$15.8 billion in 1980, or more than fivefold. During the same period, real GDP (at 1980 prices) less than doubled, and exports rose threefold. If short-term debts were considered, the gap between the growth of debt and that of GDP and exports would be greater (see table 12, Appendix).

In 1988 total external debt was expected to reach US$46 billion or about double the amount in 1981. As a result, civilian debt came close to GDP in 1987 and was forecast to surpass it in 1988. Thus, Egypt, like many developing countries, entered the final decade of the twentieth century with burdensome debt.

Most of Egypt's debt was owed to other governments or guaranteed by them, especially when military debt was taken into account. For example, in 1987 debt to private creditors was about 21 percent of the civilian total, and debt to multilateral organizations was about 17 percent of the civilian total. Prior to the peace treaty with Israel in 1979, the largest creditors were Arab countries; since 1979 the Arabs were replaced by OECD members. In 1987 Egypt owed US$10.1 billion to the United States. Of this about US$4.6 billion, or about 23 percent of Egypt's combined debt, was military debt. Within Egypt itself, the largest debtor was the government and the public sector generally. For example, public debt, apart from the military made up about 78 percent of the total; the rest was borne by private enterprises and banks.

As debt increased, Egypt became vulnerable to pressure from creditors who wanted it to repay the debts and restructure the economy. During the 1980s, prolonged, tug-of-war-like negotiations occurred between Egypt and various creditors represented by the IMF and the Paris Club.

Before concluding agreements with other creditors, Egypt had first to win the endorsement of the IMF on the soundness of its financial position. In return for a financial package to ease repayment terms, the IMF policy requires that a government undertake a macroeconomic stabilization program, known as the IMF conditionality, that touches basically on every aspect of the economy. The program consists of two interlinked components, one external and the other internal. The external component applies to the reduction of the trade deficit, in Egypt's case through the devaluation of the Egyptian pound to make exports more competitive. The internal component is far-reaching and aimed at minimizing the role of the state in the economic process. It calls for, among other things, appreciable cuts in the budget deficit, elimination of price controls, and the closing of inefficient public enterprises with the ultimate goal of privatization.

Although there was a growing consensus in Egypt on the need for reform, many interests conflicted and experts differed on the best course. Because of their colonial experience, Egyptians were generally sensitive to having their economic policies dictated by outsiders. As far back as 1966, Nasser rejected on nationalist grounds an IMF "background stabilization program" much more modest than subsequent ones.

The demand for cutting the budget, which would have entailed mainly reducing the subsidies of basic commodities, was officially resisted as politically destabilizing. Within the cabinet itself, there were different voices. For instance, while the minister of agriculture supported dismantling price controls so as to raise the incomes of his constituency, the farmers, the minister of food and supply opposed dismantling them on the ground that lack of such controls would hurt his main constituency, urban consumers.

The fear of political instability was not the only reason for resistance to restructuring. Politically significant Egyptian groups, including public-sector employees, some leading intellectuals, and ruling party functionaries, viewed with suspicion attempts to weaken drastically the role of government and the public sector. Egypt, they said, had a weak state for more than a century and free trade for an even longer period, yet the country remained underdeveloped. They pointed to the wasteful economic behavior of the private sector during the *infitah* and the way this policy widened the income gap between rich and poor. Finally, they referred to the successes of Japan, the Republic of Korea (South Korea), and Taiwan, where strong partnerships between the state and the private sector propelled economic growth.

Private-sector entrepreneurs themselves were little interested in certain aspects of reform. They considered state intervention necessary in such areas as tariff protection against foreign competition, stabilization of input prices, increased savings, and investment in infrastructure. Although they wanted to see less red tape and the simplification of investment procedures, they were able to turn market restrictions to their advantage through manipulation. Their relationship to the public sector was often more symbiotic than adversarial. For example, in the mid-1980s the poultry industry—which had grown astronomically since the mid-1970s as a result of private investment by entrepreneurs, government officials, and military officers—wanted the government to ban egg imports and to limit new farms and emergency low-interest loans to offset what it saw as market saturation. Poultry farm owners resorted to a massive slaughter of 4 to 5 million chickens to dramatize their demand.

In spite of these constraints and because of the economic difficulties and mounting debt and deficit, the government since the mid-1980s had no alternative but to come to terms with the IMF and its creditors. In the negotiations, disputes often centered on the pace and scope of restructuring, not on the need for it. Finally, after intense bargaining and pressure on the IMF by the United States, which was concerned about the impact of the Cairo security police riots in February 1986, an agreement was signed in May 1987. The agreement was considered lenient by IMF standards, although not by the Egyptians. For example, it involved Egypt's agreement to lower its budget deficit to 10 percent of GDP, a ceiling that the government found arbitrary. The IMF allowed Egypt to keep the official rate of £E1 = US$1.43 for pricing oil, cotton exports, and rice but stressed the need for eventually eliminating the multiple exchange-rate system.

In return, the government was to obtain SDR250 million, or about US$327 million, much less than the US$1.5 billion standby credit Egypt had applied for in 1986. More important, the agreement paved the way for an arrangement with Paris Club creditors to alleviate Egypt's debt. Toward the end of May, the Paris Club approved a ten-year rescheduling, with a five-year grace period. The arrangement also covered arrears outstanding at the end of 1986, in addition to interest and principal repayments due between the beginning of 1987 and June 1988 on all guaranteed debts contracted before the end of October 1987.

The government subsequently implemented many changes, including raising energy and food prices, setting higher and market-determined prices for farm production with the exception of cotton, and trimming budget and trade deficits (see The Role of Government, this ch.). The IMF and Paris Club members, however, were not satisfied with the pace of reform and expressed their concern that Egypt was delivering much less than it had promised. Egypt wanted to extend the period of arrears and payments on publicly guaranteed loans to the end of 1989 instead of June 1988 as was stipulated in the 1987 agreement with the Paris Club. A new round of negotiations began, and an accord with the IMF was anticipated in July 1989. The deadline passed inconclusively, and the marathon bargaining was continuing in early 1990.

Irrespective of the conclusion of these negotiations, Egypt entered the closing decade of the twentieth century facing an enormous economic challenge. Economic growth was unable to keep up with that of population, and inflation was eating into the modest income of many Egyptians. The government introduced uneven reforms in pricing and other policies, but more effective reform was needed, especially in the stagnant and outmoded industrial field and the notoriously inefficient bureaucracy. Although Egyptian agricultural yields were respectable, they could be enhanced substantially. Revenues from oil, the Suez Canal, workers' remittances, and tourism—the main sources of foreign currency—were expected to grow, if at all, at low rates. Egypt had to propel its agriculture and industry forward if it were to achieve a self-sustaining growth and feed and create jobs for a rapidly growing population.

*　　*　　*

Basic data on the Egyptian economy are available in the English-language editions of the annual *Statistical Yearbook* of the Central Agency for Public Mobilization and Statistics and the more carefully produced quarterly *Economic Bulletin* of the National Bank of Egypt. The World Bank's wealth of statistics on the structure of the economy are summed up in the annual *World Tables*. The International Monetary Fund's publication, *Directions of International Trade,* is a good source for trade statistics, as is its *International Financial Statistics* for finance. Information on agriculture is available in the *Production Yearbook* of the United Nations Food and Agriculture Organization.

Two of the most concise and insightful sources on the contemporary Egyptian economy are *The Egyptian Economy, 1952-72* by

Robert Mabro, and *Foreign Trade Regimes and Economic Development* by Bent Hansen and Karim Nashashibi. The latter covers the post-World War II period until the late 1960s. Mahmoud Abdel-Fadil's *The Political Economy of Nasserism* gives a rigorous analysis of the economy, especially employment, during Nasser's presidency. Unfortunately, no similar sources exist for the Sadat or Mubarak periods. *The Egypt of Nasser and Sadat* by John Waterbury is considered the basic text for the 1952–80 political economy.

Several books offer treatment of specific sectors. Industrialization is discussed insightfully in *The Industrialization of Egypt, 1939–73* by Robert Mabro and Samir Radwan. A synthesis of the modern history of Egyptian agriculture is given in *Egypt's Agricultural Development, 1800–1980* by Alan Richards. The World Bank issues occasional policy-oriented studies; one of the most comprehensive is *Trade, Exchange Rate, and Agricultural Pricing Policies in Egypt* (2 volumes) by Jean-Jacques Dethier. This work also offers a wealth of statistics for the period between 1960 and 1985.

Journalistic updates on the state of the Egyptian economy are available in special reports issued by three London-based periodicals: Economist Intelligence Unit's *Country Report: Egypt; Financial Times;* and *Middle East Economic Digest.* Finally, the Egyptian Arabic language weekly, *Al Ahram al Iqtisadi* is an indispensable source on the economic debate within Egypt itself. (For further information and complete citations, see Bibliography.)

Chapter 4. Government and Politics

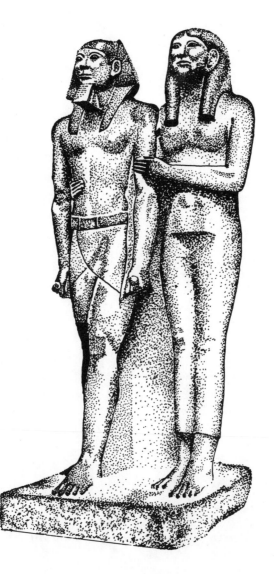

Mycerinus (Menkure) and queen, Giza, ca. 2500 B.C.

THE MODERN EGYPTIAN STATE is the product of a historically rooted political culture and of the state-building efforts of its founding leaders, Gamal Abdul Nasser and Anwar as Sadat. Egypt has been governed by powerful centralized rule since ancient times, when the management of irrigated agriculture gave rise to the pharaohs, absolute god-kings. This experience produced a propensity toward authoritarian government that has persisted into modern times. Although the contemporary Egyptian state remained in essence authoritarian, such rule was not accepted unconditionally. Its legitimacy depended on adherence to certain public expectations. Egypt's centuries of subordination to foreign rule, its long struggle for independence, and its continuing dependency on other countries generated a powerful nationalism that made national legitimacy crucial to the acceptance of the authoritarian state. Moreover, after the Arab invasion in the seventh century A.D., many expected the state to rule on behalf of the true faith and community and according to Islamic norms of justice; as a result, the state sought to legitimize itself in Islamic terms. Finally, in more recent years, the spread of political consciousness put rulers under growing pressure to accommodate demands for participation.

The 1952 Revolution against the traditional monarchy, led by Gamal Abdul Nasser's group of nationalist-reformist Free Officers, gave birth to the contemporary republic. Nasser forged the new state, suppressing the rudiments of pluralism and creating a president-dominated, military-led authoritarian bureaucratic regime with a single party and a subordinated parliament, press, and judiciary. Nasser's charismatic leadership and the populist achievements of the 1952 Revolution—particularly land reform, social welfare, and a nationalist foreign policy—legitimized the new regime. Nasser gave the state a broader base of support than it had hitherto enjoyed, a base that embraced a populist coalition of the army, the bureaucracy, the middle class, and the masses.

Nasser's successor, Anwar as Sadat, adapted the state to a "post-populist" era. The major vulnerabilities of the Nasser regime were its lack of strong support among the Egyptian landed and business classes and, after the 1967 defeat by Israel, its alienation from the United States, the superpower whose support was needed to resolve the conflict with Israel. Although Sadat assumed power as Nasser's vice president and was a veteran of the revolution, he soon reoriented the policies of the state to reconcile it with the need for support from the Egyptian middle class and for a good relationship with the United States. While retaining the essential structures of the Nasserist state, he carried out a limited political liberalization and an economic and diplomatic *infitah* (opening or open door; see Glossary) to the West. This shifted the state's base of support from reliance on Nasser's populist coalition to a reliance on the landed and business classes internally and an American alliance externally. The political system remained essentially authoritarian but with a greater tolerance of political pluralism than under Nasser; thus, parliament, opposition parties, interest groups, and the press all enjoyed greater, though still limited, freedom.

Husni Mubarak, Sadat's vice president, inherited power on the basis of constitutional legitimacy at Sadat's death. He consolidated Sadat's limited political liberalization and maintained the major lines of Sadat's policies while trying to overcome some of their excesses and costs.

As revolutionary legitimacy was eclipsed by the passage of time, the legal powers enshrined in the Constitution of 1971 became a more important source of legitimacy. The Constitution, a descendant of the 1956 constitution drafted under Nasser, largely reinforced authoritarian traditions. It established a mixed presidential-parliamentary-cabinet system, but the president is constitutionally the center of power. The president is supreme commander, declares war, concludes treaties, proposes and vetoes legislation, and may rule through decree under emergency powers that have been regularly delegated by parliament. He appoints the prime minister and the cabinet, which may issue "decisions" having the force of law. Under the Constitution, the People's Assembly has the power to legislate and to nominate the president, and other branches of government are responsible to the assembly. But it has never effectively exercised these constitutional checks on the executive.

The Dominant Executive and the Power Elite

The Presidency

The presidency is the command post of Egypt's dominant executive branch of government and the linchpin of the political elite. Nasser established and assumed the office, endowing it with broad legal powers and with his personal charisma. He made it the most institutionalized part of the political system, against which all other elite institutions—party, parliament, press, even the military—have proved impotent. The Constitution of 1971 gives legal expression to this reality, vesting vast executive authority in the president.

Succession procedures for the transfer of presidential power appeared relatively institutionalized since Nasser. The incumbent vice president has twice succeeded to the presidency. In each case the vice president was a military officer; thus, the line of succession stayed within the institution that founded the republic. Formally, a single presidential candidate was nominated by parliament and confirmed by (unopposed) national plebiscite. In practice, behind-the-scenes intraelite politics determined the outcome. Sadat was expected to be nominal head of a collective leadership and had to defeat a coalition of Nasser's left-wing Free Officer lieutenants to assume full control of the office. The backing of most of the professional military and of senior bureaucrats recruited from upper-class families was important. But the legality with which Nasser had endowed the office itself was critical to Sadat's victory; it was Sadat's legal prerogative that allowed him to purge his opponents from their state offices and that rallied the army in support of him. Sadat made Husni Mubarak, an air force officer who had distinguished himself in the October 1973 War, his vice president. Although politically inexperienced, Mubarak grew in the job. On Sadat's death, the political elite closed ranks behind him, and a smooth succession took place. Mubarak's 1987 reelection manifested the continued institutionalization of presidential authority. Mubarak did not appoint a vice president, perhaps reluctant to designate a successor and possible rival so early in his presidency. Had a succession crisis arisen, there would have been no obvious successor.

The president has broad constitutional powers. The president appoints vice presidents, prime ministers, and the Council of Ministers—the cabinet or "government." He enjoys a vast power of patronage that makes legions of officials beholden to him and ensures the loyalty and customary deference of the state apparatus. Presidential appointees include army commanders, the heads of the security apparatus, senior civil servants, heads of autonomous agencies, governors, newspaper editors, university presidents, judges, major religious officials, and public sector managers. Through the Council of Ministers, over which he may directly preside, the president commands the sprawling state bureaucracy and can personally intervene at any level to achieve his objectives if the chain of command proves sluggish. Because the levers of macroeconomic policy—banks, the budget, and the large public sector—are under government control, broad responsibility for running the economy is within the presidential domain. This responsibility carries with it heavy burdens, because as head of the state the president is expected to provide for the welfare of the vast numbers of people dependent on it.

A large presidential bureaucracy, managed by a ministerial level appointee, is a personal instrument of control over the wider bureaucracy. It is made up of personal advisers, troubleshooters, and lieutenants with specialized supervisory functions. Under Nasser it had bureaus for intelligence, economic planning, presidential security, administrative control, and foreign affairs. Under Sadat it swelled into a small bureaucracy made up of about 4,000 functionaries, many of them supporting the elaborate entourage and presidential household he created. Stretching out from this presidential bureaucracy are a multitude of presidentially appointed specialized national councils for production, social affairs, science, and the like, which bring the state and interest groups together under presidential patronage and expand presidential influence into every branch of society (see fig. 6).

The president bears primary responsibility for defense of the country and is the supreme commander of the armed forces. Having, to date, always been an ex-officer, he typically enjoys personal influence in the military. He presides over the National Security Council, which coordinates defense policy and planning, and he may assume operational command in time of war. He may declare war with the approval (in practice automatically given) of the parliament, conclude treaties, and issue decrees on national security affairs. Foreign policy is a ''reserved sphere'' of the presidency. Presidents have typically been preoccupied with foreign policy and have personally shaped it.

Finally, the president is chief legislator, the dominant source of major policy innovation. The president can legislate by decree during ''emergencies,'' a condition loosely defined, and when parliament is not in session. He can also put proposals to the people in plebiscites that always give such propositions overwhelming approval. Finally, the president normally controls a docile majority in parliament, which regularly translates his proposals into law. His control of parliament stems from his ability to dismiss it at will and from his leadership of the ruling party that dominates parliament. He also enjoys a legislative veto.

The President and the Power Elite

The actual use of presidential power has evolved through the changing relationship between the chief executive and the rest of the power elite. The style of presidential leadership determined how the president controlled the elite. Nasser headed and ruled through a tightly knit team of officer-revolutionaries with a certain shared vision. Moreover, as a charismatic leader with wide popular support, he stood above and balanced off the elites and frequently used his popular support to curb them. Thus, he was able to make the presidency a highly activist, interventionist office in the service of a revolution from above that ran roughshod over the interests of the dominant classes. He did have to contend with a certain intra-elite rivalry. The other senior Free Officers who had helped him make the revolution were entitled to be consulted in decision making; many of them served as powerful vice presidents, overseeing ministers in various sectors of government activity. Field Marshal Abdul Hakim Amir, Nasser's close colleague and the number-two man in the regime, came close to making the army his personal "fiefdom." But in the end, those who challenged Nasser were purged, and generally he enjoyed nearly unquestioned presidential authority.

Sadat transformed the charismatic, activist presidency into a sort of "presidential monarchy." His formation of a kind of "royal family" of influential relatives in his entourage; the traditional legitimacy he resurrected; the essentially conservative objectives of his policies; and the use of clientelism and corruption, traditional techniques of rule all amounted to a traditionalization of authority. The main issue of intraelite politics under Sadat was resistance inside the establishment to the president's drive to reverse many of Nasser's policies. The popular support won in the October 1973 War gave Sadat a free hand during the crucial period of redirection (1974–76). He also built a strong client network of politicians allowed to enrich themselves by often illicit manipulations of the economic opening his policies afforded and, hence, they had a big stake in his course. His shrewd patrimonial (see Glossary) manipulations—the constant rotation of elites in and out of office while playing them against each other—also helped him dominate the elite. The authoritarian political structure was crucial to Sadat's enterprise; the regime, lacking traditions of mass participation, largely kept the major decisions inside elite circles where the presidency was the dominant force.

Sadat's support also rested on a kind of tacit "social contract" with his elite and upper-class supporters under which he had to curb the arbitrary power of the state and the presidency. On the one hand, Sadat retained freedom in foreign policy, where personal impulses often seemed to override professional advice and the ultimate powers of the authoritarian presidency were never overtly challenged. On the other hand, Sadat relaxed the state's control over society and the political arena and curbed the interventionist role the presidency had played under Nasser. Although Sadat retained the last word, he refrained from intervening in many domestic policy matters, allowing the bourgeoisie growing scope

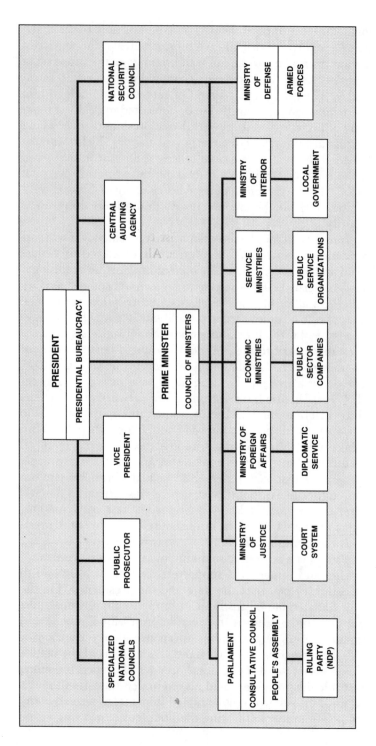

Figure 6. The Presidency, January 1990

to advance its interests. Thus, a hybrid of traditional and legal-rational authority emerged: a presidential monarchy presiding over a power-sharing alliance between the state and its bourgeois constituency. Sadat's patrimonial excesses and his occasionally arbitrary imposition of major policies retarded the consolidation of this power-sharing experiment, but it was institutionalized under his successor.

Under Mubarak, the authoritarian presidency remained the centerpiece of the state, although he was a less dominant figure than his predecessors. He did not create an elite core comparable in power to the ones they created; he lacked the mission and revolutionary comrades of a Nasser and the patronage network of a Sadat. Indeed, he came to power amid at least two power centers, the military and the ''Sadatists'' in the elite. Although he lessened his dependence on them by bringing in conservative Nasserites, backing technocratic elements in the bureaucracy, and encouraging the political opposition, he carried out no massive purge of the elite.

Mubarak has used his power in the least activist way of Egypt's three presidents. In contrast to Nasser and Sadat who sought to reshape Egypt, Mubarak sought stability and incremental change and lacked the ideological vision and political will to tackle boldly the country's intractable problems. Much more than his predecessors, Mubarak governed by intraelite consensus, a cautious balancing of contrary pressures and demands. He also delegated considerable authority to his ministers; indeed, he sometimes remained above the fray, refraining from personally identifying with or, in the face of opposition, strongly backing some of his own government's policies. In the running of government, a pragmatic managerial style stressing legality and technocracy replaced the patrimonialism and personalism of Sadat's rule. Foreign policy, made in consultation with professional diplomats, was no longer the victim of presidential impulse. In some ways, Mubarak's caution made him a man appropriate to a time of rising constraints on state power. Having no ''mission'' comparable to that of Nasser or Sadat, Mubarak could afford to be more tolerant of opposition, and because his legitimacy rested squarely on legality, he had a greater interest in respecting the law. The scope of presidential power clearly narrowed, but, being less threatening, this power was also less challenged than under Nasser and Sadat. Indeed, Mubarak's personal integrity and genuine commitment to limited democratization made him the most widely acceptable leader in a regime enjoying little popular trust.

The Prime Minister, the Council of Ministers, and the Policy-making Process

The prime minister is the president's primary lieutenant, charged with implementing his policies through the bureaucracy. Although the prime minister and his cabinet are formally accountable to parliament and are expected to submit to legislative questioning, they were, in practice, appointed and removed by the president, not by parliament. Under Nasser, when key Free Officers headed strategic ministries, the cabinet was a center of some power, but subsequently it became merely the staff of the president. Although the president might preside over cabinet meetings, the cabinet was not a collegial decision-making body; instead, the president tended to make key decisions in ad hoc consultations with ministers and advisers in a given issue area.

Egypt's policy-making process was very much dominated by the executive branch, and the heart of the process was the interaction between the presidency and the Council of Ministers. This top executive level decided on all policy proposals, whether they originated in the bureaucracy, with influential personalities, or with interest groups. It was also the arena in which all major political decisions were made, relatively free from institutionalized constraints or pressure from other parts of the political system or the public. Major policy innovations were typically launched by the president, perhaps under the influence of close personal advisers or the pressure of a major problem or crisis and most likely after consultation with ministerial experts. Particularly when a major policy decision was in the making, the president might encourage opinion groups to develop in the cabinet. These groups would advocate different policy options, but although the policies might seriously affect different segments of society, the opinion groups were not really representatives of those segments. Moreover, the president had the first and the last word in deciding among the groups.

The cabinet itself was, nevertheless, an arena of intraelite politics because presidents, engrossed in major political decisions, often left the day-to-day business of government to their ministers, intervening only to give general instructions or when something went wrong. Such mid-level policy making might be set in motion by the proposals of individual ministries, often generated by high civil servants or even by the interests of persons associated with a particular ministry, such as public sector managers or the various professional syndicates. These proposals might set off factional bargaining within the cabinet and high bureaucracy. Elite factions might take the form of *shillas,* small groups bound by friendship or family ties, heading client networks that stretched down through the bureaucracy and competed for control of offices and the personal and venal benefits that often went with them.

Typically, there was a split in the cabinet between presidential appointees and the clients the prime minister brought on board. In the late 1970s, the cabinet was reportedly split between followers of Vice President Mubarak and Prime Minister Mustafa Khalil. Sometimes factionalism took the form of bureaucratic rivalries between ministries over programs, resources, and jurisdictions; such bureaucratic struggles decided a good part of "who got what" in a country where the state sector was still at the center of the economy. As societal interests became stronger at the expense of government, policy making came more often to take the form of "trial balloons" in which the government or a faction of ministers tested public reaction to an initiative and often backed down if opposition was too strong. If intraelite conflict could not be settled in the cabinet or if a ministerial initiative invited excessive public reaction, the president was likely to intervene, perhaps dismissing a particular minister or faction.

The cabinet was also empowered to plan, coordinate, and control the work of the ministries in implementing policy, and to follow up, evaluate, and inspect policy implementation. Toward these ends, it was divided into two layers, with an inner cabinet of deputy prime ministers responsible for coordinating several functionally related ministries in the full cabinet that composed the outer layer. The independent Central Auditing Agency was responsible for financial control.

The Road to Power: Recruitment and Composition of the Elite

Within the Egyptian elite, a core elite had even more power than the broader ministerial elite. The overwhelming dominance of presidential power in Egypt meant that influence flowed, above all, from closeness to the president; his confidants, whether they held high office or not, were usually counted among the core elite.

Under Nasser, these men were fellow military revolutionaries such as Abdul Hakim Amir, Anwar as Sadat, Kamal ad Din Husayn, Abdul Latif Baghdadi, Zakariyya Muhi ad Din, and Ali Sabri. Several prominent civilians, such as press magnate Mohamed Hassanain Heikal and industry czar Aziz Sidqi, also had influence on the president and exerted power in their own domains. But the military clearly dominated the state, and most technocrats were mere executors of policy. Between the 1952 Revolution and the late Sadat era, however, there was a continual attrition in the ranks of the Free Officers; many fell out with Nasser, many were purged by Sadat during the succession struggle with Ali Sabri, and others retired thereafter. Of the twenty-six Free Officers politically active in 1970, only eight were absorbed into Sadat's ruling group, whereas a number of others emerged as leaders of the political opposition to his regime, notably Khalid Muhi ad Din on the left and Kamal ad Din Husayn in the nationalist center.

Under Sadat the top elite ceased to be dominated by the military and was transformed into a much more heterogeneous group. To be sure, certain old Free Officer colleagues and several top generals remained in the inner circle. Vice President Mubarak was a member of the inner core. Among other officers in the top elite, generals Ahmad Ismail Ali, Abdul Ghani al Gamasi, and Kamal Hassan Ali played important and extended roles. But civilians far outnumbered the military. Prime ministers such as Abdul Aziz Hijazi, Mamduh Salim, and Mustafa Khalil enjoyed real power during their tenures. Minister of Foreign Affairs Ismail Fahmi was a close confidant of the president until they fell out over Sadat's trip to Jerusalem. Interior ministers such as Mamduh Salim and Nabawi Ismail were key members of the elite in a regime plagued by constant dissidence. Certain minister-technocrats enjoying influence over key decisions or sectors belonged to the core elite; among these were Deputy Prime Minister for Economic Affairs Abdul Munim Qaysuni, long-time Minister of Petroleum Ahmad Izz ad Din Hilal, and Minister of Power Ahmad Sultan. But it was men such as Osman Ahmad Osman (also seen as Uthman Ahmad Uthman) and Sayyid Marii (also seen as Sayyid Marei), representatives of the business and agrarian bourgeoisies, who seemed to have enjoyed the most intimate confidence of the president, whether they held top office or not.

Osman was perhaps the second most powerful man in Sadat's Egypt. A multimillionaire capitalist, he and his family presided over a huge business empire spanning the public and private sectors. He held office for a time, as minister of reconstruction, but his relatives were in and out of a multitude of public offices. Through the marriage of a son to one of Sadat's daughters, he was virtually incorporated into the president's family and appeared to use his influence to favor business in general as well as his own fortunes. Another influential member of Sadat's ''family'' by marriage was Sayyid Marii, a technocrat from a landowning family. He had presided over Nasser's agrarian reform, but in the 1970s he helped steer Sadat toward both political and economic liberalization. He ran the official party and the parliament on Sadat's behalf for extended periods and was a force behind the multiparty initiative.

President Husni Mubarak
Courtesy Embassy of Egypt,
Washington

President Mubarak opening
the People's Assembly
in the early 1980s
Courtesy Embassy of Egypt,
Washington

Mubarak tried to distance himself from these core Sadatists, and many were pushed from the center of power. Mubarak's inner core was headed by two advisers in the presidency with diplomatic service backgrounds. Usamah al Baz, a former diplomat who directed the president's Office for Political Affairs and was reputedly a secret Nasserite, or supporter of Arab socialism, seemed to enjoy political influence with the president; Mustafa Faqi was another close adviser. Ismat Abdul Majid's extended tenure as minister of foreign affairs indicated that he had the trust of the president and gave him considerable influence in the foreign policy bureaucracy. Yusuf Wali, a former agricultural bureaucrat, headed the ruling party and was Mubarak's chief political troubleshooter.

After the dismissal of Kamal Hassan Ali, a general of conservative proclivities who had served Sadat, Mubarak's prime ministers were technocrats trained in economics and lacking personal political bases. Ali Lutfi was a long-time minister of finance, and Atif Sidqi was a top state auditor. Mubarak generally upgraded the role of technocrats in his inner circle at the expense of the "wheeler-dealer" politicians of the Sadat era. On the one hand, Atif Ubayd, a minister of cabinet affairs backed by the United States, was thought to be prime ministerial material but was passed over; on the other hand, officials who served Nasser but were pushed out by Sadat made a certain comeback. Still, the *infitah* bourgeoisie who supported and benefited from Sadat's rule remained powerful in the Mubarak regime, particularly entrenched in the interstices of state and business. One sign of their continued power was their ability to block attempts to legalize a Nasserist party. The continuing coercive base of the state was reflected in three major figures close to the center of power. Field Marshal Abdul Halim Abu Ghazala was long reputed to be the number-two man in the regime and was said to have been offered the vice presidency in acknowledgment of the fact. The hardline face of the regime was presented by tough and disliked ministers of interior, notably Hassan Abu Basha and Zaki Badr, whose campaigns against the opposition contained elements of dissent yet drew the heat away from the president. Mubarak's ability to dismiss both top army and police generals indicated the consolidation of his control over the elite.

Because the command posts of the bureaucracy were levers of power and patronage in Egypt, the cabinet as a whole could be taken as the second rank of the top elite, just below the core around the president. Recruitment into the cabinet remained the main road into the elite, and arrival there was either an opportunity to build power or a confirmation of seniority and influence in the bureaucracy or military. Moreover, the formation of the cabinet was a key opportunity for coopting into the regime important personalities and interests from outside the state apparatus.

The change in the composition of cabinets from the Nasser era to the post-Nasser period indicated a shift in the paths to power. Under Nasser, the military, and particularly members of the Free Officers, constituted a privileged recruitment pool from which strategic ministries were filled, although apolitical technocrats recruited from the bureaucracy and the universities also filled a significant proportion of ministerial posts. Under Sadat and Mubarak, the military declined as a main recruitment channel into the cabinet. Whereas the military supplied one-third of the ministerial elite and filled 40 percent of ministerial positions under Nasser, in Sadat's post-1973 "*infitah* governments," military representation dropped to about 10 percent; the percentage remained limited under Mubarak.

It was still possible for prominent officers to attain high political office, however. The minister of defense position, a preserve of a senior general, remained one of the most powerful posts in the regime and could be a springboard to wider political power. General Kamal Hassan Ali moved from minister of defense to minister of foreign affairs and finally to prime minister under Sadat and Mubarak. Perhaps the single most important ladder to power under Sadat was the combination of an engineering degree with a career in the bureaucracy and public sector. Persons with such backgrounds made up around one-fourth of Sadat's ministers after the initiation of *infitah* and seemed to be the chief beneficiaries of the decline of military dominance in politics. The relative eclipse of the army was also paralleled by the rise of professional police officers into the top elite. One, Mamduh Salim, became prime minister, and others wielded great power as ministers of interior and ministers of local government. Academia was an important channel of recruitment in all three regimes. Professionals, such as doctors and lawyers, and, increasingly, private business people became eligible for recruitment by service in party and parliamentary politics and made up about one-fourth of the ministerial elite in the late Sadat era. Although the roads to power diversified after Nasser, access by middle class military officers probably narrowed during the period between his era of rule and post-Nasser Egypt, which upper- and upper-middle class personalities dominated.

Elite Ideology

A dominant ideology has generally bound the Egyptian political elite, but its content changed significantly over time. Under Nasser this ideology was revolutionary nationalism, but thereafter the ideology of the 1952 Revolution was gradually replaced by a new conservative consensus that reflected the interests of an establishment with no interest in further radical change. Sadat pioneered this ideological transformation via the October Working Paper, which outlined his view of Egypt's new course after the October 1973 War; through a ''de-Nasserization'' propaganda campaign launched in the mid-1970s; and by subsequent efforts to revive the legitimacy of capitalism and to justify his Western alignment. Under Mubarak, Nasser's heritage was symbolically revered, but Sadat's revision of that heritage had by no means been reversed.

Nasserism was built on Egypt's opposition to ''imperialist influence'' in the Arab world and on a belief in the benefits of pan-Arab unity. Nationalism required the creation of a strong state with a powerful military and the mission of defending the Arab world against imperialism and Zionism. Under Sadat, Arab nationalist challenges to Western interests and to Israel were replaced by a stress on cooperation with the Western powers and on regional peace. For a period in the late Sadat era when Egypt's separate peace with Israel isolated the country from the other Arab states, a palpable anti-Arabism radiated from elite circles. Sadat insisted that the attempts of the Arab rulers to ostracize Egypt were doomed because they had no practical alternative to Egypt's course and Egypt remained the heart of the Arab world. Egypt's role was now to lead the Arabs to peace, and the treaty with Israel was a first step toward an overall just peace. Under Mubarak the Nasserist vision of Egyptian leadership of the Arabs was again vigorously promoted. But far from being a promoter of radical nationalism, Egypt weighed in on the side of moderation and stability in the Arab world.

The elite's conception of the proper nature of Egyptian society underwent a considerable change after the Nasser era. Under Nasser Egypt was seen as a revolutionary society in which the reduction of inherited inequalities was a major ideal. In the economic sphere, Nasser advocated Arab socialism. This policy laid heavy stress on state planning and the public sector as the engines of economic development and guarantors of national self-sufficiency and economic independence. The state also assumed responsibility for ensuring the basic needs of the people and for an equitable distribution of wealth. Several populist reforms redistributed national resources to the benefit of the middle and lower classes.

Under Sadat socialism was denounced as a vehicle of envy and extremism; instead, Sadat promoted a traditional concept in which society was seen as an extension of the patriarchal family and characterized by harmony among classes and belief in religion. In the economic sphere, the elite argued that the state had assumed too many responsibilities at the expense of private initiative. Capitalism had to be revived and the public sector, no longer seen as the cutting edge of development, had to be reduced to a mere support for private enterprise. Egalitarianism and redistribution were thought to have gone too far, to the detriment of economic growth. Private initiative had to be liberated from stultifying state controls; those who distinguished themselves were to be allowed rewards and individuals with capital permitted to "earn freely without limits." The pursuit of self-interest, formerly castigated, was now relegitimized. Capitalist development, it was argued, would bring "trickle-down" benefits for the masses in place of their dependence on state-supported programs.

This ideological thrust, in part a reaction against Nasserism, was, however, tempered by a more moderate strain of thinking that became more influential under Mubarak. The moderate view was not convinced that laissez-faire was the cure to all of Egypt's ills; it insisted on a continuing role for state regulation and progressive taxation to curb the inegalitarian tendencies of the market and the social conflict and political instability that these tendencies generated. Indeed, under Mubarak a limited Nasserist restoration could be seen in the return to the concept of the state as autonomous guardian of the public interest, in the continuing defense of the public sector, and in a new stress on bringing the excesses of the *infitah* bourgeoisie under state control. Mubarak sought a balance between liberal and statist factions in the elite, rejected calls to dismantle the public sector, and called for an "equal partnership" between the public and private sectors. Generally, the elite agreed on the need to avoid both the "anarchic individualism" of unregulated capitalism and the class conflict promoted by Marxism.

Finally, in the political sphere, Nasser had created a powerful authoritarian state; this concentration of power was legitimized by the charisma of the leader and the revolutionary mission of the country. Under Sadat the legitimacy formula was changed. On the one hand, it was retraditionalized as Sadat sought to infuse his office with patriarchal authority and the aura of religion. He promoted himself as the "believing president" and was constantly seen at prayer; more and more, the state sought to legitimize its authority in Islamic terms. But on the other hand, both Sadat and Mubarak also sought to root legitimacy in constitutionalism and democracy. Egypt had moved, Sadat declared, to a state of laws and institutions rather than to one of people. Under Mubarak democratization became the main legitimacy formula. Nevertheless, it was limited. The masses were held not to be prepared for full-blown democracy; lacking sufficient responsibility and consciousness, they were susceptible to "alien" (leftist) or "fanatical" (Islamist) ideas. Strong presidential tutelage, the careful channeling of political discourse through regime-managed institutions, and limits on overt attempts to "incite" the masses were needed for the sake of social peace. By the Mubarak era, this new conservative consensus seemed to bind the elite, effacing ideological divisions. But the consensus did not prevent elite rivalries over personal power or disagreements over specific issues.

Politics among Elites

Military Politics

A major issue of Egypt's elite politics was the role of the military in the state. Nasser's Free Officers founded republican government and led Egypt's 1952 Revolution from above. Presidents continued to be ex-military men. But as Egypt entered a postrevolutionary phase, Sadat successfully demilitarized the state and depoliticized the officer corps. Without losing control of the military, Sadat was able to change it from the dominant leadership group in the state into a professional force subordinate to legal authority, radically curtailing its policy-making role, even in defense matters. This change was paralleled by a deradicalization that ended the army's role as "defender of the revolution" and as defender of the Arab nation against imperialism.

Long-term developments that were maturing before Sadat took power facilitated his effort. As many Free Officers acquired wealth and married into great families, they were deradicalized. If the Free Officers had originally been the vanguard of the rising middle class against the traditional upper class, by the late 1970s senior officers had become part of a new establishment. Many officers blamed the 1967 defeat on Nasser, the Soviet Union, and socialist measures. They resented Nasser's scapegoating of the high command for the army's failures. In addition, because the defeat could plausibly be blamed on military involvement in politics, it discredited the military's claim to political leadership and enhanced the prestige of nonpolitical professional officers. Nasser stressed professional competence in the post-1967 reconstruction of the army, and many officers themselves became impatient with political involvement that could detract from the mission of defending the front and recovering the land and honor lost in 1967.

The fall of scores of politicized officers in the succession struggle with Sadat—in particular, the group around Marshal Abdul Hakim Amir after the June 1967 War (Arab-Israeli war, also known as the Six-Day War) and the Ali Sabri group—removed the most powerful and politicized Free Officers and dissipated remaining radical sentiment in the ranks of the officer corps. In the succession struggle, Minister of War General Muhammad Fawzi stood with the leftist Sabri faction and tried to mobilize the military against Sadat by accusing him of selling out to the United States. Chief of Staff General Muhammad Sadiq and the rest of the top brass, however, stood with Sadat and neutralized Fawzi. No doubt the military's stand was affected by the unpopularity of Sabri's effort to build up the state party as a counterweight to the military, his identification with the unpopular Soviet advisory mission, and Sadat's promise to reinstate officers unfairly blamed for the 1967 defeat. But the long tradition of presidential authority established under Nasser seemed the decisive factor in rallying the professional military to Sadat's side. And this victory went far to reinforce the legal supremacy of presidential authority over all other state institutions.

Nevertheless, Sadat was thereafter embroiled in and won two other power struggles with top generals who contested his defense and foreign policies. In 1972 General Sadiq, then minister of war, seemed to challenge presidential prerogatives. Sadiq considered himself entitled, given his role in Sadat's victory and his Free Officer status, to a share in decision-making power. He used rewards, promotions, and the mobilization of anti-Soviet sentiment in the army to build a personal power base. Sadat viewed Sadiq as a mere member of his staff and saw his anti-Soviet advocacy and his links with Libya's Colonel Muammar al Qadhafi, whom Sadat deeply distrusted, as encroachments on presidential authority. Most serious, Sadiq objected to Sadat's plans for a limited war in Sinai to seize a strip of land across the Suez Canal as a prelude to negotiations with Israel. Believing Egypt unprepared for such an ambitious venture, he argued, in a tense meeting of the high command, against any military action, a course untenable for Sadat. Sadat's move against Sadiq was a classic example of his strategy of control over the military. He waited until he had first expelled the Soviet advisers, thus winning for himself the acclaim of anti-Soviet elements and taking the wind out of Sadiq's sails. He obtained the support of other top commanders, especially Chief of Staff Saad ad Din Shazli, who had quarreled with Sadiq over authority in the high command, rallied the field commanders by accusing Sadiq of ignoring orders to prepare for war, and quickly replaced Sadiq with General Ahmad Ismail Ali, a personal friend who lacked political ambition. With the help of these allies, Sadat foiled a pro-Sadiq coup attempt.

Not long after, Sadat faced another challenge, this time from General Shazli. The two men quarreled over the conduct of the October 1973 War, each holding the other responsible for the Israeli breakthrough onto the west bank of the Suez Canal. After the war, Shazli was a leading opponent of the decision to rely on the United States at the cost of weakening Egypt's military ability to take action. Sadat rallied the support of other top officers against Shazli, including then Minister of War Ismail, Air Force Commander Husni Mubarak, and Chief of Operations General Abdul Ghani Gamasi. Shazli enjoyed considerable support in the military but either would not or could not mobilize it before the high command decimated his followers in a wave of purges from corps and division commanders on down. While some of his top generals were in the future to disagree with Sadat's policies, none would again overtly challenge them, and when he chose to dismiss them, they offered no resistance.

The army, however, was not free of disaffection. Some junior officers who had risked their lives in the "crossing" of the Suez Canal believed Sadat had sold out the gains won on the battlefield. There were recurring signs of Nasserite and Islamic tendencies in the ranks thereafter. But most officers remained loyal for several reasons: the legitimacy Sadat won in the October 1973 War, in which the army had redeemed its lost honor; the realization that the alternative to Sadat might be another war in which this gain might be sacrificed; and the privileges and new American weapons Sadat lavished on the officer corps. The stake in *infitah* business some officers acquired, the acceptance of professionalism among most senior officers, and Sadat's practice of rotating senior commanders had, by the end of his presidency, seemingly reduced the military from leaders of the regime to one of its main pillars.

Under Mubarak the military remained a powerful corporate actor in the political system, and the case of Minister of Defense Abdul Halim Abu Ghazala manifested both the power and limits of the military establishment. Mubarak was initially less careful than Sadat to rotate military chieftains and to balance them with rival officers or with strong civilian politicians. As a result, Abu Ghazala, an ambitious politicized and conservative general, appeared to establish unprecedented power and acknowledged status as the number-two man in the regime. He positioned himself as champion of arms spending, resisting all decreases in the defense budget and pushing for greater autonomy for the armed forces in the political system. He widened the role of the army in the economy, making it a font of patronage, subcontracting to the private sector, and establishing close relations between the Egyptian arms industry and

United States arms suppliers. Abu Ghazala also presided over the growth of privileged facilities for the military, a development that made him something of a hero in the ranks. He appeared to stake out positions independent of the president, apparently objecting to Mubarak's soft-line handling of the *Achille Lauro* terrorist incident in October 1985. Whereas the president sought to step back from the close alliance with Washington, Abu Ghazala was known for his intimate connections to influential Americans.

In 1987 the army had to be called out when the riots of the security police left the government otherwise defenseless. Having saved the regime, Abu Ghazala seemed to have strengthened his position. He even carried influence in the appointment of cabinet ministers. But Abu Ghazala lacked the crucial control over military appointments needed in order to turn the army into a personal fiefdom; Mubarak, waking up to the danger, had by 1987 positioned his own men as chief of staff and as minister of war production. Perhaps aided by Abu Ghazala's loss of United States support over an arms smuggling scandal, Mubarak had no difficulty removing him from his post in 1989. Generally, Mubarak tried to curb military aggrandizement that diminished the civilian sector. The professionalization of the officer corps, its tradition of respect for legal legitimacy, and the reluctance of an army lacking in national vision or ambition to assume responsibility for Egypt's problems made it unlikely that any top general could carry the officer corps in an overt challenge to Mubarak.

The Politics of Economic Strategy

The most important decision taken by the Egyptian government since Nasser was Sadat's *infitah* to foreign and domestic private capital. While the stagnation of the early 1970s raised the issue of economic reform, the decision to implement *infitah* did not take place in a political vacuum. A number of different elite factions prescribed different solutions to the economic problems. A handful of Marxists favored a "deepening" of the socialist experiment. Another small group called for a rapid move to free-market capitalism. The third, statist (see Glossary) trend, led by Prime Minister Aziz Sidqi, stood for a controlled role for private and foreign capital compatible with the dominance of the public sector. In May 1973, Sadat dismissed Sidqi, who was an influential possible rival associated with the Nasser era, and before long outstanding leftists, such as Minister of Planning Ismail Sabri Abdullah, were also forced out. The dominant thinking that emerged advocated creation of a new foreign sector, restriction of the public sector to large industry and infrastructure, and the opening of all other sectors to private capital. Some of

Sadat's closest confidants, major figures of the Egyptian bourgeoisie such as Osman Ahmad Osman and Sayyid Marii, played major roles in swinging him toward this option. The legitimacy won in the October 1973 War gave him the strength to make this break with Nasserism.

Egypt's state-dominated economy, Sadat declared, was too burdened by military spending and bureaucratic inertia to mobilize the resources for an economic recovery. But postwar conditions, namely the diplomatic opening to the United States and the new petrodollars in Arab hands, presented a unique opportunity to spark a new economic take-off combining Western technology, Arab capital, and Egyptian labor.

An *infitah* would also consolidate Sadat's support among the Egyptian landed and business classes and among the state elite who had enriched themselves in office and were seeking security and investment outlets for their new wealth. In addition, Sadat viewed *infitah* as essential to winning United States commitment to Egypt's recovery of the Sinai Peninsula from Israel.

Abdul Aziz Hijazi, a long-time minister of finance and liberal economist with links to Western and Arab capital, was appointed prime minister in 1974, charged with implementing the *infitah*. To neutralize resistance inside the state, Sadat encouraged a "de-Nasserization" campaign in which all those who had grievances against socialism publicly attacked it for having ruined the economy. As the emerging ills of *infitah*—inflation and corruption—generated discontent over the new course, Hijazi was sacked, and Mamduh Salim, Sadat's police "strong man," took over as prime minister with a mission to push ahead with *infitah*, overruling those who were obstructing it and those who were abusing it.

Once *infitah* was established as Egypt's economic strategy, intra-elite conflicts centered on its proper scope and management. These conflicts typically pitted liberalizing economists, who were convinced that a fully capitalist economy would be more efficient than an economy incorporating a public sector, against more statist-minded bureaucrats and state managers, who wanted to reform, rather than to dismantle, the public sector. The latter were often allied with politicians fearful of public reaction to the rollback of populist measures such as subsidies and public-sector employment. One major episode in this conflict came in 1976 over pressures from the International Monetary Fund (IMF—see Glossary) and foreign banks to cut subsidies and devalue the Egyptian pound (for value of the Egyptian pound—see Glossary) as necessary steps in the liberalization of the economy. Sadat's minister of economy, Zaki Shafii, and his minister of finance, Ahmad Abu Ismail, fearful of the consequences on the mass standard of living, urged him to resist pressures for rapid reform. But other economists, chief among them Abdul Munim Qaysuni, argued that Egypt could not afford costly welfare programs if it were to revitalize its productive bases. Top Western bankers, such as David Rockefeller and William Simon, urged Sadat to go beyond half measures if he wanted to make the *infitah* a success. Sadat overruled his own ministers and replaced them with a new team headed by Qaysuni, who began to cut the subsidies. But decision makers had misjudged their political environment. The subsidy cuts triggered the 1977 food riots, which shattered much of the support Sadat had carefully built up. The government backed down and did not again attempt such a radical cut in the social safety net for the poor.

Managing *infitah* remained the major problem of public policy under Mubarak. Rather than producing a dynamic capitalist alternative to Nasserite statism, *infitah* had stimulated a consumption boom that put Egypt in debt and made it heavily dependent on external revenues, which declined in the mid-1980s, plunging the country into economic crisis. Mubarak insisted that *infitah* would be reformed, not reversed, but the government's freedom of action was limited by conflicting domestic constraints. The interests created under Nasser remained obstacles to capitalist rationalization and belt-tightening. The public sector was still the main engine of investment, and public sector managers and unionized labor tenaciously defended it. The bureaucracy, employing a large portion of the middle class, was a formidable constituency. Meanwhile, Egypt's huge army had not been demobilized, and, indeed, Sadat had bought its acquiescence to his policy by replacing weapons from the Soviet Union with more expensive arms from the United States, for which the military showed a voracious appetite. Marshal Abu Ghazala rejected demands by Prime Minister Ali Lutfi that he pay off Egypt's military debts from revenues of arms sales overseas; instead he plowed funds into subsidized apartments, shops, and sports clubs for the officer corps. Populist "rights" acquired under Nasser had grown into a tacit social contract by which the government provided subsidized food to the masses in return for their tolerance of growing inequality. The contrast between the conspicuous new wealth and the mass poverty generated a moral malaise, making Egypt's debt a political issue. "*We're* asked to pay the debt," chanted demonstrators in 1986, "while *they* live in palaces and villas." Thus, attacking populist policies seemed likely to fuel Islamist political activism.

Infitah had itself, however, created interests resistant to reform. A larger and richer bourgeoisie was unprepared to give up opportunities for enrichment or to trim its level of consumption. Any reversal of the course that so favored this class would have cost the regime its strongest social support. Indeed, the increasing power of the bourgeoisie was manifest in its successful veto of several government reform initiatives. Prime Minister Ali Lutfi was expected to produce difficult reforms but was stymied by powerful business interests. The ability of the regime to raise domestic revenues to cope with the financial imbalance was limited because those who could pay represented the government's own support base. Thus, when importers staged demonstrations against increased customs duties, the government rescinded the duties, and the ruling party parliamentary caucus turned back its own government's proposal to tax lucrative urban real estate interests.

Caught between rich and poor, the regime opted for incrementalism. It gradually shaved subsidies, replacing the one piaster (see Glossary—about one United States cent) loaf of bread with a supposedly better quality, higher priced loaf; raising electricity prices; and eliminating subsidies on feed corn. The regime also partially reformed the exchange rate and raised taxes on imported luxuries. But, unable to undertake radical reform, it chiefly concentrated on negotiations with creditors for a rescheduling of debts, lower interest rates, and new loans to support the balance of payments, merely postponing the day of reckoning.

The growing power of the bourgeoisie and the determination of Mubarak's state to maintain its independence from this class was reflected in another case of economic policy making, a battle over control of foreign currency. The government wanted this control in order to protect the value of the Egyptian pound. In 1985 Minister of Economy Mustafa Said tried to close down black-market money changers who absorbed most workers' remittances but was dismissed when foreign currency dried up and business demanded his head. In 1986 the Lutfi government fell because of a bid by the governor of the Central Bank, Ali Nijm, to rein in the Islamic investment companies that also dealt in foreign currency. The new power of this rising independent bourgeoisie resulted from its ability to disrupt the economy, its payoffs to the press, and its connections to the political opposition and inside the elite itself. In 1988 Prime Minister Atif Sidqi personally led the government's efforts while the companies mobilized the Muslim Brotherhood (Al Ikhwan al Muslimun; also known as the Brotherhood) and the New Wafd Party in defense of the private sector. Aided by financial scandals that damaged depositor confidence, the government brought the companies under its regulative sway, but they retained considerable autonomy. Whereas Mubarak's state was no longer a mere

*Aswan High Dam made possible large land reclamation
and electric power generation projects.*
Courtesy Susan Becker

champion of bourgeois interests as was the state under Sadat, neither
had it regained the power over society of Nasser's days.

Despite the power of elites, they did not operate in a vacuum.
Many of their decisions were reached in response to economic pressures that sharply limited their options. They also had to consider
the political consequences of their decisions. The major change from
Nasser's era was that the bourgeoisie acquired the capacity to advance and defend its interests in the system; the 1977 riots made
clear, however, that mass reaction must also be included in regime
calculations. Thus, while the Egyptian state remained essentially
authoritarian, decision makers could not ignore societal wishes, nor
could they escape environmental constraints.

The Bureaucracy and Policy Implementation

Egypt's public bureaucracy was an enormous establishment en-
compassing at least thirty ministries and hundreds of public agencies and companies. There were ministries devoted to the traditional
tasks of governance, such as the Ministry of Interior, charged with
the maintenance of internal order, and the ministries of defense,
finance, foreign affairs, and justice. There was also a multitude
of ministries charged with managing the economy and promoting

development, such as the ministries of economy and foreign trade, industry, international investment and cooperation, irrigation, petroleum, planning, power, and reconstruction. Others provided public services, such as the ministries of culture, education, health, and manpower and training. There was also a vast public sector. Under Nasser, 62 public authorities and public service organizations responsible to various ministries presided over about 600 public companies. Public authorities were holding companies coordinating profit-oriented public sector firms of similar function, whereas public service organizations were nonprofit in orientation.

Below the politically appointed ministers and deputy ministers was the civil service. It was ranked in six grades, the most senior ranks being first undersecretary, undersecretary, and general manager. Under the Nasser regime, efforts to reform and modernize the traditional civil service raised the professional qualifications of senior civil servants and opened the service to wider recruitment from the educated middle class. But to curb favoritism, seniority rather than performance was made the main criterion for advancement. In addition, Nasser used the bureaucracy to provide employment for university graduates. The reform of the bureaucracy soon fell behind its expansion in size and functions, making Egypt an overadministered society. Sadat pared back the state's control over the economy but failed to restrain the growth of the state bureaucracy and allowed its standards and efficiency to decline. The bureaucracy mushroomed from 1.2 million at the end of the Nasser era to 2 million at the end of Sadat's rule (20 percent of the work force) and 2.6 million in 1986.

The bureaucracy had a number of outstanding achievements to its credit. The special ministries and agencies set up under Nasser to build the Aswan High Dam, to carry out agrarian reform, and to operate the Suez Canal had the budgets to recruit quality personnel and carried out their missions with distinction. But by the Sadat era, the bureaucracy and the public sector were afflicted with a multitude of pathologies that made them more of a burden on, rather than an instrument of, development. The Council of Ministers generally failed to provide the strong administrative leadership needed to coordinate the sprawling state apparatus, and therefore its various parts often worked at cross-purposes. Many middle rank bureaucrats were statists at odds with the liberalization initiatives from the top. There was a general breakdown in performance and discipline in the public service; employees generally could not be dismissed, pay was dismal except at the highest levels, and most officials moonlighted after putting in only a few hours each day at work. The excessive number of employees charged with the same job made it impossible to distinguish conscientious officials from timeservers. Under these conditions, little responsibility could be delegated to lower bureaucrats, and little initiative was expected of them.

Infitah-era policies also enervated government planning and control of the public sector. Abolishing the public authorities created under Nasser as layers between the ministries and public sector firms was supposed to give the latter greater freedom of management, but instead it brought a decline in financial accountability without really allowing managers to respond to a free market. The partial "privatization" of public sector companies cost the treasury. Government investments in joint ventures with the private or foreign sector often escaped the control of government auditors and ended up in the pockets of the officials, ex-officials, and private business partners who ran the companies. The bureaucracy was afflicted with corruption. At senior levels there were periodic scandals over embezzlement and acceptance of commissions; at lower levels, petty graft was rampant. This propensity toward corruption damaged the regime's effort to manage its most crucial and costly welfare program. The theft of subsidized commodities was facilitated by official collusion, from the clerks of government retail outlets to the high officials of the Ministry of Supply. The decline of the bureaucracy also had deleterious economic consequences; the public sector suffered from an erosion in management, while bureaucratic red tape remained an obstruction to the private and foreign sectors. The latter often had to pay off officials to negotiate the complex webs of administrative requirements.

Local Government

Local government traditionally enjoyed limited power in Egypt's highly centralized state. Under the central government were twenty-six governorates (sing., *muhafazah;* pl., *muhafazat*). These were subdivided into districts (sing., *markaz;* pl., *marakaz*) and villages (sing., *qaryah;* pl., *qura*) or towns (see fig. 1). At each level, there was a governing structure that combined representative councils and government-appointed executive organs headed by governors, district officers, and mayors, respectively. Governors were appointed by the president, and they, in turn, appointed subordinate executive officers. The coercive backbone of the state apparatus ran downward from the Ministry of Interior through the governors' executive organs to the district police station and the village headman (sing., *umdah;* pl., *umadah*).

Before the revolution, state penetration of the rural areas was limited by the power of local notables, but under Nasser, land reform reduced their socioeconomic dominance, and the incorporation of peasants into cooperatives transferred mass dependence from landlords to government. The extension of officials into the countryside permitted the regime to bring development and services to the village. The local branches of the ruling party, the Arab Socialist Union (ASU), fostered a certain peasant political activism and coopted the local notables—in particular the village headmen—and checked their independence from the regime.

State penetration did not retreat under Sadat and Mubarak. The earlier effort to mobilize peasants and deliver services disappeared as the local party and cooperative withered, but administrative controls over the peasants remained intact. The local power of the old families and the headmen revived but more at the expense of peasants than of the state. The district police station balanced the notables, and the system of local government (the mayor and council) integrated them into the regime.

Sadat took several measures to decentralize power to the provinces and towns. Governors acquired more authority under Law Number 43 of 1979, which reduced the administrative and budgetary controls of the central government over the provinces. The elected councils acquired, at least formally, the right to approve or disapprove the local budget. In an effort to reduce local demands on the central treasury, local government was given wider powers to raise local taxes. But local representative councils became vehicles of pressure for government spending, and the soaring deficits of local government bodies had to be covered by the central government. Local government was encouraged to enter into joint ventures with private investors, and these ventures stimulated an alliance between government officials and the local rich that paralleled the *infitah* alliance at the national level. Under Mubarak decentralization and local autonomy became more of a reality, and local policies often reflected special local conditions. Thus, officials in Upper Egypt often bowed to the powerful Islamic movement there, while those in the port cities struck alliances with importers.

The Subordinate Branches: The Regime and Its Constituency

The Egyptian state was by no means "captured" by Egypt's bourgeoisie; it retained its essential autonomy and often put its own interests ahead of those of the upper classes, whether the issue was control of the economy or the need to placate the masses and maintain social peace. But, beginning under Sadat, the regime gradually came to share power with the business, landed, and professional strata that made up a large portion of the most politically active public and represented its main constituency. This power sharing was essentially channeled through parliament, interest groups, the judiciary, and the press.

Parliament

Egypt had a two-chamber legislature made up of the lower People's Assembly (Majlis ash Shaab), which was the locus of legislative power, and the upper Consultative Council (Majlis ash Shura). Power in the People's Assembly was concentrated in the hands of the leadership, an elected speaker and the chairs of the specialized committees into which the assembly was divided. The president and prime minister began each legislative session, which lasted seven months, with an overview of government policy. Laws proposed by the executive or by legislators were first considered in committee and then, with the consent of the legislative leadership, by the full assembly.

The early parliaments under Nasser were dominated by officials and by owners of medium-sized property. In the 1960s, the regime decreed that half the seats had to be reserved for the lower classes; thus, in each electoral district, one seat was filled by a worker or peasant and the other by a professional or official. Although this provision was never repealed, in practice, since Nasser, those who filled peasant seats were actually either clients of notables or wealthy peasants enriched by such ventures as labor contracting, while most "worker" deputies were trade union officials or government employees. There was no sign of any parliamentary voice speaking for the have-nots, save the occasional leftist intellectual who managed to get a seat but carried no weight. Beginning in 1979, a third seat, to be filled by a woman, was added in thirty constituencies, but this provision was abolished in the 1980s under conservative Islamic influence. The president appointed ten Copts to parliament to make sure this minority had some representation (see Coptic Church, ch. 2).

Constitutional practice put parliament at a great disadvantage in relation to the executive. The president is above parliamentary authority and appoints the prime minister and his government. Constitutionally, parliament must approve the government. Moreover, it can remove a minister by a vote of no-confidence. It can also, in theory, similarly challenge the prime minister and his cabinet; if it does so, the president must dissolve the government or obtain its endorsement in a popular referendum. In practice, however, governments have changed exclusively at the will of the president and never following a vote of no-confidence. The president can legislate by decree when parliament is not in session and can bypass parliament through a government-controlled plebiscite.

255

Sadat carried out some of his most politically controversial initiatives independently of parliament, including his 1978 repression of the New Wafd Party and his 1979 promulgation of a liberal law of personal status that was resisted by Muslim opinion.

The cabinet and even individual ministers enjoyed, on the authority of very loosely worded laws, what in effect amounted to decree power, which they used to make crucial decisions, including the cut in subsidies that touched off the 1977 riots. The budget must be accepted or rejected in toto by parliament unless the executive consents to amendments. The executive must present its policy agenda to parliament, and ministers are subject to interpolation, but parliament regularly approves executive initiatives.

Because defense and foreign policy matters are reserved to the executive, defense budgets are never debated in parliament. Likewise, during negotiations over the peace treaty with Israel, Sadat rejected, without repercussions, nearly unanimous parliamentary resolutions to break off the negotiations, to give the Arab Defense Pact priority over the treaty, and to permit normalization of relations with Israel to proceed only within the framework of a comprehensive settlement.

The president's trusted confidants were the legislative leaders, and they easily set the agenda. The ruling party, subordinate to the president, dominated the assembly and in a number of cases ousted its own parliamentary peers when their criticism antagonized the government. Many deputies were economically dependent on the government; in the 1980s a third of them were employed by the state. Because the executive can dissolve parliament and through its control of the ruling party and the electoral process replace incumbents with more docile deputies, the legislature was really at the president's mercy. When opposition parties appeared in parliament, it became a less submissive body, but the members of the large government majority did not view challenging the executive as part of their role. Generally, the legislature, lacking all traditions of independence or collective solidarity, had only the most modest capacity to check the government or hold it accountable.

Nevertheless, as limited political liberalization advanced, parliament played a growing, if still subordinate, role in the political system. Two changes fostered this role: first, the government relegated authority over lesser matters to parliament and, along with it, wider scope for debate and expression; second, opposition parties were permitted to win seats in parliament.

The chief result of this liberalization was that parliament became an arena through which the state shared power with its constituency, the dominant landed and business classes, allowing them to articulate their interests, albeit generally within the broader lines of presidential policy. Thus, parliamentary committees were breeding grounds for an endless stream of initiatives that sought to roll back state control or populist regulation of the private sector. For example, the Planning and Budget Committee demanded that the private sector get a fair share of foreign exchange and bank credit, that public sector shares be sold to investors, and that public industry be confined to areas private firms could not undertake. The Housing Committee pressured the Antiquities Department to divest itself of land coveted by developers. The Religious Affairs Committee became a sounding board for conservative religious opinion, pushing Islamization measures, and proposing bans on alcohol, Western films, and even belly dancing. Parliament also played some role in the budgetary process by which public resources were allocated and on a number of occasions blocked measures to levy taxes on wealthy farmers and business people.

Parliament had no record of deciding the big issues, but occasionally it became an arena for debating them. When the regime wished to change policy, parliament was sometimes the arena for testing the waters or for discrediting old policies as a prelude to launching new ones. Sadat encouraged parliament under his confidant, Sayyid Marii, to criticize the statist Sidqi government and used parliament as a vehicle of his de-Nasserization campaign. Once opposition parties took their seats in parliament, they attempted, with mixed success, to raise issues in opposition to government policy.

Parliament also played an ''oversight'' role, calling attention to shortcomings in the performance of the bureaucracy or bringing constituent grievances to government attention. Ministers were constantly criticized over market shortages and service breakdowns, and deputies who took their role seriously spent a great deal of time intervening with the bureaucracy on behalf of constituents. On occasion, parliament challenged the probity of actions by ministers and high officials. It attacked the Sidqi government over irregularities in the arrangements of a major oil pipeline project and the Khalil government over the awarding of a telecommunications contract. A project to build a resort near the pyramids, although involving persons close to President Sadat, was investigated and rejected in parliament. Whereas such parliamentary activities could serve the leader as a useful way of controlling the bureaucracy and as a safety valve for redress of grievances, if deputies went too far, they invited a reaction. Sadat was so irritated by the rise of parliamentary criticism that in 1979 he dissolved the People's Assembly

257

and called new elections, in which the regime, by a combination of fraud and intimidation, made sure its main critics lost their seats.

For those deputies willing to exercise their political skills in support of the government, however, parliamentary seats could be stepping-stones to political influence and elite careers. Parliamentary seats allowed deputies to act as brokers between government and their constituency, might serve as a base from which to cultivate strategic connections in government, and became something of a political apprenticeship by which certain more influential deputies became eligible for ministerial office. Parliament also served as a repository for high officials out of office who wished to keep their hand in the political pot. Judging by the number of candidates who sought parliamentary seats, these seats were worthwhile for developing connections in the capital and influence at home.

A second chamber was added to the legislature in the late 1970s when the Central Committee of the ASU was transformed into the Consultative Council, essentially an advisory chamber of notables and retired officials. In 1980 the membership was overhauled; 70 members were appointed by the president, and the ruling party won all 140 elected seats. In 1989 the ruling party again took all seats.

The Judiciary, Civil Rights, and the Rule of Law

The Egyptian legal system was built on both the sharia (Islamic law) and the Napoleonic Code introduced during Napoleon Bonaparte's occupation and the subsequent training of Egyptian jurists in France. Until they were abolished in the 1940s, consular courts and mixed courts (of foreign and Egyptian jurists), products of the capitulations, had jurisdiction over cases involving foreigners. Until the 1952 Revolution, there was a separate system of religious courts that applied the law of personal status, ruling in matters of marriage, divorce, and inheritance. Sharia courts had jurisdiction over Muslims while the Coptic minority had its own communal courts. Under the republic, religious courts were abolished and their functions transferred to the secular court system, although religious law continued to influence the decisions of these courts, especially in matters of personal status. In 1990 Egypt's court system was otherwise chiefly secular, applying criminal and civil law deriving primarily from the French heritage. In the 1970s and 1980s, however, Muslim political activists had fought with some success to advance the impact of the sharia in adjudication; for example, they were influential in reversing a liberal law of personal status decreed under Sadat that had expanded the rights of women. They also achieved the passage of a constitutional amendment making the sharia in principle the sole source of legislation, a potential ground for ruling unconstitutional a whole corpus of secular law.

Under the Constitution, the executive is prohibited from "interfering" in lawsuits or in the affairs of justice. Judges are appointed for life and cannot be dismissed without serious cause. This provision did not deter Nasser from a wholesale purge of politically hostile judges in the late 1960s, but his action was the exception. Under Sadat, who sought to replace revolutionary with constitutional legitimacy, the role of the judiciary was largely respected. Although often annoyed by their rulings in political cases, Sadat eschewed any purge of judges and resorted instead to the creation of exceptional courts for political offenses; for its part, the judiciary was able to ensure that a majority of appointees to these courts be trained judges. The presidency, nevertheless, continued to enjoy considerable influence over the judiciary since judicial appointments are a presidential prerogative. Judges were considered functionaries of the Ministry of Justice, which administered and financed the court system. The president headed the Supreme Council of Judicial Organs, which established regulations governing the judiciary.

The base of the court system was made up of district tribunals, single-judge courts with jurisdiction over minor civil and criminal cases. (Minor civil cases involved less than £E250, and minor criminal cases were punished by less than three years' imprisonment.) Over these there was in each governorate at least one tribunal of first instance, which was composed of a presiding judge and two sitting judges. These tribunals of first instance dealt with serious crimes and heard appeals from district courts. Seven higher-level courts of appeals in Cairo (Al Qahirah), Alexandria (Al Iskandariyah), Tanta, Asyut, Mansurah, Ismailia (Al Ismailiyah), and Bani Suwayf were divided into criminal and civil chambers; the former tried certain felonies, and the latter heard appeals against judgments of the tribunals of first instance. The Court of Cassation in Cairo heard petitions on final judgments rendered by the courts of appeals, made on grounds of defective application of the law or violation of due process. It had a president, fifteen vice presidents, and eighty justices. Alongside these courts of general jurisdiction were special courts, such as labor tribunals and security courts, headed by the Supreme State Security Court, which heard cases involving political and military security. A three-level hierarchy of administrative courts adjudicated administrative disputes among ministries and agencies and was headed by the Council of State. The Office of the Public Prosecutor, headed by the attorney general and staffed by his public prosecutors, supervised the enforcement of criminal law judgments. At the apex of the judiciary was the Supreme Constitutional Court made up of a chief justice and nine justices. It settled disputes between courts and rendered binding interpretations in matters that were grave enough to require conformity of interpretation under the Constitution.

The rule of law expanded in the post-Nasser era, and judges became a vigorous force defending the legal rights of citizens against the state. Nonpolitical personal rights, much restricted under Nasser, were effectively restored under Sadat. It was a sign of the new political climate he fostered that not only were private property rights considered inviolable but also the courts proved zealous in defending the rights of those charged with abuse of public property. Political rights were less secure. In contrast to Nasser, Sadat allowed private criticism of the government, but rights of public assembly were circumscribed by draconian laws against even peaceful protest and the distribution or possession of "subversive"—normally leftist—literature. Although the courts frequently dismissed charges on such offenses, those arrested nevertheless often spent much time in jail, nor have the courts been able to restrain the regime when it wanted badly enough to end dissidence. While Islamic radicals have been regularly subjected to arbitrary arrest, the most dramatic case of the "iron fist" was the 1981 crackdown, when Sadat arrested about 1,500 of Egypt's most prominent public figures.

Under Mubarak the independence of the courts and their role in expanding constitutional rights and procedures grew. Courts overturned a ban on the New Wafd Party, threw out the Electoral Law of 1984, and declared unconstitutional a Sadat decree issued in the absence of parliament. Judges expanded the scope of press freedom by dismissing libel suits of government ministers against the opposition press and widened the scope of labor rights by dismissing charges against strikers. But the regime saw fit to ignore a Supreme Constitutional Court ruling that overturned the distribution of certain seats in parliament to the disadvantage of the ruling party. The Ministry of Interior continued to exercise sweeping powers of arrest and detention of dissidents and frequently ignored court decisions (see The Judicial System, ch. 5).

The Political Role of the Media

Under Nasser the media were brought under state control and harnessed as instruments of the revolutionary government for shaping public opinion. Radio and television, in particular, began to penetrate the villages. Nasser used them to speak directly to Egyptians in their own language, and they were major factors in his rise as a charismatic leader. Radio Cairo was a link between Nasser and his pan-Arab constituency in the Arab world and was regularly used to stir up popular feeling against rival Arab leaders. In the print media, however, the government did not speak with one voice. There were identifiable differences in the government-controlled press between those on the right of the political spectrum (*Al Akhbar,* The News), the center (*Al Ahram,* The Pyramids), and the left (*Ruz al Yusuf*). Nasser, a voracious reader, appears to have been influenced by the views expressed in the prestigious *Al Ahram,* headed by Mohamed Hassanain Heikal. Criticism in the left-wing press played a role in the drift of his policies to the left in the 1960s. Thus, the press had a certain role in transmitting opinion upward.

In the post-Nasser era, the broadcast media remained government controlled. Fairly developed radio and television facilities existed. Egypt had sixty-two mediumwave amplitude modulation (AM) radio stations, representing at least one for each major town in the country, and three shortwave transmitters that relayed programs to listeners in Egypt and overseas. Domestically, stations carried a number of national programs as well as regional programs designed for different parts of Egypt. In its foreign programs, Egypt broadcast in thirty-three languages, including the most common European languages in addition to such African languages as Amharic, Hausa, Wolof, Swahili, and Yoruba and such Asian languages as Bengali, Hindi, Indonesian, and Urdu. Egyptians were estimated to own 14 million radios in 1989 and about 3.5 million television sets. Television had two national networks, an additional channel in Cairo, and a regional "Sinai network"; programs were televised in Arabic only. The broadcast media permitted the government to blanket the country with its messages. For example, the government enjoyed a virtual monopoly at election time. To placate Muslim opinion, television programming was increasingly Islamized, and several popular preachers in alliance with the government used the electronic media to broaden their followings.

Newspapers were scarcely more autonomous: government-appointed editors were still expected to "self-censor" their product and were subject to removal when they did not. Generally, Sadat used his prerogative of editorial appointment to eject editors and journalists with left-wing views and to foster conservative voices. For example, the anti-Nasser Amin brothers, Ali and Mustafa, reappeared in the journalistic establishment, and Ibrahim Saada was permitted to turn *Al Akhbar* into a vehicle of anti-Soviet and anti-Arab propaganda. The fall of Heikal at *Al Ahram* for allegedly trying to turn the paper into a "center of power" showed Sadat was no more willing than Nasser to tolerate a major journalistic voice at variance with his policy. Sadat, however, permitted the founding of an independent opposition press that reached far fewer readers but expressed much more diverse views than the government press. *Al Ahali* (The Folk) spoke for the left, *Al Ahrar* (The Liberals) for the right, *Ad Dawah* (The Call) and later *Al Ihtisan* (Adherence) for the Muslim Brotherhood, and *Ash Shaab* (The People) for the center-left Labor Party. The government party published *Al Mayu* (May). Opposition newspapers were sometimes joined by government papers in investigative journalism that uncovered scandals embarrassing to the government. The left-wing press, in particular, carried on a campaign against the *infitah* and Sadat's foreign policy that led to the closing of *Al Ahali*.

Mubarak restored freedom to the secular press, allowed the New Wafd Party to publish *Al Wafd* (The Mission) and Nasserites to open *Sawt al Arab* (Voice of the Arabs), while repressing the Brotherhood's *Ad Dawah*. The rise of Islamist sentiment was nevertheless reflected in the proliferation of Islamist periodicals put out by the various parties, such as *Al Liwa al Islami* (The Islamic Standard) by the government party and *An Nur* (The Light) by the Liberal Party (Ahrar). One sign of the growing independence and influence of the press under Mubarak was the 1987 trial of police officers for torturing Islamic activists, a milestone in the protection of individual rights that resulted largely from public pressures generated by the press. But there were limits to the influence of the press: the circulation of the main government dailies did not exceed 1 million each, and except for *Al Wafd*, the opposition papers were all weeklies lucky to get a tenth of that figure.

Interest Groups

The widening scope for interest-group politics was one of the most significant dimensions of the limited liberalization begun under Sadat. Under the Nasser regime, which distrusted the effect of pressure groups on public policy, interest groups were brought into a corporatist system whereby their leaders were government appointed. They were thus rendered powerless to deflect the mounting state assault on private interests launched in the name of socialism. Sadat, seeking to win the support of the land-owning and educated classes, permitted their associated interest groups greater autonomy and opened greater access for them into the decision-making process. Their members turned parliament into a channel for promoting their interests, and their representatives carried weight in the system of consultative national councils. Under Mubarak the numbers and influence of interest groups grew, and although the relation between the state and these associations was by no means free of conflict, they carried much more weight in policy councils than the unorganized mass public. Of all interests,

Government television building, Cairo
Courtesy Embassy of Egypt, Washington

business made the best use of the widened scope for interest-group activity. In men such as Osman Ahmad Osman, business enjoyed the direct access to Sadat critical for steering the transition from statism. But organizations like the Chamber of Commerce and the Federation of Industries also spoke with increasing authority for their interests against both the state sector and labor. The Businessmen's Association and the Egyptian-American Chamber of Commerce united the most powerful business interests and facilitated their access to state resources. The government even encouraged formation of new business organizations, such as a joint venture investors' association and an exporters' union.

To be sure, the bourgeoisie was far from united on many issues. Business people vied for lucrative privileged deals with the public sector, and those connected to its patronage networks were much more favorable to the state than those in competition with it. Such competition included the bankers, who fought the public sector for control of foreign exchange, and others who had to pay off officials merely to operate. Clashes also occurred between the interests of importers and of local industrialists and between the secular *haute bourgeoisie* and Islamic-oriented small business.

Nevertheless, on the big issues such as *infitah,* government regulation, taxation, prices, and wages, business shared a common view.

Thus, business people and business groups were instrumental in pressuring for the widening of *infitah* under Sadat. They continually lobbied, with considerable success, for tax reductions and exemptions on the ground that the mobilization of savings and investment required these concessions. The government responded by reducing the progressive rates of the income tax and permitting a proliferation of "tax holidays" for new investment. The ability of the rich to evade taxes had become such a scandal by the end of the 1970s that Sadat declared the rich were not paying their fair share of taxes. The Chamber of Commerce lobbied aggressively against attempts by the Ministry of Supply to fix profit ceilings on imported commodities and fought back pressures from the trade unions for increases in minimum wages. Construction and real estate interests, operating through the Housing Committee of parliament, pushed through the demolition of lower-income neighborhoods to make way for luxury hotels, highways, parking lots, and office towers. The Federation of Industries launched a campaign to roll back public sector monopolies in fields where industrialists wanted to invest, while at the same time pushing for protection from foreign competition. Owners of large farms were also successful in advancing their interests. Operating through the Agricultural Affairs Committee of parliament, they won an alteration in the Law on Agrarian Relations, reducing the security of tenants and raising their rents; had public money allocated to compensate victims of the Nasserite land reforms; and won the right to bid on reclaimed state land, unrestricted by the agrarian reform ceiling.

The professional syndicates or unions also worked to defend the interests of their members. The medical syndicate, for example, lobbied to restrain the indiscriminate expansion of professional school enrollments, which it said was producing a surplus of under-trained graduates. The engineers' syndicate insisted that foreign firms be required to hire a quota of Egyptian engineers.

The actions of the journalists' and lawyers' syndicates stood out as cases where professionals took positions on wider political issues in opposition to the regime. The syndicates took these positions partly because these associations were battlegrounds between rival political forces and partly because their professional interests demanded political freedoms greater than those that the regime was willing to concede. Thus, the journalists' union long fought to expand press freedoms. Sadat inserted a trusted confidant to discipline the union, and when the strong leftist influence in the profession led to the election of a leftist, he tried unsuccessfully to abolish the union. The Mubarak regime, however, managed to reassert its control.

The lawyers' syndicate also became an independent force trouble-some to the regime. While lawyers generally applauded Sadat's liberalization and the restoration of the rule of law, he did not go far enough to please many. The union gave New Wafdist leader Fuad Siraj ad Din (also seen as Serag al Din) a forum for his attempt to resurrect his party. Siraj ad Din vigorously attacked Sadat's Law of Shame by which he attempted to outlaw all criticism ''disrespectful'' of presidential authority. Sadat finally purged the syndicate leadership when it attacked the normalization of relations with Israel. Under Mubarak the syndicate became an even more contentious defender of civil liberties; in 1986 lawyers staged a strike against the continuation of emergency laws, and in 1988 the syndicate raised a public storm when it launched a campaign against the abuse of emergency laws and illegal detentions.

Public sector managers also entered the interest group arena as the *infitah* unfolded, embodying both threats and opportunities for them. The Ministry of Industry convened assemblies in which public sector officials were allowed to vent their grievances. Seeking to compete and survive in a freer economy, they demanded discretion to raise prices as costs rose, reduction of their tax burden, and authority over personnel policy to ''link incentives to production.'' They also lobbied against a joint-venture textile factory that threatened to flood the market at the expense of the public textile industry. The managers had but limited success, however, because their desire for lower taxes clashed with the needs of the treasury, and their desire to raise prices and dismiss excess labor risked a popular reaction the government could ill afford. Public sector managers increasingly saw their salvation, therefore, in joint ventures with foreign firms that would release them from government restrictions and from the provisions of the labor code. Pushing from the other side with mixed success, the trade unions voiced the objections of public sector workers to any weakening of the labor code. The unions fought for increases in the minimum wage, too, but raises always seemed to lag behind the rising cost of living.

Generally speaking, the widened scope for interest-group politics in post-Nasser Egypt opened access for the ''haves'' to the policy process. But this was to the exclusion of, and often at the expense of, the less well connected or unorganized masses.

Controlling the Mass Political Arena

A state may control the political arena through some combination of legitimacy, coercion, and the incorporation of participation through political institutions. Nasser used charisma and coercion to impose a nationalist-populist ideological consensus on Egypt's political arena and to incorporate a broad support coalition in a single—albeit weak—party, the Arab Socialist Union (ASU). His charismatic legitimacy allowed him to balance rival social forces. For example, he used popular support to curb the bourgeoisie, rather than to accommodate their participatory propensities, and to repress those—the Wafd (Al Wafd al Misri), and the Muslim Brotherhood—that refused incorporation into his coalition. The post-Nasser regime had to reshape Egypt's political institutions in order to maintain control over the political arena without the legitimacy and coercive assets he had commanded.

Sadat resorted to a strategy mixing limited liberalization, retraditionalization, and repression. He pioneered an experiment in limited political pluralization designed to control the politically attentive public. Needing to solicit the support of the bourgeoisie in the absence of the broad mass legitimacy Nasser had enjoyed, Sadat had to address its desires for political liberalization. Moreover, as his ''rightward'' policy course shattered the consensus Nasser had built and precipitated the emergence of leftist-Nasserite opposition, Sadat sought to balance this opposition by allowing the mainstream Islamic movement and the liberal New Wafd Party to reenter the political arena. As Egypt's political arena was thus pluralized, Sadat attempted to incorporate it through a controlled multiparty system. The ASU was dismantled and opposition parties allowed to coalesce around its fragments or the remnants of resurrected prerevolutionary parties. They were expected to be ''loyal'' opposition parties that would refrain from ''destructive'' criticism of regime policy but within this limit were allowed to compete with the government party in parliamentary elections. Even Nasserites and the Marxist left were more or less accommodated within these parties, although they were vulnerable to exclusion from the system when they pushed their cases too far; indeed, ultimately, when they refused to play by his rules, Sadat suspended the experiment.

Toward the more passive masses, Sadat's strategy was to replace charismatic with traditional personal legitimacy, projecting himself as a pious and patriarchal leader and, after 1973, as a successful war hero. But as corruption and inequality spread while he pursued Westernization and accommodation with Israel, this strategy gradually failed, leaving a legitimacy vacuum that paved the way for his assassination. The absence of public mourning on his death, in stark contrast to the mass hysteria on Nasser's passing, was a measure of the decline of regime legitimacy by the end of Sadat's presidency.

Mubarak inherited a regime lacking a credible legitimizing ideology or a leading personality capable of attracting mass loyalties to the state. Indicative of the regime's ideological bankruptcy following Sadat's death was Mubarak's attempt to portray his new regime as both Nasserite and Islamic, all the while continuing Sadatist policies. In the absence of ideological legitimacy, the Mubarak regime had to restore the faltering political liberalization pioneered by Sadat. Mubarak revived opposition parties and widened freedom of political expression, particularly of the press, permitting much more unrestrained criticism of the government than was permitted under Sadat. Limited political pluralization was essential to accommodate the participatory demands of the educated upper and middle classes, and given the continuing passivity, poverty, and deference of a large part of the masses, such pluralization could be managed with less risk than the alternative of large-scale repression. Moreover, as under Sadat, liberalization was not uniformly applied to social groups. The regime sought to accommodate more conservative forces, such as the liberal bourgeoisie and conservative Islamists, while reserving selective repression for leftists, strikers, and Islamic radicals.

The "Dominant Party System"

In Egypt's "dominant party system," a big ruling party straddling the center of the ideological spectrum was flanked by small opposition "parties of pressure" on its left and right.

The Ruling Party

The ruling National Democratic Party (NDP) was a direct descendant of Nasser's Arab Socialist Union, albeit shorn of the left-wing intellectuals and politicized officers who dominated it in the 1960s. By the 1980s, it incorporated the ruling alliance of senior bureaucrats, top police and army officers, business people, and large landowners who dominated the governorates. Most of these elites had a foot in both state and society, combining public office and private assets. The party's official ideology expressed this social composition: it stood for a middle way between socialism and individualistic capitalism. This middle way would be compatible with a large public sector, in which the many senior bureaucrats and state managers had a stake, and with the growing private and foreign capitalism, on which both officials and proregime business people were thriving. The party's ideology was generally too vague and ambivalent to determine government policy, but it authentically expressed the stake of its constituents in both a massive state and an open economy. The relative balance between the party's elements shifted over time; under Sadat the *infitah* bourgeoisie rose to prominence, while Mubarak shifted the balance in favor of the state bourgeoisie and the old pre-1952 aristocracy.

The NDP, lacking developed organization and ideological solidarity, was a weak party, in many ways more an appendage of government than an autonomous political force. But it performed useful functions for both the regime and its membership. Although the bureaucracy and academia remained the principal channels of elite recruitment, party credentials and service became a factor in such cooptation, and the party represented a ladder of recruitment for the private sector bourgeoisie. The party did not make high policy, and many of the policy recommendations of its committees, such as calls for the application of the sharia and abolition of the public sector, were simply ignored by the government. But its parliamentary caucus assumed considerable authority over lesser matters: it was the source of a constant stream of initiatives and responses to government meant to defend or to promote the interest of its largely bourgeois constituency. Thus, the NDP incorporated major segments of the most strategic social forces into the ruling coalition; it conceded no accountability to them but provided enough privileged access to satisfy them.

The party lacked a strong extragovernmental organization, enjoyed little loyalty from its members, and had few activists; indeed, police officials played a prominent role in its leadership, and in the governorates the Ministry of Interior seemed to act for the party in the absence of a real apparatus. But by way of the client networks of progovernment notables, the party brought a portion of the village and urban masses into the regime's camp, denying the opposition access to them. The party also nominally incorporated large numbers of government employees and managed to place its partisans in the top posts of most of the professional and labor syndicates. The party lacked an interest in mass mobilization, and, if anything, its function was to enforce demobilization. The government had to depend on the Ministry of Interior, village headmen, and local notables to bring out the vote. But as an organizational bond between the regime and the local sub-elites that represented its core support and its linkage to wider social forces, the party helped protect the government's societal base.

The Opposition Parties

The once monolithic Egyptian political arena gave birth in the 1970s to a rich array of new political parties competing with the ruling party. While some were a "loyal" opposition and others closer to counterregime movements, all gave expression to interests and values different from those of the ruling party.

The tiny Liberal Party was formed in 1976 from a right-wing sliver of the ASU by an ex-army officer. Grouping landowners and professionals, it was to the right of the ruling party. Its ideology combined calls for the selling of the public sector, an end to subsidies, and unrestricted foreign investment with demands for further political liberalization and an attempt to mobilize God and Islam in defense of capitalism. Having little popular appeal, it operated as an elite pressure group speaking for private enterprise and generally in support of Sadat's liberalization policies.

Although also beginning as a faction of the ASU headed by a left-wing Free Officer, Khalid Muhi ad Din, the National Progressive Unionist Party (NPUP or Tagamu) evolved into an authentic opposition party of the left. It brought together, behind an ideology of nationalist populism, a coalition of Marxist and Nasserite intellectuals and trade union leaders. It defended the Nasserite heritage, rejected the alignment with the United States and the separate peace with Israel, and called for a return to Egypt's anti-imperialist role. It rejected the *infitah* as damaging to national industry and leading to foreign domination, debt, corruption, and inequality; it called for a return to development led by the public sector. It had a small but well organized base of activists.

The Socialist Labor Party (SLP or Amal) was formed in 1979 under Sadat's encouragement to displace the NPUP (which was proving too critical) as the loyal opposition party of the left. While its social composition—landlords and professionals—resembled the Liberal Party, many of its leaders were quite different in political background, having belonged to the radical nationalist Young Egypt Party (Misr al Fatat) before 1952. Despite its origin, the party, alienated by Sadat's separate peace, by the corruption in his regime, and by the excesses of *infitah,* soon moved into opposition, becoming a public sector defender critical of untrammeled capitalism and Western alignment. The SLP lacked a large organized base and relied on the personal followings of its leaders. It and the Liberal Party, in an effort to overcome their limited popular appeal, joined in 1987 with the Muslim Brotherhood in the Islamic Alliance under the slogan "Islam is the solution."

The New Wafd Party was a coalition of landowners, professionals, and merchants, led by a number of prominent leaders of the original Wafd, notably Fuad Siraj ad Din. It was the voice of the old aristocracy excluded from power by Nasser and of the wing of the private bourgeoisie still antagonistic to the state bourgeoisie that emerged in the shadow of the regime. It also enjoyed a significant following among the educated middle class. The party's main plank called for genuine political liberalization, including competitive election of the president. It demanded thorough economic liberalization to match political liberalization, including a radical reduction in the public sector, in state intervention in the economy, and in barriers to a full opening to international capitalism. Although it clashed with Sadat over the legitimacy of the 1952 Revolution, as the economic role of the state was strengthened under Mubarak, the New Wafd Party came to speak with a Sadatist slant to the "right" of the ruling NDP.

The Islamic movement was fragmented into a multitude of autonomous factions that shared the common goal of an Islamic state but differed in social origin and in tactics. Those that were willing to work through the system were allowed to organize and nominate candidates in parliamentary elections. But no Islamic party, as such, was permitted, and major sections of the movement remained in intense, often violent conflict with the regime. Thus, the movement was only partially integrated into the party system.

The mainstream of the movement, the Muslim Brotherhood, was a coalition led by ulama, merchants, and lower-middle-class student activists commanding a following in the traditional urban quarters. It was founded as a radical movement in the 1930s by Hasan al Banna, was repressed under Nasser, and reemerged in more moderate form under Sadat. Umar Tilmasani, its main leader in the Sadat era, was associated with the *infitah,* and its leader thereafter, Muhammad Hamid Abu an Nasr, was from a wealthy provincial family. The Brotherhood was split along generational lines among factions loyal to its various previous leaders. These factions included the more radical elements loyal to the founder, the conservative Tilmasani faction, and the parliamentary caucus in the late 1980s led by Mahmud al Hudaibi, son of the second Supreme Guide, or party leader. On the Brotherhood's right were wealthy conservatives who justified capitalism in the language of religion. The more activist Jamaat al Islamiyah (Islamic Associations), an amorphous movement of many small groups, were drawn from a cross-section of the student population, while the most radical Islamic groups, such as At Takfir wal Hijra (Atonement and Alienation) and Al Jihad (Holy War), were made up of educated, lower-middle-class elements and recent urban emigrants from the village (see Islam, ch. 2, Muslim Extremism, ch. 5). Various populist preachers in the traditional urban neighborhoods enjoyed broad personal followings. Whereas the movement was weak among industrial workers and peasants, it was strongly attractive to more "marginal" elements such as educated, unemployed, rural migrants and the traditional mass of small merchants and artisans. All the Islamic groups shared a rejection of both Marxism and Westernization in the name of an Islamic third way that accepted private property and profit but sought to contain their inegalitarian consequences by a moral code and a welfare state. The main ideological difference between the Islamic groups centered on the means for reaching an Islamic order; whereas moderate groups advocated peaceful proselytization, detente with the regime, and work through established institutions, radical groups pursued a more activist challenge to the secular order, and some advocated its violent overthrow.

Elections

The pluralization of the party system was accompanied by a parallel but limited opening up of the electoral system. Parliamentary elections continued to be held even after the 1952 establishment of an authoritarian system, although they were never truly competitive and played almost no role in recruitment of the top elite, which was selected from above. The elections were not meaningless, however. They were a mechanism by which the regime coopted into parliament politically acceptable local notables, and they served as a safety valve for managing the pressures for participation.

During the period of single-party elections (1957–72), government controls were tight, and candidates were screened for political loyalty by the leading Free Officers who dominated the party. Some choice was permitted among candidates, who normally were authentic local notables, and the personal prestige and resources of rival candidates often decided the outcome. In the 1960s, a dual-member constituency system was introduced, in which one of two seats was reserved for a worker or peasant. As mentioned earlier, this system was a largely unsuccessful attempt to draw the lower classes into the electoral process.

Beginning in 1976, Sadat permitted competition among three proto-parties of the left, center, and right, a major step on the road to a more open political process; scores of independents were also allowed to run. The 1979 elections, in which antigovernment candidates running against the peace treaty with Israel encountered a wall of government harassment and fraud, represented a step backward from liberalization.

The 1984 and 1987 elections under Mubarak, however, were the most open and competitive elections since 1952. There were more parties, because the New Wafd Party and the NPUP, excluded by Sadat, were readmitted, and the Muslim Brotherhood was allowed to run individual candidates under the auspices of an allied secular party. Because campaigning was freer and more extensive than ever, it was also clearer to more people that party stands on issues were important in the elections. But, as if to counter this, the government's introduction of the 1984 Election Law meant to exclude smaller parties from parliament: no party that received less than 8 percent of the vote would receive seats, and its votes would be added to the party achieving a plurality. Moreover, the dual-member constituency system was replaced with large multi-member districts in which party lists competed. This arrangement diluted the influence of local notables vis-à-vis the government but also reduced the regime's ability to coopt them because many refused to run for election under these conditions. It also ended the guarantee of half of the seats for workers and peasants. The low turnout for elections indicated that many Egyptians were unconvinced that voting under these conditions made any difference to political outcomes; although officials announced a 47 percent 1987 turnout, the number of voters was actually closer to 25 percent.

Even under the relatively open multiparty elections, the government party continued to have the upper hand and never failed to win a large majority. The government party monopolized the broadcast media, and the government tried to restrict opposition attempts to reach the voters. The Ministry of Interior ran the elections, in which the ballot was not really secret; it mobilized local headmen on the side of government; and it sometimes resorted to outright stuffing of ballot boxes. Ruling-party "toughs" and police often intimidated opposition poll watchers and voters. The government benefited from the tendency of many voters to support the government candidate out of deference to authority, hope for advantage, or realization that the opposition would not be permitted a majority. Many workers and peasants, economically dependent on a government job or agricultural services, dared not antagonize the government.

Because the scope of opposition on issues was so narrow, the personal prestige and patronage resources of candidates played a major role in swaying votes, and the government party typically coopted its candidates from local notables with such resources. Patronage could range from the distribution of chickens at election time, to the promise of government jobs or the delivery of roads and utilities to a village, to the refurbishing of the local mosque. Voters were also influenced by the prestige of wealth and profession, the well-known family name that could forge intricate patterns of family alliances, and the national-level stature that made one a local "favorite son." Only as the electoral process was pluralized did ideologies and issues come to play a role, but this role remained limited; many voters either lacked political consciousness or were unconvinced of the efficacy of issue voting in an authoritarian regime.

Buses are a major element in Cairo's transportation.
Courtesy Susan Becker

Urban middle- and working-class voters were most likely to vote on an issue basis, but in the rural areas most people cast their votes for the notables for whom they worked or for those who had the government connections best able to do them favors. Thus, the government could offset the votes of the more politically conscious with a mass of rural votes delivered on a clientage basis.

The outcomes of the four multiparty elections reflected a certain changing balance of power between government and the opposition and among the competing opposition forces. In the first multiparty elections of 1976, the government center faction won 280 of 350 seats; the right (soon-to-be Liberal Party) 12; and the left (soon-to-be NPUP), 4. In addition, there were forty-eight independents, some of whom emerged as leading opposition figures. In 1979 Sadat, having repressed the NPUP and the just-formed New Wafd Party, allowed only one supposedly loyal opposition party, the Socialist Labor Party, to compete, and the government party (the NDP) won all but thirty seats. In the 1984 elections, the New Wafd Party and the Muslim Brotherhood formed a joint ticket. The NDP got 73 percent of the vote and took 390 of 448 seats, whereas the New Wafd Party-Brotherhood alliance captured 58 seats with 15 percent of the vote and emerged as the main opposition force. The smaller parties were excluded from parliament by the 8 percent rule. In 1987 the New Wafd Party ran alone, while the small Liberal and Socialist Labor parties joined with the Muslim Brotherhood in the Islamic Alliance. The New Wafd Party won thirty-five seats and the Islamic Alliance, sixty. Thus, under Mubarak the government majority remained unchallengeable, but it had declined, and the New Wafd Party and the Islamic movement had emerged as a significant opposition presence in parliament. However, the exclusion of the NPUP from parliament, principally through the 1984 Election Law, marginalized Egypt's only unambiguously populist voice, the one force that was free of wealthy patrons or powerful economic interests and that set forth an alternative noncapitalist economic program. Parliament remained almost exclusively a preserve of the bourgeoisie. The 1987 elections marked not only the growing influence of Islam and the decline of the secular left, but also the rise of a new Islamic-secular cleavage cutting across class-based rifts and putting the regime, the NPUP, and the New Wafd Party on the same side. This cross-cutting tended to mute political conflict to the advantage of the regime.

Despite their seeming inability to win power, the opposition parties had a real function as ''parties of pressure'' in the dominant party system. They articulated the interests and values of sectors of the population ignored by the dominant party. They helped frame the terms of public debate by raising issues that would otherwise have remained off the public agenda. For opposition activists, participation offered the chance to espouse ideas, to shape public opinion, and occasionally even to influence policy because if they threatened to capture enough support, they might force the government to alter its course. The Liberal Party helped advance economic liberalization under Sadat, while the NPUP was a brake on the reversal of populist policies. The Islamists won Islamization concessions from the secular regime, whereas the New Wafd Party helped make partial political liberalization irreversible.

A party of pressure might also act as an interest group advocating particular interests in elite circles or promoting the fortunes of aspirant politicians hoping for cooptation. Mubarak's more consensual style of rule and regular consultation with opposition leaders marginally advanced their ability to influence government policy. For example, in early 1990 Mubarak bowed to an opposition campaign and removed the unpopular minister of interior, Zaki Badr. A tacit understanding existed between government and opposition: the latter knew if it went too far in challenging the regime, it invited repression, whereas the former knew if it were too unresponsive or tightened controls too much, it risked antisystem mobilization.

The primary consequence of the system in the short run was the stabilization of the regime. The divisions in the opposition allowed the regime to play them against each other. Secularists were pitted against Islamists, left against right. The opposition parties channeled much political activity that might otherwise have taken a covert, even violent, antiregime direction into more tame, manageable forms. Opposition elites, in working through the system, brought their followings into it; a sign of the regime's success was the incorporation of the three political formations that had been most independent under Sadat—the New Wafd Party, the Muslim Brotherhood, and the NPUP—into the system under Mubarak.

In the longer run, the party experiment was deepening the pluralization of the political arena. That the pluralization begun under Sadat was real was clear from the persistence of all the parties then founded. They proved to be more than personalistic or official factions and either revived some political tradition or were rooted in an underlying social cleavage or dissent on a major issue. The rough correspondence between the ideologies of the parties and their social bases indicated a "blocking out" of the political arena, moving Egyptian politics beyond a mere competition of patrons and *shillas* without social roots. This pluralization had, however, only begun to seep down to the level of the mass public, much of which remained politically apathetic or attached to traditional client networks. The dominant party system had adapted sufficiently to the level of pluralization in the 1980s to impart a crucial element of stability to the regime.

The Limits of Incorporation: The Rise of Political Islam and the Continuing Role of Repression

The social base of the state under Sadat and Mubarak was undoubtedly narrower than it had been under Nasser. In some ways, it was more solid. It rested on the hard-core support of the most strategic social force, the bourgeoisie, which had a major stake in its survival, and it at least partially incorporated elements of the opposition through the party/interest group structure created under limited liberalization. Yet, although the parties articulated interests, they did not, as in strong party systems, incorporate a large mobilized public or the interests of the masses into the making of public policies. There was still an institutional gap between public wishes and policy outcomes; decisions, still made in limited elite circles, therefore enjoyed little societal support. Moreover, the regime still lacked the ideological legitimacy to win the loyalty of the masses. By the middle of the 1980s, as economic expansion gave way to austerity, the challenge of mass control became ever more burdensome. The limits of the regime's capacity to incorporate dissident factions left the door open to the rise of a counter-elite in the form of the Islamic movement, and the regime had to continue to rely on coercion and repression to stave off dissent and rebellion.

The development of the Islamic movement in the 1980s was the most significant change in the political arena and one with the potential to transform the system. Sadat originally unleashed the movement against his leftist opponents, but as Westernization and the *infitah* advanced, the Islamic movement became a vehicle of opposition, sometimes violent, to his regime. He attempted to curb it, but under Mubarak it took on new dimensions. The more violent messianic groups, such as Al Jihad, were the targets of continual repression and containment, apparently only partly successful. Their destabilizing potential was indicated by their role in the assassination of Sadat, a major rebellion they mounted in Asyut at that time, a 1986 wave of attacks on video shops and Westernized boutiques, and assassination attempts against high officials. The regime responded by arresting thousands of these radical activists. Another Islamic body, the Jamaat al Islamiyah, recovered the control of the student unions Sadat tried to break. In the mid-1980s, they won twice the number of votes of the NDP in student union elections, and the secular opposition was squeezed out. The left made inroads in their dominance toward the end of the decade, however. Radical groups belonging to Jamaat al Islamiyah tried to impose a puritanical, sometimes anti-Coptic, Islamic regime on the campuses and in the towns of Upper Egypt, where local government sometimes bowed to their demands. More moderate groups in Jamaat al Islamiyah could turn out large disciplined crowds for public prayer, the nearest thing to a mass demonstration that the regime reluctantly permitted. A major contest was waged over Egypt's 40,000 mosques; the government sought to appoint imams but had too few reliable candidates, while the movement sought to wrest control of these major potential centers of Islamic propaganda.

The influence of Islamic groups in poor urban neighborhoods seemed to grow in the 1980s. In 1985 when parliament rejected immediate application of the sharia, Islamic agitation led by Shaykh Hafiz Salama swept Cairo, and in the late 1980s bitter clashes occurred in Ayn Shams between a kind of Islamic ''shadow government'' there and the security forces. Although Islamic militants were certainly a minority and were even resented by a good portion of the public, their activism in a largely passive political arena gave them great power. The government tried to drive a wedge between the more militant youth groups and the Islamic mainstream; thus, in 1989 Shaykh Muhammad Mutwalli Sharawi, a prestigious and popular preacher, was brought to denounce the use of violence in the name of Islam.

The Islamic mainstream, possessed of increasing cohesion, organization, and mobilizational capability, rapidly took advantage of the legitimate channels of activity opened by the regime under Mubarak. The mainstream Muslim Brotherhood and its conservative cousins were incorporated into parliament; they infiltrated the parties, the judiciary, and the press; and they generally put secular forces on the defensive. The more the secular opposition proved impotent to wrest a share of power from the regime, the more dissidents seemed to turn to political Islam as the only viable alternative. A dramatic indicator of this was the substantial representation Islamists won in the professional syndicates, especially the doctors' union, traditionally bastions of the liberal, upper-middle class; only the lawyers' and journalists' unions resisted their sway. Victories indicative of Islamic influence included the reversal of Sadat's law of personal status that gave women some modest rights, a decision by certain state companies to cease hiring women so they could take their "proper place in the home," and a constitutional amendment making sharia the sole basis of legislation. Islamic sentiment and practices were widespread in the 1980s. Filling the vacuum left by the withering of state populism, the Islamic movement constructed an alternative social infrastructure—mosques, clinics, cooperatives—to bring the masses under Islamic leadership.

The movement was backed by the power of Islamic banking and investment houses, an enigmatic development that possibly was filling the gap left by the decline of the state economy. Claiming to represent an alternative economic way, these Islamic banks initially seemed better positioned than government or foreign banks to mobilize the savings of ordinary people. Yet, while the Islamic movement grew up in opposition to Westernization and the *infitah,* these institutions were linked to entrepreneurs enriched in the oil states who made huge profits on the same international connections and through many of the same speculative financial, black-market, and tertiary enterprises *infitah* had encouraged. As scandals shook public confidence in them, the government moved to curb their autonomy. But their tentacles reached into the political system. They were major contributors to the ruling NDP and had forged alliances with the New Wafd Party and the Islamic Alliance as well. It was unclear by 1990 whether the effect of Islamic banking institutions would be to incorporate ordinary Egyptians into a more indigenous, broader-based capitalism adjusted to the *infitah* regime, to provide the economic basis for an alternative socio-political order, or to prove a mere flash in the pan. The regime's mix of hostility and wary tolerance toward them suggested it was not sure itself.

The Islamic movement thus emerged as a powerful cross-class political alliance, a potential counterestablishment. As its economic and political power grew, however, there were signs that its anti-regime populism was being overshadowed by the emergence of a bourgeois leadership preaching conservative values: class deference, respect for elders, female submission, the right to a fair profit, and the superiority of the private sector. To the extent that its program thus became indistinguishable, except in symbolism, from regime policies, a gap threatened to separate this leadership from its plebeian following, splitting or enervating the movement. If the bourgeois leadership prevailed, the outcome was likely to be a gradual cooptation of the Islamic movement and Islamization of the regime rather than Islamic revolution.

To the extent control mechanisms proved inadequate, a role remained for coercion and repression in the political system. Under Nasser coercive controls were very tight although largely directed at the upper class and limited numbers of middle-class opposition activists. Sadat initially relaxed controls, particularly over the bourgeoisie, but when opposition became too insistent, he did not hesitate to repress it. His massive 1981 purge showed how quickly the regime could change from conciliation to repression. Under the more tolerant Mubarak regime, political freedoms were still unequally enjoyed. Dissent within regime institutions was tolerated, but when it crossed the line into mass action—such as Islamic street demonstrations for implementation of sharia and anti-Israeli protests—it was regularly repressed. Strikes were also regularly smashed with the use of force. The regime continued to round up leftist and Islamic dissidents, charging them with belonging to illegal organizations or spreading antigovernment propaganda, apparently part of a strategy to keep dissent within manageable bounds. Indeed, the regime went so far as to arrest whole families of political dissidents and to hold them as virtual hostages in order to pressure suspects to surrender.

The security apparatus, more massive than ever, contained the main episodes of violent challenge to the regime—notably the food riots and localized Islamic uprisings at Sadat's death. The Ministry of Interior presided over several coercive arms including the General Directorate for State Security Investigations (GDSSI), the domestic security organization, and the gendarmerie-like Central

Security Forces; behind the police stood the army itself (see Internal Security, ch. 5). But there were signs that these forces were neither totally reliable nor effective. In the 1977 riots, the army reputedly refused to intervene unless the government rescinded the price rises, and scattered Nasserite and Islamic dissidence in the military continued in the 1980s. There were rivalries between the army and the Ministry of Interior, and disagreements inside the latter over whether dialogue or the iron fist could best deal with opposition. In 1986 the CSF itself revolted. Although the rebellion had no political program and was mainly sparked by worsening treatment of the lower ranks, it signaled that the use of conscripts from the poorest sectors of society to contain radical opposition to a bourgeois regime was ever more risky. Yet the regime continued thereafter to use the CSF against students, strikers, and Islamic militants. Finally, the assassination of Sadat after his crackdown on12the opposition showed that coercion could run two ways; according to its perpetrators, their purpose was "to warn all who come after him and teach them a lesson."

Foreign Policy
The Determinants of Foreign Policy

Geopolitics inevitably shaped Egypt's foreign policy. Egypt occupies a strategic position as a landbridge between two continents and a link between two principal waterways, the Mediterranean Sea and the Indian Ocean. It must therefore be strong enough to dominate its environment or risk becoming the victim of outside powers. Its security is also linked to control of the Nile, on whose waters its survival depends. It has, therefore, had historical ties with Sudan and has sought satisfactory relations with the states on Sudan's southern borders, Uganda and Zaire. The landbridge to Asia, route of potential conquerors, had also to be secured, and Egyptian rulers traditionally tried to project their power into Syria and Arabia, often in contest with other powers in Anatolia (present-day Turkey), or the Euphrates River valley (present-day Iraq). In contemporary times, Israel, backed by a superpower, located on Egypt's border, and blocking its access to the east, was perceived as the greatest threat to Egyptian security.

Egypt was also politically strategic. As Nasser saw it, with considerable justice, Egypt was potentially at the center of three "circles," the African, the Arab, and the Islamic. Egypt viewed itself as playing a major role in Africa and, beyond that, was long a leading mover in the wider Third World camp and a major advocate of neutralism and nonalignment. This geopolitical importance made the country the object of interest to the great powers, and when Egypt was strong enough, as under Nasser, allowed it to play the great powers against each other and win political support and economic and military aid from all sides. Even the weakened Egypt of Mubarak was able to parlay its strategic importance in the Arab-Israeli conflict and as a bulwark against Islamic political activism into political support and economic aid from both the West and the Arab world.

A second constant that shaped Egypt's foreign policy was its Arab-Islamic character. To be sure, Egypt had a long pre-Islamic heritage that gave it a distinct identity, and in periods such as the British occupation it developed apart from the Arab world. Egypt's national identity was never merged in an undifferentiated Arabism; Egyptians were shaped by their own distinct geography, history, dialect, and customs. But the content of Egyptian identity was indisputably Arab-Islamic. Egypt was inextricably a part of the Arab world. It was the largest Arabic-speaking country and the intellectual and political center to which the whole Arab world looked in modern times. It was also a center of Islamic civilization, its Al Azhar University one of Islam's major religious institutions and its popular culture profoundly Islamic. Although a portion of the most Westernized upper class at times saw Egypt as Mediterranean or pharaonic (see Glossary), for the overwhelming majority, Egypt's identity was Arab-Islamic.

Indeed, Egypt saw itself as the leader of the Arab world, entitled to preeminence in proportion to the heavy burdens it bore in defense of the Arab cause. This Arab-Islamic identity was a great asset for Egyptian leaders. To the extent that Egyptian leadership was acknowledged in the Arab world, this prestige bolstered the stature of the ruler at home, entitled Egypt to a portion of Arab oil wealth, and gave credence to Egypt's ability to define a common Arab policy, hence increasing the country's strategic weight in world affairs. This leadership position also meant that Egypt was a natural part of the inter-Arab power balance, typically embroiled in the rivalries that split the Arab world and a part of the solidarities that united it. In the 1950s, modernizing, nationalist Egypt's rivals were traditional pro-Western Iraq and Saudi Arabia, and its main ally was Syria. In the 1970s, an alliance of Egypt, Syria, and Saudi Arabia led the Arab world in its search for peace with honor; when Sadat made a separate peace, Syria became Egypt's main rival. The country's Arab-Islamic identity also put certain constraints on foreign-policy decision makers: to violate it risked the legitimacy of the whole regime.

Finally, Egypt's foreign policy was pulled in contrary directions by the ideals of anti-imperialist nonalignment and the webs of dependency in which the country was increasingly enmeshed. Egypt's long history of subordination to foreign rulers, especially European imperialism, produced an inferiority complex, an intense anti-imperialism, a quest for dignity, and, particularly under Nasser, a powerful national pride among Egyptians. Egypt's national ideal was to be independent of both East and West, to be a strong prosperous state, to stand up to Israel, and to lead the Arab world. Yet, as a poverty-stricken developing country and a new state actor in the international power game, Egypt could not do without large amounts of economic aid and military assistance from the advanced economies and the great powers. Such dependency, of course, carried heavy costs and threats to national independence. The problem of dependency could be minimized by diversifying aid sources, and Nasser initially pursued a policy of balance between East and West, which won aid from both sides and minimized dependence on any one.

United States support for Israel after the June 1967 War made Egypt ever more dependent on the Soviet Union for military aid and protection, but this dependence was, in part, balanced by increasing financial aid from the conservative Arab oil states. By the late 1970s, Sadat, in choosing to rely on American diplomacy to recover Egyptian land from Israel and in allowing his ties to the Soviet Union and the Arab world to wither, had led Egypt into heavy economic and military dependency on the United States. This dependency, by precluding foreign-policy decisions displeasing to Israel and Washington, sharply limited Egypt's pursuit of a vigorous Arab and independent foreign policy. The basic dilemma of Egypt's foreign policy was that its dependence on foreign assistance conflicted with its aspiration for national independence and its concept of its role as an Arab-Islamic and traditionally nonaligned entity.

Foreign Policy Decision Making

The great risks and opportunities inherent in Egypt's foreign relations made it inevitable that foreign policy dominated the leader's political agenda. Performance on foreign policy could make or break the leadership. Nasser's charisma was rooted above all in his nationalist victories over "imperialism," and the decline of Nasserism was a direct function of Egypt's 1967 defeat by Israel; similarly, Sadat's achievements in the October 1973 War gave him legitimacy, whereas his separate peace with Israel destroyed it.

It was not surprising, therefore, that foreign policy was virtually a "reserved sphere" of the presidency. Nasser concentrated and

281

personalized foreign policy decision making in his own hands, taking alone such crucial decisions as the nationalization of the Suez Canal. Sadat asserted a similar prerogative; a major issue in the power struggle with left-wing Free Officers after Nasser's death was Sadat's insistence on his right to make independent foreign policy decisions, such as his offer to open the Suez Canal in return for a partial Israeli withdrawal from its banks and his decision to join the Federation of Arab Republics with Libya and Syria. Once he consolidated his power, Sadat continued the tradition of presidential decision making in foreign policy, making many decisions in defiance of elite opinion and in disregard of professional military and diplomatic advice. In crucial negotiations over Sinai I and Sinai II, the disengagement agreements with Israel after the October 1973 War, he excluded his top advisers from key sessions with United States secretary of state Henry Kissinger and overrode their objections to many details of these agreements. He made his momentous decision to go to Jerusalem without even bothering to create an elite consensus behind him. As a result, both the minister of foreign affairs and his deputy resigned. Sadat allowed his top generals little say at Camp David. His unilateral concessions so often undermined the hand of his diplomats in the negotiations over the peace treaty with Israel that they sought to keep the Israelis away from him. Mubarak inherited the tradition of presidential dominance in foreign policy, but he seemed to make his decisions in closer consultation with his advisers, such as Usamah al Baz, Butrus Butrus Ghali, and Minister of Foreign Affairs Ismat Abdul Majid.

Despite presidential dominance, the Egyptian foreign policy bureaucracy was the most sophisticated and influential in the Arab world. Under the minister of foreign affairs was a minister of state for foreign affairs, a position long held by Butrus Ghali. Under them were a first undersecretary and a series of other undersecretaries in charge of geographical areas (America, Africa, Asia, Europe) and functional departments (economic affairs, cultural affairs, and the like). Al Ahram's Center for Political and Strategic Studies acted as a think tank in support of decision makers. Career diplomats were recruited chiefly through competitive examinations and trained at the Egyptian Diplomatic Institute. In 1982 Egypt had diplomatic relations with 95 foreign countries and had more than 1,000 diplomatic service officers.

The Development of Foreign Policy

Despite certain constants, Egyptian foreign policy underwent substantial evolution shaped by the differing values and perceptions of the country's presidents and the changing constraints and

Tolls from ships on the Suez Canal are a major source
of Egypt's foreign exchange.
Courtesy Embassy of Egypt, Washington

opportunities of its environment. Under Nasser the core of the regime's ideology and the very basis of its legitimacy was radical nationalism. Nasser sought to end the legacy of Egypt's long political subordination to Western imperialism, to restore its Arab-Islamic identity diluted by a century of Westernization, and to launch independent national economic development. He also aimed to replace Western domination of the Arab states with Egyptian leadership of a nonaligned Arab world and thus to forestall security threats and to enhance Egypt's stature as head of a concert of kindred states.

Nasser's foreign policy seemed, until 1967, a qualified success. He adeptly exploited changes in the international balance of power, namely the local weakening of Western imperialism, the Soviet challenge to Western dominance, and the national awakening of the Arab peoples, to win a series of significant nationalist victories. The long-sought British withdrawal from Egypt, the defeat of the security pacts by which the West sought to harness the Arabs against the Soviet Union, the successful nationalization of the Suez Canal, and the failure of the 1956 French-British-Israeli invasion put Egypt at the head of an aroused Arab nationalist movement and resulted in a substantial retreat of Western control from the

Middle East. This policy also won political and economic benefits internally. The Arab adulation of Nasser was a major component of the regime's legitimacy. It was as leader of the Arab world that Egypt won substantial foreign assistance from both East and West.

Nasser's success was, of course, only relative to the failure of previous Arab leaders, and his policies had mounting costs. The other Arab regimes were unwilling to accept Egyptian hegemony and, although largely on the defensive, worked to thwart Nasser's effort to impose a foreign policy consensus on the Arab world. The effort to project Egyptian influence drained the country's resources; Egyptian intervention in support of the republican revolution (1962–70) in the Yemen Arab Republic (North Yemen) was particularly costly. Generally, Nasser's Egypt failed to become the Prussia of the Arab world, but it played the decisive role in the emergence of an Arab state system independent of overt foreign control.

Pan-Arab leadership, however, carried heavy responsibilities, including above all the defense of the Arab world and the championing of the Arab and Palestinian cause against Israel. These responsibilities, which entailed grave economic burdens and security risks, eventually led Nasser into the disastrous June 1967 War with Israel. Nasser did not seek a war, but he allowed circumstances to bring on one that caught him unprepared. Nasser's challenge to Western interests in the region had earned him accumulated resentment in the West, where many perceived him as a Soviet client who should be brought down. At the same time, a rising Syrian-Palestinian challenge to Israel was peaking, threatening to provoke an Israeli attack on Syria. Despite an unfavorable military balance, Nasser, as leader of the Arab world, was obliged to deter Israel by mobilizing on its southern front. The mobilization opened the door to an Israeli "first strike" against Egypt. The rapid collapse of the Egyptian army in the war showed how far Nasser's foreign policy ambitions had exceeded his capabilities. Israel occupied Egypt's Sinai Peninsula. The same nationalist foreign policy by which Nasser had ended the Western domination of Egypt had led him into a trap that entrenched a new foreign presence on Egyptian soil.

Nasser's response to the crisis was twofold. In accepting the plan of United States secretary of state William P. Rogers, he signaled Egypt's readiness for a peaceful settlement of the Arab-Israeli conflict. This meant the acceptance of Israel and acknowledged the role of the United States as a dominant power broker in the Middle East. Convinced that diplomacy alone, however, would never recover Sinai and skeptical of United States intentions, he launched a major overhaul and expansion of the armed forces and in the

War of Attrition (1969–70) contested Israel's hold on the Sinai Peninsula. But the shattering of Egyptian self-confidence in the 1967 defeat, the growing belief that the Soviet Union would not supply the offensive weapons for a military recovery of Sinai, and the conviction that the United States would keep Israel strong enough to repulse any such recovery combined to convince a growing portion of the Egyptian political elite that the United States "held the cards" to a solution and that Cairo would have to come to terms with Washington.

Sadat came to power ready for a diplomatic opening to the West, a political solution to the crisis, and a compromise settlement, even if it were a partial one. He sought a United States-sponsored peace, believing that only those who provided the Israelis with the means of occupation had the means to end it. The expulsion of the Soviet advisers from Egypt in 1972 was in part an effort to court American favor. He also struck a close alliance with the conservative Arab oil states, headed by Saudi Arabia, whose influence in Washington, money, and potential to use the "oil weapon" were crucial elements in building Egyptian leverage with Israel. Once it was clear that Egypt's interests would be ignored until Egyptians showed they could fight and upset a status quo comfortable to Israel and the United States, Sadat turned seriously to war as an option. But rather than a war to recapture Sinai, he decided on a strictly limited one to establish a bridgehead on the east bank of the Suez Canal as a way of breaking the Israeli grip on the area and opening the way for negotiations. Such a limited war, Sadat calculated, would rally the Arab world around Egypt, bring the oil weapon into play, challenge Israel's reliance on security through territorial expansion, and, above all, pave the way for a United States diplomatic intervention that would force Israel to accept a peaceful settlement. The price of an American peace, however, would almost certainly be an end to Egypt's anti-imperialist Arab nationalist policy.

The October 1973 War did upset the status quo and ended with Egyptian forces in Sinai. But because Israeli forces had penetrated the west bank of the Suez Canal, Sadat badly needed and accepted a United States-sponsored disengagement of forces. Sinai I removed the Israelis from the west bank but, in defusing the war crisis, also reduced Arab leverage in bargaining for an overall Israeli withdrawal. In subsequently allowing his relations with the Soviet Union and Syria to deteriorate and hence decreasing the viability of war as an option, Sadat became so dependent on United States diplomacy that he had little choice but to accept a second partial and separate agreement, Sinai II, in which Egypt recovered further territory but was allowed a mere token military force in

Sinai. This agreement so undermined Arab leverage that negotiations for a comprehensive peace stalled. A frustrated Sadat, hoping to win world support and weaken Israeli hard-liners, embarked on his trip to Jerusalem. Even if Israel refused concessions to Syria or the Palestinians, it might thereby be brought to relinquish Sinai in return for a separate peace that took Egypt out of the Arab-Israeli power balance.

At Camp David and in the subsequent negotiations over a peace treaty, Sadat found out just how much his new diplomatic currency would purchase: a return of Sinai and, at most, a relaxation of Israeli control over the West Bank (''autonomy''), but no Palestinian state (see Peace with Israel, ch. 1). By 1979 Egypt was finally at peace. But because the separate peace removed any remaining incentive for Israel to settle on the other fronts, Egypt was ostracized from the Arab world, forfeiting its leadership and the aid to which this had entitled the country.

Simultaneously, as Sadat broke his links with the Soviet Union and the Arab states and needed the United States increasingly to mediate with the Israelis, to provide arms, and to fill the aid gap, Sadat moved Egypt into an ever closer alliance with the United States. Particularly after the fall of the shah of Iran, he openly seemed to assume the role of guardian of United States interests in the area. Joint military maneuvers were held, facilities granted to United States forces, and Egyptian troops deployed to prop up conservative regimes, such as that of Zaire. Sadat seemingly reasoned that Washington's support for Israel derived from its role in protecting United States interests in the area, and if he could arrogate that role to himself, then Egypt would be eligible for the same aid and support and the importance of Israel to Washington would decline. The Egypt that had led the fight to expel Western influence from the Arab world now welcomed it back.

Mubarak's main foreign policy challenge was to resolve the contradiction between the standards of nationalist legitimacy established under Nasser and the combination of close United States and Israeli connections and isolation from the Arab world brought on by Sadat's policies. It took Mubarak nearly a decade to make any significant progress, however, because Sadat's legacy proved quite durable. The regime's dependence on the United States was irreversible: for arms, for cheap food to maintain social peace, and—especially as oil-linked earnings plummeted—for US$2 billion in yearly aid to keep the economy afloat. Dependency dictated continuing close political and military alignment largely aimed at radical nationalist forces in the Arab world—not at Israel, Egypt's traditional enemy since 1948. Mubarak had to maintain the Israeli connection despite the lack of progress toward a comprehensive peace or recognition of Palestinian rights. He remained passive during the 1982 Israeli invasion of Lebanon, a major blow to the Arab world made possible largely by Israel's no longer needing to station substantial forces along the southern front as a result of the Camp David Accords. This invasion and the Israeli raids on Iraq in 1981 and on Tunis in 1986 showed how Sadat had opened the Arab world to Israeli power as never before.

Mubarak did recover some foreign policy independence. He rejected pressures from the United States government in late 1985 and early 1986 for joint action against Libya, and he restored Cairo's diplomatic relations with Moscow. Moreover, he had some leverage over the United States: Washington had invested so much in Egypt and gained so much from Sadat's policies—defusing the threat of an Arab-Israeli war, rolling back the influence of the Soviet Union and radicals in the Arab world—that it could not afford to alienate the regime or to let it go under.

The continuing Israeli-American connection deepened Egypt's crisis of nationalist legitimacy, however. Israel was widely seen in Egypt as having "betrayed" the peace by its rejection of Palestinian rights; its attempt to keep the Sinai enclave of Taba; and its attacks on Iraq, Lebanon, and Tunis. Evidence of the Egyptians' deep resentment of Israeli policy was demonstrated by the way they made a folk hero of Sulayman Khatir, a policeman who killed Israeli tourists in 1985. Egyptians also resented economic dependency on the United States, and the United States' forcing down of an Egyptian aircraft after the *Achille Lauro* incident in October 1985 was taken as a national insult and set off the first nationalist street disturbances in years. This sentiment did not become a mass movement able to force a policy change despite demands by opposition leaders and isolated attacks on Israeli and American officials by disgruntled "Nasserist" officers. But few governments anywhere have been saddled with so unpopular a foreign policy.

What saved the regime was that Mubarak's astute diplomacy and the mistakes of his rivals allowed him to achieve a gradual reintegration of Egypt into the Arab world without prejudice to Egypt's Israeli links. The first break in Egypt's isolation came when Yasir Arafat's 1983 quarrel with Syria enabled Egypt to extend him protection and assume patronage of the Palestinian resistance. Then the Arab oil states, fearful of Iran and of the spread of Shia Islamic activism, looked to Egypt for a counterbalance. Thus, Mubarak was able to demonstrate Egypt's usefulness to the Arabs and to inch out of his isolation. Egypt's 1989 readmission to the League of Arab States (Arab League) crowned his efforts.

Mubarak's Egypt viewed its role in the Arab world as that of a mediator, particularly in trying to advance the peace process between Israel and the Arabs. Thus, the regime invested its prestige in the 1989 attempt to bridge differences between Israel and the Palestinians over West Bank elections. By 1990 these efforts had not resolved the stalemate over Palestinian rights, but the restoration of ties between Egypt and Syria amounted to a Syrian acknowledgment that Egypt's peace with Israel was irreversible. Thus, Egypt's rehabilitation as a major power in the Arab world was completed, undoing a good bit of the damage done to regime legitimacy under Sadat.

After Egypt had established its alliance with the United States, the formerly significant roles of non-Arab powers in Egyptian foreign policy waned. Relations with Western Europe remained important, if secondary. With some success, Egypt regularly sought the intervention of West European governments with its international creditors. When the United States commitment to pushing the peace process beyond Camp David stalled, Egypt also looked to Europe to pressure Israel, but the Europeans were, in this respect, no substitute for Washington.

The role of the Soviet Union dwindled even more dramatically. Under Nasser, Moscow was Cairo's main military supplier and political protector and a main market and source of development assistance; Soviet aid helped build such important projects as the Aswan High Dam and the country's steel industry. Without Soviet arms Egypt would have been helpless to mount the October 1973 War that broke the Israeli grip on Sinai. But Sadat's 1972 expulsion of Soviet advisers and his subsequent reliance on the United States to recover the rest of Sinai soured relations with the Soviet Union. Wanting American diplomatic help and economic largesse, Sadat had to portray Egypt to United States interests as a bulwark against Soviet threats; under these conditions Soviet relations naturally turned hostile and were broken in 1980. Under Mubarak amicable—but still low-key—relations were reestablished. Mubarak sought better Soviet relations to enhance his leverage over the United States, but Moscow was in no position to offer a credible threat to American influence.

In 1990 Mubarak governed a state that was the product of both persistence and change. Continuity was manifest in the durability of the structures built by Nasser. The authoritarian presidency remained the command post of the state. Nasserist policies—from Arab nationalism to the food subsidies and the public sector—created durable interests and standards of legitimacy. Under Sadat Egypt had accommodated itself to the dominant forces in the regime's environment; in Sadat's "postpopulist" regime, charisma, social reform, and leadership of the Arab world achieved by Nasser gave way to their opposites. Sadat had also adapted the state to new conditions, altering the goals and style of presidential power and liberalizing the political structure. The survival of most of Sadat's work under Mubarak suggested that, more successfully than Nasser, he had partially institutionalized it in a massive political structure, an alliance with the dominant social forces, and a web of constraints against significant change. Under Mubarak the state's ability to manipulate its environment retreated before rising societal forces and powerful external constraints. But Mubarak also consolidated the limited liberalization of the political system and restored an Arab role for Egypt. Although it cost the concession of its initial ideology, the Egyptian state resulting from the Nasser-led 1952 Revolution had shown a remarkable capacity to survive in the face of intense pressures.

Yet Sadat's innovations, in stimulating rising autonomous forces while narrowing regime options, had set change in motion. Although the massive bureaucratic state was sure to persist, the capitalist forces unleashed by the *infitah* contained the seeds of countervailing power, the social basis for further political liberalization. The widening inequality and social mobilization precipitated by capitalist development threatened, however, to produce growing class conflicts. In a regime with precarious legitimacy, these conflicts could spell instability or revolution and could require continuing authoritarian control. Should rising economic constraints force the government to abandon the residues of populism, such a regime might have an ever more repressive face. If this increasing repression were accompanied by accommodation between the regime and political Islam, the end might be conservative rule by consensus; otherwise, a crumbling of the secular state under pressures from the street and defections within could still produce a new Islamic order. At the beginning of the 1990s, however, the regime was continuing its established course, avoiding radical turns to left or right, and mixing doses of limited liberalization, limited repression, and limited Islamization.

* * *

Still the most insightful overviews of the Nasser regime are Anouar Abdel-Malek's Marxist interpretation, *Egypt: Military Society*, Richard Hrair Dekmejian's elite-centered analysis, *Egypt under Nasir*, Nazih Ayubi's *Bureaucracy and Politics in Contemporary Egypt*, and P.J.

Vatikiotis's *The Egyptian Army in Politics*. Robert Stephens's *Nasser: A Political Biography* is the best biography of Nasser, masterfully situating his personal role in the wider political context. Raymond A. Hinnebusch, Jr.'s *Egyptian Politics under Sadat* is the only comprehensive overview of the Sadat era, and Robert Springborg's *Mubarak's Egypt* is the only one on the current era.

A number of major works that bridge several eras are recommended. John Waterbury's political economy study, *The Egypt of Nasser and Sadat,* is essential reading. The work edited by Gouda Abdel-Khalek and Robert L. Tignor, *The Political Economy of Income Distribution in Egypt,* updates the political economy picture into the late Sadat era. Springborg gives cultural and social dimensions to politics in his analysis of family and patrimonial politics, *Family Power and Politics in Egypt,* while Hamied Ansari's *Egypt: The Stalled Society* and Leonard Binder's *In a Moment of Enthusiasm* argue the centrality of the rural notables. Henry Clement Moore's elite study, *Images of Development,* is a story of technocracy derailed by patrimonialism. Patrimonialism is also identified as the undoing of the revolution in Raymond Baker's *Egypt's Uncertain Revolution under Nasser and Sadat* and J.P. Vatikiotis's *Nasser and His Generation.* Muhammed Hassanain Haikal has written a number of illuminating "insider" accounts from a Nasserist point of view, in particular *The Road to Ramadan* and *The Autumn of Fury.* Sadat's autobiography, *In Search of Identity,* looks at many of the same issues and events through different eyes. Useful studies with narrower, more in-depth foci include Iliya Harik's *The Political Mobilization of Peasants,* Richard H. Adams's *Development and Social Change in Rural Egypt,* Adeed Dawisha's *Egypt in the Arab World,* and Gilles Kepel's *Muslim Extremism in Egypt.* (For further information and complete citations, see Bibliography.)

Chapter 5. National Security

Hawk at entrance to the hypostyle hall of the Temple of Edfu (Idfu)

EGYPT IS LOCATED in a region characterized by tension and conflict. Since Egypt's war with Israel in 1973, however, the threat of military confrontation with neighboring countries has steadily subsided. As of 1990, the government was in the process of reducing the size of its armed forces relative to the size of the population. At the same time, the armed forces were modernizing their command structure and updating their arms and equipment. With 448,000 troops, Egypt in 1990 remained one of the major military powers in the Middle East.

The four services—the army, navy, air force, and Air Defense Force—included conscripts and some volunteers. The average conscript served three years in the military, although people who had completed higher education served shorter terms. The military also had a liberal exemption policy.

Since the Free Officers' coup in 1952, career military officers have headed Egypt's government, and senior officers have played an influential role in the nation's affairs. The military's involvement in government has diminished since the 1970s, although ranking members of the officer corps have continued to fill the positions of minister of defense (who served concurrently as commander in chief of the armed forces) and minister of interior.

Egypt's military leaders enjoyed a reputation for competence and professionalism; many of these leaders had advanced training at foreign military institutes and combat experience as junior officers during the October 1973 War.

As of 1990, much of the military was still equipped with arms provided by the Soviet Union between the late 1950s and mid-1970s. In 1979 the United States began supplying Egypt with arms. With the exception of Israel, Egypt was the largest recipient of United States military aid during the 1980s. Its impressive stock of weaponry from all sources nevertheless did not match that of Israel in terms of modern armor and combat aircraft.

Egypt has made substantial progress in expanding its own arms industry, but this progress depended on assistance from several Western countries. During the 1980s, the army began to play an important role in Egypt's development efforts; it built roads, irrigation and communications systems, and housing. It also produced food and industrial products. These activities demonstrated that the military could be an asset to the country even during periods of peace.

The country faced no threat of invasion as of early 1990, but extreme Islamic groups fanned internal tensions. The police and the government's intelligence service were fairly successful in controlling Muslim extremists' activities, which included arson and attempts to assassinate government officials.

During the 1980s, elements of the military were involved in activities aimed at destabilizing the government. Religious conspirators in the army, seeking to overthrow the government, assassinated President Anwar as Sadat in 1981. But overall, the armed forces remained loyal to the regime and supported the peaceful transition of power from Sadat to the vice president and former air force commander Husni Mubarak. Troops again upheld internal order in 1986 by quashing riots of conscripts from the Central Security Forces, a paramilitary police body, protesting against harsh treatment.

Military Heritage

It was not until the period of the New Kingdom (1552–664 B.C.) that standing military units were formed, including the appearance of chariotry and the organization of infantry into companies of about 250 men. Egyptian armies then became militarily involved in the Near East, contending for Syria and Palestine. By the later periods beginning in the seventh century B.C., foreign mercenaries formed the core of Egyptian military power. From the time Greek rule was established in 332 B.C. until 1952 A.D., the country was subject to foreign domination. Under the successive control of Persian, Greek, Roman, Arab, Turkish, French, and British forces, the Egyptians remained disdainful of the military. In 1951 a prominent Egyptian author described military service as ''an object of ridicule, a laughingstock which is to be avoided whenever possible.'' He added that the military was ''left for the poor and uneducated'' and called it ''a derisory profession commanding contempt rather than honor or pride.''

Under Muhammad Ali, the Albanian soldier who governed Egypt during the first half of the nineteenth century, a conscripted Egyptian army pursued campaigns on behalf of the Ottoman sultan in the Arabian Peninsula, Sudan, and Greece. In a disagreement over the control of Syria, his army, consisting of more than 250,000 Egyptians, advanced nearly to Constantinople (formerly Byzantium; present-day Istanbul) before the European powers pressured him into withdrawing (see Muhammad Ali, 1805–48, ch. 1). After the deaths of Muhammad Ali and his son, Ibrahim, Egypt's military strength declined, and the country slipped increasingly under European control. In 1879 a nationalist revolt erupted over proposed restrictions to prevent Egyptians from entering the officer corps. Ahmad Urabi, an Egyptian colonel, led the countrywide uprising which was suppressed after British troops crushed the Egyptians in 1882.

The British began their era of domination in Egypt and assumed responsibility for defending the country and the Suez Canal, which were of particular interest to the British Empire. The British disbanded the Egyptian army, and recreated it by incorporating Egyptian units staffed by British officers into British commands. British regiments remained to defend the canal. To mobilize personnel for the Egyptian units, the British resorted to irregular conscription among the fellahin (peasants), who went to great lengths to avoid military service. Potential conscripts, however, could make a cash payment in lieu of service. This practice resulted in units that were staffed mostly by the poorest members of society. Egyptians who became officers were almost always from wealthy and distinguished families.

Egyptian nationalism intensified after World War I, and with certain reservations, Britain granted Egypt independence in 1922. Britain transferred command over the armed forces to Egyptians but retained a British inspector general at the top. The Anglo-Egyptian Treaty of 1936, however, eliminated this vestige of British control. Egypt then expanded the army, making enrollment in the Military Academy and a subsequent army career much more attainable and desirable for young middle-class Egyptians.

The Egyptian Military in World War II

Before World War II, military service was compulsory for men between the ages of nineteen and twenty-seven, but because of the limited size of the army—about 23,000 in 1939—few were actually conscripted. During World War II, Egypt's army grew to about 100,000 troops. Britain maintained a strong influence in the military and provided it with equipment, instruction, and technicians. Under the terms of the 1936 treaty, British troops remained in the country to defend the Suez Canal. During the war, Egypt became the principal Allied base in the Middle East.

Egypt severed relations with the Axis powers soon after the outbreak of World War II but remained technically neutral until near the end of the war. The Italians first brought the war to Egypt in 1940 but were repelled by the British. In late 1941, the German Afrika Korps entered western Egypt and threatened the country and the canal. But the British Eighth Army defeated the German force at Al Alamayn in October 1942. Some Egyptians flew patrol duty in British planes with British pilots during the war, and Egypt inaugurated a naval service with a few patrol boats supplied by Britain. Egyptians were used primarily for guard duty and logistical tasks rather than for combat. Some Egyptian officers favored Germany as a way to end Britain's influence in the country. (The British had imprisoned Anwar as Sadat because of his pro-German activities.) Aware of such sentiments, the British command was reluctant to employ Egyptian units in combat even after King Faruk formally declared war against the Axis in February 1945.

First Arab-Israeli War

During the First Arab-Israeli War (1948-49), an Egyptian invasion force of 7,000 men crossed the Palestinian border at Rafah on the Mediterranean coast and at Al Awja (Nizzana) farther inland (see fig. 7). They soon reached Ashdod, less than thirty-five kilometers from Tel Aviv. But by the time the first truce ended in mid-July, the Israelis had reinforced their positions, beating off Egyptian attacks and recovering territory to protect Jewish settlements in the Negev. By the fall of 1948, the Israelis put Egypt's 18,000 troops deployed in Palestine on the defensive and penetrated the Sinai Peninsula. Egypt and Israel concluded an armistice under United Nations (UN) auspices at the end of 1948 and later agreed on a cease-fire line that generally followed the prewar boundary between Palestine and Sinai. But Egyptian forces still occupied and administered the narrow coastal strip of southwestern Palestine, the Gaza Strip.

The venality and ineffectiveness of the Faruk regime were the main causes of Egypt's failures in the war. Although inexperienced, Egypt's troops had performed well in defensive operations before being driven back by the Israelis.

A coup d'état in 1952 toppled Faruk's regime and brought to power younger officers of the Free Officers' movement (see The Revolution and the Early Years of the New Government, 1952–56, ch. 1). From then on, Egypt gave priority to the development of the military. In 1955 the government enacted the National Military Service Law, which aimed at reforming and upgrading the armed forces.

The 1956 War

After President Gamal Abdul Nasser's seizure of the Suez Canal in July 1956, the British, French, and Israelis began coordinating an invasion. On October 29, 1956, the Israelis struck across Sinai toward the canal and southward toward Sharm ash Shaykh to relieve the Egyptian blockade of the Gulf of Aqaba. At the crossroads of Abu Uwayqilah, thirty kilometers from the Israeli border, and at the Mitla Pass, Egyptian troops resisted fiercely, repelling several attacks by larger Israeli forces. British and French forces bombed Egyptian air bases, causing Nasser to withdraw Egyptian troops from Sinai to protect the canal. At the heavily fortified complex of Rafah in the northwestern corner of Sinai and at other points, the Egyptians carried out effective delaying actions before retreating. Egypt vigorously defended Sharm ash Shaykh in the extreme south until two advancing Israeli columns took control of the area. At Port Said (Bur Said), at the north end of the canal, Egyptian soldiers battled the initial British and French airborne assault, but resistance quickly collapsed when allied forces landed on the beach with support from heavy naval gunfire.

The performance of many of the Egyptian units was determined and resourceful in the face of the qualitative and numerical superiority of the invaders. Nasser claimed that Egypt had not been defeated by the Israelis but that it had been forced to abandon Sinai to defend the canal against the Anglo-French attacks. According to foreign military observers, about 1,650 of Egypt's ground forces were killed in the campaign. Another 4,900 were wounded, and more than 6,000 were captured or missing.

Respect for the armed forces grew in response to Nasser's rise to political preeminence in the Arab world, his widespread support among Egyptians, hostility toward Israel, and the broadened base of military service. But Egypt's army suffered a psychological setback in September 1962 when it intervened unsuccessfully in a civil war in what later became the Yemen Arab Republic (North Yemen) (see Egypt and the Arab World, ch. 1). Nasser moved large numbers of Egyptian troops into the country after a group of Yemeni army officers staged a coup against the royalist regime. The number of Egyptian troops in the country rose from 20,000 in 1963 to 70,000 by 1965. The Egyptians, who were not well trained or equipped for battle in Yemen's rugged mountain terrain, failed to defeat the royalists. Some of Egypt's best troops were still stalemated in Yemen when Israel attacked Egypt in 1967.

The June 1967 War

In the eleven years leading up to the June 1967 War (also seen as the Arab-Israeli War and the Six-Day War), the military had been intensively trained for combat and outfitted with new Soviet weapons and equipment. Despite these preparations, the war proved to be a debacle for Egypt. Although there had been many indications that an attack was imminent, the Israelis still took Egypt by surprise on June 5, when their aircraft approached from the Mediterranean at low altitudes to avoid detection by radar and

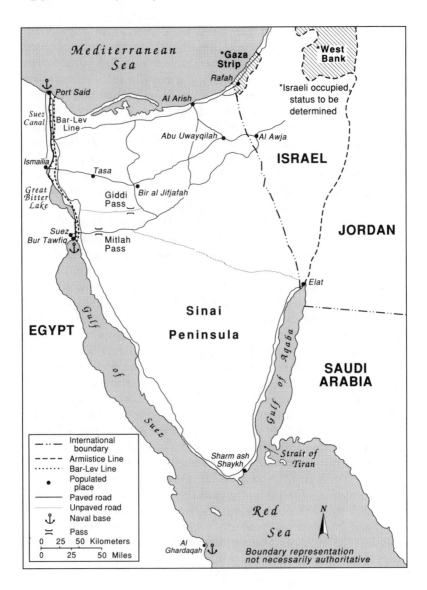

Figure 7. Principal Military Installations in the Sinai Peninsula, 1989

attacked the Egyptian air force while it was still on the ground. Within three hours, the Israelis had destroyed 300 Egyptian combat aircraft, including all of Egypt's 30 long-range bombers. Israel focused its ground attack on the heavily fortified Sinai road junction of Abu Uwayqilah as it had done in 1956. After a fierce battle, the Israelis overwhelmed Egyptian forces in fewer than twelve hours. The devastating air attacks and initial Israeli ground successes panicked Egyptian commander in chief Field Marshal Abdul Hakim Amir into withdrawing army units from Sinai to the west bank of the Suez Canal. Staff officers later persuaded Amir to rescind his order, but by that time all the main elements of the four frontline divisions had already begun retreating westward. At several points, rearguard actions delayed Israeli advances, but Israeli forces managed to block bottlenecks in the Giddi Pass and the Mitla Pass and at Bir al Jifjafah and prevented the escape of Egyptian troops and equipment. The Israeli air force bombed and strafed thousands of Egyptian tanks, guns, and vehicles caught in the bottleneck.

After four days of intensive fighting, Israel controlled the entire Sinai Peninsula up to the east bank of the canal. Egypt acknowledged that of approximately 100,000 troops in Sinai, 10,000 soldiers and 1,500 officers were casualties. Observers estimated that about half of the dead had succumbed to thirst or exhaustion in the desert. A further 5,000 soldiers and 500 officers were captured, many of whom were wounded. Israel also destroyed or captured about 700 of Egypt's 930 tanks. Popular support for the military subsided rapidly after the June 1967 War, and morale within the forces plunged to its lowest level since before the military takeover of 1952. Although individually and in some cases as units the Egyptians often performed bravely, the Israeli army again demonstrated the self-reliance of its unit leaders, its better training, and the superior use of its armor.

War of Attrition and the October 1973 War

After conquering Sinai, the Israelis constructed the Bar-Lev Line, a series of thirty-three small, heavily fortified observation posts atop sand ramparts eight to ten meters high along the east bank of the Suez Canal. They built a second sand embankment several kilometers behind the first one. Both embankments had firing ramps for roving armored patrols. In January 1969, Egypt began the War of Attrition with an intensive eighty-day bombardment along the whole canal. Israeli positions along the Bar-Lev Line survived the attack but suffered heavy damage. Egypt followed the attack with commando raids on the line itself and against Israeli patrols and rear installations. Israel launched a severe reprisal that included bombing raids against military and strategic targets deep in the interior of Egypt. The relative ineffectiveness of Egypt's Soviet SA-2 high-altitude surface-to-air missiles (SAMs) against the Israeli raids necessitated the introduction of low-level SA-3 SAMs, manned mostly by Soviet technicians. Egypt reinforced the new missiles with more than 100 MiG–21 aircraft flown by Soviet pilots. Egypt's revitalized air defense system succeeded in destroying a considerable number of Israeli aircraft. Still, in the only major battle between Israeli and Soviet fighters, the Israeli air force quickly prevailed. In August 1970, a cease-fire negotiated by the United States with Soviet support ended the fighting between Israel and Egypt.

Sadat, who succeeded Nasser in September 1970, assumed the responsibility of managing the international and domestic pressures that were impelling Egypt and the Middle East toward another war. Although the Soviets had replaced the enormous amounts of arms and equipment lost during the June 1967 War, Sadat and other Egyptian military leaders had become wary of the Soviet military's increasing influence on national affairs. In mid-1972 Sadat dismissed most of the Soviet advisers as part of his preparations for recovering Sinai. In January 1973, Egypt began planning a top-secret project known as Operation Badr in conjunction with Syria.

Early in the afternoon of October 6, 1973, Egypt launched the operation with a massive artillery barrage against Israeli positions on the eastern bank of the Suez Canal. Water cannons mounted on pontoons sliced gaps in the high sandbank of the Bar-Lev Line, permitting armored vehicles to cross on assault craft. By midnight ten bridges and fifty ferries had carried 80,000 Egyptian troops across the waterway and one kilometer beyond the embankment. Almost all of the armor of the Egyptian Second Army and Third Army crossed the following day. By October 9, the Egyptian bridgeheads were seven to ten kilometers east of the canal. The Soviet-supplied antitank missiles and rockets repulsed the initial Israeli counterattacks. The newer Soviet SAMs protected Egyptian forces from Israeli air attacks, but as Egyptian troops advanced beyond the missile defenses, they were exposed to punishing air attacks.

On October 14, Egyptian armored columns took the offensive to try to seize the main routes leading to Tasa and the Giddi and Mitla passes. In the largest tank battle since World War II, the Egyptian attack failed when Israeli gunnery proved superior, and the Israelis' defensive positions gave them an added advantage. Mounting a strong counterattack, the Israelis thrust toward the canal and narrowly succeeded in crossing it just north of Great Bitter Lake. Egyptian forces on the east bank heavily contested Israel's weak link to the canal bridgehead, but by October 19, the Israelis succeeded in breaking out west of the canal. Stubborn Egyptian defenses prevented the loss of the cities of Ismailia (Al Ismailiyah)

*United Nations Emergency Force and Israeli officers meeting with
beduins in southern Sinai Peninsula, 1975
Courtesy United Nations, Y. Nagata*

and Suez at the southern end of the canal until a UN cease-fire
took effect on October 24, 1973. Before the cease-fire, however,
the Israelis had isolated the Egyptian Third Army on the east bank
of the canal.

Under a disengagement agreement reached on January 17, 1974,
Israel withdrew its forces from west of the canal while Egyptian
forces withdrew from the east bank to a depth of about eight kilometers. The agreement also provided for a United Nations Emergency Force (UNEF) to occupy a north-south buffer strip about
eight kilometers wide and allowed a limited number of Israeli troops
to occupy a similar zone to the east of the UNEF.

Although Egypt's armed forces suffered severely in the October
1973 War, the losses were not nearly as heavy as they had been
in 1967. Of the combined strength of 200,000 in Egypt's Second
and Third armies, approximately 8,000 men were killed in combat. Egypt also lost more than 200 aircraft, 1,100 tanks, and large
quantities of other weapons, vehicles, and equipment. Despite these
losses, the effect of the war on the armed forces was as exhilarat-
ing as the defeat in 1967 had been debilitating. Although they had
not recovered Sinai, their initial successes in securing the east bank
of the canal had an important positive psychological impact on the

armed forces. The war enabled Egypt to negotiate from strength rather than from the abject weakness of the post-1967 period. At the same time, Egypt had proved that it was capable of successful military planning and of inflicting painful losses on Israel.

Security Concerns and Strategic Perspectives

After the disengagement agreement of 1974, the threat of an Israeli attack on Egypt diminished significantly, and a second disengagement agreement was concluded in 1975. In 1979 Egypt and Israel signed a treaty of peace under which Israel agreed to withdraw its forces in stages from the Sinai Peninsula, further reducing the likelihood of a new conflict between the two countries.

Nevertheless, Egypt's experience of four wars with Israel continued to shape the thinking of Egyptian military planners. In 1986 Egyptian commander in chief Abdul Halim Abu Ghazala asserted that Israel still embraced a strategy of maintaining military strength superior to that of all of its neighbors combined. Egypt's policy, he declared, was to "neutralize" this strength so that it could not be used for aggressive purposes threatening the security of the Arab states.

A chain of Egyptian fortifications east of the Suez Canal was manned by the equivalent of about one-half of a mechanized division, which was less than Egypt was permitted under the peace treaty. Annual military exercises practiced reinforcement of Sinai by the five Egyptian divisions that could be quickly deployed across the canal. Egypt's deployments in the area had a defensive character, however, and its forces west of the canal occupied permanent bases that had existed for many years.

In addition to its concern about Israel, Egypt's 1,000-kilometer border with Libya remained a problem for Egyptian defense planners in 1990 despite a campaign of reconciliation by Libya's leader, Muammar al Qadhafi. Egypt believed that Qadhafi had amassed a stockpile of Soviet weaponry beyond any foreseeable defensive needs and was seeking additional advanced weaponry, including Soviet MiG-29 combat fighters and medium-range missiles. Libya had an estimated 40,000 troops backed by modern tanks, missiles, and combat aircraft at air bases adjacent to the Egyptian-Libyan border. Although Qadhafi announced in May 1988 that all combat forces would be pulled back from the border, the Egyptian minister of defense claimed in 1989 that a major part of the Libyan army was still deployed along the border zone.

Sudan, Egypt's neighbor to the south, presented no direct military problem for Egypt. The border between the two countries was unguarded except for policing to prevent smuggling and drug trafficking. Because the two countries shared a long cultural and political history, Egypt regarded Sudanese territory as providing added depth to the country's strategic defenses. Egypt was reportedly concerned about the coup in Sudan in June 1989 that brought to power a group of military officers identified with Islamism. The deterioration of Sudan's economy and internal security, accentuated by the mismanagement of the military junta, posed the danger of instability on Egypt's southern flank.

Egypt's role in Sudan was linked to its general policy promoting African regional stability and moderation. Egypt provided military assistance and advisers to Nigeria, Somalia, and Zaire and focused on Africa in marketing the products of its defense industry. Egypt sold arms to African nations that agreed to use them only for national defense rather than for domestic control over their citizens.

Egypt believed that the Red Sea was of vital interest to the country's strategic objectives because this body of water was closely associated with the security of the Suez Canal. Egypt believed, moreover, that any threats to the security of the nations surrounding the Persian Gulf or on the Arabian Peninsula could signal a threat to its own security. Against threats from Iran, Egypt had pledged its support to the states of the Gulf Cooperation Council (GCC), including Saudi Arabia, Kuwait, Bahrain, Qatar, the United Arab Emirates, and Oman. Egypt also expressed a willingness to play a larger role in the Persian Gulf through the provision of military advice, training, and sales of arms and equipment. Egypt chose, however, not to participate in a joint Arab force, which had been proposed to protect the GCC states against Iran. Egypt provided large quantities of arms to Iraq during the Iran-Iraq War, and thousands of Egyptians were working in Iraq.

The Military in National Life

The military became one of the most important factors in Egyptian politics after the overthrow of the monarchy in 1952. Nasser appointed members of the officer corps to senior positions in the bureaucracy and public sector to help implement his social revolution. But in the later years of the Nasser regime, fewer military figures occupied high government posts. Even fewer held posts during the Sadat and Mubarak regimes. Nevertheless, senior generals on active service continued to hold the key positions in agencies responsible for national security—the Ministry of Defense and the Ministry of Interior—as of early 1990.

After the June 1967 War, which tarnished the reputation of the military leadership, Nasser purged many officers from government.

Sadat further reduced the military's influence in government by removing strong military figures who were liable to challenge his policies and by insisting on greater professionalism in the event of renewed conflict with Israel. He appointed fewer active or retired officers to high positions, although he named air force commander Husni Mubarak as vice president. Sadat was careful, however, to protect the career interests of professional soldiers and to provide for the material requirements of the military. Although the size of the armed forces had decreased after peace with Israel, the officer complement remained intact. Egypt's expanding relationship with the United States after 1974 assured a continued supply of modern weapons.

The performance of the army during the October 1973 War helped restore the military's prestige and served to justify Sadat's emphasis on professionalism instead of involvement in civilian politics (see Politics among Elites, ch. 4). The military leadership's views continued to have an important influence on the formulation of defense and national security policies. Opposition politicians, who had become more vocal during the Mubarak regime, insisted upon open debate on defense strategy, the privileges of the officer corps, and the share of national resources allocated to defense.

The armed forces played a role in maintaining domestic stability, although only under the most compelling circumstances had they actually been called upon in a domestic crisis. These occasions included the violent 1977 food riots and an uprising of conscripts of the Central Security Forces in Cairo (Al Qahirah) and other cities in 1986 (see Police, this ch.). The military leadership noted pointedly that the army units returned to their barracks as soon as both emergencies had ended. The efficiency and professionalism the armed forces demonstrated during these emergencies reinforced the public's perception that the army was the ultimate safeguard against militant Islamists or others who might threaten civil authority.

Mubarak's firm control over the military enabled him to restrict the influence of the officer corps over political decision making. His encouragement of democratizing tendencies in the political system led to previously unexpressed public criticism of the military's privileges and its demands on the economy. Much of the debate over the military's role during the Mubarak regime centered on Abu Ghazala, Mubarak's close collaborator, who was named minister of defense before Sadat's death in 1981 and was promoted to field marshal and deputy prime minister in 1982. Under Abu Ghazala, the military's growing involvement in Egypt's industrial, military, and agricultural sectors offset the military's diminishing role in politics (see Production of Civilian Goods, this ch.). With substantial economic resources and the means to earn revenues independently of the budget, the defense sector was able to maintain a high degree of financial autonomy. Despite the government's fiscal austerity, Abu Ghazala was able to purchase expensive modern weaponry during the 1980s and to undertake vast housing projects to improve the living conditions of both officers and enlisted personnel. Widely regarded as the natural successor to Mubarak as president, Abu Ghazala was careful not to appear to be a political rival to Mubarak or to undercut the president's authority. He nevertheless spoke out on nonmilitary matters, apparently with Mubarak's consent, and developed a network of contacts with civilian business leaders.

In April 1989, Mubarak abruptly appointed General Yusuf Sabri Abu Talib as minister of defense and commander in chief and assigned Abu Ghazala the vague position of assistant to the president. Most observers believed that Abu Ghazala had been dismissed for corrupt financial dealings as well as for a scandal over smuggling arms from the United States; others believed that Mubarak considered him too influential. One effect of Mubarak's dramatic action, however, was to strengthen civilian primacy over the military. Abu Ghazala's successor, Abu Talib, had earned a reputation as an efficient manager in his previous post as governor of Cairo. When Abu Talib took up his new post, he indicated that he intended to introduce greater financial accountability into defense programs and to limit the military's involvement in economic activities that were not directly related to defense and that competed with the private sector. Abu Talib was also charged with bringing corruption in the armed forces under control.

The Armed Forces

According to Articles 180 to 183 of the Constitution of 1971, the armed forces "shall belong to the people" and are required "to defend the country, to safeguard its territory and security, and to protect the socialist gains of the people's struggle." The Constitution allows only the government to have armed forces; it forbids organizations or groups from establishing a military or paramilitary force. The Constitution also refers to the defense of the homeland as a "sacred duty" and mandates compulsory conscription.

The Constitution designates the president of the republic as supreme commander of the armed forces and empowers the president to declare war or a state of emergency as long as the People's Assembly (Majlis ash Shaab; formerly the National Assembly) concurs. The four presidents who have held the office since the 1952

Revolution—Muhammad Naguib, Nasser, Sadat, and Mubarak—have all been military officers and have played decisive roles in matters affecting security and the armed forces. The Constitution establishes the National Defense Council as the president's principal advisory body for all matters relating to the country's security. The Constitution provides no rules for membership in the council, but it does designate the president as the council's chairman. In practice, however, the National Defense Council was rarely mentioned; the president and the minister of defense usually dealt informally with national security matters. On issues of broad significance, other members of the cabinet might also be present to offer their views.

The post of commander in chief of the armed forces had customarily been combined with the offices of minister of defense and minister of military production. The Ministry of Defense dealt with budgetary, administrative, industrial, and policy matters affecting the military. It also handled affairs related to reserve officers and veterans. The senior deputy to the commander in chief, the chief of staff of the armed forces, was responsible for current operations of the armed forces. The Military Operations Authority, headed by the army commander, served as a combined services coordinating and control center. The commanders of the navy, air force, the Air Defense Force, and the two field armies worked under the direction of the chief of staff. These lines of command, however, were not always strictly observed, especially under operational conditions (see fig. 8).

The commander in chief of the armed forces held the rank of a full general, except in the case of Abu Ghazala, who was promoted to field marshal in recognition of his importance in the national security establishment. In 1990 the chief of staff of the armed forces and the commander in chief of the Air Defense Force were lieutenant generals. The naval and air force commanders held the ranks of vice admiral and air marshal, the air force equivalent of lieutenant general, respectively. The chief of the Military Operations Authority and the commanders of the two field armies were major generals.

Army

The army has always been the largest and most important branch of the armed forces. The army had an estimated strength of 320,000 in 1989. About 180,000 of these were conscripts. Before the June 1967 War, the army divided its personnel into four regional commands. After the 1967 debacle, the army was reorganized into two field armies—the Second Army and the Third Army, both of which were stationed in the eastern part of the country. Most of the remaining troops were stationed in the Nile Delta region, around the upper Nile, and along the Libyan border. These troops were organized into eight military districts. Commandos and paratroop units were stationed near Cairo under central control but could be transferred quickly to one of the field armies if needed. District commanders, who generally held the rank of major general, maintained liaison with governors and other civil authorities on matters of domestic security.

The army's principal tactical formations in 1988 were believed to include four armored divisions (each with two armored brigades and one mechanized brigade); six mechanized infantry divisions (each with two mechanized brigades and one armored brigade); and two infantry divisions (each with two infantry brigades and one mechanized brigade). Independent brigades included four infantry brigades, three mechanized brigades, one armored brigade, two air mobile brigades, one paratroop brigade, and the Republican Guard armored brigade. These brigades were augmented by two heavy mortar brigades, fourteen artillery brigades, two surface-to-surface missile (SSM) regiments, and seven commando groups, each consisting of about 1,000 men.

Although disposition of the forces was secret, foreign military observers estimated that five Egyptian divisions were in camps west of the Suez Canal while half a division was in Sinai. The Second Army was responsible for the area from the Mediterranean Sea to a point south of Ismailia; the Third Army was responsible from that point southward to the Red Sea. The government deployed the armies in this way partly because of a desire to protect the canal and the capital from a potential Israeli invasion and partly because the housing facilities and installations for the two armies had long been located in these areas. The commander of the Western District controlled armored forces supplemented by commando, artillery, and air defense units (possibly totaling the equivalent of a reinforced division) that were stationed at coastal towns in the west and in the Western Desert (also known as the Libyan Desert) facing Libya.

Even though the Egyptian military became oriented toward the West after the October 1973 War, it still had large amounts of Soviet equipment in its arms inventory. As of 1989, an estimated five of the twelve divisions and portions of other units had made the transition to American equipment and order of battle. The stock of main battle tanks consisted of 785 M60A3s from the United States, together with more than 1,600 Soviet-made T–54, T–55, and T–62 models. Some of these older Soviet tanks were being refitted in the West with 105mm guns, diesel engines, fire-control systems,

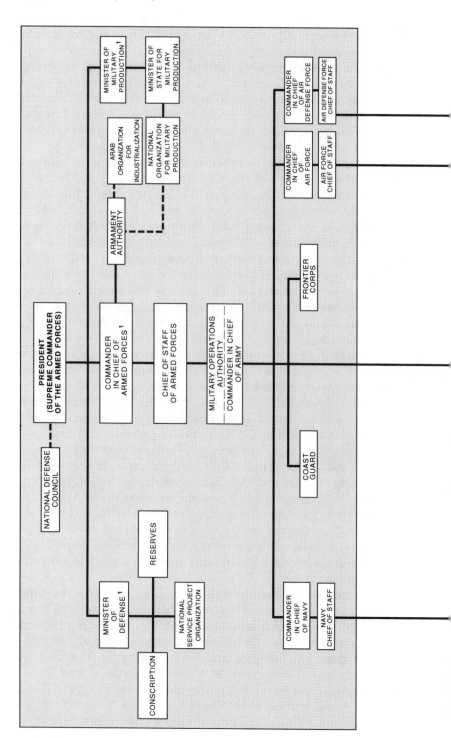

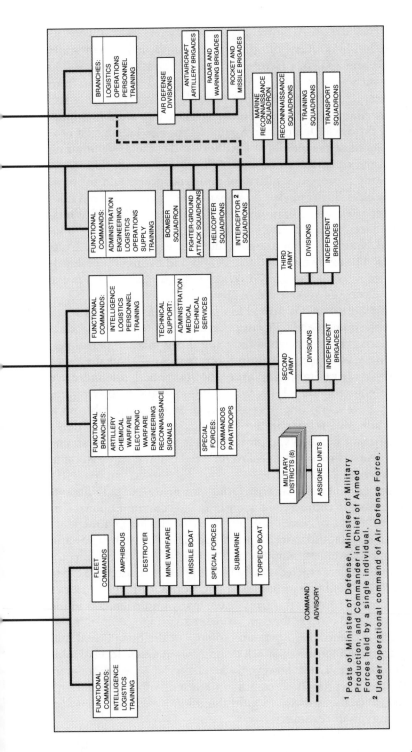

Figure 8. Organization of National Defense, 1989

and external armor. Armored personnel carriers (APCs) consisted of 1,000 M–113A2s from the United States, more than 1,000 BTR–50s and OT–62s from the Soviet Union, and about 200 Fahds, which were manufactured in Egypt based on a design from the Federal Republic of Germany (West Germany). The army also had more than 700 infantry combat vehicles that were manufactured by the Soviet Union and Spain. Egypt also launched a program to increase the mobility of artillery and rockets by mounting them on the chassis of tanks and APCs.

The army possessed a variety of antitank rockets and missiles, including older Soviet models, Egyptian rocket systems derived from the Soviet ones, and Milan missiles from France, Swingfire missiles produced in Egypt under British license, and TOW (tube-launched, optically sighted, wire-guided) missiles from the United States. The army mounted the TOWs and Swingfires on locally built jeeps. A plan to add TOWs to Fahd APCs was still at the prototype stage (see table 13, Appendix).

During the 1980s, the armed forces implemented a program to improve the quality and efficiency of the combat units by introducing modern armaments while reducing the number of personnel. The army was expected to lose more personnel than the other branches of the military. The army, however, had little incentive to cut its enlisted strength because doing so would further reduce the need for officers, who were already in excess of available positions. Moreover, service in the army helped relieve the nation's unemployment situation and provided some soldiers with vocational training. Nevertheless, plans called for a reduction in army strength by as much as 25 percent.

During each of the wars with Israel, the army had demonstrated weaknesses in command relationships and communications. Under the influence of Soviet military doctrine, higher commanders had been reluctant to extend operational flexibility to brigade and battalion commanders. Rigidity in planning was another shortcoming. Commanders reacted slowly in battlefield situations; the system did not encourage initiative among frontline officers. Prior to the October 1973 War, the army made many improvements in the way it prepared officers for combat. Moreover, the complex planning that preceded the Egyptian crossing of the Suez Canal and the execution of the initial attack demonstrated a high level of military competence. Later, however, when Israel launched its counterattack, the Egyptian high command reacted with hesitation and confusion, enabling Israel to gain the initiative in spite of determined Egyptian resistance.

Decision making in the army continued to be highly centralized during the 1980s. Officers below brigade level rarely made tactical decisions and required the approval of higher-ranking authorities before they modified any operations. Senior army officers were aware of this situation and began taking steps to encourage initiative at the lower levels of command.

A shortage of well-trained enlisted personnel became a serious problem for the army as it adopted increasingly complex weapons systems. Observers estimated in 1986 that 75 percent of all conscripts were illiterate when they entered the military and therefore faced serious obstacles when trying to learn how to use high-techlology weaponry. Soldiers who had acquired even the most basic technical skills were eager to leave the army as soon as possible in search of higher-paying positions in the civilian sector. By United States standards, the army underutilized its noncommissioned officers (NCOs), many of whom were soldiers who had served a long time but had not shown any special aptitude. Officers with ranks as high as major often conducted training that would be carried out by NCOs in a Western army. In a move to retain well-trained NCOs, the army in the 1980s started providing career enlisted men with higher pay, more amenities, and improved living conditions.

The Frontier Corps, a lightly armed paramilitary unit of about 12,000 men, mostly beduins, was responsible for border surveillance, general peacekeeping, drug interdiction, and prevention of smuggling. In the late 1980s, the army equipped this force with remote sensors, night-vision binoculars, communications vehicles, and high-speed motorboats.

Air Force

As of 1989, the Egyptian air force had more than 500 combat aircraft and 30,000 personnel, of which 10,000 were conscripts. Its front-rank fighters consisted of sixty-seven multimission F–16 A/Cs and thirty-three F–4Es from the United States, as well as sixteen Mirage 2000s from France. A large inventory of older MiG aircraft (some of which were Chinese versions assembled in Egypt) backed up the more modern fighters. The air force had fitted many of the MiGs with advanced Western electronics, including radars, jamming equipment, and Sidewinder and Matra air-to-air missiles. The Air Defense Force exercised operational control of about 135 MiG interceptors, although its aircraft and personnel remained part of the air force. Egypt also planned to exchange crude oil for fifty Pucara light ground-attack fighters from Argentina. The air force operated seventy-two combat helicopters and a number of electronic-monitoring, maritime-patrol, reconnaissance, and

311

early-warning aircraft. Some of these aircraft were capable of detecting low-flying targets at great distances (see table 14, Appendix).

When the Soviet Union became Egypt's principal arms supplier in the 1950s, it also played a preeminent role in advising and training the Egyptian air force. Much of the Soviet influence on the air force's structure and organization still prevailed in the 1980s, although training and tactics were affected by the changeover to Western equipment and the advanced training provided by the United States and other Western countries. Flying units were organized into air brigades that were headquartered at a single base. Brigades officially consisted of three squadrons that each had sixteen to twenty aircraft. Many brigades, however, had only two squadrons. With its headquarters at Heliopolis near Cairo, the air force had about seventeen principal air bases out of a total of forty major installations, as well as reserve and auxiliary bases.

After the June 1967 War and again after the October 1973 War, Egypt had to rebuild totally its air force. Only a few hours after the June 1967 War began, Israel had virtually wiped out the Egyptian air force. The government later tried and imprisoned the commander of the air force and a few other officers and purged many other senior officers. The combat efficiency of the air force, which had dropped almost to nil as a consequence of the war and its aftermath, was restored by renewed deliveries from the Soviet Union and intensified Soviet-led training of pilots and crews.

When Egypt initiated the October 1973 War, the air force was much better prepared for its mission. Egypt's air reconnaissance along the Suez Canal and its air strikes against Israeli strong points provided essential support to the ground forces that were crossing the canal. The air force then shifted to Israeli targets in Sinai and engaged in frequent dogfights over Suez and Port Said. Despite the courage and competence of the pilots, Egypt's air force suffered the loss of more than 200 aircraft in eighteen days of combat. Egypt and Syria together lost an estimated twelve aircraft for every aircraft lost by Israel.

When the war ended, Sadat repeatedly pressed the Soviets to replace Egypt's losses with more advanced aircraft that could rival the American aircraft being flown by the Israelis. Angered by Soviet delays, Sadat ordered Mirage 5 aircraft from France and, later on, F–4E fighters from the United States. Deliveries of the latter began in mid-1979. In addition, two batches of more advanced F–16s were delivered between 1986 and 1989. Delivery of a third batch, which would bring the total number of F–16s in operational units to 120, was to begin in 1991. As of 1990, Egypt was negotiating a fourth batch of forty-six aircraft. Egypt originally planned to purchase forty Mirage 2000s from France, but as of late 1989 no decision had been reached on acquiring the remaining aircraft. With the cooperation of Chinese and Western manufacturers, Egypt developed a major domestic industry that assembled aircraft and produced parts (see Defense Industry, this ch.).

Navy

Although the navy was the smallest branch of the military, it was large by Middle Eastern standards. After some years of neglect, in 1989 the navy was in the process of modernization. The navy's diverse and challenging missions included protection of more than 2,000 kilometers of coastline on the Mediterranean and Red seas, defense of approaches to the Suez Canal, and support for army operations. The navy had been built mostly with Soviet equipment during the 1960s but in the early 1980s acquired a number of vessels from China and Western sources. In 1989 the navy had 18,000 personnel, not including 2,000 members in the Coast Guard. Three-year conscripts accounted for about half of the personnel. Principal bases were at Alexandria (Al Iskandariyah), Port Said, and Marsa Matruh on the Mediterranean Sea, at Port Tawfiq (Bur Tawfiq) near Suez, and at Al Ghardaqah and Bur Safajah on the Red Sea. Some fleet units were stationed in the Red Sea, but the bulk of the force remained in the Mediterranean. Navy headquarters and the main operational and training base were located at Ras at Tin near Alexandria.

The Egyptian navy was only peripherally involved in the series of conflicts with Israel. During the 1956 War, Egyptian destroyers and torpedo boats engaged larger British vessels in a move aimed at undermining the amphibious operations of the British and French. The Egyptian blockade of ships in the Strait of Tiran that were headed toward Israel helped precipitate the June 1967 War, but Egypt's navy played only a minor role in the overall conflict. The navy's most significant action occurred in October 1967, a few months after the cease-fire, when an Egyptian missile boat sank one of Israel's two destroyers in Egyptian territorial waters off Port Said.

In the October 1973 War, Egypt blocked commercial traffic to Elat in the Gulf of Aqaba by laying mines; it also attempted to blockade Israeli ports on the Mediterranean. When Israel succeeded in enticing Egyptian missile craft into action, Israeli gunboats equipped with superior Gabriel missiles sank a number of Egyptian units. Both navies shelled and carried out rocket attacks against each other's shore installations, but neither side experienced any extensive damage.

313

Egypt maintained satisfactory operational standards for older ships at its own naval workshops and repair facilities; many ships were outfitted at these facilities with newer electronic equipment and weapons. During the 1980s, the navy focused on upgrading submarine and antisubmarine warfare, improving minesweeping capabilities, and introducing early-warning systems. Libya's mining of the Red Sea in 1984 focused attention on the need to protect shipping lanes leading to the Suez Canal and the need for more advanced mine countermeasure vessels. The navy periodically tested its effectiveness during joint operations with friendly foreign fleets. Egypt regularly carried out exercises with French and Italian naval units and with ships of the United States Sixth Fleet in a series known as "Sea Wind." Exercises were also scheduled to be held with Britain in 1990.

The navy's main operational subdivisions were the destroyer, submarine, mine warfare, missile boat, and torpedo boat commands. The most up-to-date combat vessels of the navy were two Descubierta-class frigates built in Spain and commissioned in 1984. The frigates were equipped with Aspide missiles and Stingray torpedoes for antisubmarine operations and with Harpoon SSMs. The navy commissioned two Chinese frigates of the Jianghu class in the same period. The navy had ten Romeo-class submarines, of which eight were operational, four provided by the Soviet Union and four by China. Four of the submarines were undergoing modernization in an Egyptian shipyard under contract with an American firm. Modernization included refitting the vessels so they could fire Harpoon SSMs and Mk 37 torpedoes. In 1989 Egypt purchased two Oberon-class submarines from Britain. These submarines would require refitting and modernization before entering Egyptian service. Most of the navy's considerable fleet of fast-attack craft armed with missiles or torpedoes came from the Soviet Union or China. The most modern of these craft, however, were six Ramadan-class missile boats built in Britain in the early 1980s and mounted with Otomat SSMs (see table 15, Appendix).

The Coast Guard was responsible for the onshore protection of public installations near the coast and the patrol of coastal waters to prevent smuggling. Its inventory consisted of about thirty large patrol craft (each between twenty and thirty meters in length) and twenty smaller Bertram-class coastal patrol craft built in the United States.

The navy lacked its own air arm and depended on the air force for maritime reconnaissance and protection against submarines. The air force's equipment that supported the navy included twelve Gazelle and five Sea King helicopters mounted with antiship and antisubmarine missiles. In mid-1988 the air force also took delivery of the first of six Grumman E–2c Hawkeye aircraft with search and side-looking radar for maritime surveillance purposes.

Air Defense Force

After most of the country's aircraft was destroyed on the ground in 1967, the military placed responsibility for air defense under one commander. Responsibility had previously been divided among several commands. Egypt patterned its new Air Defense Force (ADF) after the Soviet Air Defense Command, which integrated all its air defense capabilities—antiaircraft guns, rocket and missile units, interceptor planes, and radar and warning installations.

In 1989 the ADF had an estimated 80,000 ground and air personnel, including 50,000 conscripts. Its main constituents were 100 antiaircraft-gun battalions, 65 battalions of SA–2 SAMs, 60 battalions of SA–3 SAMs, 12 batteries of improved Hawk SAMs (I–Hawk), and 1 battery of Crotale missiles. Each battalion had between 200 and 500 men, and from four to eight battalions composed a brigade. Gun and missile sites were located along the Suez Canal, around Cairo, and near some other cities to protect military installations and strategic civilian targets. The ADF deployed some of its more mobile weapons in the Western Desert as a defense against possible Libyan incursions.

Progress was being made on a national air-defense network that would integrate all existing radars, missile batteries, air bases, and command centers into an automated command and control system. The ADF planned to link the system to the Hawkeye early warning aircraft.

A large share of the ADF's antiaircraft artillery, SAMs, and radar equipment was imported from the Soviet Union. As of 1989, the most modern weapons in the air defense system were the 108 medium-altitude I–Hawk SAMs acquired from the United States beginning in 1982. These weapons were supplemented by 400 older Soviet-made SA–2 SAMs with a slant range of forty to fifty kilometers and about 240 SA–3s, which provided shorter-range defense against low-flying targets. A British firm helped the ADF modernize the SA–2s. In addition, Egypt was producing its own SAM, the Tayir as Sabah (Morning Flight), based on the design of the SA–2. The ADF had mounted sixty Soviet SA–6 SAMs on tracked vehicles as tactical launchers. Sixteen tracked vehicles provided mobile launching platforms for its fifty French-manufactured Crotale SAM launchers. Egypt was also introducing its own composite gun-missile-radar system known as Amun (skyguard), integrating radar-guided twin 23mm guns with Sparrow and Egyptian Ayn as Saqr SAMs (see table 16, Appendix).

Training and Education

Army recruits followed a basic training program that included, when necessary, some remedial literacy training. After specialized training, recruits participated in the annual cycle of training that commenced at the small unit level and culminated in army-wide exercises. Individuals who volunteered to continue in service as NCOs attended a command school followed by specialized training and eventually became eligible for enrollment in an advanced career school for senior NCOs. Recruits in the navy and air force followed a similar program of basic training followed by specialized training. The navy, however, required shipboard service before specialization.

Five academies trained cadets (midshipmen) for commissioning as regular officers. The academies included the Military Academy, the Naval Academy, the Air Force Academy, the Military Technical Academy, and the Air Defense Academy. The oldest of these, the Military Academy, was located in Cairo, having been founded after Egyptian independence in 1922, when British influence in the military was still strong. In 1936 the Military Academy extended eligibility for admission to young men of lower-middle-class and peasant families. Graduates of the academy after the change in admissions policy went into effect included Nasser, Sadat, and seven others of the group known as the Free Officers who later led the 1952 military coup that toppled Egypt's monarchy.

Candidates applying for admission to the Military Academy were required to have a general secondary school certificate showing above-average grades. The academy based admissions decisions on the results of a competitive academic examination, a stringent physical examination, and a physical fitness test. Sons of military and police personnel and sons and brothers of men killed in action automatically received extra points in the scoring process. The Military Academy's curriculum included comprehensive undergraduate training and specific training in combat arms. Graduates of the three-year program were commissioned as second lieutenants. Newly commissioned army officers received branch training at schools operated by the infantry, artillery, armor, and several other branches.

The Naval Academy, located at the Ras at Tin naval base, offered an academic course comparable to the one offered by the Military Academy. The program at the Naval Academy, however, also included shipboard training during cruises that lasted from one to

Egyptian army members participating in joint United States-Egyptian Exercise Bright Star, 1982 Courtesy United States Department of Defense

three months. On graduation, midshipmen were commissioned as ensigns. Engineers, communications specialists, and other technicians also graduated from the Naval Academy after following separate curricula. The Air Force Academy, about sixty kilometers northeast of Cairo at Bilbays, had a curriculum of theoretical, technical, and scientific subjects plus up to 200 hours of flying instruction. In 1988 the Air Force Academy reduced the period of study from four to three years. The academy also eased the requirement of a superior secondary school academic record to emphasize student's aptitude for flying through a series of tests. On successful completion of flight training and the academic program, graduates were commissioned as pilots or navigators; those who did not qualify were given administrative assignments in the air force or, in some cases, were transferred to another service.

The Military Technical Academy (also known as the Armed Forces Technical College), was located at Heliopolis. It educated technical officers for all armed forces and therefore reduced the need for foreign technical advisers. The Military Technical Academy's admissions office had more stringent entrance requirements than the Military Academy; applicants had to have a superior academic record in secondary-school science courses. Applicants to the Military Technical Academy also faced more difficult qualifying examinations in science and mathematics. Because of their intensive curriculum, graduates were commissioned as first lieutenants. Selected civilians who made a commitment to government service could also enroll in the Military Technical Academy. Under Abu Ghazala, the Military Technical Academy was upgraded by the grant of scarce resources for research in spite of retrenchment at civilian research facilities. The Academy of Military Medicine trained health workers and medical professionals. In 1986 the People's Assembly passed legislation calling for the development of a new Military Academy for Administrative Sciences. The Air Defense Academy, which opened in Alexandria in 1974, required five years of study leading to a bachelor's degree in engineering. Additional training followed on individual air defense systems.

The Command and General Staff College was founded in Cairo in 1939 as the Army Staff College, a name still frequently used. The school provided training in staff duties and command responsibilities for selected officers, usually majors and junior lieutenant colonels. The college provided intensive study of tactics, logistics, operations planning, and administration. The duration of the academic program was about eighteen months. Graduates received masters' degrees in military science and were considered qualified for assignment to staff positions at the division level and higher or to command a battalion or brigade. Completion of the staff college or an appropriate educational equivalent was a prerequisite for acceptance to senior military colleges.

Named in honor of Egypt's president at the time, the Nasser High Military Academy was founded in 1965. It was dedicated to the advanced education of senior officers of the armed forces and selected civilian government officials. It encompassed both the Higher War College and the National Defense College and was the summit of the officer education system. Studies at the Higher War College lasted for one year and emphasized familiarity with Egypt's military, economic, and international situation. This institution, which prepared students to participate in the formulation of Egypt's foreign and defense policies, awarded its graduates doctoral degrees in military sciences and national strategy. Foreigners were not permitted to enroll, but special courses were held for officers of friendly countries, such as Iraq, Somalia, Sudan, and Tunisia. In addition, beginning in 1980 the college held a number of symposia on African strategic issues and invited participants from most of the African countries.

The National Defense College admitted qualified applicants who were either senior officers or ranking civilians from state and public-sector institutions. The college gave preference to persons with a master's degree. The academic program, which lasted eleven months, emphasized national strategic planning and mobilization problems to develop a civilian's capabilities to hold a leadership position in state agencies.

Egypt started sending selected officers abroad for advanced training as early as the 1930s. Between the mid-1940s and mid-1950s, hundreds of Egyptian officers attended schools in Britain, France, and the United States. When the Soviet Union became the chief supplier of Egypt's arms and equipment, it became the focal point of foreign military training. After Egypt severed relations with Britain and the United States in 1967, training abroad was conducted almost exclusively in the Soviet Union, although a few officers continued to attend French schools. Although some officers believed that the standard of instruction in Soviet institutions was seriously deficient, nearly all Egyptian officers below the rank of major general at the time of the October 1973 War had attended staff schools or received specialized training in the Soviet Union. Since the 1970s, Egypt sent almost all of its advanced military students to institutions in Western countries.

Conscription and Reserves

The Constitution mandates conscription but provides a variety of options for national service. Conscripts may be required to serve in the armed forces, the police, the prison-guard service, or a military economic service unit. In 1988 almost 12.5 million men were between the ages of fifteen and forty-nine. More than 8 million of these men were considered fit for military service. Although 519,000 men reached the draft age of twenty each year, only about 80,000 of these men were conscripted to serve in the armed forces. Women were not subject to conscription.

Volunteers earned considerably higher salaries and twice as much leave time as conscripts. Those conscripts who chose to reenlist were often among the less qualified. The result of this situation was a scarcity of NCOs with the proper level of proficiency. The navy and the air force had a smaller conscript-to-volunteer ratio, but these branches of the military faced similar problems. In all services senior NCOs could become candidates for commissions after eight years of duty. These NCOs usually were those with functional specialties who could qualify as warrant officers.

Conscripts served three years of active duty after which they remained in reserve for an additional period. Conscripts with degrees from institutions of higher education had to serve only eighteen months. The government required all males to register for the draft when they reached age sixteen. The government delineated several administrative zones for conscription purposes. Each zone had a council of military officers, civil officials, and medical officers who selected draftees. Local mayors and village leaders also participated in the selection process. After the council granted exemptions and deferments, it chose conscripts by lot from the roster of remaining names. Individuals eligible to be inducted were on call for three years. After that period, they could no longer be drafted.

Although it was no longer possible for a prospective conscript to pay a fee in lieu of service, he could still apply for an exemption. Men employed in permanent government positions, an only remaining son whose brothers had died in service, men employed in essential industries, and family breadwinners were all eligible for exemptions.

The military authorities did not give strong emphasis to maintaining reserve forces. Foreign military observers believed that the reserves would be of minimal value in the event of an emergency. An estimated 335,000 men were in the reserves in the early 1980s (300,000 army and ADF, 15,000 navy, and 20,000 air force). The total was expected to decline to about 200,000 by the early 1990s.

Conditions of Service

Between 1981 and 1989, commander in chief Abu Ghazala established his popularity with the armed forces by substantially improving the living conditions of military careerists. The cabinet approved periodic pay increases, but salaries were not as high as in the private sector. Still, the combination of salaries and benefits provided officers with a comfortable living. As of 1989, it was less common for officers to hold second jobs. Many retired officers, however, were employed in the state-owned defense production sector. Officers' special privileges included the opportunity to purchase cars at reduced prices, access to superior health care and hospitals, visits to specially designated resort areas, and club memberships. Officers shopped at clean, well-stocked commissaries that carried duty-free or subsidized foods, which were often unavailable on the local market. Children of career personnel received preferential treatment when they applied for admission to institutions of higher learning. Under Abu Ghazala, ordinary soldiers received a narrower range of benefits, but their housing, rations, and uniforms improved. Soldiers seemed well-fed and neatly turned out. NCOs earned salaries that were high enough for them to afford adequate accommodations for their families. Draftees' living conditions remained far less favorable. Their monthly earnings amounted to less than US$10 in the late 1980s.

To attract people to the uniformed services, the military began offering recruits comfortable apartments in new "military cities." Most of these cities were located in the desert just outside Cairo and other major cities and near the Suez area, where there was a high concentration of military installations. As of 1986, the military had built thirteen of these cities and was constructing another ten. The largest of these was Nasser City near Heliopolis, where an estimated 250,000 people lived in 1986. Other military cities were designed to accommodate as many as 150,000 residents, including troops in new barracks. Each city generally included a large number of apartment blocks, as well as primary schools, high schools, nurseries, mosques, supermarkets, social clubs, banks, a water purification system, and solar heating.

The military raised some of the capital needed to erect the military cities from the sale of valuable land it owned in the center of Cairo. With subsidized prices and favorable loan terms, career military personnel could typically buy an apartment for £E12,000 as of 1986 (for value of the Egyptian pound, see Glossary), with down payments ranging from £E1,000 to £E3,000, amortized over thirty years. Some officers profited by subletting their apartments to civilians. In addition, land was made available within the military cities for construction of civilian apartment blocks. As of 1986, construction in military cities accounted for 5 percent of all Egyptian residential construction.

Defense Spending

The burden of defense expenditures on the economy was difficult to assess because the military did not make this information public and did not provide details to the People's Assembly as part of the annual budget. The last time defense outlays were made public was in 1983, when the minister of finance stated that the military would receive £E2.1 billion (about US$3 billion at the 1983 rate of exchange) in fiscal year (FY—see Glossary) 1983. The amount was 22 percent higher than the amount for the preceding year and equaled 13 percent of total central government expenditures. In early 1989, Abu Ghazala indicated that military expenditures amounted to £E2.4 billion or 10 percent of total government spending.

According to estimates published in *The Military Balance, 1989–1990* by the London-based International Institute for Strategic Studies, Egypt's actual military expenditures were much higher than official figures. According to the institute, defense outlays amounted to about £E4 billion in FY 1988 and £E4.7 billion in FY 1989. The institute's estimates, however, did not include funds received directly from other sources, such as the United States, which contributed US$1.3 billion each year. The military also received an undisclosed amount from Saudi Arabia and earned foreign exchange from exports of domestically manufactured military equipment. The military reportedly produced as much as 60 percent of its consumable requirements (food, uniforms, and other goods) at its own farms and factories, but it was not clear whether the value of this production was fully reported in the budget.

According to estimates compiled by the United States Arms Control and Disarmament Agency (ACDA), Egypt's military expenditures fell to about US$4 billion annually between 1979 and 1981 because of Sadat's decision to cut the military budget by half in the wake of the peace accord with Israel. In 1982, the year after Abu Ghazala took office, defense expenditures rose sharply to US$7.4 billion, according to the ACDA. Defense expenditures tapered off during the subsequent five years to US$6.5 billion as the nation's mounting financial difficulties necessitated retrenchment in all budget categories. The ACDA estimates, calculated in constant 1987 dollars, included arms imports and foreign military aid.

The ACDA data also indicated that military expenditures as a share of gross national product (GNP—see Glossary) had fallen from 22.8 percent in 1977 to 9.2 percent in 1987. Military expenditures as a share of all central government expenditures had fallen from more than 40 percent in 1977 to 22.3 percent in 1987. Annual

*United States Air Force A–10
Thunderbolt shares an Egyptian
airfield with a Soviet-built
Egyptian Armed Forces
"Hip-C" helicopter.
Exercise Bright Star
Courtesy United States
Department of Defense*

*United States Army paratrooper
works with his Egyptian Army
counterpart prior to a
simulated combat air assault.
Exercise Bright Star
Courtesy United States
Department of Defense*

per capita military expenditures fell from US$229 in 1977 to US$126 in 1987 (expressed in constant 1987 dollars). Repayments on military credits extended by the United States, France, West Germany, Spain, Britain, and other countries amounted to about US$1 billion a year—Egypt's total foreign debt-servicing obligations amounted to US$4 billion a year.

Compared with the Middle East as a whole, Egypt's defense expenditures were relatively modest. In 1987 average military expenditures in the region amounted to 11 percent of GNP and 32 percent of total central government expenditures. Per capita military expenditures in the region totaled US$396 (Syria, Iraq, and Iran were on a wartime footing when these figures were compiled).

Military Justice

The Military Justice Law of 1966 superseded a code of military justice that the British enacted in 1893. Three major concepts underlay the 1966 law: military law must be consonant with the general law of the land; crimes committed by military personnel (such as theft and embezzlement) were especially serious because they could endanger national security; and the armed forces should be role models for the rest of the country and should set ethical standards by promptly punishing personnel who violate laws.

The 1966 law spelled out different legal procedures for administrative violations, misdemeanors, and felonies; this system was similar to the one used throughout the country for civilians. The military court system was similar to most Western military court systems but had courts whose size and authority varied according to the level of command. Military personnel had the right of trial before military courts even for common crimes against civilians. This arrangement, however, was under debate in the late 1980s because many civilians doubted military judges' qualifications and the efficacy of the military courts. Military courts also had jurisdiction in cases involving offenses against military personnel and property. Since 1958 the country's state of emergency has entitled the president to refer civilian cases to military courts when the offenses involved issues of national security.

The accused had the right to defense by an officer or by a civilian attorney. Verdicts, announced in open session, were not final until a higher authority approved them. The ultimate authority was the president, who could delegate his authority to the minister of defense or another official. The accused also had the right of appeal. The 1966 law outlawed cruel punishment, such as flogging, and established maximum sentences for various categories of crimes.

The 1966 law authorized the death penalty for treason, murder, and the destruction or sabotage of weapons or equipment of the armed forces. A 1970 amendment to the law defined twelve treasonable offenses that could be punished by execution. These offenses included misconduct before the enemy, surrendering or abandoning installations or troops to the enemy, and giving aid and comfort to the enemy. In addition, anyone abetting any of the twelve treasonable crimes through error or negligence or contributing to dereliction of duty could be sentenced to life imprisonment at hard labor. Confiscation of government property for private use was also punishable by life imprisonment.

Uniforms and Insignia

Egyptian military uniforms were similar to British uniforms. Each branch of the military had dress, service or garrison, and field uniforms. Dress uniforms were worn mostly on formal occasions. The service uniform was worn for daily duty. The service uniform for the ground forces was khaki cotton; personnel in the air force wore blue, and the navy wore navy blue in winter and white in summer. Egyptian officers purchased their uniforms, but enlisted personnel received a standard uniform issue, which consisted of service and field uniforms, fatigues, and in some cases, dress uniforms.

Rank insignia were similar for the army, navy, and air force. The grade structure had seventeen ranks ranging from private to general. Each rank had a counterpart in all services. Commissioned officers in the army and navy wore gold insignia on shoulder boards; officers in the air force wore silver ones. Army enlisted personnel wore green stripes; air force enlisted personnel wore blue stripes on the upper sleeve (see fig. 9).

Armed Forces Production

Production of Civilian Goods

Beginning in 1978 the armed forces launched a number of enterprises that produced goods for military and civilian use. The National Service Project Organization (NSPO) controlled these enterprises. The government set up the NSPO to help reorient the military toward national economic development efforts as the military's role in defense diminished after the 1979 peace treaty with Israel. Moreover, government officials believed that national security would be bolstered if the military achieved a degree of self-sufficiency in food and other essential supplies.

Agriculture, the most important sector of military production, accounted for £E488 million in production in FY 1985, the last

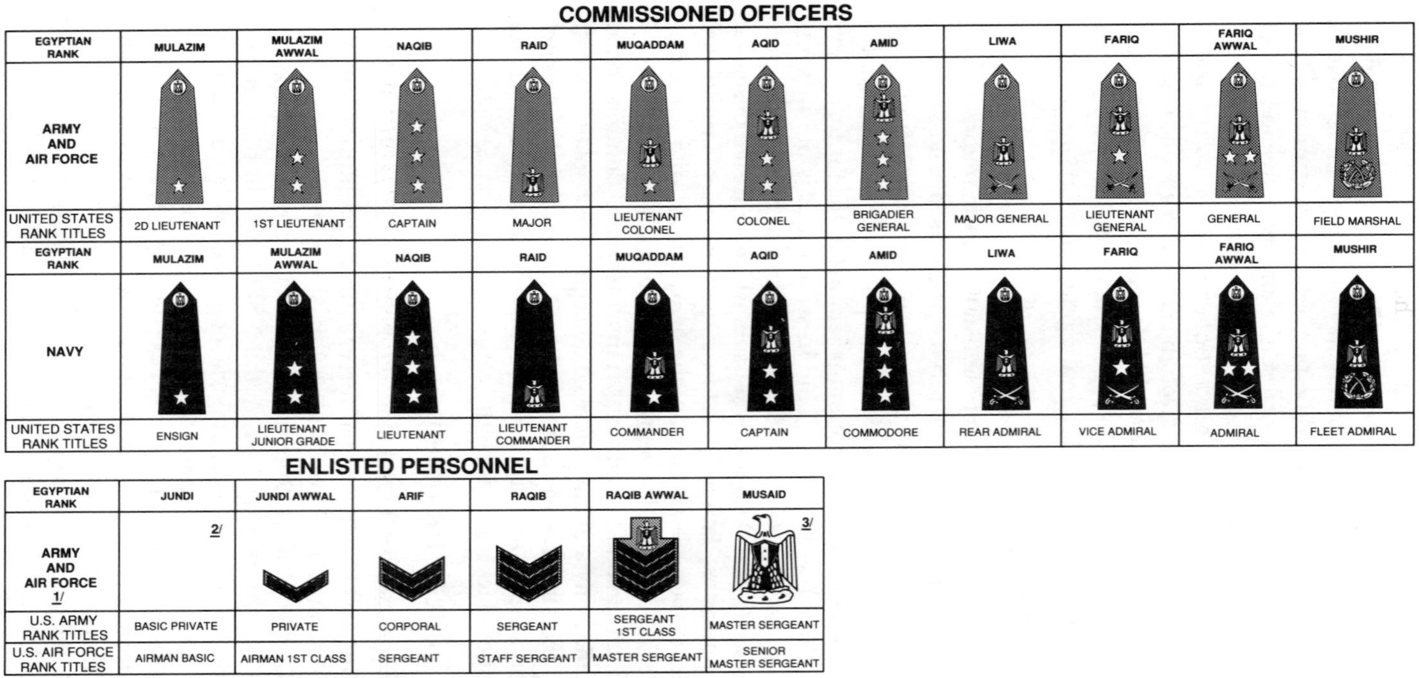

COMMISSIONED OFFICERS

EGYPTIAN RANK	MULAZIM	MULAZIM AWWAL	NAQIB	RAID	MUQADDAM	AQID	AMID	LIWA	FARIQ	FARIQ AWWAL	MUSHIR
ARMY AND AIR FORCE											
UNITED STATES RANK TITLES	2D LIEUTENANT	1ST LIEUTENANT	CAPTAIN	MAJOR	LIEUTENANT COLONEL	COLONEL	BRIGADIER GENERAL	MAJOR GENERAL	LIEUTENANT GENERAL	GENERAL	FIELD MARSHAL
EGYPTIAN RANK	MULAZIM	MULAZIM AWWAL	NAQIB	RAID	MUQADDAM	AQID	AMID	LIWA	FARIQ	FARIQ AWWAL	MUSHIR
NAVY											
UNITED STATES RANK TITLES	ENSIGN	LIEUTENANT JUNIOR GRADE	LIEUTENANT	LIEUTENANT COMMANDER	COMMANDER	CAPTAIN	COMMODORE	REAR ADMIRAL	VICE ADMIRAL	ADMIRAL	FLEET ADMIRAL

ENLISTED PERSONNEL

EGYPTIAN RANK	JUNDI	JUNDI AWWAL	ARIF	RAQIB	RAQIB AWWAL	MUSAID
ARMY AND AIR FORCE 1/	2/					3/
U.S. ARMY RANK TITLES	BASIC PRIVATE	PRIVATE	CORPORAL	SERGEANT	SERGEANT 1ST CLASS	MASTER SERGEANT
U.S. AIR FORCE RANK TITLES	AIRMAN BASIC	AIRMAN 1ST CLASS	SERGEANT	STAFF SERGEANT	MASTER SERGEANT	SENIOR MASTER SERGEANT

Note: 1/ Navy insignia not known. 2/ No rank insignia. 3/ Worn on wrist.

Figure 9. Military Ranks and Insignia, 1990

year for which data were available. The output of nonmilitary manufactured goods amounted to £E347 million in FY 1985, construction £E174 million, and other goods and services £E144 million. Military-operated facilities (including dairy and poultry farms, fisheries, cattle feedlots, vegetable and fruit farms, bakeries, and food-processing plants) accounted for 18 percent of the nation's total food production in FY 1985. The military consumed much of the food it produced, selling the surplus in commissaries and through civilian commercial channels.

Military-operated manufacturing enterprises included factories that produced clothing, doors, window frames, stationery, pharmaceutical packaging, and microscopes. Abu Ghazala planned to develop a military-operated automobile assembly plant with assistance from General Motors Corporation, but the government shelved the idea because of widespread criticism on both economic and political grounds.

The military was also involved in a number of infrastructure projects. It installed more than 40 percent of the new telephone links covered in the First Five-Year Plan (FY 1982–86). It constructed power lines, sewers, bridges, and overpasses in Cairo and elsewhere. It also participated in land reclamation projects.

Many career military officers disapproved of the military's role in national economic development projects; they believed that the armed forces should concentrate on the nation's security. Others, however, believed the projects improved the military's image and made the armed forces seem more efficient than the public sector. Senior officers argued that these projects had no effect on combat capabilities because the soldiers employed on them were not physically qualified for normal military functions. The precise number of troops detailed to economic development was not disclosed, although observers have estimated that tens of thousands of troops were so engaged. Food production employed 5,000 service personnel, including about 500 officers, in 1986. In the same year, Abu Ghazala announced that he would assign 30,000 conscripts to newly created development regiments after they received special training following basic training.

Opposition politicians and some business people complained that the military competed with the private sector in the country's development efforts. Critics argued that the private sector would be at a disadvantage as long as the armed forces were exempt from taxes, import licenses, and business permits and were not held accountable for profits or losses. Some business people, however, liked the military's growing role in the economy because many of them

327

were awarded lucrative contracts from the military for a variety of goods and services.

Defense Industry

Egypt was the most important manufacturer of weapons and military components among the Arab countries. State-owned enterprises, under control of the Armament Authority headed by a major general, were the main domestic producers of Egypt's defense systems. The Armament Authority was responsible for selecting, developing, and procuring military systems. Acting on behalf of the military's branches, the authority assigned production to domestic factories or contracted with external suppliers.

As early as 1949, Egypt unveiled plans to develop its own aircraft and armaments industry with the industrial base that emerged during World War II when British and American forces placed orders for equipment. Egypt entered into a number of joint venture projects to produce European-designed aircraft. The most successful of these led to the Jumhuriya basic flight trainer, of which about 200 were eventually made. In 1962 Egypt undertook a major program with the help of West German technicians to design and build a supersonic jet fighter, but the government terminated the project because of financial strains caused by the June 1967 War. In a separate program assisted by West German scientists and technicians, the air force built prototypes of three SSM designs. These designs, however, were never put into operational use.

During the 1970s and 1980s, Egypt expanded and diversified its production of arms to achieve partial self-sufficiency and to develop an export market in the Middle East and Africa. In addition to manufacturing small arms and ammunition, Egypt had begun producing or assembling more advanced weapons systems through licensing and joint venture agreements with companies based in the United States and Western Europe. Egyptian technicians and scientists developed several indigenous weapons systems.

The National Organization for Military Production within the Ministry of Military Production supervised a number of manufacturing plants, which were usually named after their location. These plants included the Abu Zaabal Company for Engineering Industries, which produced artillery pieces and barrels; the Abu Zaabal Tank Repair Factory, which overhauled and repaired tanks and would eventually become the producer of Egypt's main battle tank; the Al Maadi Company for Engineering Industries, which produced light weapons, including the Egyptian version of the Soviet AK–47 assault rifle; the Hulwan Company for Machine Tools, which produced mortars and rocket launchers; the Hulwan Company for

Engineering Industries, which produced metal parts for ammunition, shells, bombs, and rockets; the Heliopolis Company for Chemical Industries, which produced artillery ordnance, bombs, and missile warheads; and the Banha Company for Electronic Industries, which produced communications devices.

In 1975 Egypt, Qatar, Saudi Arabia, and the United Arab Emirates founded the Arab Organization for Industrialization (AOI) and capitalized the new organization with more than US$1 billion. These countries set up the AOI to establish an Arab defense industry by combining Egypt's managerial ability and industrial labor force with the Arab countries' oil money and foreign technology. The bulk of the arms manufacturing was intended to take place in Egypt. But the AOI foundered before it could become a major arms producer because the Arab states broke relations with Egypt over Sadat's peace initiatives with Israel. Egypt kept the AOI functioning in spite of a 1979 proclamation by Saudi Arabia dissolving the body. Some of the AOI's members have renewed military contacts, but as of 1989, the AOI had not been restored to its original status.

The AOI had operated as an independent enterprise since 1979 and was exempt from Egyptian taxes and business restrictions. The AOI consisted of nine companies, five wholly owned by Egypt and four joint ventures. The Egyptian plants manufactured missiles, rockets, aircraft engine parts, armored personnel carriers, electronics, radar, communications gear, and assembled aircraft. A joint venture with French firms assembled Gazelle combat helicopters and helicopter engines. A joint venture with the British manufactured the Swingfire antitank guided missile, while another venture with the Chrysler Corporation produced jeeps.

As of 1990, Egypt did not manufacture its own aircraft, but it assembled Tucano primary trainers from Brazil, Chenyang fighters from China, and Alpha Jet trainers designed in France and West Germany. Egyptian technicians had also reverse engineered and modified two Soviet SAMs—the Ayn as Saqr (a version of the SA-7) and the Tayir as Sabah (a version of the SA-2). Egyptian shipyards had produced eight fast attack naval craft fitted with British armaments and electronics.

The only armored vehicle in production was the Fahd four-wheeled APC, although the United States and Egypt planned to coproduce 540 Abrams M1A1 main battle tanks over a ten-year period beginning in 1991. The project would be funded largely through United States military aid; the United States would also supply the engines and fire control systems. According to some reports, Egypt was reconsidering the project because of its high cost. But as of late 1989, Egypt appeared to be going forward with the plan.

In September 1989, Egypt had reportedly dropped out of the Condor II project, cosponsored with Argentina and Iraq, to develop an intermediate-range (800-kilometer) SSM. Earlier that year, officials in the United States had arrested several persons, including two military officers attached to the Embassy of Egypt in Washington, in connection with the illegal export of missile technology and materials needed to produce rocket fuel and nose cones.

In March 1989, United States and Swiss officials claimed that Egypt had imported from Switzerland the main elements of a plant capable of manufacturing poison gas. Mubarak denied that Egypt had either the facilities or the plans for producing chemical weapons.

The main purchaser of Egyptian defense products had been Iraq. In the early 1980s, Iraq was desperate to replace Soviet military equipment lost during the early stages of the war with Iran. Iraq blunted Iranian attacks with the Saqr 18, the Egyptian version of the Soviet BM-21 122mm multiple rocket launcher.

Egypt sold a smaller volume of weapons to Kuwait and other Persian Gulf states. In 1988 Kuwait was reported to have ordered about 100 Fahd armored personnel carriers; Oman and Sudan ordered smaller quantities of these carriers. Because Egypt considered the value of its military exports confidential, it omitted this information from its published trade statistics. According to ACDA, Egypt exported US$340 million worth of military equipment in 1982, declining to an average of US$70 million annually in the years from 1985 to 1987. The ACDA data was considered conservative. Other estimates have placed Egyptian defense exports as high as US$1 billion in 1982 and US$500 million annually in 1983 and 1984, when deliveries to Iraq were at their peak.

International observers believed that Egypt has not engaged in efforts to develop a nuclear weapons capability. Egypt had a small nuclear research reactor that was built with Soviet assistance, but the Soviets controlled the disposal of the facility's spent fuel. In any event, the facility was not capable of producing a significant amount of weapons-grade material. Egypt signed the Treaty on the Non-Proliferation of Nuclear Weapons (NPT) in 1968 but delayed ratifying it, presumably because the government had evidence that Israel had embarked on a nuclear weapons program. In 1975 the United States agreed in principle on a program to supply Egypt with power reactors. The plan was subject to a trilateral safeguards agreement signed by the United States, the International Atomic Energy Agency, and Egypt. Although financing problems stalled construction of power reactors from the United States, Egypt ratified the NPT in 1981, in order to be able to conclude agreements with other countries for the construction of atomic energy production facilities.

Foreign Military Assistance

Between 1955 and 1975, the Egyptian armed forces depended heavily on the Soviet Union. The Soviet Union provided Egypt with grants and loans to pay for equipment, training, and the services of large numbers of military advisers. The Soviets initially supplied outmoded equipment from surplus stocks to help Egypt replenish its forces after the 1956 War, but in the early 1960s, the Soviet Union began furnishing up-to-date MiG-21 fighter aircraft, SA-2 SAMs, and T-54 tanks. The Soviet Union and the German Democratic Republic (East Germany) supplied large numbers of trainers and technicians, and Egypt sent many of its officers to Soviet military institutions to learn new organizational and strategic doctrines.

Egypt's defeat in the June 1967 War deepened the Soviet Union's involvement in Egypt's military (see War of Attrition and the October 1973 War, this ch.). By the early 1970s, the number of Soviet personnel in Egypt had risen to nearly 20,000. They participated in operational decisions and served at the battalion and sometimes even company levels.

Soviet advisers' patronizing attitudes, Moscow's slow response to requests for more sophisticated equipment, and Cairo's desire for more freedom in preparing for a new conflict were considered by observers as some of the reasons for Sadat's decision to expel most Soviet military personnel in July 1972. The Soviet Union continued to provide equipment, spare parts, and replacements for equipment lost during the October 1973 War, but Sadat was becoming increasingly disenchanted with Egypt's reliance on Soviet weaponry. In March 1976, Sadat asked the People's Assembly to abrogate the 1971 Soviet-Egyptian Treaty of Friendship and Cooperation.

After Egypt and Israel signed their peace treaty in 1979, the United States strove to increase deliveries of armaments to Egypt and to provide the country with American military advisers and training. By 1989 this aid averaged US$1.3 billion a year and had totaled more than US$12 billion. Egypt was the second largest recipient of United States military aid after Israel, which received US$1.8 billion annually. The United States supplied a number of major weapons systems, including F-4 and F-16 fighter aircraft, C-130 transports, E-2C Hawkeye electronic surveillance aircraft, M60A3 tanks, M-113A2 APCs, I-Hawk antiaircraft missile batteries, and improved TOW antitank missiles. The United States military assistance program for FY 1990 included initial funding for M1A1 tank coproduction, attack helicopters, and equipment to enhance command, control, and communications systems. Under the concurrent military education and training program of US$1.7 million for FY 1990, 174 Egyptian military personnel would receive training.

The United States stationed 1,200 military personnel in Egypt as of mid-1989. The presence of a large number of United States advisers in Egypt was a source of some political friction. The United States planned gradually to reduce the number in conjunction with the long-term Egyptian goal of self-sufficiency.

Starting in 1981, the United States and Egypt had held joint military exercises every other year under the name of Operation Bright Star. The two countries conducted the largest of these maneuvers near the Suez Canal in 1987 with 9,000 ground, air, and sea personnel from each country. In alternate years, the two countries also held combined air and sea exercises.

In 1981 Egypt agreed to allow the United States Rapid Deployment Force (currently called the United States Central Command) to use Egypt's base at Ras Banas on the Red Sea in the event that a friendly Arab nation needed help in repelling an armed attack. Preparations were made to upgrade the base by installing fuel-storage tanks, lengthening runways, and building barracks and docks. In 1984, however, the project was shelved because of disagreements over who would manage construction and because the United States Congress insisted that Egypt provide a formal guarantee of access to the base. Mounting distrust among the Egyptian public over close strategic ties with the United States was an underlying factor in abandoning the project. Egypt nonetheless indicated that the United States would still have access to the base if help were needed by a friendly Arab government.

Egypt was indebted to the United States for about US$4.5 billion, incurred at high interest rates in the late 1970s and early 1980s, for the purchase of military equipment. Beginning in 1984, the United States provided all of its military assistance in grant form. The interest payments on the earlier debt amounted to as much as US$600 million in a single year. Saudi Arabia and Kuwait helped Egypt maintain its initial payments, and in 1989 Egypt was negotiating a rescheduling of the debt at lower rates with the help of private banks (see Debt and Restructuring, ch. 3).

Although as of early 1990 the United States continued to be Egypt's main supplier of military equipment, Egypt's policy of diversifying its sources of weaponry led it to enter into cooperative

United States Army M-2 Bradley Infantry Fighting Vehicles maneuver in the Egyptian desert during Exercise Bright Star, 1987.
Courtesy United States Department of Defense

military relations with a number of other countries. Egypt acquired much of its modern aircraft from France, in some cases assembling them in Egypt. Egypt was engaged in a number of coproduction projects with Britain as well and assembled the Tucano primary trainer in cooperation with Brazil. Egypt acquired Chinese versions of Soviet-designed aircraft and submarines. Although an insufficient supply of replacement parts of the large arsenal of outdated Soviet equipment continued to present a problem, Egypt entered into a new understanding with the Soviet Union in 1986 to permit resumption of a modest flow of parts. Moscow also agreed to relax the terms of repayment of Cairo's military debt to the Soviet Union—estimated to be between US$5 billion to US$7 billion—over twenty-five years without interest. According to ACDA, the value of arms transfers to Egypt between 1983 and 1987 amounted to about US$7.8 billion, of which US$3.4 billion came from the United States, US$1.6 billion from France, US$550 million from China, US$340 million from the Soviet Union, US$270 million from Italy, US$200 million from Britain, US$60 million from West Germany, and the remaining US$1.4 billion from unidentified sources.

Internal Security

The level of violence in Egypt as a result of political or criminal activity has been below that of many countries of the Middle East. Periodic outbreaks of unrest have occurred as manifestations of popular discontent with economic conditions. These protests have mainly been localized or regional in scope and have been brought under control by the military when the forces of public order proved unable to deal with them. Rarely have political disturbances occurred on a national scale sufficient to threaten the existing political structure.

Although opposition to Nasser and Sadat was often widespread, security forces usually managed to contain the discontent. Riots and mass demonstrations plagued the Sadat administration. Students and intellectuals demonstrated against the protracted negotiations over the return of Sinai, Egypt's cooperation with the United States, and what they regarded as an unduly moderate stance regarding Arab-Israeli issues. Economic discontent led to violence on several occasions. For example, the 1977 food riots broke out when the government proposed to eliminate subsidies, thus raising the price of many common food items. The violence posed a serious challenge to the regime, forcing Sadat to restore the subsidies. Mubarak attempted to relieve some of the tension that had been building up in Egypt by permitting increased political expression, at least through officially sanctioned channels. He also sought to relieve social unrest through the retention of food subsidies. In 1986, however, riots by the Central Security Forces threatened to break down public order. Loyal units of the armed forces successfully contained the unrest (see Police, this ch.).

Religiously inspired activism was the source of much of the internal violence that occurred during the 1980s. Muslim extremists had a wide following, but only a few of them were actually involved in assaults against governmental institutions. In general, Egypt's security forces demonstrated a capacity to suppress widespread violence among Muslim extremists. As of early 1990, most observers believed that the majority of the population had rejected these radical but factionalized fringe groups and that these groups presented no immediate threat to the political system.

Muslim Extremism

The main organization advocating the establishment of an Islamic government in Egypt was the Muslim Brotherhood (Al Ikhwan al Muslimun; also known as the Brotherhood). The Brotherhood, founded in 1928, was closely linked to groups that opposed the

British and the monarchy in the 1940s. It also provided some of the ideas that inspired the Free Officers' coup in 1952. The government suppressed the Brotherhood after some of the organization's members were suspected of involvement in an assassination attempt against Nasser in 1954. In an attempt to offset the strength of Egypt's political left, Sadat permitted the reemergence of the Brotherhood. He freed hundreds of Brotherhood members who had been jailed for political reasons. Shifting to nonviolent tactics, the dominant elements of the Brotherhood sought respect and attempted to permeate the government and its institutions with Brotherhood adherents. Because it was a religious party, it could not participate directly in elections. Still, it ran a number of candidates in the 1984 and 1987 elections in alliances with other opposition parties. The Brotherhood's successful campaign in 1987, in which it captured thirty-eight seats in the People's Assembly, indicated an intensifying pro-Islamist sentiment in Egypt (see Islam, ch. 2; The Limits of Incorporation: The Rise of Political Islam and the Continuing Role of Repression, ch. 4).

The Brotherhood represented the mainstream of the Islamic movement, in comparison with the estimated fifty more radical Islamic groups, collectively known as the Jamaat al Islamiyah (Islamic Associations), that operated clandestinely. Most of these other groups sought to overthrow the state and to reorder society in accordance with the sharia (Islamic law—see The Judicial System, this ch.). They also sought to reject Western political and social influence and to promote Arab militancy against Israel. In 1981 the followers of Al Jihad (Holy War) in the armed forces were responsible for the assassination of Sadat during a military parade. As a result of the assassination, the military dismissed 30 officers and 100 enlisted men because of their extreme religious views. An offshoot of Al Jihad, Baqaya Jihannam (Survivors of Hell), attempted in 1987 to assassinate the former minister of interior and a prominent editor. Religious extremists, some of whom were military officers, also set fire to video rental shops, movie theaters, pharmacies, shops selling alcohol, automobiles, and Coptic churches (see Coptic Church, ch. 2). Some soldiers had stolen arms and ammunition from military stocks. Nonetheless, the government insisted on the ability of the intelligence services to keep radical groups from infiltrating the military.

Radical Islam drew adherents from various social classes and particularly among university students. By the 1980s, Muslim student organizations started to dominate campus life and have a strong influence over faculties and university administrations. The total number of activists was believed to be several hundred thousand but the membership in clandestine organizations was small, with estimates ranging from 3,000 to 20,000. Activists involved in violence were thought to number as few as 1,000.

The government was fairly successful in controlling underground movements in a series of crackdowns during each of which authorities arrested as many as 1,500 activists. Most of these activists were released after interrogation. The government did, however, prosecute some of these activists on charges ranging from undermining the security of the state to terrorism. Police carried out an effective surveillance program that included infiltration of campus groups and monitoring the activities of extremist leaders in Egypt and abroad. The police also closely watched twenty-five mosques that were suspected of being the headquarters of outlawed political groups and storage places for arms.

Leftist Organizations

Since the early 1950s, Egypt has banned the Communist Party of Egypt (CPE), which was formed in 1921. The National Progressive Unionist Organization (a bloc of leftist factions including some Marxists), however, was legal. Egyptian communism has traditionally been a general movement of leftist factions rather than the platform of a cohesive single party. Before the 1952 Revolution, the movement was represented by the CPE as well as smaller groups with names such as the Egyptian Movement for National Liberation, the Spark, the Vanguard, the Marxist League, and the New Dawn.

After the overthrow of the monarchy, Marxist groups endorsed the new regime but withdrew their support when the Revolutionary Command Council declared that Marxism was dangerous to state security and imprisoned many leftists. When Soviet Premier Nikita S. Khrushchev visited Cairo in 1964, Nasser released all imprisoned leftists. During the remainder of the 1960s, most leftists abandoned their illegal groups and joined the government party, the Arab Socialist Union (ASU). Many occupied important positions, but their views and activities could not exceed the bounds of government tolerance. In 1971 Sadat dismissed a number of Marxists and known Soviet sympathizers from the ASU. Sadat again purged leftists from the ASU after he expelled Soviet advisers from Egypt in 1972 and after riots later that year and in early 1973. Sadat blamed them for inciting unrest. After the 1977 food riots and the 1986 police conscripts' riots, some observers blamed communist involvement, but most observers believed the riots were almost entirely spontaneous. An underground group, Thawrat Misr (Egypt's Revolution, also known as Thawrat Misr an Nassiriyah or Egypt's Nasserist Revolution), took credit for the murder of two

Israeli diplomats and the attempted murders of several Israeli and United States embassy personnel between 1984 and 1987. In 1986 a number of members of the CPE were sentenced to prison for one to three years for producing and possessing subversive publications. Later that year, forty-four members of a secret leftist group, Al Ittijah ath Thawri (Revolutionary Tendency), were arrested on charges of planning to overthrow the regime and replace it with a Marxist system.

As of 1990, Egyptian left-wing groups remained factionalized. The CPE existed, but its membership was believed to be minuscule. Other organizations, with names such as the Egyptian Communist Workers' Party, the Popular Movement, the Revolutionary Progressive Party, and the Armed Communist Organization, claimed to be part of the leftist underground. Foreign observers believed that the potential threat of these groups to the security of the state was insignificant in comparison to the potential threat of Islamic extremists.

Police

The Nasser and Sadat administrations initiated a number of police and law-enforcement reforms. They strengthened police organization and improved public security. According to official statements, the incidence of serious crimes decreased because of these changes. Nevertheless, the tight political security enforced under Nasser created a police state. Although controls were greatly eased by Sadat, widespread dislike of the police persisted.

Egypt's national police had a wide variety of functions and responsibilities. The national police was responsible for maintaining law and order, preventing and detecting crime, supporting the court system through the collection of evidence, and other police duties, including processing passports, screening immigrants, operating prisons, controlling traffic, guarding special events and celebrities, suppressing smuggling and narcotics trafficking, preventing political subversion and sabotage, guarding transport and utility installations, preventing black marketing, and participating in civil defense.

Turkish and French systems influenced the organization of Egypt's police force until the late nineteenth century, when the British modified the system. The national-level police force, set up in 1883, was trained and staffed by British officials and became the basis for the system that was still used in 1990. In 1922, when the British, with reservations, relinquished sovereignty to the Egyptians, the police became a virtual private agency of the monarch, and police administration became even more highly centralized.

After the 1952 Revolution (which was supported by the police), all police functions were placed under the direction of the Ministry of Interior.

As of early 1987, the size of the regular police force was reported to be about 122,000; an estimated 40,000 positions were unfilled because police jobs paid poorly and offered few benefits. A typical policeman in 1986 earned between £E60 and £E70 (US$30 to US$35) a month. Salaries in real terms were lower in 1986 than in 1976. According to one Egyptian analysis, police salaries were low in part as a result of excessive allocations of funds for other purposes. The Ministry of Interior's budget had increased 400 percent over an eight-year period, but much of this money was spent on equipment used primarily for controlling riots.

The low salaries encouraged many police officers to accept small bribes (in exchange for overlooking traffic citations, for example) to compensate for their unrealistically low wages. At a higher level, police corruption took the form of complicity in drug smuggling. The creation of law-enforcement bodies within the ministries of supply, transportation, and finance, and within the customs service diminished the authority of the police. According to one source, Egypt had thirty-four separate police forces as of 1986.

Organization

Sadat's administration divided the functions of the police and public security among four deputy ministers of interior. The minister himself retained responsibility for state security investigations and overall organization. The deputy minister for public security oversaw sections responsible for public safety, travel, emigration, passports, port security, and criminal investigation. Responsibilities assigned to the deputy minister for special police included prison administration, the Central Security Forces, civil defense, police transport, communications, traffic, and tourism. The deputy minister for personnel affairs was responsible for police-training institutions, personnel matters for police and civilian employees, and the Policemen's Sports Association. The deputy minister for administrative and financial affairs had charge of general administration, budgets, supplies, and legal matters.

Commissioned police ranks resembled ranks in the army. The highest-ranking police officer was a major general and ranks descended only to first lieutenant. Below first lieutenant, however, was the grade known as lieutenant-chief warrant officer, followed by three descending grades of warrant officers. Enlisted police held the grades of master sergeant, sergeant, corporal, and private. Police

Cairo street scene with traffic police officer
Courtesy Susan Becker

rank insignia were the same as those used by the army, and uniforms were also similar.

In each governorate (sing., *muhafazah;* pl., *muhafazat*), a director of police commanded all police in the jurisdiction and, with the governor, was responsible for maintaining public order. Both the governor (a presidentially appointed figure) and the director of police reported to the Ministry of Interior on all security matters; the governor reported directly to the minister or to a deputy, and the director of police reported to the ministry through regular police channels. In the subdivisions of the governorate, district police commandants had authority and functions that were similar to the director at the governorate level. In urban areas, police had modern facilities and equipment, such as computers and communications equipment. In smaller, more remote villages, police had less sophisticated facilities and equipment.

Training

Almost all commissioned officers were graduates of the Police College at Cairo. All police had to complete a three-month course at the college. The Police College was established in 1896 under British influence. It had developed into a modern institution equipped with laboratory and physical-training facilities. The police force also sent some officers abroad for schooling. From the mid-1950s to the mid-1970s, the force sent most of its overseas students to training institutions in the Soviet Union. By the early 1980s, the force starting sending student officers for training in Western countries.

The curriculum of the Police College included security administration, criminal investigation, military drills, civil defense, fire fighting, forensic medicine, communications, cryptology, first aid, sociology, anatomy, and the French and English languages. Political orientation, public relations, and military subjects (such as infantry and cavalry training), marksmanship, leadership, and field exercises were also included. Graduates of the two-year program received a bachelor of police studies degree and were commissioned first lieutenants. Advanced officer training was given at the college's Institute for Advanced Police Studies, completion of which was required for advancement beyond the rank of lieutenant colonel. The college conducted its three-month course for enlisted ranks in a military atmosphere but emphasized police methods and techniques.

Central Security Forces

About 300,000 members of the paramilitary Central Security Forces (CSF) augmented the police force. The CSF was responsible for guarding public buildings, hotels, strategic sites (such as water and power installations), and foreign embassies. They also helped direct traffic and control crowds. Formed in 1977 to obviate the need to call upon the armed forces to deal with domestic disturbances, the CSF grew rapidly to 100,000 members when Mubarak took office. The government had hoped that the CSF would counterbalance the military's power, but the force never served this function. Poorly educated conscripts from rural areas who failed to meet the standards for army service filled the ranks of the CSF. Officers often treated the conscripts harshly and frequently humiliated them. Conscripts commonly lived in tents and sometimes lacked beds, adequate plumbing, and electricity.

The Central Security Forces rioted in 1986 when a rumor spread that their term of service would be extended from three years to four years. They set hotels and nightclubs on fire in the tourist areas of Cairo and near the pyramids at Giza (Al Jizah) and destroyed automobiles. Army units restored order after the rioting had gone on for four days and had spread to other cities. When the uprising ended, hundreds of people were dead or wounded, and about 8,000 CSF conscripts were missing. The CSF as a result dismissed more than 20,000 conscripts.

The minister of interior subsequently promised a series of reforms in the CSF, including a reduction in the number of people to be drafted into the force. He also promised to raise training standards, improve health care, and eliminate illiteracy. He doubled conscripts' wages (which had been lower than the wages of army conscripts) to £E12 a month. Nevertheless, as of 1987, living conditions appeared to have improved only marginally and the size of the force decreased by only 10 percent. The government continued to use the CSF as the main force for dealing with student disturbances, intimidating industrial strikers and peasant demonstrators, and curbing gatherings of Islamic activists.

Intelligence Services

Internal security was the responsibility of three intelligence organizations: General Intelligence, attached to the presidency; Military Intelligence, attached to the Ministry of Defense; and the General Directorate for State Security Investigations (GDSSI), under direct control of the minister of interior. Any of these agencies could undertake investigations of matters pertaining to national security, but the GDSSI was the main organization for domestic security matters. After the Sadat era, the tendency of military intelligence to encroach on civilian security functions had been curbed.

Nasser established a pervasive and oppressive internal security apparatus. The security police detained as many as 20,000 political prisoners at a time and discouraged public discussions or meetings that could be construed as unfriendly to the government. The security police recruited local informants to report on the activities and political views of their neighbors. Under Sadat intelligence forces were less obtrusive but still managed to be well informed and effective in monitoring subversives, opposition politicians, and foreigners. The security police's failure to uncover the plot leading to Sadat's assassination tarnished the reputation of the force. The security police also seemed to be taken by surprise by the CSF riots and failed to prevent other disorders such as a series of assassination attempts by radical Islamists in the late 1980s.

The authorities have never revealed the personnel strength of the GDSSI, which played an important role in government by influencing policy decisions and personnel matters. The GDSSI engaged routinely in surveillance of opposition politicians, journalists, political activists, foreign diplomats, and suspected subversives. The GDSSI focused on monitoring underground networks of radical Islamists and probably planted agents in those organizations. According to some sources, the GDSSI had informants in all government departments and public-sector companies, labor unions, political parties, and the news media. The organization was also believed to monitor telephone calls and correspondence by the political opposition and by suspected subversives.

In the past, the regime had given the GDSSI considerable leeway in maintaining political control and using emergency laws to intimidate people suspected of subversion (see The Judicial System, this ch.). The GDSSI remained in 1990 the primary organ for combatting political subversion even after Mubarak and the judiciary took several steps to limit the organization's power.

The GDSSI was accused of torturing Islamic extremists to extract confessions. In 1986 forty GDSSI officers went on trial for 422 charges of torture that were brought by Al Jihad defendants. After lengthy legal wrangling, the court absolved all the GDSSI officers in mid-1988. The judgment concluded that the GDSSI had indeed tortured Al Jihad members but said there was insufficient evidence to link the particular GDSSI officers on trial with the torture.

Crime and Punishment

The Judicial System

Egypt based its criminal codes and court operations primarily on British, Italian, and Napoleonic models. Criminal court procedures had been substantially modified by the heritage of Islamic legal and social patterns and the legacy of numerous kinds of courts that formerly existed. The divergent sources and philosophical origins of these laws and the inapplicability of many borrowed Western legal concepts occasioned difficulties in administering Egyptian law. The Criminal Procedure Code of 1950 prescribed the jurisdiction of various courts and provided basic guidance for the conduct of investigations and trial procedures.

The Muslim Brotherhood and other Islamist groups brought demands on the government to adopt Islamic sharia. Government officials argued that adopting Islamic sharia was not necessary because 95 percent of Egypt's laws were already consistent with or derived from Islamic law. In 1985 the People's Assembly rejected demands for the immediate adoption of the sharia but supported a recommendation to review all statutes and change the ones that conflicted with Islamic law. This process, which was expected to continue for years, necessitated the review of approximately 6,000 laws and 10,000 peripheral legal acts.

The criminal code listed three main categories of crime: contraventions (minor offenses), misdemeanors (offenses punishable by imprisonment or fines), and felonies (offenses punishable by penal servitude or death). Lower courts handled the majority of the cases that reached adjudication and levied fines in about nine out of ten cases. At their discretion, courts could suspend fines or imprisonment (when a sentence did not exceed one year). At the village level, a village headman, an *umdah* (pl., *umada*), representing the central authority was responsible for maintaining order. The *umdah* could also adjudicate some minor offenses and impose short prison sentences.

Capital crimes that carried a possible death sentence included murder, manslaughter occurring in the commission of a felony, arson or the use of explosives that caused death, rape, treason, and endangerment of state security. Few convictions for capital crimes, however, resulted in execution. The supreme court, the mufti (see Glossary) of Egypt, and the president reviewed each death sentence. In 1987 Egypt executed six individuals for murder and two others for abduction and rape.

The investigation of a crime was a sort of preliminary trial, and the results of the investigation determined the disposition of the case. The Office of the Public Prosecutor, an institution under the Ministry of Justice, conducted investigations. After an investigation with the help of police officials from the district involved, the public prosecutor could decide to drop a case if the charges were not serious enough to warrant a trial.

Egypt's laws required that a detained person be brought before a magistrate and formally charged within forty-eight hours or released. The accused was entitled to post bail and had the right to be defended by legal counsel. Searches could not be conducted without a warrant. Trials were open to the public, but the court could choose to hold all or part of the hearing in camera "in order to preserve public order or morals." According to the United States Department of State's *Country Reports on Human Rights Practices,* Egypt's judiciary acted independently and carefully observed constitutional and legal safeguards in arrests and pretrial custody. The Emergency Law of 1958 outlined special judicial procedures for some cases. The law enabled authorities to circumvent the increasingly independent regular court system in cases where people were charged with endangering state security. The law applied primarily to Islamic radicals but also covered leftists suspected of political violence, drug smugglers, and illegal currency dealers. It also allowed detention of striking workers, pro-Palestinian student demonstrators, and relatives of fugitives.

The Emergency Law of 1958 authorized the judicial system to detain people without charging them or guaranteeing them due process while an investigation was under way. After thirty days, a detainee could petition the State Security Court to review the case. If the court ordered the detainee's release, the minister of interior had fifteen days to object. If the minister overruled the court's decision, the detainee could petition another State Security Court for release after thirty more days. If the second court supported the detainee's petition, it released the detainee. The minister of interior could, however, simply rearrest the detainee. The government commonly engaged in this practice in cases involving Islamic extremists.

The State Security Courts preserved most procedural safeguards. They barred secret testimony, upheld defendants' rights to be represented by an attorney, and gave attorneys access to the prosecution's investigations. Trials were usually in public, except in some cases involving political violence. Convicted persons could appeal to the Court of Cassation (see The Judiciary, Civil Rights, and the Rule of Law, ch. 4). The State Security Courts drew their judges from the ranks of the senior judiciary.

In most cases, detainees were released after a period of interrogation and were never brought to trial. In mid-1989 the minister of interior stated that a total of 12,000 individuals had been detained under the Emergency Law of 1958 during the preceding three years. As of early 1990 the government acknowledged that it was detaining 2,411 individuals, 813 of whom were being held on political charges.

In certain instances, civilian suspects could be turned over to military courts for trial on the basis of a presidential order. This practice was the subject of a constitutional challenge initiated in 1989.

In 1980 the government created a separate judicial institution, the Court of Ethics, together with its investigating arm, the Office of the Socialist Prosecutor, to investigate complaints of widespread corruption in government. The court was charged with trying offenses against "socialist values," which included corruption and illegal business practices. The Office of the Socialist Prosecutor served as watchdog against abuses by government officials; approved the credentials of candidates for office in the trade union movement, professional syndicates, and local government councils; and performed security checks on senior government appointees.

Incidence of Crime

Ordinary crime, that is, crime unconnected to political dissent or sectarian strife, was perceived to be a major problem during the 1980s, although it was difficult to demonstrate a strong upsurge in criminal activity on the basis of the limited data available. Minor

*Immigration officer checking
passport of one of about
2 million tourists
who visit annually
Courtesy Embassy
of Egypt, Washington*

crimes, such as petty theft, pickpocketing, and purse snatching, were widespread in the streets of metropolitan Cairo, but violence in the commission of these crimes was uncommon. In rural areas, crime victims generally sought retribution without going to the authorities, especially in cases where the honor of an individual or a family was tarnished. An informal analysis found that more than half the murder cases in rural areas occurred within the family and commonly involved issues of passion, honor, or vengeance.

Reliable official statistics on crime were not available, but an Egyptian report to Interpol, the international police organization, in 1988 recorded 784 murders, 364 serious assaults, 189 morals offenses, and 322 robberies involving violence. Thefts totaled 19,964, including 1,397 auto thefts but only 14 armed robberies. There were 1,313 cases of fraud and 10,559 drug offenses. The police claimed to have solved more than 90 percent of the major crimes and 75 percent of the thefts. The level of criminal activity reported appeared to be surprisingly low and the success rate in solving crimes unusually high, particularly in light of the belief that urban crime was escalating. The police recorded a total of more than 1,500,000 infractions of all kinds; presumably this included petty crimes and misdemeanors and such offenses as evasion of price controls.

In an interview in late 1989, the director of security for Cairo attributed higher crime rates to bad economic conditions, high unemployment, population growth, and changes in social norms. In 1988 Cairo experienced sharp increases in the theft of cars and other goods, offenses by women and juveniles, kidnappings, and vice cases. Bank robberies, gang activity, and other violence continued to be uncommon, however.

White-collar crime, smuggling, black marketing in currency, and other economic offenses were rampant and increased under the Sadat and Mubarak regimes. Sadat established special commissions to investigate official corruption. Soon after taking office, Mubarak condemned favoritism and graft and replaced several cabinet members whom he thought were inadequate in their efforts to detect and expose corruption. Nevertheless, economic crimes continued to be widespread. These crimes included embezzlement, tax and customs evasion, illegal currency transactions, smuggling and trading contraband, diversion of subsidized goods, "leakages" from free trade zones, kickbacks, and bribes to officials. In 1986 Egyptian officials arrested about 102,000 individuals for "supply violations," which included petty infringements by shopkeepers and vendors, such as their failure to observe price controls. Some of these violations, however, involved large enterprises engaged in major infractions, often with the connivance of government officials.

Drug Trafficking

The use of narcotics became an increasingly serious problem in Egypt during the 1980s. Some officials estimated that as many as 2 million Egyptians were users of illegal drugs as of 1989. Many of these users were students and children of wealthy parents. Many people used cocaine or heroin, while others used opium or hashish, which Egyptians have commonly smoked for centuries. According to one source, Egypt had about 250,000 heroin addicts in 1988. Police claimed that drug use was spreading at a frightening pace and that the rising cost of narcotics was causing addicts to commit crimes to obtain money for drugs.

A large amount of the hashish and opium sold in Egypt was produced domestically. In 1988 and 1989, however, Egyptian authorities seized large shipments of heroin and other drugs that were probably produced in Lebanon and Pakistan. An estimated 300 kilograms of heroin were sold in Egypt in 1988. In 1984 (the latest year for which data were available) an estimated 264,000 kilograms of hashish and 2,000 kilograms of opium were sold. The value of the illegal drugs sold in 1988 was estimated at US$1 billion.

Law-enforcement authorities were more successful in arresting people who sold drugs on the streets—typically owners of kiosks where cigarettes were normally purchased—than major drug dealers, who were apparently able to buy immunity by bribes to high officials. The government had begun punishing drug violations more severely and had proposed subjecting some offenders to the death penalty. Egypt convicted about 3,500 people on charges of narcotics trafficking in 1982. About 2,500 of these individuals received sentences ranging from six months to one year; about 1,000 persons received sentences of five years or less, and 15 received life sentences at hard labor. By 1988 Egypt had imposed much stiffer penalties. A woman from Britain, for example, received a twenty-five-year sentence for smuggling a small amount of heroin into the country.

The Penal System

Prison administration was under the jurisdiction of the Ministry of Interior. Prison officials were usually graduates of police or military schools. The main categories of penal institutions were penitentiaries, general prisons, district jails, and juvenile reformatories. Criminals receiving heavy sentences were sent to penitentiaries where they faced hard labor and strict discipline. Penitentiaries could subject prisoners to solitary confinement only as a disciplinary measure for bad behavior. General prisons housed offenders who were sentenced to more than three months. District jails usually housed prisoners who were sentenced for up to three months. Village police stations had jail facilities that they used only for temporary incarceration. As of the mid-1980s, Egypt had three major penitentiaries and twenty-seven general prisons.

After the 1952 Revolution, Egypt implemented some reforms in the quality of penal administration. The government built hospitals in major prisons and provided separate facilities for women. Prisons adopted the concept of rehabilitation; juvenile prisoners received special attention; and, in cases of need, provision was made for assisting a prisoner's family.

Egyptian prisons were overcrowded; facilities designed to hold fewer than 20,000 prisoners housed about 30,000. Most of the prisons were built in the early twentieth century and needed complete renovation or replacement. Six prisons were under construction in 1988 in nonresidential areas, where space was available for farming and dairying by convict laborers.

According to the United States Department of State's *Country Reports on Human Rights Practices for 1987,* prison conditions and treatment varied considerably. Some institutions lacked adequate medical and sanitary facilities. Tora Prison near Cairo, where convicted members of Al Jihad were incarcerated, had a particularly bad reputation. Other prisons provided better living conditions and offered inmates recreational programs and vocational training. In its 1987 report, the Arab Human Rights Organization criticized what it termed "supervision" of the prison system by officers of the GDSSI.

In an interview appearing in a Cairo newspaper in August 1988, then Minister of Interior Zaki Badr acknowledged that "conditions inside the prisons are terrible . . . the prisons are a hotbed of drug and monetary crimes . . . even more so among the guards themselves." He said that the penal system planned to implement modern methods of prison security, improve communication systems among guards, and install electronic closed-circuit television monitoring systems and special measures to ensure efficiency and discipline among prison officers and guards.

According to the 1988 report of the human rights organization Amnesty International, there were many allegations of torture and poor treatment of detainees, particularly in parts of the Tora Prison complex. Torture was apparently inflicted to obtain confessions in 1987 after a series of assassination attempts against high officials. Egypt has refused to allow representatives from groups such as the Arab Human Rights Organization and the International Red Cross to inspect the country's prisons and meet with prisoners. Members of the People's Assembly who represented opposition parties were also refused access to the prisons. A report by the Egyptian Organization for Human Rights in early 1990 claimed that there was a marked increase in the use of torture in 1989, not only against members of subversive organizations but also against ordinary citizens with no political affiliations. Muhammad Abd al Halim Musa replaced Badr as minister of interior in January 1990. Badr had long been criticized for harsh repression of Islamic extremists and violations of civil liberties. Egyptian human rights activists hoped that his successor would adopt more moderate policies and improve the treatment of prisoners.

*　*　*

A number of articles on the modern role, mission, and equipment of the Egyptian armed forces are included in the December 1989 issue of *Defense and Foreign Affairs* under the heading "Defense in Egypt." Additional material, some of it no longer current, can be found in the article on Egypt by Gwynne Dyer and John Keegan in the compendium *World Armies*. In *Fighting Armies*, G.P. Armstrong summarizes Egypt's military doctrine, fighting qualities, and perception of national security. Trevor N. Dupuy's *Elusive Victory* evaluates the performance of the Egyptian armed forces in the successive wars with Israel. *The Military Balance, 1989–1990,* published by the International Institute for Strategic Studies in London, provides the most reliable data on current force strengths and weapons.

Robert Springborg's *Mubarak's Egypt* assesses the influence of Abu Ghazala on the Egyptian armed forces during the 1980s and the importance of the new military-operated production enterprises. Contrasting interpretations of the status of the military under Mubarak are presented by Robert B. Satloff in *Army and Politics in Mubarak's Egypt* and by Ahmed Abdallah in an article, "The Armed Forces and the Democratic Process in Egypt," in *Third World Quarterly.* In *Egyptian Politics under Sadat,* Raymond A. Hinnebusch, Jr. provides an account of the depoliticization of the military during the 1970s. The criminal justice system, the application of the Emergency Law, and prison conditions are appraised in the United States Department of State's annual *Country Reports on Human Rights Practices.* The significance of the Islamic activist movement as a potential threat to internal security has been analyzed in numerous studies, including Springborg's book previously mentioned, an article by former United States Ambassador to Egypt Hermann Frederick Eilts, "Egypt in 1986," in the *Washington Quarterly,* an article by Yahya Sadowski, "Egypt's Islamist Movement: A New Political and Economic Force," in *Middle East Insight,* and the book by Thomas W. Lippman, *Egypt after Nasser.* A brief commentary by Lillian Craig Harris in *Middle East International* is notable for its conclusion that the threat to the political system by religious zealotry remains remote. (For further information and complete citations, see Bibliography.)

Appendix

Table 1. Metric Conversion Coefficients and Factors

When you know	Multiply by	To find
Millimeters	0.04	inches
Centimeters	0.39	inches
Meters	3.3	feet
Kilometers	0.62	miles
Hectares (10,000 m²)	2.47	acres
Square kilometers	0.39	square miles
Cubic meters	35.3	cubic feet
Liters	0.26	gallons
Kilograms	2.2	pounds
Metric tons	0.98	long tons
	1.1	short tons
	2,204	pounds
Degrees Celsius (Centigrade)	9 divide by 5 and add 32	degrees Fahrenheit

Table 2. Enrollment by Education Level and Sex, 1985–86

Level	Male	Female	Total
Primary	3,397,779	2,605,071	6,002,850
Intermediate	1,274,137	860,870	2,135,007
Secondary			
General	355,454	213,912	569,366
Technical	526,283	351,116	877,399
Total secondary	881,737	565,028	1,446,765
Teacher training	34,113	50,474	84,587
University	445,963	215,384	661,347

Source: Based on information from *The Middle East and North Africa, 1989,* London, 1989, 395.

Table 3. Gross Domestic Product by Sector,
Selected Years, 1952-87
(in percentages)

Sector	1952	1968	1975	1980	1983	1985	1987
Agriculture	33 [1]	29 [1]	27	18	16	15	15
Industry	13 [1]	23 [1]	30	37	34	35	34
Services	53 [1]	50 [1]	43	45	50	50	51
TOTAL [2]	100	100	100	100	100	100	100
Value [3]	983 [1]	1,813 [1]	9,508	15,740	19,629	22,253	23,424

[1] At 1959-60 current market prices; all other years are 1980 prices at factor cost.
[2] Figures may not add to total because of rounding.
[3] In millions of Egyptian pounds (for value of the Egyptian pound—see Glossary).

Source: Based on information from Bent Hansen and Karim Nashashibi, *Foreign Trade Regimes and Economic Development,* New York, 1975, 12-13; and World Bank, *World Debt Tables, 1988-89,* Baltimore, 1989, 236-39.

Table 4. Government Budgets, Selected Years, 1979–88
(in millions of Egyptian pounds) [1]

	1979	1983	1985	1988
Revenues				
Central government				
Taxes				
Imports	904	1,920	1,700	3,200
Consumption	568	1,302	1,600	3,174
Business profit	659	1,506	2,300 }	
Personal income	55	129	150 {	5,972 [2]
Property	29	14	12	
Other	213	492	750 }	
Total taxes	2,428	5,363	6,512	12,346
Profits				
Petroleum company	631	1,066	950	781
Suez Canal	148	285	280	306
Other	222	n.a.	n.a.	2,688
Total profits	1,001	n.a.	n.a.	3,775
Local government and other				
public authorities	386	550	703	1,150
Self-financing investments	350	1,628	1,731	4,243
Total revenues	4,165	10,371	11,992	1,514
Expenditures				
Wages	2,375	2,620	3,440	5,515
Subsidies	1,370	2,875	2,766	1,813
Deficit of public enterprises	229	193	300	n.a.
Interest (domestic)	n.a.	1,111	1,700	2,366
Armed forces	642	1,982	1,769	2,469
Other	n.a.	2,504	3,485	n.a.
Gross public investment	2,587	5,518	6,358	7,780
Total expenditures	n.a.	16,803	19,818	28,733
Gross deficit (–)	2,168	6,432	7,826	7,219
Expenditures as percentage of GDP [3]	50	70	60	49
Revenues as percentage of GDP	33	33	36	37
Gross deficit as percentage of GDP	17	27	24	12

n.a.—not available.
[1] For value of the Egyptian pound—see Glossary.
[2] Aggregate figure for four categories.
[3] GDP—gross domestic product.

Table 5. Monetary Survey,
Selected Years, 1980–88
(in millions of Egyptian pounds) [1]

	1980	1984	1986	1988
Deposits				
Time savings and foreign				
currency deposits	3,589	10,884	21,127	33,969
Other [2]	4,112	7,924	11,511	16,082
Total deposits	7,701	18,808	32,638	50,051
Domestic credit				
Central government	8,248	14,733	19,484	28,186
Public sector	3,310	7,479	10,175	13,651
Private sector	2,174	8,284	12,888	17,330
Other [3]	333	1,057	2,200	19,485
Total domestic credit	14,065	31,553	44,747	78,652
Money supply [4]				
Foreign currency	2,367	6,529	11,493	21,608
Other	7,997	19,400	25,609	32,941
Total money supply	10,364	25,929	37,102	54,549
Consumer price index	100	172	239	336

[1] For value of the Egyptian pound—see Glossary.

[2] Includes government, demand, and import deposits.

[3] Includes institutions similar to banks.

[4] Includes combined currency in circulation, private demand deposits, time deposits (including foreign currency), and post office saving deposits.

Source: Based on information from International Monetary Fund, *Financial Statistics,* Washington, 1987, 318–20; and International Monetary Fund, *Financial Statistics,* Washington, 1989, 308–10.

Table 6. Employment Distribution by Sector, Selected Years, 1966–86
(in thousands)

Sector	1966 [1]	1976 [1]	1983	1986 [1]
Agriculture [2]	4,447	4,224	4,385	4,542
Industry [3]	1,140	1,257	1,696	1,954
Trade	559	1,016	1,188	1,187
Construction	206	434	724	336
Transportation and communications	340	422	464	581
Other services	1,602	2,276	4,012	3,818
TOTAL	8,294	9,629	12,469	12,418

[1] Census year.
[2] Includes fishing.
[3] Includes mining, manufacturing, and electricity.

Source: Based on information from United States, Department of Commerce, International Trade Administration, *Marketing in Egypt,* Washington, December 1981, 6; Khalid Ikram, et al., *Egypt: Economic Management in a Period of Transition,* Baltimore, 1980, 134–35; and National Bank of Egypt, *Economic Bulletin,* 40, Nos. 1–2, 1987.

Table 7. Cropped Area, Selected Years, 1952–87
(in thousands of *feddans*) [1]

Cropped Area	1952	1974	1980	1987
Winter crops [2]	4,364	4,980	4,926	5,098
Summer crops [3]	3,026	5,101	5,045	4,842
Fall crops [4]	1,824	667	803	854
Fruit orchards	94	273	361	616
TOTAL	9,308	11,021	11,135	11,410

[1] See Glossary.
[2] Main crops include wheat, beans, barley, onions, and clover (for fodder).
[3] Main crops include cotton, rice, millet, and sugarcane.
[4] Main crop is corn.

Table 8. Major Crop Production, Selected Years, 1974–87

Crop	1974 Area [1]	1974 Output [2]	1980 Area	1980 Output	1987 Area	1987 Output
Clover	2,797	49	2,711	54	2,714	55
Cotton	1,453	1,204	1,245	1,408	980	978
Corn	1,387	2,640	1,905	3,231	1,811	3,367
Wheat	1,370	1,884	1,326	1,736	1,373	2,721
Rice	1,051	2,244	972	2,382	983	2,279
Vegetables	895	6,520	1,027	8,013	1,024	9,964
Fruits	320	2,068	437	3,757	616	3,666

[1] In thousands of *feddans* (see Glossary).
[2] In tons.

Table 9. Planned Public and Private Investment, FY 1987–91 Five-Year Plan (in millions of Egyptian pounds) [1]

Investment	Public	Private	Total
Industry and mining	5,791	6,400	12,191
Housing	167	6,600	6,767
Transportation and communications	4,703	1,400	6,103
Electricity	4,761	0	4,761
Other public utilities	4,017	0	4,017
Agriculture	852	2,650	3,502
Health and education	2,427	85	2,512
Irrigation and drainage	1,435	0	1,435
Petroleum products	1,115	0	1,115
Other	3,233	865	4,098
TOTAL [2]	28,500	18,000	46,500

[1] For value of the Egyptian pound—see Glossary.
[2] Figures may not add to total because of rounding.

Source: Based on information from *Egypt's Second Five-Year Plan for Socio-Economic Development (1987/88–1991/92), with Plan for Year One (1987/88)*, Cairo, 1987, 165.

Table 10. Value of Foreign Trade,
Selected Years, 1979–88
(in millions of United States dollars)

	1979	1983	1985	1988
Exports (f.o.b.) [1]				
Cotton	348	314	414	310
Other agriculture	198	159	140	123
Oil (domestic companies)	1,880	2,807	2,891	1,553
Oil (foreign companies)	948	1,357	1,890	1,501
Textiles	267	199	294	455
Other manufacturing	351	411	447	803
Total exports	3,992	5,247	6,076	4,745
Imports (c.i.f.) [2]				
Food and other agriculture	1,677	2,393	2,711	1,734
Oil and other energy	243	493	469	208
Other consumer goods	845	1,218	1,875	1,997
Intermediate goods	1,725	2,322	3,064	3,693
Capital goods	2,315	3,193	3,475	3,007
Total imports	6,805	9,6191	1,594	10,639
Trade deficit	−2,813	−4,372	−5,518	−5,894
Terms of trade [3]				
Export price index	67	95	76	71
Import price index	91	94	90	110
Terms of trade [3]	74	102	84	65

[1] f.o.b.—free on board.

[2] c.i.f.—cost, insurance, and freight.

[3] Terms of trade means export price index divided by import price index. Index used is 1980 = 100.

Table 11. Summary of Balance of Payments,
Selected Years, 1979–88
(in millions of United States dollars)

	1979	1985	1988
Current account			
Exports of goods and nonfactor services			
Tourism	602	409 [1]	1,170 [2]
Suez Canal	589	897	1,323 [2]
Other	4,210	7,405	6,066
Total	5,401	8,711	8,559
Imports of goods and nonfactor services			
Foreign oil companies	−531	−814	n.a.
Other	−8,250	−12,870	n.a.
Total	8,781	−13,684	−12,491
Trade balance	−3,380	−4,973	−3,932
Net factor income			
Interest [3]	−428	−2,437	−1,229
Other	n.a.	−847	−766
Total	n.a.	−3,284	−1,995
Net current transfers			
Workers' remittances	2,445	3,496	3,386
Other	n.a.	26	22
Total	n.a.	3,522	3,408
Current account balance [4]	−1,915	−4,735	−2,519
Trade balance as percentage			
of GDP [5]	−19.8	−14.3	−10.4
Current account balance as			
percentage of GDP [4]	−11.2	−13.6	−6.6
Capital account			
Long-term capital inflows			
Direct investment	1,375	1,289	993
Official capital grants	n.a.	1,171	980
Net long-term loans [6]	n.a.	−133	1,813
Other net long-term inflows	−20	0	1
Total	2,527	2,327	3,787

Table 11.—Continued

	1979	1985	1988
Total other net items			
Net short-term capital	n.a.	-5	203
Errors and omissions	n.a.	1,555	-1,070
Other	n.a.	0	1
Total	n.a.	1,550	-868
Change in reserves [7]	-37	-858	-400

n.a.—not available.

[1] Income from EgyptAir moved from this item to nonfactor services.

[2] Projected.

[3] Includes interest on arrears and estimates of interest on military as well as short-term debt.

[4] Current account balance consists of total of trade balance, net factor income, and net current transfers.

[5] GDP—gross domestic product.

[6] Includes arrears on Western military debt.

[7] Change in reserves consists of total of current account balance, long-term capital inflows, and total other net items.

Table 12. External Debt, Selected Years, 1982–88 [1]
(in millions of United States dollars)

	1982–83	1984–85	1986–87	1988 [2]
Civilian debt				
Medium- and long-term	18,230	20,841	26,527	29,921
Short-term	4,857	5,196	4,737	4,737
Interest arrears	670	1,060	964	537
Total	23,757	27,097	32,228	35,195
By creditor				
Official	17,135	19,510	24,950	28,155
Private	6,622	7,587	7,278	7,040
Total	23,757	27,097	32,228	35,195
By borrower				
Public sector	18,430	21,180	26,641	35,195
Private sector	527	650	984	n.a.
Domestic banks	4,800	5,267	4,603	n.a.
Total	23,757	27,097	32,228	n.a.
As percentage of GDP [3]	88	87	101	109
As percentage of exports				
of goods and services	312	357	471	438
Military debt	4,675	6,975	9,750	10,800
TOTAL	28,432	34,072	41,978	45,995

n.a.—not available.
[1] Figures are annual averages for periods indicated.
[2] Projected.
[3] GDP—gross domestic product.

Source: Based on information from Institute of International Finance, *Egypt: Country Report,*
88, No. 2, Washington, August 15, 1988, 3.

Table 13. Major Army Equipment, 1989

Type and Description	Country of Origin	Inventory
Tanks		
M60A3	United States	785
T-54/-55	Soviet Union	1,040
T-62	-do-	600
PT-76 (light)	-do-	15
Armored vehicles		
BRDM-2, scout car	-do-	300
BMP-1, infantry combat	-do-	220
BMR-600P, wheeled, various configurations	Spain	250
Armored personnel carriers		
Walid, four-wheeled	West Germany, Egypt	1,000
Fahd, four-wheeled	-do-	200
BTR-50/OT-62	Soviet Union	1,075
M-113A2	United States	1,000
Towed artillery		
M-31/-37, 122mm	Soviet Union	48
M-1938, 122mm	-do-	400
D-30, 122mm	Egypt	220
M-46, 130mm	Soviet Union	440
M-1937, 152mm	-do-	12
Multiple rocket launchers		
VAP-80-12, 80mm	Soviet Union	
BM-21/Saqr 18, 122mm	Soviet Union, Egypt	
M-51 on Praga truck chassis	Czechoslovakia	about 300
BM-13-16, 132mm	Soviet Union	
BM-14-16, 140mm	-do-	
BM-24, 240mm	-do-	
Surface-to-surface missile launchers		
FROG-7, 60 km range	Soviet Union	12
Scud-B, 300 km range	-do-	9
Saqr D-3000, 80 km range	Egypt	n.a.
Saqr D-6000, 122mm	-do-	n.a.
Mortars		
M-43, 120mm	Soviet Union	450
M-43, 160mm	-do-	100
M-1953, 240mm	-do-	24
Antitank guided missile launchers		
AT-1 Snapper	-do-	800
AT-2 Swatter	-do-	200
AT-3 Sagger	-do-	1,400
Milan	France	220
Swingfire	Britain, Egypt	200
I-TOW	United States	520
Recoilless rifles		
B-11, 107mm	Soviet Union	n.a.

Table 13.—Continued

Type of Description	Country of Origin	Inventory
Air defense guns		
ZPU-2/-4, 14.5mm	Soviet Union	n.a.
ZU-23-2, 23mm	-do-	460
ZSU-23-4, 23mm, self-propelled	-do-	110
Nile, 23mm	Egypt	45
M-1939, 37mm	Soviet Union	150
S-60, 57mm	-do-	300
ZSU-57-2, 57mm, self-propelled	-do-	40
Surface-to-air missile launchers		
SA-7/Ayn as Saqr/SA-9, shoulder-fired	Soviet Union, Egypt	1,200
M-54 Chaparral, self-propelled	United States	22

n.a.—not available.

Source: Based on information from *The Military Balance, 1989-1990*, London, 1989, 98;
DMS Market Intelligence Reports, *DMS Foreign Military Markets—Middle East/Africa*,
Greenwich, Connecticut, 1989; and *Military Technology and Economics (Miltech)*, Bonn,
January 1989, 1985.

Table 14. Major Air Force Equipment, 1989

Type and Description	Country of Origin	Inventory
Fighter-ground attack aircraft		
Mirage 5E2	France	16
F–4E Phantom	United States	33
Shenyang J–6 (MiG-19)	China, Egypt	76
Alpha Jet	France, West Germany	15
MiG-17 Fresco	Soviet Union	30
Fighter-interceptor aircraft		
MiG-21 Fishbed	-do-	83
Shenyang J–7 (MiG-21F)	China, Egypt	52
F–16A/C Fighting Falcon	United States	67
Mirage 5E	France	54
Mirage 2000C	-do-	16
Reconnaissance aircraft		
Mirage 5 SDR	-do-	6
MiG-21 Fishbed	Soviet Union	14
Bombers		
Tu–16 Badger	-do-	9
Electronic warfare		
EC–130H Hercules	United States	2
Beech 1900	-do-	2
Airborne early warning		
E–2C Hawkeye	-do-	5
Transport aircraft		
C–130H Hercules	-do-	19
An-12 Cub	Soviet Union	5
DHC–5D Buffalo	Canada	5
Training aircraft		
Shenyang J–6 (MiG-19)	China, Egypt	16
Alpha Jet	France, West Germany	29
L–29 Delfin (being replaced)	Czechoslovakia	20
Gumhuriya	Egypt, West Germany	36
EMB–312 Tucano	Brazil, Egypt	40
Mirage 5 SDD	France	5
Mirage 2000B	-do-	3
F–16B D Fighting Falcon	United States	13
DHC–5 Buffalo	Canada	4
Attack helicopters		
Gazelle	France, Egypt	72

Table 14.—Continued

Type and Description	Country of Origin	Inventory
Transport helicopters		
CH–47C Chinook, heavy	Italy	15
Mi-6, heavy	Soviet Union	6
Mi-8, heavy	-do-	27
Mk-1, Commando, medium	Britain	23
Hiller UH–12E, light (training)	United States	17
Mi-4, light	Soviet Union	12
Naval helicopters		
Sea King, antisubmarine	Britain	5
Gazelle, antiship	France, Egypt	12

Source: Based on information from *The Military Balance, 1989–1990*, London, 1989, 99; and Aviation Advisory Services, *International Air Forces and Military Aircraft Directory*, Essex, United Kingdom, 1989, 33–37.

Table 15. Major Navy Equipment, 1989

Type and Description	Country of Origin	Inventory	Commissioned or Delivered
Destroyers			
A1 Fatah, British Z class, 1,730 tons (training)	Britain	1	Transferred 1955; modernized 1964.
Frigates			
Descubierta class, 1,480 tons, Harpoon surface-to-surface missiles (SSMs)	Spain	2	Commissioned 1984.
Jianghu class, 2,000 tons, HY-2 Silkworm SSMs	China	2	Commissioned 1984–85.
Black Swan class, 1,925 tons (training)	Britain	1	Transferred 1949.
Submarines			
Romeo class, 1,400 tons (four being modernized with Harpoon SSMs and Mk 37 torpedoes)	Soviet Union, China	10	Transferred 1966–69 and 1982–84.
Whiskey class, 1,080 tons (being retired)	Soviet Union	2	Transferred 1957 and 1962.
Fast-attack craft, missile			
Ramadan class, 307 tons, Otomat SSMs	Britain	6	Commissioned 1981–82.
Osa-I class, 210 tons, SS-N-2A Styx SSMs	Soviet Union	7	Delivered 1966–68.
October class, 82 tons, Otomat SSMs	Egypt	6	Refitted 1978–81 in Britain.
Hegu class, 80 tons, Chinese version of Styx missile	China	6	Delivered 1984.
Fast-attack craft, torpedo			
Shershen class, 170 tons	Soviet Union	6	Delivered 1967–68.
Shanghai II class, 155 tons	China	4	Transferred 1984.
Hainan class, 392 tons	-do-	8	Transferred 1983–84.
Landing ships, multipurpose			
Polnochny A class, 800 tons	Soviet Union	3	n.a.
Vydra class, 600 tons	-do-	9	n.a.
SMB-1 class, 360 tons	-do-	2	n.a.
Minesweepers			
T-43 class, 580 tons	-do-	3	Transferred 1970.
Yurka class, 520 tons	-do-	4	Transferred 1969.
T-301, 180 tons (inshore)	-do-	2	Transferred 1962.

Table 15.—Continued

Type and Description	Country of Origin	Inventory	Commissioned or Delivered
Coast Guard			
Large patrol craft	Various	32	n.a.
Bertram coastal patrol craft	United States	20	n.a.

Source: Based on information from *Jane's Fighting Ships, 1989-90,* Alexandria, Virginia, 1989, 148-55.

Table 16. Major Air Defense Force Equipment, 1989

Type and Description	Country of Origin	Inventory
Antiaircraft guns		
20mm, 23mm 37mm, 40mm, 57mm, 85mm, and 100mm	Various	2,500
Surface-to-air missile (SAM) launchers		
SA-2	Soviet Union	400
SA-3	-do-	240
SA-6	-do-	60
Improved Hawk	United States	108
Crotale	France	50
Air defense systems	Italy, United	18
Amun (Skyguard)—Sparrow and Ayn as Saqr SAMs with 35mm radar-guided guns	States, Egypt	

Source: Based on information from *The Military Balance, 1989-1990,* London, 1989, 99.

Bibliography

Chapter 1

Abdel-Fadil, Mahmoud. *Employment and Income Distribution in Egypt, 1952-1970.* (University of East Anglia Discussion Paper No. 4.) n.d.

Abdel-Malek, Anouar. *Egypt: Military Society.* New York: Vintage Books, 1968.

Aldred, Cyril. *The Egyptians.* London: Thames and Hudson, 1984.

_____. *Egypt to the End of the Old Kingdom.* New York: McGraw-Hill, 1976.

Aly, Abdel Moneim Said. *Back to the Fold? Egypt and the Arab World.* (Occasional Papers Series.) Washington: Center for Contemporary Arab Studies, Georgetown University, 1988.

Armour, Robert A. *Gods and Myths of Ancient Egypt.* Cairo: American University in Cairo Press, 1986.

Badran, Margot. "Dual Liberation: Feminism and Nationalism in Egypt, 1870s-1925," *Feminist Issues,* 8, No. 1, Spring 1988, 15-34.

Baer, Gabriel. "Social Change in Egypt, 1800-1914." Pages 135-61 in P.M. Holt (ed.), *Political and Social Change in Modern Egypt.* London: Oxford University Press, 1968.

_____. *Studies in the Social History of Modern Egypt.* Chicago: University of Chicago Press, 1969.

Beinin, Joel, and Zachary Lockman. *Workers on the Nile: Nationalism, Communism, Islam, and the Egyptian Working Class, 1882-1954.* Princeton: Princeton University Press, 1987.

Bell, H. Idris. *Egypt From Alexander the Great to the Arab Conquest.* Oxford: Clarendon Press, 1948.

Butler, Alfred. *The Arab Conquest of Egypt.* New York: AMS Press, 1973.

Cole, Juan Ricardo. "Feminism, Class, and Islam in Turn-of-the-Century Egypt." *International Journal of Middle East Studies,* 10, No. 2, May 1979, 387-407.

Crecelius, Daniel. *The Roots of Modern Egypt.* Minneapolis: Bibliotheca Islamica, 1981.

Davis, Eric. *Challenging Colonialism: Bank Misr and Egyptian Industrialization, 1920-1941.* Princeton: Princeton University Press, 1983.

Deeb, Marius. *Party Politics in Egypt: The Wafd and Its Rivals, 1919-1939.* London: Ithaca Press, 1979.

Dekmejian, Richard Hrair. *Egypt under Nasir: A Study in Political Dynamics.* Albany: State University of New York Press, 1971.

Erman, Adolf. *Life in Ancient Egypt.* (Trans., H.M. Tirard.) New York: Dover, 1971.

Frankfort, Henri. *The Birth of Civilization in the Near East.* Bloomington: Indiana University Press, 1959.

Freedman, Robert O. *Soviet Policy Toward the Middle East since 1970.* (3d ed.) New York: Praeger, 1982.

Gazetteer of Egypt. (2d ed.) Washington: Defense Mapping Agency, August 1987.

Goldberg, Ellis. *Tinker, Tailor, and Textile Worker: Class and Politics in Egypt, 1930–1952.* Berkeley: University of California Press, 1986.

Gran, Peter. *Islamic Roots of Capitalism.* Austin: University of Texas Press, 1979.

Groupe de Recherches et d'Etudes sur le Proche-Orient. *L'Egypte d'aujourd'hui: Permanence et changements, 1805–1976.* Paris: Centre National de la Recherche Scientifique, 1977.

Haikal, Muhammed Hasanain. *Autumn of Fury: The Assassination of Sadat.* New York: Random House, 1983.

———. *The Road to Ramadan.* New York: Readers Digest Press, 1975.

Hinnebusch, Raymond A., Jr. *Egyptian Politics under Sadat: The Post-Populist Development of an Authoritarian-Modernizing State.* (Rev. ed.) Boulder, Colorado: Lynne Rienner, 1988.

Hirst, David. *The Gun and the Olive Branch.* (2d ed.) London: Faber and Faber, 1984.

Hirst, David, and Irene Beeson. *Sadat.* London: Faber and Faber, 1981.

Hoffman, Michael H. *Egypt Before the Pharaohs: The Prehistoric Foundations of Egyptian Civilization.* New York: Knopf, 1979.

Holt, P.M. *Egypt and the Fertile Crescent, 1516–1922.* Ithaca: Cornell University Press, 1966.

Holt, P.M. (ed.). *Political and Social Change in Modern Egypt.* London: Oxford University Press, 1968.

Holt, P.M., Ann K.S. Lambton, and Bernard Lewis (eds.). *The Cambridge History of Islam.* Cambridge: Cambridge University Press, 1970.

Hopwood, Derek. *Egypt: Politics and Society, 1945–1984.* Boston: Allen and Unwin, 1985.

Hourani, Albert. *Arabic Thought in the Liberal Age, 1798–1939.* Cambridge: Cambridge University Press, 1984.

Hunter, Robert. *Egypt under the Khedives, 1805–1879: From Household Government to Modern Bureaucracy.* Pittsburgh: University of Pittsburgh Press, 1984.

Irwin, Robert. *The Middle East in the Middle Ages: The Early Mamluk Sultanate, 1250–1382.* London: Croom Helm, 1986.

Issawi, Charles. *The Economic History of the Middle East.* Chicago: University of Chicago Press, 1966.

Kamil, Jill. *The Ancient Egyptians.* Cairo: American University in Cairo Press, 1984.

Kissinger, Henry. *Years of Upheaval.* Boston: Little, Brown, 1979.

Lane-Poole, Stanley. *Egypt During the Middle Ages.* London: Methuen, 1925.

Lenczowski, George. *The Middle East in World Affairs.* (4th ed.) Ithaca: Cornell University Press, 1980.

Lewis, Bernard. "Egypt and Syria." Pages 175–232 in P.M. Holt, Ann K.S. Lambton, and Bernard Lewis (eds.), *The Cambridge History of Islam.* Cambridge: Cambridge University Press, 1970.

McDermott, Anthony. *Egypt from Nasser to Mubarak: A Flawed Revolution.* London: Croom Helm, 1988.

Marsot, Afaf Lutfi al-Sayyid. *Egypt in the Reign of Muhammad Ali.* Cambridge: Cambridge University Press, 1984.

_____. "Muhammad Ali's International Politics." Pages 153–73 in *L'Egypte au XIXe siècle.* Groupe de Recherches et d'Etudes sur le Proche Orient. Paris: Centre National de la Recherche Scientifique, 1982.

_____. "The Revolutionary Gentlewomen in Egypt." Pages 261–76 in Louise Beck and Nikki Keddie (eds.), *Women in the Muslim World.* Cambridge: Harvard University Press, 1978.

Mitchell, Timothy. *Colonizing Egypt.* Cambridge: Cambridge University Press, 1988.

Noshy, Ibrahim. *The Coptic Church.* Washington: Ruth Sloane Associates, 1975.

Owen, Roger. "Egypt and Europe: From French Expedition to British Occupation." Pages 195–209 in Roger Owen and Bob Sutcliffe (eds.), *Studies in the Theory of Imperialism.* London: Longman Group, 1972.

_____. *The Middle East in the World Economy.* London: Methuen, 1981.

Radwan, Samir. *Capital Formation in Egypt.* London: Ithaca Press, 1974.

Ramadan, Abd el-Azim. "Social Significance of the Urabi Revolt." Pages 187–96 in *L'Egypte au XIXe siècle.* Groupe de Recherches et d'Etudes sur le Proche Orient. Paris: Centre National de la Recherche Scientifique, 1982.

Raymond, André. *Artisans et commerçants au Caire au XVIIIe siècle.* Damascus: Institut Français de Damas, 1974.

Scholch, Alexander. *Egypt for the Egyptians.* London: Ithaca Press, 1981.

———. "The Formation of a Peripheral State: Egypt: 1854–1882." Pages 175–85 in *L'Egypte au XIXe siècle.* Groupe de Recherches et d'Etudes sur le Proche Orient. Paris: Centre National de la Recherche Scientifique, 1982.

Smith, W. Stevenson. *The Art and Architecture of Ancient Egypt.* (Rev., with additions by William Kelly Simpson). New York: Penguin Books, 1981.

Springborg, Robert. *Mubarak's Egypt: Fragmentation of the Political Order.* Boulder, Colorado: Westview Press, 1989.

Terry, Janice. *The Wafd: 1919–1952.* London: Third World Centre for Research and Publishing, 1982.

Trigger, B.G., B.J. Kemp, D. O'Connor, and A.B. Lloyd. *Ancient Egypt: A Social History.* Cambridge: Cambridge University Press, 1983.

Tucker, Judith. *Women in Nineteenth-Century Egypt.* Cambridge: Cambridge University Press, 1985.

Vatikiotis, P.J. *The History of Egypt from Muhammad Ali to Sadat.* Baltimore: Johns Hopkins University Press, 1980.

Waterbury, John. *The Egypt of Nasser and Sadat: The Political Economy of Two Regimes.* Princeton: Princeton University Press, 1983.

Watt, W. Montgomery. *Muhammad at Mecca.* Oxford: Clarendon Press, 1960.

———. *Muhammad at Medina.* Oxford: Clarendon Press, 1962.

Wissa Wassef, Ceres. *Egypt.* New York: Scala Books, 1983.

Chapter 2

Abaza, Mona. *The Changing Image of Women in Rural Egypt.* (Cairo Papers in Social Science, No. 10.) Cairo: American University in Cairo Press, 1987.

Abdel-Fadil, Mahmoud. *Development, Income Distribution, and Social Change in Rural Egypt, 1952–1970.* (Department of Applied Economics, Occasional Papers, No. 45.) London: Cambridge University Press, 1975.

Abdel-Khalek, Gouda, and Robert L. Tignor (eds.). *The Political Economy of Income Distribution in Egypt.* New York: Holmes and Meier, 1982.

Abu-Lughod, Janet. *Before European Hegemony: The World System, A.D. 1250–1350.* New York: Oxford University Press, 1989.

———. *Cairo: 1001 Years of the City Victorious.* Princeton: Princeton University Press, 1971.

Abu-Lughod, Lila. "Bedouins, Cassettes, and Technologies of Public Culture," *Middle East Report,* No. 159, July–August 1989, 7–11, 47.

_____. *Veiled Sentiments: Honor and Poetry in a Bedouin Society.* Berkeley: University of California Press, 1986.

Adams, Michael. *The Middle East.* (Handbooks to the Modern World Series.) New York: Facts on File, 1988.

Akhavi, Shahrough. "Egypt: Neo-Patrimonial Elite." Pages 69–113 in Frank Tachau (ed.), *Political Elites and Political Development.* New York: Wiley, 1975.

Aldridge, James. *Cairo.* Boston and Toronto: Little, Brown, 1969.

al-Guindi, Fadwa. "Veiling *Infitah* with Muslim Ethic," *Social Problems,* 28, 1981, 465–83.

Ansari, Hamied. *Egypt: The Stalled Society.* Albany: State University of New York Press, 1986.

_____. "The Islamic Militants in Egyptian Politics," *International Journal of Middle East Studies,* 16, No. 1, 1984, 123–44.

_____. "Sectarian Conflict in Egypt and the Political Expediency of Religion," *Middle East Journal,* 38, No. 3, Summer 1984, 397–418.

Aulas, Marie-Christine. "Sadat's Egypt: A Balance Sheet," *MERIP Reports,* 12, No. 107, July-August 1982, 6–11, 14–15, 18.

Ayrout, Henry Habib. *The Egyptian Peasant.* (Trans., John Alden Williams.) Boston: Beacon Press, 1963.

Ayubi, Nazih. *Bureaucracy and Politics in Contemporary Egypt.* London: Ithaca Press, 1980.

Baker, Raymond. *Egypt's Uncertain Revolution under Nasser and Sadat.* Cambridge: Harvard University Press, 1978.

Banks, Arthur (ed.). *Political Handbook of the World, 1986.* Binghamton: State University of New York Press, 1986.

Bannerman, Patrick. *Islam in Perspective: A Guide to Islamic Society, Politics, and Law.* London: Routledge for Royal Institute of International Affairs, 1988.

Beinin, Joel, and Zachary Lockman. *Workers on the Nile: Nationalism, Communism, Islam, and the Egyptian Working Class, 1882–1954.* Princeton: Princeton University Press, 1987.

Berque, Jacques. *Egypt: Imperialism and Revolution.* (Trans., Jean Stewart.) (Books That Matter Series.) New York: Praeger, 1972.

Binder, Leonard. *In a Moment of Enthusiasm: Political Power and the Second Stratum in Egypt.* Chicago: University of Chicago Press, 1978.

Chaichian, Mohammad A. "The Effects of World Capitalist Economy on Urbanization in Egypt, 1800–1970," *International Journal of Middle East Studies,* 20, No. 1, February 1988, 23–43.

Committee on Population and Demography. *The Estimation of Recent Trends in Fertility and Mortality in Egypt.* (National Academy of Science Panel on Egypt, Report No. 9.) Washington: National Academy Press, 1982.

Egypt. Central Agency for Public Mobilization and Statistics. *Population, Housing, and Establishment Census, 1986.* Cairo: CAPMAS, 1987.

"Egypt." Pages 921–42 in *The Europa Yearbook, 1986: A World Survey.* London: Europa, 1986.

"Egypt." Pages 367–408 in *The Middle East and North Africa, 1989.* London: Europa, 1989.

"Egypt." Pages 156–61 in Arthur Banks (ed.), *Political Handbook of the World, 1986.* Binghamton: State University of New York Press, 1986.

"Egypt's *Infitah* Bourgeoisie," *Middle East Report,* No. 142, September-October 1986, 39–40.

Farah, Nadia Ramsis. *Religious Strife in Egypt: Crisis and Ideological Conflict in the Seventies.* Montreux, Switzerland: Gordon and Breach Science, 1986.

Fernea, Elizabeth Warnock, and Robert Fernea. *The Arab World: Personal Encounters.* Garden City: Anchor Press/Doubleday, 1985.

Fernea, Elizabeth Warnock (ed.). *Women and the Family in the Middle East: New Voices of Change.* Austin: University of Texas Press, 1985.

Fisher, W.B. "Egypt." Pages 480–93 in *The Middle East: A Physical, Social, and Regional Geography.* (6th ed.) London: Methuen, 1971.

———. "Egypt: Physical and Social Geography." Pages 364–67 in *The Middle East and North Africa, 1989.* London: Europa, 1989.

Gazetteer of Egypt. (2d ed.) Washington: Defense Mapping Agency, August 1987.

Geiser, Peter. *The Egyptian Nubian: A Study in Social Symbiosis.* Cairo: American University in Cairo Press, 1986.

Goldberg, Ellis. *Tinker, Tailor, and Textile Worker: Class and Politics in Egypt, 1930–1952.* Berkeley: University of California Press, 1986.

Goldschmidt, Arthur, Jr. *Modern Egypt: The Formation of a Nation-State.* Boulder, Colorado: Westview Press, 1988.

Hammam, Mona. "Egypt's Working Women: Textile Workers of Chubra el-Kheima," *MERIP Reports,* No. 82, November 1979, 3–7.

Harik, Iliya. *The Political Mobilization of Peasants: A Study of an Egyptian Community.* Bloomington: Indiana University Press, 1974.

Harris, Lillian Craig (ed.). *Egypt: Internal Challenges and Regional Stability.* London: Routledge and Kegan Paul, 1988.

Hatem, Mervat. "Egypt's Middle Class in Crisis: The Sexual Division of Labor," *Middle East Journal,* 42, No. 2, Summer 1988, 407–22.

_____. "Toward the Study of the Psychodynamics of Mothering and Gender in Egyptian Families," *International Journal of Middle East Studies,* 19, No. 3, August 1987, 287–306.

Hinnebusch, Raymond A., Jr. *Egyptian Politics under Sadat: The Post-Populist Development of an Authoritarian-Modernizing State.* (Rev. ed.) Boulder, Colorado: Lynne Rienner, 1988.

Hirschhorn, Norbert. "Appropriate Health Technology in Egypt," *Middle East Report,* No. 161, November–December 1989, 26–28.

Hussein, Aziza. "Recent Amendments to Egypt's Personal Status Law." Pages 229–32 in Elizabeth Warnock Fernea (ed.), *Women and the Family in the Middle East: New Voices of Change.* Austin: University of Texas Press, 1985.

Ibrahim, Barbara Lethem. "Cairo's Factory Women." Pages 293–99 in Elizabeth Warnock Fernea (ed.), *Women and the Family in the Middle East: New Voices of Change.* Austin: University of Texas Press, 1985.

Ibrahim, Ibrahim. "Religion and Politics under Nasser and Sadat, 1952–1981." Pages 121–34 in Barbara Freyer Stowasser (ed.), *The Islamic Impulse.* London: Croom Helm, 1987.

Ibrahim, Saad Eddin. "Anatomy of Egypt's Militant Islamic Groups: Methodological Note and Preliminary Findings," *International Journal of Middle East Studies,* 12, No. 4, December 1980, 423–53.

_____. "Egypt's Islamic Militants," *MERIP Reports,* 12, No. 103, February 1982, 5–14.

Juynboll, Gautier (trans.). *The History of al-Tabari: The Conquest of Iraq, Southwestern Persia, and Egypt,* 13. (Biblioteca Persica Series.) Albany: State University of New York Press, 1989.

Kepel, Gilles. *Muslim Extremism in Egypt: The Prophet and the Pharaoh.* (Trans., Jan Rothschild.) Berkeley: University of California Press, 1986.

Khadduri, Majid. *Modern Libya: A Study in Political Development.* Baltimore: Johns Hopkins University Press, 1963.

Khafagy, Fatma. "Women and Labor Migration: One Village in Egypt," *MERIP Reports,* No. 124, June 1984, 17–21.

LaTowsky, Robert. "Egyptian Labor Abroad: Mass Participation and Modest Returns," *MERIP Reports,* No. 123, May 1984, 11–18.

McDermott, Anthony. *Egypt from Nasser to Mubarak: A Flawed Revolution.* London: Croom Helm, 1988.

The Middle East and North Africa, 1989. London: Europa, 1989.

Momen, Moojan. *An Introduction to Shi'i Islam.* New Haven: Yale University Press, 1985.

Mortimer, Edward. *Faith and Power: The Politics of Islam.* New York: Random House, 1982.

Myntti, Cynthia. "Medical Education: The Struggle for Relevance," *Middle East Report,* No. 161, November–December 1989, 11–15.

Nasr, Seyyed Hossein. *Traditional Islam in the Modern World.* London: KPI, 1987.

Orfalea, Gregory. *Before the Flames: A Quest for the History of Arab Americans.* Austin: University of Texas Press, 1988.

Peretz, Don. *The Middle East Today.* (2d ed.) Hinsdale, Illinois: Dryden Press, 1971.

Piscatori, James (ed.). *Islam in the Political Process.* Cambridge: Cambridge University Press, 1983.

Richards, Alan. *Egypt's Agricultural Development, 1800–1980: Technical and Social Change.* Boulder, Colorado: Westview Press, 1982.

_____. "Egypt's Agriculture in Trouble," *MERIP Reports,* No. 84, January 1980, 3–13.

Rodenbeck, Max. "Revolution of Goodwill," *Middle East International* [London], No. 342, January 20, 1989, 12–13.

_____. "Stamping on Extremists," *Middle East International* [London], No. 341, January 6, 1989, 12–13.

_____. "Trouble at the Mill," *Middle East International* [London], No. 357, August 25, 1989, 13.

Rugh, Andrea B. *Family in Contemporary Egypt.* Syracuse: Syracuse University Press, 1984.

_____. "Women and Work: Strategies and Choices in a Lower-Class Quarter of Cairo." Pages 273–88 in Elizabeth Warnock Fernea (ed.), *Women and the Family in the Middle East: New Voices of Change.* Austin: University of Texas Press, 1985.

Saab, Gabriel. *The Egyptian Agrarian Reform, 1952–1962.* London: Oxford University Press, 1967.

Springborg, Robert. *Family, Power, and Politics in Egypt: Sayed Bey Marei—His Clan, Clients, and Cohorts.* Philadelphia: University of Pennsylvania Press, 1982.

_____. *Mubarak's Egypt: Fragmentation of the Political Order.* Boulder, Colorado: Westview Press, 1989.

Stork, Joe. "Political Aspects of Health," *Middle East Report,* No. 161, November–December 1989, 4–10.

Taylor, Elizabeth. "Egyptian Migration and Peasant Wives," *MERIP Reports,* No. 124, June 1984, 3–10.

Tyson, James. "Letter From Siwa," *Middle East International* [London], No. 352, June 9, 1989, 24.

Wahba, Mourad. "Social Aspects." Pages 11–30 in Lillian Craig Harris (ed.), *Egypt: Internal Challenges and Regional Stability.* London: Routledge and Kegan Paul, 1988.

Waterbury, John. *The Egypt of Nasser and Sadat: The Political Economy of Two Regimes.* Princeton: Princeton University Press, 1983.

Wikan, Unni. *Life among the Urban Poor of Cairo.* (Trans., Ann Henning.) New York: Tavistock, 1980.

_____. "Living Conditions among Cairo's Poor: A View from Below," *Middle East Journal,* 39, No. 1, Winter 1985, 7–26.

Williams, Caroline. "Islamic Cairo: Endangered Legacy," *Middle East Journal,* 39, No. 3, Summer 1985, 231–46.

Zaalouk, Malak. *Power, Class, and Foreign Capital in Egypt: The Rise of the New Bourgeoisie.* London: Zed Books, 1989.

Chapter 3

Abdel-Fadil, Mahmoud. *Development, Income Distribution, and Social Change in Rural Egypt, 1952–1970.* (Department of Applied Economics, Occasional Papers, No. 45.) Cambridge: Cambridge University Press, 1975.

_____. *The Political Economy of Nasserism.* (Department of Economics, Occasional Papers, No. 52.) Cambridge: Cambridge University Press, 1980.

Ahmed, Sadiq. *Public Finance in Egypt: Its Structure and Trends.* (Staff Working Papers, No. 639.) Washington: World Bank, 1984.

Amin, Galal Ahmad. "External Factors in the Reorientation of Egypt's Economic Policy." Pages 285–315 in Malcolm Kerr and El Sayed Yassin (eds.), *Rich and Poor States in the Middle East: Egypt and the New Arab Order.* Boulder, Colorado: Westview Press, 1982.

Bedding, James. "Money Down the Drain," *New Scientist* [London], No. 1660, April 15, 1989, 34–38.

Bremer, Jennifer. *New Lands Concepts, Paper 2: Rethinking an AID Assistance Strategy for the New Lands of Egypt.* Washington: Development Alternatives, 1981.

Central Bank of Egypt. *Economic Review* [Cairo], 27, No. 1, 1987.

Charnock, Anne. "The Greening of Egypt," *New Scientist* [London], 23, January 23, 1986, 44–48.

Choucri, Nazli. "The Hidden Economy: A New View of Remittances in the Arab World," *World Development* [London], 14, No. 6, June 1986, 697–712.

Commander, Simon. *The State and Agricultural Development in Egypt since 1973.* London: Ithaca Press for Overseas Development Institute, London, 1987.

Cuddihy, William. *Agricultural Price Management in Egypt.* (Staff Working Paper No. 388.) Washington: World Bank, 1980.

Dalrymple, Dana G. *Development and Spread of High-Yielding Rice Varieties in Developing Countries.* (Bureau of Science and Technology Series.) Washington: Agency for International Development, 1986.

_____. *Development and Spread of High-Yielding Wheat Varieties in Developing Countries.* (Bureau of Science and Technology Series.) Washington: Agency for International Development, 1986.

Dethier, Jean-Jacques. *Trade, Exchange Rate, and Agricultural Pricing Policies in Egypt.* (2 vols.) Washington: World Bank, 1989.

Economist Intelligence Unit. *Country Report: Egypt, 1987-88.* London, 1988.

Egypt. Central Agency for Public Mobilization and Statistics. *Statistical Yearbook, 1952-1987.* Cairo: CAPMAS, 1988.

"Egypt." Page 617 in George Kurian (ed.), *Encyclopedia of the Third World,* 1. New York: Facts on File, 1987.

"Egypt: Economy." Pages 384-96 in *The Middle East and North Africa, 1990.* London: Europa, 1989.

Elmusa, Sharif S. "Dependency and Industrialization in the Arab World," *Arab Studies Quarterly,* 8, No. 3, 1986, 253-67.

Gotsch, Carl, and Wayne Dyer. "Rhetoric and Reason in the Egyptian 'New Lands,'" *Food Research Institute Studies,* 18, No. 2, 129-36.

Habeeb, William Mark (ed.), *U.S.-Egyptian Relations in an Era of Economic Constraints,* Washington: Middle East Institute and Institute for National Strategic Studies, 1988.

Hansen, Bent and Karim Nashashibi. *Foreign Trade Regimes and Economic Development: Egypt.* New York: Columbia University Press for National Bureau of Economic Research, 1975.

Hopkins, Nicholas. *Agrarian Transformation in Egypt.* Boulder, Colorado: Westview Press, 1987.

_____. "Mechanized Irrigation in Upper Egypt: The Role of Technology and the State in Agriculture." Pages 223-47 in B.L. Turner and Stephen Bush (eds.), *Comparative Farming Systems,* New York: Guilford, 1987.

Husayn, Adil. *Al-Iqtisad al-Misri min al-Istiqlal ila al-Tabaiyah* (The Egyptian Economy from Independence to Dependency). Cairo: Dar al-Mustaqbal al-Arabi, 1982.

Ibrahim, Ibrahim (ed.), *Arab Resources.* Washington: Center for Contemporary Arab Studies, Georgetown University, 1983.

Ikram, Khalid, et al. *Egypt: Management in a Period of Transition.* Baltimore: Johns Hopkins University Press for the World Bank, 1980.

Institute of International Finance. *Egypt: Country Report,* 88, No. 1, Washington: January 26, 1988.

_____. *Egypt: Country Report,* 88, No. 2, Washington: August 15, 1988.

_____. *Egypt: Country Report.* 89, No. 1, Washington: February 8, 1989.

International Monetary Fund. *Financial Statistics,* 40. Washington: 1987.

_____. *Financial Statistics,* 42. Washington: 1989.

International Rice Research Institute. *Rice Farming Systems: New Directions.* (Proceedings of 1987 international symposium at the Rice Research and Training Center, Sakha, Egypt.) Manila: 1988.

Jane's World Railways, 1989-90. (Ed., Allen Geoffrey.) Coulsdon, Surrey, United Kingdom: Jane's Information Group, 1989.

Kishk, M.A. "Land Degradation in the Nile Valley," *Ambio,* 15, No. 4, 1986, 226-30.

Korayem, Karima. *The Impact of Economic Adjustment Policies on the Vulnerable Families and Children in Egypt.* Cairo: UNICEF, 1987.

Kubursi, Atif. "Arab Agricultural Productivity: A New Perspective." Pages 71-101 in Ibrahim Ibrahim (ed.), *Arab Resources.* Washington: Center for Contemporary Arab Studies, Georgetown University, 1983.

Lesch, Ann M. "Egyptian Politics in the 1990s." Pages 12-26 in William Mark Habeeb (ed.), *U.S.-Egyptian Relations in an Era of Economic Constraints.* Washington: Middle East Institute and Institute for National Strategic Studies, 1988.

Mabro, Robert. *The Egyptian Economy, 1952-72.* Oxford: Clarendon Press, 1974.

Mabro, Robert, and Samir Radwan. *The Industrialization of Egypt, 1939-1973: Policy and Performance.* Oxford: Clarendon Press, 1976.

National Bank of Egypt. *Economic Bulletin* [Cairo], 40, Nos. 1-2, 1987.

Oweiss, Ibrahim. "Egypt's Current Economic Situation." Pages 2-11 in William Mark Habeeb (ed.), *U.S.-Egyptian Relations in an Era of Economic Constraints,* Washington: Middle East Institute and Institute for National Strategic Studies, 1988.

Pleskovic, Boris. "Interindustry Flows in a General Equilibrium Model of Fiscal Incidence: An Application to Egypt," *Journal of Policy Modeling,* 11, No. 1, Spring 1989, 157-77.

Richards, Alan. *Egypt's Agricultural Development, 1800-1980: Technical and Social Change.* Boulder, Colorado: Westview Press, 1982.

_____. *Food Problems and Prospects in the Middle East.* (Occasional Paper Series.) Washington: Center for Contemporary Arab Studies, Georgetown University, 1984.

Richards, Alan, and Philip Martin. "Introduction." Pages 1–14 in Alan Richards and Philip Martin (eds.), *Migration, Mechanization, and Agricultural Labor Markets in Egypt.* Boulder, Colorado: Westview Press, 1983.

Sadowski, Yahya. "The Sphinx's New Riddle: Why Does Egypt Delay Economic Reform?" *American-Arab Affairs,* 22, Fall 1987, 28–40.

Scobie, Grant M. *Food Subsidies and the Government Budget in Egypt.* (Working Papers on Food Subsidies, No. 2.) Washington: International Food Policy Research Institute, 1985.

Sennitt, Andrew G. (ed.). *World Radio TV Handbook, 1990,* 44. Hvidovre, Denmark: Billboard, 1990.

Sherbiny, Naiem, and Ismail Serageldin. "Expatriate Labor and Economic Growth: Saudi Demand for Egyptian Labor." Pages 225–57 in Malcolm Kerr and El Sayed Yassin (eds.), *Rich and Poor States in the Middle East: Egypt and the New Arab Order.* Boulder, Colorado: Westview Press, 1982.

Springborg, Robert. *Mubarak's Egypt: Fragmentation of the Political Order.* Boulder, Colorado: Westview Press, 1989.

Tucker, Judith. *Women in Nineteenth-Century Egypt.* Cambridge: Cambridge University Press, 1985.

United Nations. Food and Agriculture Organization. *World Hunger.* Rome: 1980.

United States. Department of Commerce. International Trade Administration. *Marketing in Egypt.* Washington: GPO, December 1981.

Vivian, Cassandra (ed.). *Cairo, a Practical Guide.* (6th ed.) Cairo: American University in Cairo Press, 1986.

Voll, Sarah. "Egyptian Land Reclamation since the Revolution," *Middle East Journal,* 34, No. 2, Spring 1980, 127–48.

von Braun, Joachim, and Hartwig de Haen. *The Effects of Food Price and Subsidy Policies on Egyptian Agriculture.* (Research Report No. 42.) Washington: International Food Policy Research Institute, 1983.

Waterbury, John. *The Egypt of Nasser and Sadat: The Political Economy of Two Regimes.* Princeton: Princeton University Press, 1983.

Wolfe, Ronald (trans.). *Egypt's Second Five-Year Plan for Socio-Economic Development (1987/88–1991/92), with Plan for Year One (1987/88).* Cairo: Professional Business Services, 1987.

World Bank. "Egypt," *Trends in Developing Economies.* Washington: 1989, 129–34.

_____. *World Tables, 1988–89.* Baltimore: Johns Hopkins University Press, 1989.

World Resources Institute and International Institute for Environment and Development. "Food and Agriculture." Pages 51–67 and 271–84 in *World Resources, 1988–89,* Washington: 1989.

(Various issues of the following publications were also used in the preparation of this chapter: *Al Ahram* [Cairo]; *Al Ahram al Iqtisadi* [Cairo]; *Egypte Contemporaine* [Cairo]; *Financial Times* [London]; *International Financial Statistics; Middle East Economic Digest* [London]; *Middle East Report;* and *World Development Report.*)

Chapter 4

Abdallah, Ahmed. *The Student Movement and National Politics in Egypt.* London: Saqi Books, 1985.

Abdel-Fadil, Mahmoud. *Development, Income Distribution and Social Change in Rural Egypt, 1952–1970.* (Department of Applied Economics, Occasional Papers, No. 45.) Cambridge: Cambridge University Press, 1975.

_____. *The Political Economy of Nasserism.* (Department of Economics, Occasional Papers, No. 52.) Cambridge: Cambridge University Press, 1980.

Abdel-Khalek, Gouda, and Robert L. Tignor (eds.). *The Political Economy of Income Distribution in Egypt.* London: Holmes and Meier, 1982.

Abdel-Malek, Anouar. *Egypt: Military Society.* New York: Vintage Books, 1968.

Adams, Richard H. *Development and Social Change in Rural Egypt.* Syracuse: Syracuse University Press, 1986.

Ajami, Fouad. *The Arab Predicament: Arab Political Thought and Practice since 1967.* Cambridge: Cambridge University Press, 1981.

_____. "The Open Door Economy: Its Roots and Welfare Consequences." Pages 469–516 in Gouda Abdel-Khalek and Robert L. Tignor (eds.), *The Political Economy of Income Distribution in Egypt.* London: Holmes and Meier, 1982.

Akhavi, Shahrough. "Egypt: Diffused Elite in a Bureaucratic Society." Pages 223–65 in I. William Zartman (ed.), *Political Elites in Arab North Africa.* New York: Longman, 1982.

_____. "Egypt: Neo-Patrimonial Elite." Pages 69–113 in Frank Tachau (ed.), *Political Elites and Political Development in the Middle East.* New York: Wiley, 1975.

al-Guindi, Fadwa. "The Mood in Egypt," *Middle East Insight,* 4, Nos. 4-5, 1986, 30-39.

Altman, Israel. "Islamic Movements in Egypt," *Jerusalem Quarterly* [Jerusalem], 10, 1979, 87-105.

Ansari, Hamied. *Egypt: The Stalled Society.* Albany: State University of New York Press, 1986.

Aulas, Marie Christian. "Sadat's Egypt," *New Left Review,* 98, 1976, pp. 84-95.

_____. "Sadat's Egypt: A Balance Sheet." Pages 6-18 in *MERIP Reports,* No. 107, July-August 1982.

Ayubi, Nazih. *Bureaucracy and Politics in Contemporary Egypt.* London: Ithaca Press, 1980.

_____. "Implementation Capability and Political Feasibility of the Open Door Policy in Egypt." Pages 349-413 in Gouda Abdul Khalek and Robert L. Tignor (eds.), *The Political Economy of Income Distribution in Egypt.* London: Holmes and Meier, 1982.

_____. "The Political Revival of Islam: The Case of Egypt," *International Journal of Middle East Studies,* 12, No. 4, December 1980, 481-99.

Baker, Raymond. *Egypt's Uncertain Revolution under Nasser and Sadat.* Cambridge: Harvard University Press, 1978.

Beinin, Joel, and Zachary Lockman. *Workers on the Nile: Nationalism, Communism, Islam, and the Egyptian Working Class, 1882-1954.* Princeton: Princeton University Press, 1987.

Berger, Morroe. *The Arab World Today.* New York: Doubleday, 1962.

_____. *Bureaucracy and Society in Modern Egypt.* Princeton: Princeton University Press, 1957.

Berque, Jacques. *Egypt: Imperialism and Revolution.* (Trans., Jean Stewart.) (Books That Matter Series.) New York: Praeger, 1972.

Bianchi, Robert. "Businessmen's Associations in Egypt and Turkey," *Annals,* 482, November 1985, 147-54.

_____. "The Corporatization of the Egyptian Labor Movement," *Middle East Journal,* 40, No. 3, Summer 1986, 429-44.

Binder, Leonard. "Egypt: The Integrative Revolution." Pages 396-449 in Lucian Pye and Sidney Verba (eds.), *Political Culture and Political Development.* Princeton: Princeton University Press, 1965.

_____. *The Ideological Revolution in the Middle East.* New York: Wiley, 1964.

_____. *In a Moment of Enthusiasm: Political Power and the Second Stratum in Egypt.* Chicago: University of Chicago Press, 1978.

_____. "Political Recruitment and Participation in Egypt." Pages 217-40 in Joseph LaPalombara and Myron Weiner (eds.),

Political Parties and Political Development. Princeton: Princeton University Press, 1966.

Brown, William. *The Last Crusade: A Negotiator's Middle East Handbook.* Chicago: Aldine, 1980.

Buttner, Friedemann. "Political Stability Without Stable Institutions: The Re-Traditionalization of Egypt's Policy," *Orient,* 20, 53–76.

Cooper, Mark. "Egyptian State Capitalism in Crisis: Economic Policies and Political Interests, 1967–1971," *International Journal of Middle East Studies,* 10, No. 4, 1979, 481–516.

————. *The Transformation of Egypt.* Baltimore: Johns Hopkins University Press, 1982.

Cremeans, Charles D. *The Arabs and the World: Nasser's Arab Nationalist Policy.* New York: Praeger, 1963.

Critchfield, Richard. *Shahhat: An Egyptian.* Syracuse: Syracuse University Press, 1978.

Dawisha, Adeed. *Egypt in the Arab World: The Elements of Foreign Policy.* New York: Wiley, 1976.

Dawisha, Adeed, and I. William Zartman. *Beyond Coercion: The Durability of the Arab State.* London: Croom Helm, 1988.

Deeb, Marius. *Party Politics in Egypt: The Wafd and Its Rivals, 1919–1939.* London: Ithaca Press, 1979.

Dekmejian, Richard Hrair. *Egypt under Nasir: A Study in Political Dynamics.* Albany: State University of New York Press, 1971.

————. "Marx, Weber, and the Egyptian Revolution," *Middle East Journal,* 30, No. 2, Spring 1976, 158–72.

————. *Patterns of Political Leadership: Egypt, Lebanon, Israel.* Albany: State University of New York Press, 1975.

Dessouki, Ali E. Hillal. "Policy Making in Egypt: A Case Study of the Open Door Policy," *Social Problems,* 28, No. 4, April 1984, 410–16.

————. "The Politics of Income Distribution in Egypt." Pages 55–87 in Gouda Abdel-Khalek and Robert L. Tignor (eds.), *The Political Economy of Income Distribution in Egypt.* London: Holmes and Meier, 1982.

Entelis, John P. "Nasir's Egypt: The Failure of Charismatic Leadership," *Orbis,* 28, No. 2, 1974, 451–64.

Fahmi, Ismail. *Negotiating for Peace in the Middle East.* Baltimore: Johns Hopkins University Press, 1983.

Goldschmidt, Arthur, Jr. *Modern Egypt: The Formation of a Nation-State.* Boulder, Colorado: Westview Press, 1988.

Groupe de Recherches et d'Etudes sur le Proche-Orient. *L'Egypte d'aujourd'hui: Permanence et changements, 1805–1976.* Paris: Centre National de la Recherche, 1977.

Haikal, Muhammed Hasanain. *Autumn of Fury: The Assassination of Sadat.* New York: Random House, 1983.

_____. *Nasir: The Cairo Documents.* London: New English Library, 1971.

_____. *The Road to Ramadan.* New York: Readers Digest Press, 1975.

_____. *The Sphinx and the Commissar.* New York: Harper and Row, 1978.

Halpern, Manfred. *The Politics of Social Change in the Middle East and North Africa.* Princeton: Princeton University Press, 1963.

Harik, Iliya. "Continuity and Change in Local Development Policies in Egypt," *International Journal of Middle East Studies,* 16, No. 1, 1984, 43–66.

_____. "Mobilization Policy and Rural Change in Egypt." Pages 287–334 in Iliya Harik and Richard Antoun (eds.), *Rural Politics and Social Change in the Middle East.* Bloomington: Indiana University Press, 1972.

_____. "Opinion Leaders and the Mass Media in Rural Egypt," *American Political Science Review,* 65, No. 3, September 1972, 731–40.

_____. *The Political Mobilization of Peasants: A Study of an Egyptian Community.* Bloomington: Indiana University Press, 1974.

_____. "The Single Party as a Subordinate Movement: The Case of Egypt," *World Politics,* 26, No. 1, October 1973, 80–105.

Harik, Iliya, and Richard Antoun (eds.). *Rural Politics and Social Change in the Middle East.* Bloomington: Indiana University Press, 1972.

Heaphey, James. "The Organization of Egypt: Inadequacies of a Non-Political Model of Nation-Building," *World Politics,* 26, 1965, 80–105.

Hendriks, Bertus. "Egypt's New Political Map: Report from the Election Campaign," *Middle East Report,* No. 147, July–August 1987, 23–31.

Hill, Enid. *Mahkama! Studies in the Egyptian Legal System,* London: Ithaca Press, 1979.

Hinnebusch, Raymond A., Jr. *Egyptian Politics under Sadat: The Post-Populist Development of an Authoritarian-Modernizing State.* (Rev. ed.) Boulder, Colorado: Lynne Rienner, 1988.

_____. "From Nasir to Sadat: Elite Transformation in Egypt," *Journal of Middle East and South Asian Studies,* 7, No. 1, Fall 1983, 24–49.

_____. "The Re-emergence of the Wafd Party: Glimpses of the Liberal Opposition in Egypt," *International Journal of Middle East Studies,* 16, No. 1, 1984, 99–121.

Hirst, David, and Irene Beeson. *Sadat.* London: Faber and Faber, 1981.

Hussein, Mahmoud. *Class Conflict in Egypt.* New York: Monthly Review Press, 1973.

Ibrahim, Saad Eddin. "Anatomy of Egypt's Militant Islamic Groups: Methodological Note and Preliminary Findings," *International Journal of Middle East Studies,* 12, No. 4, December 1980, 423-53.

Issawi, Charles. *Egypt in Revolution: An Economic Analysis.* New York: Oxford University Press, 1963.

Kepel, Gilles. *Muslim Extremism in Egypt: The Prophet and the Pharaoh.* (Trans., Jan Rothschild.) Berkeley: University of California Press, 1986.

Kerr, Malcolm. *The Arab Cold War: Abd al-Nasir and His Rivals.* London: Oxford University Press, 1971.

Kerr, Malcolm, and El Sayed Yassin (eds.). *Rich and Poor States in the Middle East: Egypt and the New Arab Order.* Boulder, Colorado: Westview Press, 1982.

LaPalombara, Joseph, and Myron Weiner (eds.). *Political Parties and Political Development.* Princeton: Princeton University Press, 1966.

Lenczowski, George (ed.). *Political Elites in the Middle East.* Washington: American Enterprise Institute, 1975.

Mabro, Robert. *The Egyptian Economy, 1952-1972.* Oxford: Clarendon Press, 1974.

Mansfield, Peter. *Nasser's Egypt.* Baltimore: Penguin Books, 1969.

Mayfield, James. *Rural Politics in Nasir's Egypt.* Austin: University of Texas Press, 1971.

Mitchell, Richard. *The Society of the Muslim Brothers.* London: Oxford University Press, 1969.

Moore, Henry Clement. "Authoritarian Politics in Unincorporated Society: The Case of Nasser's Egypt," *Comparative Politics,* 6, No. 2, January 1974, 193-218.

_____. *Images of Development: Egyptian Engineers in Search of Development.* Cambridge: Massachusetts Institute of Technology Press, 1980.

_____. "Money and Power: The Dilemma of the Egyptian Infitah," *Middle East Journal,* 40, No. 4, Autumn 1986, 634-50.

O'Brien, Patrick. *The Revolution in Egypt's Economic System: From Private Enterprise to Socialism, 1952-1965.* London: Oxford University Press, 1966.

Owen, Roger. "Mubarak's Dilemma," *MERIP Reports,* No. 117, September 1983, 12-27.

Post, Erika. "Egypt's Elections." *Middle East Report,* No. 147, July-August 1987, 17-22.

Pye, Lucian, and Sidney Verba (eds.). *Political Culture and Political Development*. Princeton: Princeton University Press, 1965.

Radwan, Samir. *Agrarian Reform and Rural Poverty: Egypt, 1952–1972*. Geneva, Switzerland: ILO, 1977.

Riad, Mahmoud. *The Struggle for Peace in the Middle East*. London: Quartet Books, 1982.

Richards, Alan. "Ten Years of Infitah: Class, Rent, and Policy Stasis in Egypt," *Journal of Development Studies*, 20, No. 4, July 1984, 323–38.

Sadat, Anwar. *In Search of Identity: An Autobiography*. New York: Harper and Row, 1978.

Sennitt, Andrew G. (ed.). *World Radio TV Handbook, 1990*, 44. Hvidovre, Denmark: Billboard, 1990.

Shazli, Saad. *The Crossing of the Suez*. San Francisco: American Mideast Research, 1980.

_____. *Mubarak's Egypt: Fragmentation of the Political Order*. Boulder, Colorado: Westview Press, 1989.

_____. "Patrimonialism and Policy Making in Egypt: Nasir and Sadat and the Policy for Reclaimed Lands," *Middle Eastern Studies* [London], 15, No. 1, 26, January 1979, 49–59.

Springborg, Robert. *Family Power and Politics in Egypt: Sayed Bey Marei—His Clan, Clients, and Cohorts*. Philadelphia: University of Pennsylvania Press, 1982.

_____. "Patterns of Association in the Egyptian Political Elite." Pages 83–107 in George Lenczowski (ed.), *Political Elites in the Middle East*. Washington: American Enterprise Institute, 1975.

_____. "The President and the Field Marshal: Civil-Military Relations in Egypt Today." *Middle East Report*, No. 147, July–August 1987, 5–16.

_____. "Professional Syndicates in Egyptian Politics," *International Journal of Middle East Studies*, 9, No. 3, 1978, 275–95.

Stephens, Robert. *Nasser: A Political Biography*. New York: Simon and Schuster, 1974.

Tachau, Frank (ed.). *Political Elites and Political Development in the Middle East*. New York: Wiley, 1975.

Tripp, Charles, and Roger Owen (eds.). *Egypt under Mubarak*. London: Routledge, 1989.

Tucker, Judith, and Joe Stork. "Mubarak's Transition." *MERIP Reports*, No. 107, July–August 1982, 3–6.

Udovitch, L. (ed.). *The Middle East: Oil, Politics, and Hope*. Lexington, Massachusetts: Lexington Books, 1976.

Vatikiotis, P.J. *The Egyptian Army in Politics: Pattern for New Nations?* Bloomington: Indiana University Press, 1961.

_____. *Nasser and His Generation.* New York: St. Martin's Press, 1978.

Waterbury, John. *Egypt: Burdens of the Past, Options for the Future.* Hanover, New Hampshire: American Universities Field Staff, 1976.

_____. *The Egypt of Nasser and Sadat: The Political Economy of Two Regimes.* Princeton: Princeton University Press, 1983.

_____. "Egypt: The Wages of Dependency." Pages 291–351 in L. Udovitch (ed.), *The Middle East: Oil, Politics, and Hope.* Lexington, Massachusetts: Lexington Books, 1976.

_____. "The Soft State and the Open Door: Egypt's Experience with Economic Liberalization, 1974–1984," *Comparative Politics,* 18, No. 1, October 1985, 65–83.

Yaari, Ehud. "Sadat's Pyramid of Power," *Jerusalem Quarterly* [Jerusalem], 14, 1980, 110–21.

Yoram, Peri. *Between Battles and Ballots, Israel's Military in Politics.* Cambridge: Cambridge University Press, 1983.

Zartman, I. William (ed.). *Political Elites in Arab North Africa.* New York: Longman, 1982.

Chapter 5

Abdallah, Ahmed. "The Armed Forces and the Democratic Process in Egypt," *Third World Quarterly* [London], 10, No. 4, October 1988, 1452–67.

Amnesty International Report, 1988. London: Amnesty International, 1988.

Armstrong, G.P. "Egypt." Pages 147–65 in Richard A. Gabriel (ed.), *Fighting Armies: Antagonists in the Middle East: A Combat Assessment.* Westport, Connecticut: Greenwood Press, 1983.

Brassey's Defence Yearbook, 1989. London: Brassey's, 1989.

Copley, Gregory R. (ed.). "Defense in Egypt," *Defense and Foreign Affairs,* 17, No. 12, December 1989.

Cowell, Alan. "A Poor Land Torn by a Rich Craving," *New York Times,* May 20, 1989, I4.

DMS Market Intelligence Reports. *DMS Foreign Military Markets— Middle East/Africa.* Greenwich, Connecticut: Defense Marketing Services, 1989.

Dunn, Michael C. "Arming for Peacetime: Egypt's Defense Industry Today," *Defense and Foreign Affairs,* 15, Nos. 10–11, October–November 1987, 20–24.

_____. "Mother of the World: Egypt in Mubarak's Second Term," *Defense and Foreign Affairs,* 18, Nos. 10–11, October–November 1987, 11–15.

Dupuy, Trevor N. *Elusive Victory: The Arab-Israeli Wars, 1947–1974.* New York: Harper and Row, 1978.

Dyer, Gwynne, and John Keegan. "Egypt." Pages 162–73 in John Keegan (ed.), *World Armies.* Detroit: Gale Research, 1983.

"Egypt." Pages 305–15 in Gregory R. Copley (ed.), *Defense and Foreign Affairs Handbook, 1989.* Alexandria, Virginia: International Media, 1988.

"Egypt." Pages 102–6 in George Thomas Kurian (ed.), *World Encyclopedia of Police Forces and Penal Systems.* New York: Facts on File, 1989.

"Egypt." Pages 143–49 in Charles Miller (ed.), *Air Forces of the World, 1988–89.* Geneva, Switzerland: Interavia, 1988.

"Egyptian Air Force and Egyptian Air Defence Command." Pages 33–37 in *International Air Forces and Military Aircraft Directory.* Stapleford Air Field [Essex, United Kingdom]: Aviation Advisory Services, 1989.

Eilts, Hermann Frederick. "Egypt in 1986: Political Disappointments and Economic Dilemmas," *Washington Quarterly,* 10, No. 2, Spring 1987, 113–28.

Gabriel, Richard A. (ed.). *Fighting Armies: Antagonists in the Middle East: A Combat Assessment.* Westport, Connecticut: Greenwood Press, 1983.

Gawrych, George W. "The Egyptian High Command in the 1973 War," *Armed Forces and Society,* 13, No. 4, Summer 1987, 535–57.

Gold, Dore. *America, the Gulf, and Israel: CENTCOM (Central Command) and Emerging U.S. Regional Security Policies in the Middle East.* (Jaffee Center for Strategic Studies, Tel Aviv University Study No. 11). Boulder, Colorado: Westview Press, 1988.

Harris, Lillian Craig. "Egypt: The Constraints on Revolution," *Middle East International* [London], No. 313, November 21, 1987, 16–17.

Hill, Enid. *Mahkama! Studies in the Egyptian Legal System.* London: Ithaca Press, 1979.

Hinnebusch, Raymond A., Jr. *Egyptian Politics under Sadat: The Post-Populist Development of an Authoritarian-Modernizing State.* (Rev. ed.) Boulder, Colorado: Lynne Rienner, 1988.

International Air Forces and Military Aircraft Directory. Stapleford Air Field [Essex, United Kingdom]: Aviation Advisory Services, 1989.

International Crime Statistics, 1987–1988. St. Cloud, France: International Criminal Police Organization (Interpol) General Secretariat, n.d.

Jabber, Paul. "Egypt's Crisis, America's Dilemma," *Foreign Affairs,* 64, No. 5, Summer 1986, 960–80.

Jane's Fighting Ships, 1989–90. (Ed., Richard Sharpe.) Alexandria, Virginia: Jane's Information Group, 1989.

Joint Publications Research Service—JPRS (Washington). The following items are from the JPRS series:

Translations on the Near East/South Asia.

"Cairo's Security Chief Interviewed on Crime," *Akhir Saah* [Cairo], January 11, 1989 (JPRS 89-016, March 3, 1989, 16–21).

"Narcotics Traffic, Organized Financial Crime Grow," *Al Yaqzah al Arabiyah* [Cairo], May 1989 (JPRS 89-016-L, July 28, 1989, 7–8.).

"Political Violence Phenomenon in Egypt: Qualitative, Analytical, and Comparative Study, 1952-87," *Al Mustaqbal* [Beirut], November 1988 (JPRS 89-006, January 26, 1989, 19- 24.).

"Zaki Badr Defends Prison Measures, Emergency Law, Himself," *Al Akhbar* [Cairo], August 31, 1988 (JPRS 88-082, November 21, 1988, 114.).

Keegan, John (ed.). *World Armies.* Detroit: Gale Research, 1983.

Kurian, George Thomas (ed.). *World Encyclopedia of Police Forces and Penal Systems.* New York: Facts on File, 1989.

Kutter, Wolf D., and Glenn M. Harned. "Interoperability with Egyptian Forces," *Infantry,* 75, No. 1, January–February 1985, 1,517.

Levran, Aharon, and Zeev Eytan. Pages 125–34 in Aharon Levran (ed.), *The Middle East Military Balance, 1986.* Boulder, Colorado: Westview Press, 1987.

Lippman, Thomas W. *Egypt after Nasser.* New York: Paragon House, 1989.

McDermott, Anthony. *Egypt from Nasser to Mubarak: A Flawed Revolution.* New York: Croom Helm, 1988.

Middleton, Drew. "U.S. Aides Say Egypt Lacks Ability to Handle Weapons," *New York Times,* February 21, 1986, A8.

The Military Balance, 1989–1990. London: International Institute for Strategic Studies, 1989.

Military Technology and Economics (Miltech). Bonn: January 1989.

Miller, Charles (ed.). *Air Forces of the World, 1988–89.* Geneva, Switzerland: Interavia, 1988.

Miller, Judith. "Cairo's Army Has New Job: Milk the Cow," *New York Times,* November 29, 1985, I14.

The Multinational Force and Observers. Rome: Office of Public Affairs, Multinational Force and Observers, 1987.

1987 Yearbook on International Communist Affairs. (Ed., Richard F. Staar.) Stanford, California: Hoover Institution Press, 1987.

Pajak, Roger F. *Nuclear Profileration in the Middle East: Implications for the Superpowers*. (National Security Affairs Monograph Series, No. 82-1.) Washington: National Defense University Press, 1982.

Perlmutter, Amos. *Egypt: The Praetorian State*. New Brunswick, New Jersey: Transaction Books, 1974.

Perry, Glenn E. "Egypt." Pages 429-322 in Richard F. Staar (ed.), *1987 Yearbook on International Communist Affairs*. Stanford, California: Hoover Institution Press, 1987.

Sadowski, Yahya. "Egypt's Islamist Movement: A New Political and Economic Force," *Middle East Insight*, 4, No. 4, 1987, 37-44.

Satloff, Robert B. *Army and Politics in Mubarak's Egypt*. Washington: Washington Institute for Near East Policy, 1988.

Schuler, G. Henry M. (ed.). *Egypt and Nuclear Technology: The "Peace Dividend."* (Significant Issues Series 5, No. 9.) Washington: Center for Strategic and International Studies, Georgetown University, 1983.

Seib, Gerald F. "Double Duty: Egypt Army Provides Bridges, Roads, Goods—and Much Stability," *Wall Street Journal*, 208, No. 89, November 4, 1986, 1,7.

Springborg, Robert. *Mubarak's Egypt: Fragmentation of the Political Order*. Boulder, Colorado: Westview Press, 1989.

_____. "The President and the Field Marshal: Civil-Military Relations in Egypt Today," *Middle East Report*, No. 147, July–August 1987, 5-16.

United States. Arms Control and Disarmament Agency. *World Military Expenditures and Arms Transfers, 1988*. Washington: GPO, 1989.

_____. Department of Defense. *Congressional Presentation for Security Assistance Programs, Fiscal Year 1990*. Washington: 1989.

_____. Department of State. *Country Reports on Human Rights Practices for 1987*. (Report submitted to United States Congress, 102d, 1st Session, Senate, Committee on Foreign Relations, and House of Representatives, Committee on Foreign Affairs.) Washington: GPO, February 1988.

_____. Department of State. *Country Reports on Human Rights Practices for 1988*. (Report submitted to United States Congress, 103d, 1st Session, Senate, Committee on Foreign Relations, and House of Representatives, Committee on Foreign Affairs.) Washington: GPO, February 1989.

Vatikiotis, P.J. *The Egyptian Army in Politics: Pattern for New Nations?* Bloomington: Indiana University Press, 1961.

Yaari, Ehud. "Israel's Egypt Problem," *Washington Post,* March 13, 1988, C5.

(Various issues of the following publications were also used in the preparation of this chapter: *Defense and Foreign Affairs; Economist* [London]; Foreign Broadcast Information Service, *Daily Report, Middle East, South Asia; Jane's Defence Weekly* [London]; Joint Publications Research Service, *Near East/Africa Report; Keesing's Record of World Events* [Edinburgh]; *Middle East International* [London]; *New York Times;* and *Washington Post.*)

Glossary

Egyptian pound (£E)—Consists of 100 piasters. In early 1990, the pound was worth between US$1.00 and US$1.50 depending on the exchange rate that applied; the informal market rate was £E = US$0.40.

feddan(s)—Equals 1.038 acres.

FY (fiscal year)—Since July 1, 1980, July 1 through June 30.

GDP (gross domestic product)—A value measure of the flow of domestic goods and services produced by an economy over a period of time, such as a year. Only output values of goods for final consumption and investment are included because the values of primary and intermediate production are assumed to be included in final prices. GDP is sometimes aggregated and shown at market prices, meaning that indirect taxes and subsidies are included; when these have been eliminated, the result is GDP at factor cost. The word *gross* indicates that deductions for depreciation of physical assets have not been made. *See also* GNP.

GNP (gross national product)—The gross domestic product (GDP—*q.v.*) plus the net income or loss stemming from transactions with foreign countries. GNP is the broadest measure of the output of goods and services by an economy. It can be calculated at market prices, which include indirect taxes and subsidies. Because indirect taxes and subsidies are only transfer payments, GNP is often calculated at factor cost, removing indirect taxes and subsidies.

imam—A word used in several senses. In general use and in lower case, it means the leader of congregational prayers; as such it implies no ordination or special spiritual powers beyond sufficient education to carry out this function. It is also used figuratively by many Sunni (*q.v.*) Muslims to mean the leader of the Islamic community. Among Shias (*q.v.*) the word takes on many complex meanings; in general, it indicates that particular descendant of the House of Ali ibn Abu Talib, who is believed to have been God's designated repository of the spiritual authority inherent in that line. The identity of this individual and the means of ascertaining his identity have been the major issues causing divisions among Shias.

infitah—Literally open door; refers to Anwar as Sadat's policy after the October 1973 War of relaxing government controls on

393

the economy so as to encourage the private sector and stimulate the inflow of foreign funds.

International Monetary Fund (IMF)—Established along with the World Bank (*q.v.*) in 1945, the IMF is a specialized agency affiliated with the United Nations (UN) and is responsible for stabilizing international exchange rates and payments. The main business of the IMF is the provision of loans to its members (including industrialized and developing countries) when they experience balance of payments difficulties. These loans frequently carry conditions that require substantial internal economic adjustments by the recipients, most of which are developing countries.

Ismaili Shia Islam—A subsect of Shia Islam that takes its name from Imam Muhammad ibn Ismail, the Seventh Imam. Ismaili Shia doctrine closely resembled Twelver Shia Islam with regard to observance of the sharia but also included a system of philosophy and science coordinated with religion that proved the divine origin of the imamate and the rights of the Fatimids to it. Ubaid Allah, al Mahdi, the founder of the Fatimid Dynasty, came to North Africa in the early tenth century and actively promoted the Ismaili faith. *See also* Shia.

khedive—Name given to the ruler of Egypt from 1867 to 1914. He governed as semi-independent viceroy of the sultan of Turkey.

mufti—Religious jurist who issues judgments and opinions on Islamic law and precedent.

patrimonial—Relates to an estate or any heritage from one's father or other ancestors.

pharaonic—Refers to the glories of Egypt's ancient period under the rule of the pharaohs.

piaster—See Egyptian pound.

Shia (from Shiat Ali, the Party of Ali)—A member of the smaller of the two great divisions of Islam. The Shias supported the claims of Ali and his line to presumptive right to the caliphate and leadership of the Muslim community, and on this issue they divided from the Sunni (*q.v.*) in the great schism within Islam. Later schisms have produced further divisions among the Shias over the identity and number of Imams (*q.v.*). Most Shias revere Twelve Imams, the last of whom is believed to be in hiding. Ismaili Shias are connected with the Fatimid Dynasty in Egypt; some believe that Muhammad ibn Ismail, the Seventh Imam, was the last Imam. *See also* Ismaili Shia Islam.

Special Drawing Right(s) (SDR)—A monetary unit of the International Monetary Fund (IMF) (*q.v.*) based on a basket of international currencies consisting of the United States dollar, the German deutschmark, the Japanese yen, the British pound sterling, and the French franc.

statist—One who advocates the concentration of all economic controls and planning in the hands of a highly centralized government.

Sublime Porte—Ottoman Empire palace entrance that provided access to the chief minister, representing the government and the sultan. Term came to mean the Ottoman government.

Sunni (from sunna, orthodox)—A member of the larger of the two great divisions of Islam. The Sunnis supported the traditional method of election to the caliphate and accepted the Umayyad line. On this issue they divided from the Shias (*q.v.*) in the great schism within Islam.

West Bank—The portion of Jordan west of the Jordan River and the Dead Sea that was seized by Israel in the June 1967 War (Arab-Israeli war, also known as the Six-Day War) and in 1991 remained Israeli-occupied territory.

World Bank—Informal name used to designate a group of three affiliated international institutions: the International Bank for Reconstruction and Development (IBRD), the International Development Association (IDA), and the International Finance Corporation (IFC). The IBRD, established in 1945, has the primary purpose of providing loans to developing countries for productive projects. The IDA, a legally separate loan fund, but administered by the staff of the IBRD, was set up in 1960 to furnish credits to the poorest developing countries on much easier terms than those of conventional IBRD loans. The IFC, founded in 1956, supplements the activities of the IBRD through loans and assistance designed specifically to encourage the growth of productive private enterprises in the less developed countries. The president and certain senior officers of the IBRD hold the same positions in the IFC. The three institutions are owned by the governments of the countries that subscribe their capital. To participate in the World Bank group, member states must first belong to the International Monetary Fund (IMF—*q.v.*).

Index

Abbas (Khedive), 43
Abbas Hilmi I, 31, 33
Abbasid caliphate, 4, 20, 21; destruction of, by Mongols, 24; migration of Turkish tribes during, 23; occupation of, by Turks, 24; return of Egypt to, 22
Abbasid Empire, 23
Abdin Palace, 47
Abduh, Muhammad, 45
Abdul Aziz (Sultan), 36
Abdulla, Ismail Sabri, 247
Abdul Majid, Ismat, xxxii, xxxiii, 240, 282
Abu an Nasr, Muhammad Hamid, 270
Abu an Nur, Abdul Muhsin, 71
Abu Bakr, 134
Abu Basha, Hassan, 240
Abu Ghazala, Abdul Halim, 240, 249, 304, 322; American connections of, 247; career of, 246–47, 305; concern of, over Israel, 302; dismissed, 305; institution of privileges for military, 247, 320–21; military production under, 327; Military Technical Academy under, 318
Abu Qir, 27
Abu Rudays oil fields, 80
Abu Simbel (Abu Sunbul), 12, 111, 163
Abu Sunbul. *See* Abu Simbel
Abu Talib, Yusuf Sabri, 305
Abu Uwayqilah, 296, 299
Abu Zaabal Company for Engineering Industries, 328
Abu Zaabal Tank Repair Factory, 328
ACDA. *See* United States Arms Control and Disarmament Agency
Achaemenid Empire (Persian Empire), 13
Achille Lauro hijacking, 214, 247, 287
Acre, 27, 30
Actium, battle of, 15
Ad Dawah, 262
Aden, 48
Afghanistan, 135
Africa, 135; Cairo as transshipment point for, 106; North, 134; as part of Egyptian Fatimid Empire, 21; role of Egypt in, 279
African Development Bank, xxviii

Afrika Korps, 295
afterlife, 3, 5, 10
AGIP. *See* Azienda Generale Italiana dei Petroli
agrarian reform, 67, 180, 238, 264; fertilizers and pesticides encouraged under, 196; successes of, 252
Agrarian Reform Law of 1952, 58
Agricultural Affairs Committee, 264
agricultural cooperatives, 183, 184
agricultural inputs: cost of, 196; subsidies for, 186, 196, 250
agricultural laborers, 33, 175
agricultural production: in ancient Egypt, 5; fall in, 158; insufficiency of, xxvi, 182; land suitable for, xxv; problems with, xxvi
agricultural products *(see also under names of crops),* xxv; controlled crops, 187; fruits, 192, 193, 207; kinds of, 188; vegetables, 192, 207
agricultural sector, xxv, 32; as key economic sector, 180; share of GDP, 159; stagnation in, 158
agriculture *(see also under* cropping patterns), 229; arable land, 179; area cultivated, 179; as basis for development under Muhammad Ali, 29; controls on, 169, 180; conversion to cash-crop, 32; under Fatimids, 22; food security, 181; growth of, 184; impact of import trends on, 208; irrigation projects for, 36, 193–94; mechanization of, 195; military production in, 325–27; technological changes, 193
Agriculture, Ministry of, 184
Ahmose: unification of Egypt by, 10
aid: from Arab states, 219, 280, 281; economic, xxvi, 166; military, xxvi, xxxiv; from Paris Club, xxvi; from United States, xxvi; from West, 280
AID. *See* United States Agency for International Development
Aida, 107
Air Defense Academy, 318
Air Defense Force, 315–16; commander of, 306; conscripts in, 293; military matériel of, 311; reserves of, 320;

Published Country Studies

(Area Handbook Series)

550-156	Paraguay	550-53	Thailand
550-185	Persian Gulf States	550-89	Tunisia
550-42	Peru	550-80	Turkey
550-72	Philippines	550-74	Uganda
550-162	Poland	550-97	Uruguay
550-181	Portugal	550-71	Venezuela
550-160	Romania	550-32	Vietnam
550-37	Rwanda and Burundi	550-183	Yemens, The
550-51	Saudi Arabia	550-99	Yugoslavia
550-70	Senegal	550-67	Zaire
550-180	Sierra Leone	550-75	Zambia
550-184	Singapore	550-171	Zimbabwe
550-86	Somalia		
550-93	South Africa		
550-95	Soviet Union		
550-179	Spain		
550-96	Sri Lanka		
550-27	Sudan		
550-47	Syria		
550-62	Tanzania		

☆U.S. GOVERNMENT PRINTING OFFICE: 1992 311-824/60001

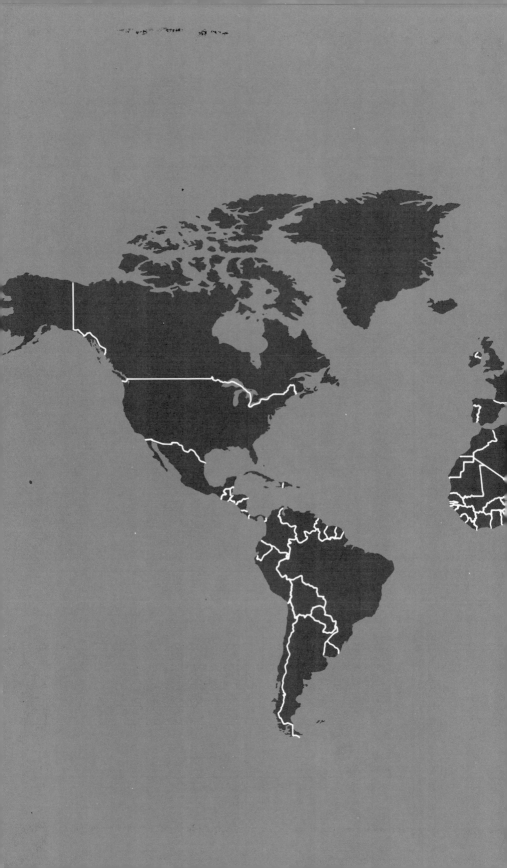